TRANSFORMING SCHOOL FOOD POLITICS AROUND THE WORLD

Food, Health, and the Environment

Series Editor: Robert Gottlieb, Henry R. Luce Professor of Urban and Environmental Policy, Occidental College

Nevin Cohen, Associate Professor, City University of New York (CUNY) Graduate School of Public Health

The full list of titles in this series is printed in the back of this book.

TRANSFORMING SCHOOL FOOD POLITICS AROUND THE WORLD

EDITED BY JENNIFER E. GADDIS AND SARAH A. ROBERT

FOREWORD BY SILVIA FEDERICI

THE MIT PRESS   CAMBRIDGE, MASSACHUSETTS   LONDON, ENGLAND

© 2024 Massachusetts Institute of Technology

This work is subject to a Creative Commons CC-BY-NC-ND license.

This license applies only to the work in full and not to any components included with permission. Subject to such license, all rights are reserved. No part of this book may be used to train artificial intelligence systems without permission in writing from the MIT Press.

The MIT Press would like to thank the anonymous peer reviewers who provided comments on drafts of this book. The generous work of academic experts is essential for establishing the authority and quality of our publications. We acknowledge with gratitude the contributions of these otherwise uncredited readers.

This book was set in Stone Serif and Stone Sans by Westchester Publishing Services. Printed and bound in the United States of America.

Library of Congress Cataloging-in-Publication Data

Names: Gaddis, Jennifer E., 1985– editor. | Robert, Sarah A., editor.
Title: Transforming school food politics around the world / edited by Jennifer E. Gaddis and Sarah A. Robert ; foreword by Silvia Federici.
Description: Cambridge, Massachusetts : The MIT Press, 2024. | Series: Food, health, and the environment | Includes bibliographical references and index.
Identifiers: LCCN 2023034503 (print) | LCCN 2023034504 (ebook) | ISBN 9780262548113 (paperback) | ISBN 9780262378819 (epub) | ISBN 9780262378802 (pdf)
Subjects: LCSH: School children—Food—Government policy—Case studies. | School children—Nutrition—Government policy—Case studies.
Classification: LCC LB3475 .T73 2024 (print) | LCC LB3475 (ebook) | DDC 371.7/16—dc23/eng/20230920
LC record available at https://lccn.loc.gov/2023034503
LC ebook record available at https://lccn.loc.gov/2023034504

10 9 8 7 6 5 4

CONTENTS

SERIES FOREWORD ix

FOREWORD xi
Silvia Federici

ACKNOWLEDGMENTS xv

INTRODUCTION xix
Jennifer E. Gaddis and Sarah A. Robert

I THE POWER AND POTENTIAL OF NATIONAL SCHOOL MEAL PROGRAMS 1

    1   A WHOLE SYSTEMS APPROACH TO SCHOOL FOOD POLICY IN JAPAN 5
        Alexis Agliano Sanborn and Katsura Omori

    2   CENTERING CHILDREN, HEALTH, AND JUSTICE IN CANADIAN SCHOOL FOOD PROGRAMS 29
        Jennifer Black, Sinikka Elliott, Rachel Engler-Stringer, Debbie Field, Brent Mansfield, Stephanie Segave, and Thibaud Liné

    3   SCHOOL FOOD POLITICS, IDENTITY, AND INDIGENEITY IN THE PERUVIAN AMAZON 53
        Emmanuelle Ricaud Oneto

II CLAIMING SPACE FOR YOUTH AND WORKER VOICES 75

    4   SUSTAINABLE FOOD EDUCATION IN FINNISH SCHOOLS THROUGH COLLABORATIVE PEDAGOGY 77
        Kristiina Janhonen, Marjaana Manninen, and Karin Hjälmeskog

- 5 **REBEL VENTURES AND YOUTH-LED FOOD INITIATIVES IN THE UNITED STATES** 95
  Raven Lewis with Jarrett Stein

- 6 **CREATING A MOBILE METHOD TO NOURISH CHILDREN IN THE UNITED STATES WITH THE "YUM-YUM BUS"** 107
  Rebecca A. Davis, A. Brooks Bowden, and Lisa Altmann

- 7 **LOCAL AND NATIONAL RESPONSES TO THE COVID-19 PANDEMIC IN THE UNITED STATES** 125
  Margaret Read, Anne Moertel, Courtney Smith, and Jennifer LeBarre

III STRUGGLING FOR JUST SCHOOL FOOD ECONOMIES 145

- 8 **CIVIL SOCIETY ACTIVISM AND GOVERNMENT PARTNERSHIPS IN INDIA** 149
  Prerna Rana

- 9 **COOPERATIVE AND SMALL-SCALE FARMING THROUGH BRAZIL'S NATIONAL PROCUREMENT STANDARDS** 169
  José Arimatea Barros Bezerra and Ludmir dos Santos Gomes

- 10 **AGROECOLOGY AND FEMINIST PRAXIS IN BRAZILIAN SCHOOL FOOD POLITICS** 185
  Sônia Fátima Schwendler, Cristiane Coradin, and Islandia Bezerra

- 11 **DIRECT URBAN-RURAL SUPPLY CHAINS FOR SOUTH KOREAN COMMUNITIES** 201
  Seulgi Son

IV TOOLS AND CAMPAIGNS FOR SYSTEMS CHANGE 217

- 12 **USING STORYTELLING IN THE UNITED STATES TO BUILD EMPATHY FOR CHANGE** 219
  Christine C. Caruso, Lucy Flores, and Amy Rosenthal

- 13 **FACILITATING THINK TANKS TO GUIDE ACTION AND ADVOCACY IN CANADIAN TEACHERS' UNIONS** 233
  Andrée Gaçoin, Michelle Gautreaux, and Anne Hales

- 14 **THE CENTER FOR ECOLITERACY'S APPROACH TO SCHOOL FOOD SYSTEMS CHANGE IN THE UNITED STATES** 251
  Anne Moertel

- 15 **DEVELOPING SOLIDARITY COALITIONS FOR UNIVERSAL SCHOOL MEALS AND LOCAL FOOD IN THE UNITED STATES** 273
  Anore Horton, Faye Mack, Betsy Rosenbluth, and Amy Shollenberger

CONCLUSION 295
Jennifer E. Gaddis and Sarah A. Robert

ANCILLARY MATERIALS 301
CONTRIBUTORS 303
INDEX 309

SERIES FOREWORD

Transforming School Food Politics around the World is the twenty-first book in the Food, Health, and the Environment series. The series explores the global and local dimensions of food systems and the issues of access, social, environmental, and food justice, and community well-being. Books in the series focus on how and where food is grown, manufactured, distributed, sold, and consumed. They address questions of power and control, social movements and organizing strategies, and the health, environmental, social, and economic factors embedded in food-system choices and outcomes. As this book demonstrates, the focus is not only on food security and well-being but also on economic, political, and cultural factors and regional, state, national, and international policy decisions. Food, Health, and the Environment books therefore provide a window into the public debates, alternative and existing discourses, and multidisciplinary perspectives that have made food systems and their connections to health and the environment critically important subjects of study and for social and policy change.

Robert Gottlieb, Occidental College

Nevin Cohen, City University of New York (CUNY) Graduate School of Public Health

FOREWORD

School food politics is one of those places where everything meets: nutrition, agriculture, institutional politics, community involvement in the life of the new generation, and state investment in social reproduction. It is a place where we can rethink what we need to give a good future to the next generation. The food children eat is the product of so many activities, interventions, and relations, each with political significance.

Food is the sustenance of life. It has been one of the most widespread, common, and ancient activities for women. Once reproductive activities go to the market, they are extremely underpaid, extremely precarious, and extremely low-valued. It pains me that so many aspects of domestic work and even cooking have become so oppressive because of the condition in which women have had to perform it. And it pains me that many feminists have internalized the devaluation of this activity.

Of course, we must make the connection between what is happening on the home front and what is happening on the agricultural farm. The industrialization of agriculture has produced a constant contamination of soil and water through pesticides and all kinds of chemical inputs. This system is producing a kind of food that is more deleterious than nutritious. What the market—and capitalism—have offered us is fast food products, which are responsible for a steady increase in obesity and disease around the world, even among young people.

When we have a food system that is driven by a logic that devalues life, that devaluation can spill over into all areas of reproductive activity. It has become extremely difficult for women, for families, and for communities to provide the kind of services, work, and resources that are necessary to produce healthy, prosperous human beings. Eating a school meal may seem to be a microscopic activity, but when we put an expanding lens on it, we see so much. *Transforming School Food Politics around the World* puts the spotlight on the whole broad network of relations that must work together simultaneously to provide the meal.

School food traverses so many questions and so many kinds of struggle. It is a microcosm of something much bigger. I'm very skeptical when I hear so many of my feminist sisters say, "social services, social services." But what kind? And who decides what they're going to look like? The state controls social wealth, so there must be all kinds of engagements with the state—conflictual and negotiation—from many different agents. We need to have a kind of social fabric, a kind of *community* fabric, that has the capacity to interfere with the state and control what kind of social services it provides and how they are organized. Otherwise, we are going to have social services that are so degraded, that are so reduced to the minimum available, that in many cases they will not fulfill the expectations we have of them.

Unless there is control over the wealth produced and how it is used, it is not possible to transform society. Schools have a very central and strategic role in this process. What happens in schools with children, and what happens with the people who are in charge of social reproduction in the schools? School food workers now work in conditions that are really inequitable because of the devaluation of reproductive work under capitalism. This is the product of a state that always gives the minimum and gives the minimum because they can get away with it. There is no conflict between the well-being of the children and the well-being of school food workers. If the children are given more or better food, this does not necessarily mean that school food workers will be overburdened or even more underpaid than before. This is an artificial conflict and a microcosm of all the conflict that we suffer now. We see this in hospitals where patients and their nurses appear as two opposite interests. It is not opposite interests but rather the state that is organizing that we fight against each other.

To break that very hellish circle, families and people in the community need to intervene. They must recognize a whole network of relations: the condition of the school food workers impacts the condition of food provision, which impacts the condition of the children. It's a question of what organizational work and what kinds of relations—affective and otherwise—need to take place for somebody to go to school, to be cared for, and to have a good lunch? "Good," not only in providing the proper nutrients but also "good" because it is organized by people who care for the child and who receive support for themselves from the community and from the state.

Many things radiate from food and from the social rituals and practices of sharing a meal. Food establishes social relationships and brings together knowledge of the body, of nature, and of cultural activities. There is creativity in the process of eating, commenting, interacting, and looking at what other people like or do not like. It is so important for students to be brought to parks, to botanical gardens, and to community gardens to learn that the vegetables are not coming from plastic, they're not coming from the supermarket, and to absorb that knowledge and that magic.

Food and love are what bring people together, so we must not forget the importance of children eating together. This collection focuses on that very beautiful topic, and the range of international perspectives make it of great value and inspiration.

Silvia Federici, April 17, 2023

Brooklyn, New York

ACKNOWLEDGMENTS

This collection is the result of three years of collaborative work. We are especially grateful to the contributors for writing rich chapters (during a global pandemic!), responding to our feedback and editorial direction, trusting us to make this collection more than the sum of its parts, and being patient with our timeline. We would also like to thank Emily Callaci for her generous introduction to Silvia Federici, and Silvia herself, whose contribution of a foreword (a gift that we treasure) foregrounds why we must think about social reproduction and feminist politics when we think about school food.

We, along with multiple contributors to this collection, wish to acknowledge the contributions of Dr. Sinikka Elliott, who passed away unexpectedly in May 2021. Dr. Elliott was a cherished colleague, scholar, writer, friend, mentor, and teacher, and we were privileged to learn from and with her while working on this book. In chapter 2, she outlines her vision for a conception of childhood that positions children as competent social actors and advocates for a world where children's voices and perspectives are heard. The authors of chapter 13 are especially grateful for Dr. Elliott's engagement with the British Columbia Teachers' Federation. Her generous and spirited engagement in their opening food security panel discussion greatly enriched their think-tank event, while her sociological research on family, social inequality, and the processes of food provisioning for families of small children continues to inspire meaningful dialogue and informed action. She will be deeply missed.

The narrative structure and storytelling within the chapters benefited enormously from the developmental feedback of Megan Pugh and the careful editorial efforts of Marissa Lanker. The manuscript also benefited from undergraduate Sarah Wack's formatting efforts. And we owe a huge thanks to graduate students Sara Trongone and Jacob DeWald for their expert assistance with the final stages of manuscript preparation: from test-reading each chapter and offering helpful feedback, to final formatting of references, and more. We are especially grateful to Beth Clevenger, Anthony Zannino, series editors Robert Gottlieb and Nevin Cohen, the anonymous peer reviewers, and the rest of the team at the MIT Press for believing in this project and supporting us through the publication process. We also thank Sally Brown for indexing the book.

Specifically, Jen would like to thank Sarah for inviting her to coedit this volume! It has been an incredible journey filled with many wonderful moments of collaboration, laughter, and life experiences. She is grateful for research support provided by the University of Wisconsin-Madison Office of the Vice Chancellor for Research and Graduate Education with funding from the Wisconsin Alumni Research Foundation. Most especially, she would like to thank her friends and family for their love and support. In particular, she is forever grateful to her husband, James, for his unwavering encouragement, kindness, and delicious cooking, and to Isobel, her daughter, for bringing joy, wisdom, curiosity (and a bit of mystery) to each day.

Sarah thanks Jen for taking a (blind?!) leap into a project during a pandemic and while still on tenure track! She will forever treasure this collaboration with her because it and she reintroduced her to the values and vision and humans that drew her to academia. Thanks to the University at Buffalo's Office of International Education Rapid Grants for Global and International Research 2022 and 2023. Inspiration emerged from the UB Gender Institute's Interventions in Social Reproduction Lecture Series. She is indebted to Marion Werner for wisdom-while-running and introducing her to the Dominican Republic's school food stakeholders. Sarah's family has grown since the publication of *School Food Politics* to include three baby bears: Agustina, Lilah, and Julia. With each of their births, her heart grew and with each day since they inspire her to be a better person, to love fiercely, and to enjoy because this is not a rehearsal. (She'll continue to work on the last item.) After seven World Cups, her love for Nicolás continues to evolve and grow. His patience, his calm, his humor, his lentils, sos u-nico, te quiero. Finally, she dedicates this book to Marjorie Robert Elam, aunt and godmother, who nourished her extended family and died prior to publication.

INTRODUCTION

Jennifer E. Gaddis and Sarah A. Robert

"When hungry, you cannot study." Youth in Buenos Aires have united around this call to action, demanding #viandasdignas (decent meals) and an end to privatization of the public education system. They are organizing for the rights of all young people to be educated and cared for through public institutions. Using their collective power, they are calling on national and local government officials to provide quality nutritional meals, invest in school building infrastructure, and a moratorium on mandatory unpaid internships at private companies. For these youth, school politics and *school food politics* are one and the same, both involving struggles with the state over public resources and educational opportunity.

To draw media attention to their cause and exert political pressure, teenagers from the Autonomous City of Buenos Aires are engaging in direct action with the government and the broader public.[1] In September and October 2022, they halted classes and, in some cases, barred teachers and staff from entering the building.

While their campaign is ongoing, these youth are transforming school food politics. They engage with each other and with their teachers through *centros de estudiantes* (student councils), which are hubs for student organizing and governance. In these educational spaces, students learn about how school food contracting works, conduct studies of food quality, and develop outreach messaging to school administrators, the media, government officials, and the public. And they question why, in a country that guarantees children and youth the right to a free public education from age four through university, their right to a free school meal ends with elementary school.

What they want is a better school food system, better for themselves and for the workers who feed them. This vision hinges on two key demands. First, the students demand that school meals be free for all students through the end of secondary school. Second, they demand new systems of accountability for government contractors and argue that contracts should be preferentially awarded to agroecological producers and cooperatives.

These Argentine students aren't alone in their desire for school food transformation. School meals are a site of social struggle and resistance in countries around the world.[2] A new wave of school food politics is happening at all scales, ranging from individual schools to the global School Meals Coalition, a pandemic-motivated initiative supported by the United Nations World Food Programme, which includes more than seventy-eight member states and a wide range of NGO partners.[3]

Taken together, the fifteen essays in this volume provide a global vista of how school food politics is transforming in productive ways, generating new answers to the foundational question Jen Sandler posed in *School Food Politics* over a decade ago: who feeds whom what, how, when, and for what purpose?[4] The answers to these questions are the direct result of food and education politics, yet the people who are most impacted by the resulting programs and policies too often experience "politics" as an abstract and distant process.

School food politics is often thought of as the purvey of corporate food lobbyists, economists, and politicians who debate the specific contours of what schools serve, to whom, and for how much. This book rejects this narrow framing of who "does" school food politics. We see the individuals, families, and local community institutions who confront imperialist-white supremacist-capitalist-patriarchal school food systems as politically powerful.[5] They are important school food stakeholders whose perspectives matter.[6] As we use the term, a stakeholder is any person or organization who has an interest—whether they recognize it or not—in the production and consumption of school meals. For a stakeholder group to successfully engage in school food politics, they must first define the problems they wish to address and find avenues for change. But *how* do stakeholders change material conditions, challenge existing power structures, and assert collective responsibility for human and ecological well-being?

GLOBAL OVERVIEW OF SCHOOL FOOD PROGRAMS

The social organization of school meals[7] varies widely across country contexts.[8] It is the product of complex, place-specific histories, and stakeholder power dynamics. The first programs that were developed from the 1850s through the 1930s, mostly began as local charitable efforts that relied heavily on volunteer labor. Many of these programs were established to address childhood hunger and malnutrition, with the goal of improving the health of students from working-class and poor households. Public and compulsory education was expanding around the world, and schools proved to be an efficient institution to reach vulnerable populations. In some countries, such as the United States (US), governments began investing in the creation and growth of community-based school meal programs, partially as an outlet for redistributing surplus agricultural commodities at home and abroad.

From the 1940s through the 1960s, the growth of not-for-profit school food programs was fueled by postwar nation-building efforts focused on children's nutrition and as a means of expanding the influence of international aid organizations (i.e., the US Agency for International Development). The United Nations' (UN) World Food Programme (WFP) further accelerated the development of school food programs in lower-income countries in the 1960s and 1970s, while some higher-income countries with existing programs focused their attention on improving the quality and nutritional profile of school meals to address growing concerns about the health impacts of feeding children highly processed foods. Since the 1990s, countries have begun to grapple with a wider range of health and sustainability concerns in relation to school food programs and UN agencies have actively worked to promote sustainable and equitable development through, for example, Home Grown School Feeding initiatives, which now feed children in forty-six countries.[9] This trend was bolstered by the

WFP's 2013 Global School Feeding Policy, which explicitly acknowledged the multiple benefits of school meal programs to different stakeholder groups and national priorities, while shifting the focus of the WFP to providing technical assistance to governments and bolstering government-led national school meal/feeding programs.[10]

Prior to the COVID-19 pandemic, 163 countries had at least one school food program, which collectively fed 388 million children.[11] And coverage was increasing globally. The closure of schools around the world due to the health pandemic illustrated on global and local scales the importance of school-based meals as much more than just a nutritional supplement. During the pandemic, many countries worked to expand their school nutrition programs and by 2022 they exceeded pre-pandemic levels, serving 418 million children daily.[12] These programs most often serve lunch, although some serve breakfast or a snack in addition to or instead of school lunch. The majority of meals and snacks are prepared on school grounds or in publicly owned centralized kitchens.[13] However, some programs contract with off-site private kitchens or serve only preprocessed items that require no preparation.[14]

As of 2021, approximately 40 percent of countries incorporated agricultural goals into their school food programs.[15] These goals directly impact what students eat. More broadly speaking, the nutritional quality of school meals is variable, but nearly all programs include grains/cereals, legumes/nuts, oil, and salt, while only 44–54 percent of programs include eggs, meat, and poultry. Wealthier nations tend to serve a greater variety of foods and more processed foods, and certain regions (i.e., South Asia, East Asia, and the Pacific) include the highest average diversity of food items in their school meal programs.[16] Most of these programs only provide food during the school year, but a small minority—including those in Cameroon, Hungary, India, Portugal, and Uruguay—also feed students during school breaks.[17] In addition to food, 87 percent of these programs provided nutrition education and 68 percent incorporated school gardens. However, higher-income countries were less likely than others to incorporate educational or agricultural goals into their school food policies.[18]

There are significant disparities in school meal access both within and across countries. Children's right to food and education is constitutionally protected or guaranteed through laws or policies in some countries.

Whether these rights are universal or restricted to certain populations (e.g., students from low-income households) and under particular conditions (e.g., in rural schools) is a central issue within school food politics. Most countries focus their efforts on feeding younger students in primary schools, but even so, their access to school meals varies substantially by region (e.g., school meal programs reach less than 15 percent of enrolled primary students in the Middle East and North Africa and 85 percent of enrolled primary students in Latin America and the Caribbean). Twenty-six countries provided school meals to at least 95 percent of enrolled primary students, but only five countries—the Czech Republic, Eswatini, Finland, Nauru, and Palau—did the same for secondary students.[19]

Several countries that we discuss in this volume—namely, Brazil, Finland, Japan, and the US—have long-standing national programs that have influenced and helped shape the organization of school meals around the world. For example, Bolivia, Ecuador, Guatemala, Honduras, and Paraguay modeled their school feeding laws after the Brazilian program.[20] And the Coalition for Healthy School Food (CHSF) in Canada, which is actively working toward the creation of a national program, is taking inspiration and lessons learned from multiple countries' programs, including Brazil, Denmark, France, Germany, Italy, Japan, the United Kingdom (UK), and the US.[21]

School meals vary in how they are conceived: either a *public good* (i.e., typically organized as a not-for-profit government-sponsored/subsidized program) or a *private commercialized service* that is offered as a convenience to students and families. For example, unlike Brazil and Japan, where school meals are seen as a public good and provided universally to students, only 20–25 percent of Danish public schools have a school food program and these are largely offered as a commercial service.[22] Most students eat from a privatized "packed-lunch-from-supermarket" supply chain, despite the recommendations of public health reports and advisory boards for the Danish government to create a national school food program.[23] And in countries like the UK and US, public school meal programs have come under fierce public criticism for their harsh and rigid means-testing eligibility criteria that restrict access to government-funded free school meals to a small percentage of students and shift the financial burden onto families that are struggling to afford the costs of food, housing, utilities, and other basic necessities.

The responsibility for financing school meal programs varies widely but is typically shared by governments and parents/caregivers. While some governments contribute only a small percentage to the cost of feeding children at school, or nothing at all, there are governments in every region of the world that provide full funding for school meal programs. In most programs worldwide, parents and/or other community members are required, or at the very least expected, to collaborate with the government to operate their local school meal programs. Many programs also rely on the students themselves to assist in preparing, serving, and cleaning up after meals.[24] Yet these important school food stakeholders typically have limited opportunities to participate in decision-making about how their programs should be designed, funded, and operated.[25]

Civil society organizations and for-profit companies are two stakeholder groups that are widely involved in school meal programs, and their relative power and influence is a central topic of school food politics. Civil society is a very broad umbrella that encompasses social movement organizations like Via Campesina that fight for food sovereignty and nongovernmental organizations like those in India that are contracted by the government to manage and prepare school meals.[26] The values and goals that civil society organizations hold for school food programs are variable and do not always advance justice, sustainability, or democracy. Moreover, civil society organizations are not universally activist in nature, and we take a more nuanced view of civil society organizations in this volume. We are, however, more critical of both the corporate food industry and public-private development organizations that reinforce existing power dynamics within food systems and extend colonial and imperialist economic development priorities.

The corporate food industry and the corporatization of public schools more broadly are intimately intertwined, as the Argentine student protesters have made clear in their #viandasdignas campaign. Neoliberal goals of creating for-profit markets out of public education through privatization and commercialization of everything, including school food, often lead to a higher prevalence of ultra processed foods and other convenience items that require limited or no onsite preparation.[27] This overarching political-economic reality makes it difficult for schools to achieve the transformative educational potential of school food programs.

Yet there are examples globally that provide inspiration for how school food programs can be designed to push back against neoliberalism by creating collective and democratic experiences for students that prioritize values of caring for each other and the world around them. In Greece, eating school meals together with one's classmates is seen to strengthen social cohesion and solidarity. Likewise, in Finland, educators and policymakers see school mealtimes as an important avenue for teaching young people about civic engagement.[28] Such efforts vary in their respect for young people's agency—a culturally specific value and priority that can be difficult to accomplish in practice within the context of top-down national school food programs. What's more, some countries are constrained by transnational trade agreements, externally imposed development priorities, and internal political-economic oligarchies that reinforce neoliberal food and education systems.

POLITICAL GOALS AND IMPACTS OF SCHOOL MEALS

Cost-benefit studies show that public school food programs can generate returns as high as US$9 for every US$1 invested through positive impacts on education, health and nutrition, poverty, and local agriculture.[29] However, the extent to which these benefits are realized depends on how school meal programs are designed and the context they operate within. While certain goals are country and context specific, some are nearly universal. These goals include improvements in child health and nutrition, school attendance, and academic achievement for the most vulnerable populations, particularly girls.

There is ample evidence that school food programs meet these goals, especially for the most vulnerable students in a society, and a widespread assumption that these programs should be funded, ideally as a cost that is included in official government budgets.[30] This evidence has been of particular concern to Brazil, Russia, India, China, and South Africa (BRICS nations), all of which are geographically vast middle-income countries with rapidly growing economies, large populations, and comparatively high levels of global influence. In Russia, this includes building out hot school meals to continue reforming a post–Soviet Union public education system, while in South Africa school meals are integral to cultivating a vision of schools as "inclusive centers of learning, care, and support."[31]

By taking a closer look at individual programs and across geographical contexts, we gain a deeper understanding of school food politics. One area that deserves closer attention is the impact of school food programs on girls and women, which we argue is vital for the development of a feminist politics of food and education. In low-income countries, school food programs are widely touted as an effective tool for improving girls' school attendance and nutrition. Across country contexts, school food programs have the potential for broader change in gender relations within households and the economy. Firstly, lunch provision at school "allowed for" more mothers to work outside the home who may have previously been expected to labor only in the home and focus on the needs of their households.[32] Secondly, because household food work is disproportionately done by mothers, they benefit from the reduced time, money, and mental labor spent on preparing lunches. Thirdly, women stand to benefit greatly from the jobs these programs generate, particularly when these jobs are well compensated, although this remains a significant global challenge.[33]

Prior to the COVID-19 pandemic, 1,668 new jobs were created for every one hundred thousand students fed by school meal programs.[34] Most of those jobs went to local community members, primarily women, who prepare and serve the food in school kitchens. They are part of a broader system of school food labor that includes the food chain workers who grow, harvest, process, and distribute ingredients; the nutritionists who develop menus; and the teachers who feed and educate students about food and nutrition. The majority of school food programs worldwide emphasize the creation of jobs or leadership opportunities for women, but, at the same time, programs in less affluent countries rely heavily on the unpaid labor of women workers.[35] And in wealthy nations such as the UK and the US—where school cooks are colloquially referred to as "lunch ladies" and "dinner ladies," respectively—the jobs are often not well compensated. However, countries in Latin America and the Caribbean are at the forefront of using social policy to ensure that women are in positions of power within school food systems, ranging from leaders of agricultural cooperatives and associations to presidents of school feeding councils.[36]

This intentional approach to women's empowerment through school food policy takes many forms and often integrates with and supports healthy, sustainable food systems and food sovereignty. For example, the Integrated Program for Sustainable School Canteens in Côte d'Ivoire supports women-led micro-agricultural projects that sell food to school canteens.[37] Similarly, Tunisian rural women's cooperatives—who are given free use of school gardens—donate 30 percent of their produce to the schools and sell the rest through other market channels.[38]

These examples are part of a broader effort to leverage the immense purchasing power of the state—through sourcing ingredients for school meals and other public programs—to drive innovations in global, regional, and local food systems that lead to better outcomes for people and the planet. This is one of the fastest-growing areas of school food politics.[39] It is actively supported by the Food and Agriculture Organization (FAO) of the United Nations. Their 2021 report outlines how public procurement can be a driver of food systems transformation. It presents examples and lessons learned from thirty-two countries in Africa, Asia, Europe, North America, and South America that are purchasing food for public programs in ways that align with the United Nations Sustainable Development Goals.[40]

A related area of school food politics focuses on food sovereignty, particularly in former colonial states and among Indigenous peoples.[41] Food sovereignty moves school food politics beyond questions of what, how, and from whom school food is procured and the role of the state in strategically directing public dollars. It asserts the fundamental human right to both policy participation (e.g., defining the goals and priorities of the food and agriculture systems one is embedded within) and to healthy, culturally relevant food that is produced through ecologically sustainable and economically just methods. For instance, Ecuador's school food policy mentions goals of sustainability and good living, which are actualized through public procurement of at least 35 percent of food purchases from peasant farming and the "popular and solidarity economy sector."[42] In North America, Indigenous peoples and their collective organizations, such as The First Nations' Development Institute's Native Farm to School Project, are advancing food sovereignty through Native farm-to-school programs that "ensure young tribal leaders can experience traditional foodways inside culturally inclusive school food systems."[43]

Food sovereignty within Native school food systems is as much a reflection of local conflict as it is a blueprint for larger-scale change. It reminds us that school food politics must do more than expand existing programs or make incremental improvements. Rather, school food politics must be connected to and act as a vehicle for challenging and changing systems of injustice, particularly in the frontline communities that are most economically and ecologically vulnerable to global challenges like the COVID-19 pandemic and climate change. This is, as we see it, the rationale behind *transforming* school food politics around the world—a project that requires us to engage with the politics of care or "the larger structural questions of thinking about which institutions, people and practices should be used to accomplish concrete and real caring tasks" and to what ends.[44]

TRANSFORMING SCHOOL FOOD POLITICS

From Native Amazonian communities in Peru (chapter 3) to megacities like Seoul, South Korea (chapter 11), this volume asserts that school food programs are a valuable form of public care that can and should become a key arena for building just and sustainable futures. This argument furthers a key point from *The Labor of Lunch* that "debates about school lunch are fundamentally about care: what it means to care well, how much care is worth, and whether caring for public goods like children and the environment should be the private responsibility of individuals in the home or a public responsibility that is collectivized and shared."[45]

Care is an activity that includes "everything that we do to maintain, continue, and repair our 'world' so that we can live in it as well as possible. That world includes our bodies, our selves, and our environment, all of which we seek to interweave in a complex, life-sustaining web."[46] As a form of government-sponsored care infrastructure, public school meal programs are a vital arena to begin renegotiating both economic and ecological relationships.[47] One way to do this is by practicing care-at-a-distance, holding distant others in emotional closeness rather than physical closeness through values-based supply chains that connect buyers with producers who emphasize fair labor standards, healthy food access, community empowerment, and ecological sustainability.[48]

As a commodified form of care nested within a fiercely contested state institution, the labor of educating and feeding children at school is tethered to a legacy of feminization, racialization, and devaluation that is common across occupations that involve care work.[49] What's more, women do the majority of food work—often for low wages or in an unpaid capacity—in countries around the world, yet they control fewer resources and hold limited decision-making power over food policy or industry practices.[50] However, they are not without agency, and in this volume, we highlight numerous ways that women are leading efforts to remake social, economic, and environmental relationships through school food politics. We conceptualize their efforts within the broad umbrella of care-centered politics, which "has the capacity to provide values and ideas, and a perspective about change that not only challenges the neoliberal political consensus and its long-standing capitalist and market-centered underpinnings but the more extreme versions of the anticare politics that neoliberalism has bred too."[51]

By using the verb "transforming" in our title, we assert a critical need to understand and do school food politics differently. We argue that a *transformative* school food politics is an inherently *feminist* politics of food and education. It is driven by inclusive policymaking processes that draw from the lived expertise of those most impacted. It is welcoming of collaborations that include a wide range of stakeholders—for example, students, their caregivers, teachers, cafeteria workers and other school support staff, labor unions, grassroots activists and nonprofit organizations, policymakers, and the private sector—while centering the voices and perspectives of the students and frontline workers who have historically held the least power in determining school food problems, policy, and practice. It pushes back against the economic devaluation of the gendered labor that goes into caring for, feeding, and educating children. Lastly, we conceptualize transformative school food politics as a distributed, transnational movement capable of learning from local, state, regional, national, and international examples.

Chapters in this collection explore both "why" and "how" school food politics shape and are shaped by these interlocking political-economic systems, providing new ways of seeing school food politics from often overlooked and ignored lived experiences. Chapter contributors offer deep and broad funds of knowledge, often drawing from their own experiences, in-depth fieldwork, or participatory research with community partners. They share creative strategies for pushing policy levers and shifting mindsets, lessons for building inclusive solidarity coalitions, and prefigurative glimpses of care-centered school food programs.

Ultimately, this book makes the case for *policy protagonism* as a necessary ingredient for both pushing elected officials and other decision-makers to invest in public education and food systems, and holding them accountable when they do not.[52] This concept, which we develop further in the next section, emerges from our need to understand how different stakeholders—youth, food chain workers, teachers, lobbyists, policymakers, state agencies, NGOs, and social movement organizations—identify policy "problems" and "opportunities" within school food systems and work toward solutions that contribute to the common good.

POLICY PROTAGONISM IN SCHOOL FOOD POLITICS

Policy protagonists assert ownership over school feeding and related policies, sometimes as individuals but often through collective action. The four attributes of policy protagonism that we draw out in this collection are (1) defining school food policy "problems," (2) seeking power and resources to address those policy-worthy problems, (3) "using" social categories and symbolic identities such as perceptions of teachers as mothers and caregivers, and, finally, (4) demanding multiple seats at the decision-making table.[53]

School food policies and systems too often emerge from a narrow framing of who possesses the knowledge and expertise to identify and define school food programming. As we show in this book, the distant and seemingly entrenched policy elites, transnational organizations, and multinational corporations do not have a monopoly on school food politics. Local school communities and solidarity networks have agency as policy protagonists: whether an Indigenous mother who prepares food for her community's children or urban Black public high school students' concern for "healthy deliciousness," those closest to school food preparation and consumption have tremendous knowledge. They assert leadership and bring overlooked assets to school food politics that can be used to define school food programming in their schools that is situated within the goals or visions of the broader community.

Identifying and defining policy problems is also part of collective action on larger scales. State- and national-level coalitions from diverse countries presented in this collection recognize school food as intertwined with other complex systems. They see school food politics as important in its own right—as vital for reimagining the infrastructure of everyday life—and as an entry point into addressing wicked problems such as climate change and poverty.[54] Some are also responding to the ongoing legacies of settler colonialism, slavery, racism, classism, misogyny, and other forms of violence and oppression through their policy protagonism.

Food politics and school food politics have been loosely framed as engagement with the state.[55] Policy protagonists do engage with state agencies and officials. They also acknowledge that power and resources for addressing policy problems lie in cross-sectoral or cross-issue coalition building. The chapters in this collection—particularly those written by practitioners involved in these coalitions—reveal to us the wide variety of stakeholders who inherently care, or can be brought to care, about school food. The chapters also make an important intervention into how we conceptualize "politics" and how we value different forms of labor. Too often, the policy work that gets done behind the scenes—cultivating relationships, acknowledging and asserting care for others, and validating the issues most salient to them—is invisible and unaccounted for as a political resource or asset. We argue that this relational and care-centered work is a necessary and powerful driver of political change.

Policy protagonists often have an astute understanding of social categories and symbolic identities (e.g., teachers as second mothers or caregivers; mothers as cooks, not chefs; youth as uninterested in healthy food; women as farmers), and they assert them to clarify the "problem" and to seek the resources to transform school food systems. For example, in Brazil (chapter 10), feminist farmers use the symbolic identity of women as "nurturers," and even though that knowledge is often overlooked or dismissed, they, too, understand and assert their valuable knowledge and positionality to make concrete changes to the pedagogy, philosophy, and practice of feeding children. And in Philadelphia, a major city in the US (chapter 5), middle and high school students expand the social category of youth as *consumers* of school meals. Through their policy protagonism, they become youth entrepreneurs—renegotiating who feeds whom, how, when, and for what purpose—with the goal of providing "healthy deliciousness" to everyone in their school community.

What these disparate efforts have in common—and what unites them as expressions of a transformative school food politics—is how individual stakeholders demand to be included in decision-making as a community or as part of a collective, eschewing the spotlight as individual heroes. Each of the following chapters does important work in helping us understand the educational and caring potential of school food.

OVERVIEW OF THE BOOK

The chapters are organized into four parts, providing guideposts for learning from the contributors about how stakeholders engage in transformative school food politics at varied levels of governance. Many authors share strategies and tactics that have been successful in pushing the state to assume responsibility for feeding children at school in ways that support community well-being. Others shed light on the challenges, power dynamics, and potential compromises inherent in transforming school food politics. It is important to note, however, that this collection offers only a partial view of school food programs and politics around the world.

In the first part, "The Power and Potential of National School Meal Programs" (chapters 1–3), we ground the volume with a discussion of the power and potential of government-funded school meal programs as an expression of national politics. In the first chapter, Alexis Agliano Sanborn and Katsura Omori discuss how Japanese school lunch became a source of national pride and global inspiration through a series of government policies and investments across the entire school food system that emphasize nutrition, taste, cultural relevance, respect, and community collaboration. Their chapter invites us to think about the politics of care, both in terms of the policy goals of Japan's universal school meal program and in the everyday actions of Japanese students who contribute to the labor of lunch—gathering, serving, and cleaning up after meals—participating in both formal and informal acts of *shokuiku* (food education).

INTRODUCTION　　　　　　　　　　　　　　　　　　　　　　　　　　xxxiii

The premise that governments should invest in the care "infrastructure of everyday life" through the creation of high-quality universal school meal programs and complementary pedagogical goals is further illuminated in chapter 2 by Jennifer Black, Sinikka Elliott, and Rachel Engler-Stringer.[56] Their chapter focuses on Canada, one of the few affluent countries without a national school food program. Responding to growing calls for state funding to support a national program coming from the Coalition for Healthy School Food, the Canadian federal government is actively debating the future of school meals. The authors collectively argue that transcending current deadlocks around the design of this program hinges on Canadian policymakers' willingness to not only treat children as competent social actors but also to reject the narrow framing of "health" as synonymous with nutrition and to actively address issues of justice and equity.

Next, chapter 3 turns our attention to the power, potential, and problematics of *Qali Warma* (Vigorous Child, in Quechua), the national school lunch program in Peru, a global south country with a history of colonization and Indigenous erasure. Emmanuelle Ricaud Oneto's chapter shows how mothers from two Amazonian Native communities, the Maijuna and the Napuruna, grapple with the constraints of the program and deploy strategies to adapt it to their community's agendas. In both communities, mothers take turns cooking the meals and play a significant role in the school food system at the local level. In doing so, they follow local logics to discretely and, at times, profoundly deviate from the official government design of the program. Navigating the frontier between appropriation and resistance on their own terms, the mothers who cook school lunches in these Amazonian communities perform both reproductive labor and political work by claiming for themselves the power to decide who feeds whom, what, how, when, and for what purpose from within the constraints of the colonial settler state.

The second part of the book, "Claiming Space for Youth and Worker Voices" (chapters 4–7), further explores the question of who holds the power to decide these important facets of school food politics, focusing on two stakeholder groups—children and the workers who feed them—whose perspectives are too often ignored in discussions of school food policy. Chapter 4 by Kristiina Janhonen, Marjaana Manninen, and Karin Hjälmeskog moves us to Finland, a country that has guaranteed all students the right to free school meals since 1948. In Finland, national curricular standards ensure that school meals and mealtimes provide lessons in health, nutrition, and manners, as well as opportunities for students to participate in planning and implementing their local school meal programs. Leaning on Dewey's pragmatist learning theory and the concept of *food sense*, the authors develop a flexible action framework using a home economics course, "Sustainability transformations in our school," that taps into the potential of both teachers and school catering staff as food educators.[57]

The need to take children seriously and recognize their agency within school food systems is further illuminated in chapter 5 by Raven Lewis, who, with Jarrett Stein, focuses on Rebel Ventures, a youth-led nonprofit organization in the US. "Rebel" youth entrepreneurs, drawn from the school district of Philadelphia, Pennsylvania, and mostly students of color, know that kids want to eat good food: food that is nutrient-dense and is grown, prepared, and shared with love. So, they have developed products that are served to fellow students throughout the school district. This chapter is one example of how youth "do" school food politics, told from the perspective of one Rebel, Raven Lewis, who shares middle and high school students' lived experiences of school food, their motivations for starting and participating in Rebel Ventures, and the impacts it has had on their lives.

In a similar vein, chapter 6 by Rebecca Davis, A. Brooks Bowden, and Lisa Altmann shows what is possible when school nutrition workers become policy protagonists. Many students and families in the US rely on government-subsidized school meals to meet their daily nutritional needs, yet these meals are much harder to access during the summer months when schools are closed. In rural North Carolina, school nutrition staff developed an innovative program called the "Yum-Yum Bus" that uses school buses converted into mobile cafeterias to deliver food and educational materials directly to children's neighborhoods. Key to the program's success, they argue, was the strategic formation of school-community partnerships and the collaborative work of a diverse group of staff from departments and positions that do not always work together or have a seat at the policy table.

The importance of frontline school nutrition staff in meeting the needs of children and communities is further emphasized by Margaret

Read, Anne Moertel, Courtney Smith, and Jennifer LeBarre in chapter 7, which charts the innovations in policy, sourcing, preparation, and service that occurred during the first two years of the pandemic to allow schools to operate the largest emergency food program in US history. Federal policy waivers allowed schools to serve all students up to age eighteen free of charge, but this temporary universal free school meal program was ended at the start of the 2022–2023 school year. This sudden end to a widely popular program bolstered existing advocacy efforts, as more and more stakeholder groups began to believe it was both necessary and feasible to continue the pandemic "free for all" school meal programs through state or federal policy changes.

Part III of the book, "Struggling for Just School Food Economies" (chapters 8–11), continues this inquiry into the dynamic nature of school food politics and its transformative potential through a careful examination of policy protagonism, care ethics, and rural-urban alliances in Brazil, India, and South Korea. All three countries operate universal free school meal programs and leverage their school food budgets to accomplish other goals related to social justice and environmental sustainability.

In chapter 8, Prerna Rana explains how the Right to Food campaign, an Indian civil society initiative started in 2001, transformed India's existing Mid-day Meal Scheme (MDMS) into the world's largest free school lunch program. With a combined strategy of grassroots community action and judicial intervention, the campaign put pressure on state governments for effective implementation of national policy and a legal recognition of children's right to food. Rana then examines other ways that civil society actors continue to shape the MDMS, from women's self-help groups that cook meals in rural villages to the philanthropic organizations that run centralized catering operations to the left-leaning trade unions that oppose such public-private partnerships. Ultimately, she reveals the tensions inherent in Indian school food politics that are hidden when the concerns of "civil society" are seen as monolithic and reminds us to think critically about the politics of different stakeholder groups.

Next, in chapter 9, José Arimatea Barros Bezerra and Ludmir dos Santos Gomes give unique insight into the experience of two smallholder farmers, Ana and João, in the Brazilian state of Ceará with ties to the Landless Workers' Movement, who formed a cooperative and became suppliers to the *Programa Nacional de Alimentação Escolar* (PNAE) [National School Feeding Program], one of the world's largest free school lunch programs. Beginning in 2009, Brazilian schools were required to purchase at least thirty percent of the food served through the PNAE from local, smallholder farmers or their collectives. The compulsory policy language of the PNAE stands out as a global example of how governments can strategically use school meal funding to support the economic viability of smallholder farmers and socially disadvantaged food producers. Achieving this transformative potential, this chapter argues, is dependent on the agroecological farming and policy protagonism of small-scale producers like Ana and João whose local efforts are key to replacing *big food* corporations with anti-capitalist alternatives.

In chapter 10, Sônia Fátima Schwendler, Cristiane Coradin, and Islândia Bezerra also explore how Brazil's PNAE has created new avenues for agroecological feminist women farmers to engage in school food politics. Using oral histories of Landless Workers' Movement members who supply agroecological food to local schools in the state of Paraná, the authors reveal not only the benefits and challenges of participating in the PNAE but also the philosophical, political, and pedagogical commitments of these women. They show how Landless Women have successfully navigated the PNAE policy certification process, thereby earning a reliable income and the independence that comes with it. In sharing the perspectives of these feminist agroecologists, this chapter makes an important contribution to the volume, theorizing the importance of care ethics and women's empowerment to the transformative potential of school food politics.

In chapter 11, Seulgi Son then asks what role municipal governments can play in driving food system transformations through school meal programs. Beginning in 2011, after several decades of civil society activism in support of food sovereignty and against the privatization of school meals, South Korea enacted a universal free, eco-friendly school lunch policy. To accomplish such a wide-reaching transformation of the existing school food system, South Korea's central, provisional, and municipal governments developed novel procurement policies and infrastructure for sourcing and distributing eco-friendly school lunch ingredients. Bolstered by this experience, the metropolitan government of Seoul, South Korea's capital city, created the Urban-Rural Coexistence Meal Service Program, an innovative effort to create short, direct supply chains between small- and mid-sized family farms in rural areas and public meal programs in urban areas. As Son's chapter reveals, transformations within school food politics can lead to greater efforts to reshape regional food economies.

In the final part of the book, "Tools and Campaigns for Systems Change" (chapters 12–15), we take a close look at tools and campaigns for systems change that have been effectively used in Canada and the US. In chapter 12, Christine C. Caruso, Lucy Flores, and Amy Rosenthal argue that stories are a powerful tool for sharing information and communicating diverse stakeholders' perspectives in ways that inspire empathy and action. They present one storytelling approach—composite narrative—as a promising method for sharing stories derived from multiple people's experiences. The authors explain how and why to use the composite narrative storytelling technique and offer three example vignettes based on data collected by the US-based nonprofit organization FoodCorps. Throughout, they emphasize the importance of incorporating an equity-centered and culturally responsive approach in all phases of research, communications, and advocacy, and demonstrate how they integrate this approach into the theories and techniques presented in the chapter.

Andrée Gaçoin, Michelle Gautreaux, and Anne Hales (chapter 13) then share how the British Columbia Teachers' Federation in Canada used facilitated think tanks to guide action and advocacy to address a longstanding issue that many teachers have witnessed and addressed daily in their classrooms: growing food insecurity among students and the abdication of government responsibility to meet this need. Grounded in a framework of union research as activist research, the authors share key themes from a union-organized think tank related to principles that can guide action and advocacy on food security in British Columbia, Canada. Importantly, this technique (virtual think tank discussion) and organizational structure (social justice union) allow teachers to come together—despite the time scarcity, overwork, fatigue, and burnout that the COVID-19 pandemic has exacerbated across the teaching profession—to engage in policy protagonism.

The next two chapters take us inside two successful state-level campaigns in the US, allowing us to learn firsthand from the nonprofit organizations that helped build multi-stakeholder coalitions in California and Vermont. These campaigns fundamentally altered the scope of school food politics in the US by offering proven templates for achieving state-level policy changes that guarantee free meals to all students and invest public dollars in farm-to-school programs that source local ingredients for school meals. In chapter 14, Anne Moertel, from the Center for Ecoliteracy, a California-based nonprofit organization that has been engaged in school food systems change for more than twenty-five years, tells the story of how California became the first state in the US to create a universal school meal program in 2021. Moertel articulates core strategies and lessons from this campaign that secured government-funding and policy commitments to provide every student with free, freshly prepared, California-grown school meals and food education opportunities.

In a complementary chapter, Anore Horton, Faye Mack, Betsy Rosenbluth, and Amy Shollenberger tell the story of the Vermont Farm Fresh School Meals for All Bill, passed in 2022, which was developed and championed by Vermont state legislators representing all three of the state's major parties. The authors are leaders in a solidarity coalition, which includes stakeholders with varying political affiliations and organizational purposes (e.g., anti-hunger, child nutrition, farm-to-school, union labor), who united to achieve this shared vision through policy protagonism at the state level. In chapter 15, they provide a history of their campaign and explain the action circles organizing model they used to pass legislation that guarantees universal free school meals, establishes a new local food purchasing incentive program, and funds the Farm to School and Early Childhood Network and grants program.

We draw the collection to a close with a conclusion in which we discuss our efforts to push the field of school food politics forward, strategies and priorities for expanding the field, and our vision for transforming school food politics through care and community.

In this contemporary moment, as school food programs around the world are being reimagined and rebuilt after the disruptions of the COVID-19 pandemic and school closures, we see both an urgent need for a more radical school food politics and an expansion in the politics of the possible. *Transforming School Food Politics around the World* charts a path forward by harnessing the collective wisdom of a diverse group of practitioners, youth, academics, and community-engaged scholars who possess vital knowledge and experiences of transforming school food politics on a scale that is relatable and translatable to other contexts. It is through a transnational dialogue, as offered in the chapters to come, that both school food scholarship and political practice are pushed in exciting new directions. We hope readers will emerge with a deeper understanding of the critical role of feminist politics of care and policy protagonism, while learning innovative strategies to inform their own efforts to change school food policy and systems.

NOTES

1. Santiago Brunetto, "'Con hambre no se puede estudiar', el reclamo de los estudiantes por el sistema de viandas porteño." *Pagina12*, September 29, 2022, https://www.pagina12.com.ar/485699-con-hambre-no-se-puede-estudiar-el-reclamo-de-los-estudiante.
2. Dorte Ruge, Irene Torres, Darren Powell, eds., *School Food, Equity and Social Justice* (New York: Routledge, 2022).
3. "About," School Meals Coalition, 2022, https://schoolmealscoalition.org/about/.
4. Jen Sandler, "Re-Framing the Politics of Urban Feeding in U.S. Public Schools: Parents, Programs, Activists, and the State," in *School Food Politics: The Complex Ecology of Hunger and Feeding in Schools around the World*, ed. Sarah A. Robert and Marcus B. Weaver-Hightower (New York: Peter Lang, 2011), 25–45.
5. bell hooks, "Cultural Criticism & Transformation" (transcript of interview, Media Education Foundation, 1997), retrieved from https://www.mediaed.org/transcripts/Bell-Hooks-Transcript.pdf.
6. See chapter 12, this volume.
7. Given the global diversity of school meals, throughout the book, different terms are used to describe programs. In some cases, authors use terms interchangeably (e.g., school nutrition worker, cafeteria manager, and school food worker), and in others they use a specific term to communicate nuances in how terms or roles are conceptualized within their own national contexts (e.g., school caterers in Finland and cook-cum-helpers in India).
8. See Jennifer Geist Rutledge, *Feeding the Future: School Lunch Programs as Global Social Policy* (New Brunswick, NJ: Rutgers University Press, 2016); Marije Oostindjer et al., "Are School Meals a Viable and Sustainable Tool to Improve the Healthiness and Sustainability of Children's Diet and Food Consumption? A Cross-National Comparative Perspective," *Critical Reviews in Food Science and Nutrition* 57, no. 18 (October 2016): 3942–3958, https://doi.org/10.1080/10408398.2016.1197180.
9. "Home Grown School Feeding," World Food Programme, retrieved March 23, 2023 from https://www.wfp.org/home-grown-school-feeding.
10. World Food Programme (WFP), *State of School Feeding Worldwide 2022* (Rome: World Food Programme, 2022), retrieved from https://docs.wfp.org/api/documents

/WFP-0000147725/download/?_ga=2.16195254.1876545415.1682432625-2142914727.1679423068, 35.

11. World Food Programme (WFP), *State of School Feeding Worldwide 2020* (Rome: World Food Programme, 2021).

12. WFP, *State of School Feeding Worldwide 2022*.

13. Global Child Nutrition Foundation (GCNF), *School Meal Programs around the World: Results from the Global Survey of School Meal Programs* (Global Child Nutrition Foundation, 2019), https://gcnf.org/wp-content/uploads/2021/03/GCNF_School-Meal-Programs-Around-the-World_Report_2021_Final.pdf.

14. GCNF, *School Meal Programs around the World*.

15. Global Child Nutrition Foundation (GCNF), *School Meal Programs around the World: Results from the 2021 Global Survey of School Meal Programs* (Global Child Nutrition Foundation, 2022), survey.gcnf.org/2021-global-survey.

16. GCNF, *School Meal Programs around the World: Results from the 2021*.

17. GCNF, *School Meal Programs around the World*.

18. GCNF, *School Meal Programs around the World: Results from the 2021*.

19. GCNF, *School Meal Programs around the World: Results from the 2021*; GCNF, *School Meal Programs around the World*.

20. Ruge, Torres, and Powell, *School Food, Equity*.

21. "School Food Programs around the World," The Coalition for Healthy School Food, retrieved March 23, 2023 from https://www.healthyschoolfood.ca/school-food-programs-around-the-world.

22. Bent Egberg Mikkelsen and Tenna Doktor Olsen, "Organic Foods in Danish Municipal School Food Systems: A Multi Stakeholder Analysis of Available Evidence on Constraints and Perspectives," in *Proceedings from the 3rd International IPOPY Conference: Novel Strategies for Climate Mitigation, Sustainability and Healthy Eating in Public Foodscapes*, ed. Bent Egberg Mikkelsen et al. (Tjele, Denmark: International Centre for Research in Organic Food Systems, 2010), 36–41, http://orgprints.org/16798/1/FoodPrint%2709_Proceedings_2nd_ed_FINAL.pdf.

23. Dorte Ruge and Mitdlarak Lennert, "School Foodscapes in Greenland and Denmark—Critical Perspectives," in *School Food, Equity and Social Justice: Critical Reflections and Perspectives*, ed. Dorte Ruge, Irene Torres, and Darren Powell (London: Routledge, 2022).

24. See chapters 1 and 4, this volume.

25. Ruge, Torres, and Powell, *School Food, Equity*.

26. See chapter 8, this volume.

27. Sarah Riggs Stapleton, "Parent Activists versus the Corporation: A Fight for School Food Sovereignty," *Agriculture and Human Values* 36, no. 4 (2019): 805–817.

28. See chapter 4, this volume.

INTRODUCTION

29. Donald A. P. Bundy et al., eds., *Re-Imagining School Feeding: A High-Return Investment in Human Capital and Local Economies* (Washington, DC: The World Bank, 2018), retrieved from https://dcp-3.org/sites/default/files/resources/CAHD_eBook.pdf.

30. Donald Bundy et al., *Rethinking School Feeding: Social Safety Nets, Child Development, and the Education Sector* (Washington, DC: The World Bank, 2009), http://dx.doi.org/10.1596/978-0-8213-7974-5.

31. World Food Programme, *State of School Feeding Worldwide 2020* (Rome: World Food Programme, 2021), 68.

32. Jennifer Geist Rutledge, *Feeding the Future: School Lunch Programs as Global Social Policy* (New Brunswick, NJ: Rutgers University Press, 2016)

33. See chapters 3, 8, 9, and 10, this volume.

34. World Food Programme, *State of School Feeding Worldwide 2020*.

35. GCNF, *School Meal Programs around the World: Results from the 2021*.

36. Ruge, Torres, and Powell, *School Food, Equity*.

37. GCNF, *School Meal Programs around the World*.

38. GCNF, *School Meal Programs around the World: Results from the 2021*.

39. See chapters 1, 9, 10, 11, 14, and 15, this volume.

40. Food and Agriculture Organization (FAO), *Public Food Procurement for Sustainable Food Systems and Healthy Diets—Volume 1*, (Rome: FAO and Alliance of Biodiversity International and CIAT, 2021).

41. See chapters 2, 3, 9, and 10, this volume.

42. Ruge, Torres, and Powell, *School Food, Equity*, 19–20.

43. "Current Projects: Native Farm to School," First Nations' Development Institute, 2022, https://www.firstnations.org/projects/native-farm-to-school/.

44. Joan C. Tronto, *Caring Democracy: Markets, Equality, and Justice* (New York: New York University Press, 2013), 139.

45. Jennifer E. Gaddis, *The Labor of Lunch: Why We Need Real Food and Real Jobs in American Public Schools* (Oakland: University of California Press, 2019), 5.

46. Berenice Fisher and Joan C. Tronto, "Toward a Feminist Theory of Caring," in *Circles of Care: Work and Identity in Women's Lives*, ed. Emily K. Abel and Margaret K. Nelson (Albany: State University of New York Press, 1990), 36–54, 40; Joan C. Tronto, *Moral Boundaries: A Political Argument for an Ethic of Care* (New York: Routledge, 1993), 103.

47. Jennifer Gaddis and Amy K. Coplen, "Reorganizing School Lunch for a More Just and Sustainable Food System in the US," *Feminist Economics* 24, no. 3 (2018): 89–112, https://doi.org/10.1080/13545701.2017.1383621.

48. Christine Milligan and Janine Wiles, "Landscapes of Care," *Progress in Human Geography* 34, no. 6 (2010): 736–754, https://doi.org/https://doi.org/10.1177/0309132510364556.

49. Paula England, Michelle Budig, and Nancy Folbre, "Wages of Virtue: The Relative Pay of Care Work," *Social Problems* 49, no. 4 (2002): 455–473.

50. Patricia Allen and Carolyn Sachs, "Women and Food Chains: The Gendered Politics of Food," *The International Journal of Sociology of Agriculture and Food* 15, no. 1 (2007): 1–23.

51. Robert Gottlieb, *Care-Centered Politics: From the Home to the Planet* (Boston, MA: MIT Press, 2022), 183.

52. Sarah A. Robert, "U.S. Teachers as Policy Protagonists in Digital Public Spaces?" *Peabody Journal of Education* 92, no. 4 (Fall 2017): 521–536.

53. Robert, "U.S. Teachers as Policy Protagonists."

54. Gottlieb, *Care-Centered Politics*.

55. For food politics, see Robert L. Paarlberg, *Food Politics: What Everyone Needs to Know* (Oxford: Oxford University Press, 2010); for school food politics, see Sarah A. Robert and Marcus B. Weaver-Hightower, eds., *School Food Politics: The Complex Ecology of Hunger and Feeding in Schools around the World* (New York: Peter Lang, 2011).

56. Gottlieb, *Care-Centered Politics*.

57. Kristiina Janhonen, Kaisa Torkkeli, and Johanna Mäkelä, "Informal Learning and Food Sense in Home Cooking," *Appetite* 130 (November 2018): 190–198. https://doi.org/10.1016/j.appet.2018.08.019.

I

THE POWER AND POTENTIAL OF NATIONAL SCHOOL MEAL PROGRAMS

Jennifer E. Gaddis and Sarah A. Robert

At the national level, state-sponsored school meal programs can be used for many aims that contribute to the common good. Beyond simply providing food, these public programs can be designed to improve children's health, education, and well-being; promote gender equity by helping to attract and keep girls in school; create new employment opportunities for workers across the school food chain; and catalyze broader food systems transformations that increase local agro-biodiversity, strengthen food sovereignty, and shift power away from multinational corporations to the communities where children are fed. Achieving these aims requires a transformation in global school food politics that counters the influence and legacy of multinational corporations and colonial powers.

The three chapters that follow engage with school food politics at the national scale and provoke questions about the cultural values, economic priorities, and contested ownership of these programs. Chapter 1, "A Whole Systems Approach to School Food Policy in Japan," shows us what is possible when countries reclaim their school meal programs, recognize them as complex sociocultural-political-economic-ecological systems, and design them in ways that emphasize collective well-being. Scratch cooking, local sourcing of ingredients, meaningful food education, and community engagement are all important features of the Japanese model, which is one of the most highly regarded in the world. Notably, within the Japanese school lunch system, children are educated both to take part in communal care (serving and cleaning up after lunchtime) and to value the labor of the many workers who feed them, care for them, and educate them. But even this system falls short of achieving the full caring potential of school meals: the program is universal, but not universally free (parents pay a fee unless they qualify for a public subsidy) and only one meal choice is offered to students, which marginalizes students who do not see themselves reflected in Japan's national culinary traditions or suffer from food allergies.[1]

Chapter 2, "Centering Children, Health, and Justice in Canadian School Food Programs," furthers our argument that the true power of school meals rests in their caring potential. As advocates work through the many tensions and negotiations inherent in designing Canada's first national school meal program, they highlight historical atrocities committed against Indigenous peoples and show how reconciliation of these past wrongs is a necessary act of care that could help build a healthier school food program for people and the environment. Further, this chapter takes seriously the notion of children as political actors and their human rights to food, care, and education. In doing so, this chapter reminds us that the social organization of school meals—who feeds whom, how, when, and for what purpose—can reflect and contribute to community self-determination. This is the ideal brought into view by the transformative school food politics we argue for in this volume. Yet, to reach this ideal, we must acknowledge and attend to the opposite outcome: that the social organization of school meals can extend the state's control over people's lives and dictate the values of the food they eat in schools.

We see this conflict arise in chapter 3, "School Food Politics, Identity, and Indigeneity in the Peruvian Amazon," which highlights the state's control over the infrastructure of daily life and pushes us to question how community autonomy can be embedded into national school food policy. Through case studies of two Native Amazonian communities, we learn how Napuruna and Maijuna mothers select, prepare, and serve school meals. We also learn the many ways they engage in policy protagonism at the hyperlocal village level by challenging and complicating Peru's "national" goals that do not meaningfully consider the sovereignty of their communities. Their actions remind us how important it is to question who defines what constitutes "care" within schools and how it should be provided—echoing discussions from chapter 2 about the need for community self-determination when making demands on the state.

Taken together, these chapters point toward important transformations in national-level school food politics, broaden the scope of who might be considered a school food "stakeholder," and give fresh insight into how diverse stakeholders can assert themselves as national-level policymakers. Perhaps most importantly, these chapters illustrate that transforming school food politics around the world requires a historical understanding of the social organization of school meals that accounts for unique national circumstances and specific political-economic challenges.

NOTE

1. Tina Moffat and Danielle Gendron, "Cooking Up the 'Gastrocitizen' through School Meal Programs in France and Japan," *Food, Culture & Society* 22, no. 1 (2018): 63–77, https://doi.org/10.1080/15528014.2018.1547587.

1

A WHOLE SYSTEMS APPROACH TO SCHOOL FOOD POLICY IN JAPAN

Alexis Agliano Sanborn and Katsura Omori

In early November, elementary school children across Japan gather in fields and school gardens to harvest daikon. Some students are particularly excited because they sowed the seeds for these hearty root vegetables themselves. Teachers prep them with instructions like "Be sure to pull the daikon out straight" or "They have deep roots, so heave with all your might!" Children's cries of amazement soon fill the air: "How heavy they are!" "I've pulled three... How about you?" Elderly neighborhood volunteers often lend a hand. Similar episodes of experiential food education occur throughout the year, as students harvest sweet potatoes, peas, and rice. After the harvest, each child receives a portion of produce to take home and enjoy. The remainder is gathered up and prepared for school lunch.

Japanese school lunch (*gakkō kyūshoku*) is regarded by specialists and the public alike for its nutritional quality, dynamic curriculum, and intentional integration into everyday life in local communities. The current design of the program is a result of two interconnected laws: the 2005 Basic Law on Food Education and the School Lunch Act of 1954—which was significantly revised in 2008.

Today, school lunch is a nearly universal program in Japan, serving 98.7 percent of elementary schools and 89.1 percent of junior high schools nationwide—over 29,000 schools in total.[1] Over 39,000 municipal food service workers prepare fresh meals for more than nine million middle and elementary school children.[2] Institutions that implement school lunch programs strive to serve all members of the student body, and those who attend the school typically partake in the meal. Students with dietary or allergy restrictions are permitted to bring their own lunches from home. Municipal governments fund the labor and operations to produce meals, while guardians cover the costs of ingredients through monthly fees ranging from US$33 to $39 per child.[3] These fees are considered part of "school costs," which guardians pay as part of their child's education. For guardians who cannot afford school lunches, local or prefectural governments subsidize the school lunch fees based on household income and size. The quality of school lunches nationwide remains relatively uniform due to government nutrition guidelines. Parents and guardians appreciate the convenience, nutrition, and affordability the lunches provide, as well as the food education (*shokuiku*) that is central to these meals. Students generally find meals tasty and satisfying.[4]

THE HISTORICAL DEVELOPMENT OF JAPAN'S SCHOOL LUNCH PROGRAM

School lunch in Japan began in the Meiji Era (1868–1912) and developed alongside universal education. The nation's earliest known school lunch service began in 1889 at Chuai Elementary School at Daitokuji Buddhist Temple in Tsuruoka City, Yamagata Prefecture. Philanthropic monks provided simple, nutritious meals for their poor and hungry students. The early meals were basic fare: rice balls, pickled vegetables, and salted salmon.[5] Over the next three decades, school lunch service expanded around the country through volunteer grassroots organizations and local networks.

By the turn of the twentieth century, the Japanese government realized that meals served in school could contribute to the development of healthy citizens.[6] In 1932, Japan's Ministry of Education provided a national subsidy to cover school lunch operations, and by 1940, lunch recipients included children in need, those with health issues, and those with undernourished or unbalanced diets.[7] School lunch had become a matter of national interest.

World War II and its aftermath saw a dramatic transformation in the scope and national priority of school lunch. As the war deepened, food access and quality around the country deteriorated, and in many places school lunch service was suspended. City dwellers were particularly hard-hit by food shortages. Under Japan's postwar occupation, school lunches were reinstated to address hunger. Beginning in December 1946, the US partnered with Japan's Ministry of Education, Ministry of Agriculture, and Ministry of Health & Welfare to launch an experimental school lunch for the urban population. By the end of the occupation, more than eight million children participated in the school lunch program.[8] These postwar years built the foundations of national nutritional standards, mechanisms for sharing expenses, and the role of school lunch committees.

As the US occupation ended in 1952, the future of the school lunch program seemed uncertain. Japan had regained its independence through the 1951 San Francisco Peace Treaty, which brought an end to two programs that had helped fund school lunch: Government Appropriation for Relief in Occupied Area (GARIOA) and Licensed Agencies for Relief in Asia (LARA).[9] Without this support, families now had to pay for students' meals out of pocket.[10] Facing a significant budget crisis, Japan's finance minister advocated for the termination of Japan's portion of government subsidies and even school lunches themselves. Parent-teacher associations nationwide urged the government to continue school meals, and even opposition political party members joined forces to propose permanent legislation.[11] Ultimately, reports of malnourished children and natural disasters hastened the passage of new legislation: the School Lunch Act in 1954. The act established four nationwide objectives:[12]

I. Promote a better understanding of diet in everyday life and cultivate desirable dietary habits;
II. Enrich school life and cultivate sociability;
III. Promote streamlining of dietary life, improvement of nutrition, and enhancement of health;
IV. Lead to a proper understanding of food production, distribution, and consumption.[13]

The School Lunch Act also included a School Lunch Enforcement Ordinance, which stipulated mechanisms of cost-sharing and details of local and national funding. Although the act initially only covered public elementary schools, by 1956, the law extended to all compulsory education.[14]

In 1955, the School Lunch Association Act established regional associations to oversee school lunch quality. After several mergers and reorganizations, these associations reemerged as the Federation of Prefectural School Lunch Associations of Japan. Staffed by an array of retirees, education administrators, food service workers, and government employees, these associations continue to administer government-commissioned services, including the procurement and distribution of food. The associations maintain no commercial purpose, and their operational costs must be approved by the Ministry of Education.[15] The associations' primary focus remains operational support, ensuring a stable supply chain relatively unencumbered by the concerns of private enterprise.

One of the defining culinary characteristics of postwar Japanese school lunch was the inclusion of bread and milk, two ingredients absent from the nation's traditional diet. During the occupation, the US donated surplus wheat flour for use in school lunches, and UNICEF supplied powdered milk to Japanese schools. Both foods were promoted by Western nations as excellent sources of vitamins and calories and helped to ameliorate malnourishment in children.[16] Even after the occupation came to an end, the Japanese government encouraged the public to eat bread, meat, and dairy to build strong bodies, and Japan continued to import US wheat for use in school lunches. Bread-based school lunches spread to every part of the country by the 1960s,[17] and milk accompanies school lunch to this day.

In the early 1980s, faced with a growing national debt and a sluggish economy, the government looked for new ways to cut spending and support the private sector.[18] As a result, in 1985, the education ministry announced it would award private companies contracts to produce school lunch.[19] This gave municipal governments the choice to either manage meal production themselves or engage private companies to prepare meals planned by a municipal nutritionist. Some communities complained about the contracted school lunch providers, and in the early 2000s, several citizen lawsuits argued that the contracts constituted an illegal use of public funds.[20] Those efforts failed, and today school lunch associations continue to partner with both public and private providers.

Faced with a severe economic recession that began in the 1990s and continued for decades, Japan embraced neoliberal policies designed to support free-market capitalism through lowered tariffs and limitations on government spending. The increasingly globalized market led to the formation of a grassroots movement focused on *chisan chisho* (local production, local consumption)[21] that emphasizes the quality and uniqueness of Japan's agricultural identity.[22] The agricultural ministry adopted *chisan chisho* in 2002 to improve the country's dismal food self-sufficiency rates, revitalize rural communities, and address food safety concerns.[23] Prefectures and municipalities now offer matching funds or subsidies for schools to partner with local farmers, create new meals with local ingredients, and use locally produced food for food education activities.[24] The *chisan chisho* movement and policy have helped revitalize local agriculture and cultivate students' sense of place through school lunch.

FOOD EDUCATION LAW AND SCHOOL LUNCH ACT REVISIONS

Ongoing health concerns related to rising rates of diabetes and obesity, coupled with the desire to support and benefit from local agriculture, contributed to the development of the 2005 Basic Law on Food Education. This law encourages individuals and organizations to promote knowledge about food and nutrition and to foster the public's ability to make appropriate food choices. Lawmakers drew inspiration from the writings of Sagen Ishizuka (1850–1909), a military doctor and early proponent of the macrobiotic diet, whose philosophy influenced, for example, the law's supplementary provision[25] "Food education is the foundation for living and is positioned as the base of intellectual, moral, and physical education." According to this precept, one should intellectually engage with food education by learning about nutrition. Physically, one should strive for a healthy diet and lifestyle. Morally, individuals should practice gratitude toward food, nature, and those who created the meal.

The resulting 2005 law had seven key objectives:

The Seven Objectives of the Basic Law on Food Education (2005)

I. To promote health in body and mind, as well as to enrich lives;
II. To develop a greater appreciation for and understanding of diets, including the natural environment and the various roles of people who produce, transport, and prepare food;
III. To develop volunteer/grassroots movements to promote food education;
IV. To encourage food education among children (as well as parents, educators, and daycare providers);

V. To reinforce dietary knowledge through food-related experiences and activities including at home, schools, and in the community;
VI. To promote awareness and appreciation of traditional Japanese food culture and food supply/demand, as well as opportunities for interaction between food producers and consumers to revitalize rural farming and fishing regions and boost food self-sufficiency in Japan;
VII. To provide information on proper diets and food safety[26]

Today, the Ministry of Agriculture, Forestry, and Fisheries (MAFF) oversees food education promotion plans in cooperation with other ministries, prefectures, and municipalities. To meet the seven objectives, prefectures develop food education plans and report progress every year. Table 1.1 shows a selection of target areas that the Basic Law on Food Education addressed starting in 2015 and their progress as of 2020. Like other pieces of Japanese legislation, the law relies on informal social consensus.[27]

In 2008, the School Lunch Act was significantly revised and changed its aim from "improvement of dietary habits" to—in keeping with the Basic Law on Food Education—the "promotion of food education."[28] Food education became an official part of the National Curriculum Standard for Japanese schools, and the School Lunch Act's objectives were reworded and expanded in order to better align with the general aims of the Basic Law on Food Education.[29] Objectives four and five of the School Lunch Act now highlight ethics through appreciation of the natural world and the people who support the food industry. The newly added sixth objective highlights the importance of Japanese culinary history.

The Seven Objectives of the Revised School Lunch Act (2008)[30]

+ indicates a new objective added in 2008

I. Sustain and improve health through proper nutrition;
II. Foster understanding, decision-making, and eating habits for an appropriate diet;
III. Enliven school life and encourage an active, social, and considerate spirit;
IV. Further appreciation of the gifts of nature that support us, foster respect of life and nature, and encourage a spirit of environmental conservation;+
V. Acknowledge how the activities of many people support the food industry and respect their hard work;+
VI. Further understanding of Japanese and local traditional cuisine;+
VII. Foster an understanding of the mechanisms of food production, transportation, and consumption

Table 1.1 A selection of food education goals and target values, 2021–2025

Food education goals	2025 target values	Target status in 2020
Percentage of people interested in food education	90% or more	83.2%
Number of mutual meals such as breakfast or dinner eaten with family members	11 times a week or more	9.6 times per week
Percentage of children who skip breakfast	0%	4.6%
Frequency that local products are discussed in the food and nutrition teacher's lessons	12 times per month or more	9.1 times per month
Average intake of vegetables per day	350 g or more	280.5 g
Percentage of citizens with agriculture, forestry, or fishery experience	70% or more	65.7%
Percentage of citizens who have basic knowledge of food safety and can apply it	80% or more	75.2%
Percentage of municipalities that have made and implemented a plan for promoting food education	100%	87.5%
Number of citizens involved in volunteer or other groups promoting food education	370,000 or more	362,000

Note: See Ministry of Agriculture, Forestry, and Fisheries (MAFF), "The Fourth Basic Plan for the Promotion of Shokuiku (Provisional Translation)" March 2021, https://www.maff.go.jp/j/syokuiku/attach/pdf/kannrennhou-30.pdf.

Taken together, the Basic Law on Food Education and the revision of the School Lunch Act objectives helped school lunch to improve health and strengthen communities more effectively.

SCHOOL LUNCH TODAY AND ITS SEVEN OBJECTIVES

In the following sections, we explore some of the ways that students, teachers, and communities are fulfilling the goals prescribed in the School

Lunch Act while addressing broader issues facing Japanese society. We want to emphasize that the examples we use are not isolated but representative of numerous parallel practices at schools across the country.

OBJECTIVE I: SUSTAIN AND IMPROVE HEALTH THROUGH PROPER NUTRITION

Good nutrition is the foundation of school lunch and is key to a child's health and development. Indeed, for some children, school lunch may be their only nutritious meal of the day. Poverty rates in Japan have steadily risen over the past thirty years, and currently one in seven children lives in poverty.[31] During breaks in the school year when meals are not provided, such as vacations and holidays, educators anecdotally report that they notice weight loss in some of their students.[32] Research has shown that vitamins and minerals provided by school lunch alone may be sufficient for students to overcome dietary deficiencies.[33]

School lunch providers follow government nutrition standards to create meals that meet one-third of a child's daily caloric requirement (530–830 calories). Lunch should provide the following quota of daily nutrition: protein (13–20 percent), lipids (20–30 percent), calcium (50 percent), and iron (40 percent), among other nutrients.[34] National guidelines state that providers should supply these nutrients from a variety of food types, including cereals, vegetables, beans, fruits, mushrooms, sea produce, seafood, meats, eggs, and dairy.[35] School lunch typically contains a main dish (protein), side dish, soup, and carbohydrates. School lunch providers strive to source the highest-quality affordable ingredients from domestic producers.

In addition to satisfying nutritional quotas, school lunch providers purposefully develop meals to prevent specific health issues. For example, in recent years, hypertension (high blood pressure) was designated a primary chronic disease in Japan,[36] and some providers are now developing low-sodium meals to cultivate students' taste in less salty foods from an early age. Schools may cook with more *dashi* (a savory stock of kelp and fermented bonito) to create naturally rich umami flavors that lessen salt use. Other providers enhance flavor through ingredients like garlic and ginger. One town in Iwate Prefecture is even experimenting with milk to increase savoriness.[37]

OBJECTIVE II: FOSTER UNDERSTANDING, DECISION-MAKING, AND EATING HABITS FOR AN APPROPRIATE DIET

School lunch providers and educators use a variety of methods to foster an "intellectual appetite." Some of their most versatile educational tools are the simple printouts of school lunch notices (*kyūshoku dayori*) and monthly school lunch menus (*kondate*), which are posted throughout school buildings and sent home with students.[38] The notices often include information from school nutritionists about health, table manners, and seasonal produce, featuring supplementary recipes for use at home. The menus highlight each ingredient's nutritional purpose, often color-coded according to its function in the body. Some school districts have even created superhero characters based on red, green, and yellow, the colors that signify the food groups, and actors occasionally produce plays for children about adventures in healthy eating.

By the early 2000s, many dieticians were already providing food and nutrition classes in schools. Revisions to the School Lunch Act clarified their roles, stating that nutrition teachers could be employed in compulsory education (elementary and junior high school) and could be hired at the discretion of the prefectural government that would bear the cost.[39] Since then, the number of nutrition teachers in schools has gradually climbed, and in 2020, there were more than 6,500 nutrition teachers across the country.[40] Generally, nutrition teachers must have a license and a college degree. They help to manage the healthfulness, hygiene, and quality of school lunches across multiple schools.[41] They also coordinate with schoolteachers to incorporate food education into the wider curriculum.

Several times a semester, nutrition or homeroom teachers lead formal food education classes on how to be a knowledgeable consumer and healthier citizen. National curriculum guidelines suggest that younger students begin by learning basic etiquette such as how to properly hold chopsticks to cut, scoop, and stir. (From the 1950s until the mid-1970s, the "spork" was the primary school lunch utensil.)[42] Teachers discuss improper table manners such as using chopsticks to pull food apart or hovering the chopsticks over food.[43] Older students learn about proper food storage methods, the difference between "expiration dates" and "best by dates," how to construct a nutritionally balanced meal, and the types of food that can exacerbate heart disease.[44] Ideally, students will carry these lessons with them into adulthood.

OBJECTIVE III: ENLIVEN SCHOOL LIFE AND ENCOURAGE AN ACTIVE, SOCIAL, AND CONSIDERATE SPIRIT

Fostering cooperation and community spirit has been a goal of school lunch since 1958 when lunchtime was designated as a "school event" and, later, a "special activity" of classroom instruction. During lunchtime, students are expected to work collaboratively just as they would during other classes. School staff members set up hot bins at lunch stations in different parts of the building, and children participate in a rotating roster of student captains (*kyūshoku tōban*) who fetch the food and bring it to the classroom where they set up a buffet and serve their fellow students. This system of captains is instituted as early as first grade, with extra time built into the schedule for young students to practice the skills they need.

Once the students and teacher are served, the lunch captains lead the class in the traditional word of gratitude: "*itadakimasu*," which translates to "I humbly partake." No one can begin their meal before this word is spoken. Children then take approximately twenty minutes to eat lunch, listen to lunchtime announcements, and talk with their classmates. As lunch period draws to a close, captains lead their classmates in the closing phrase of thanksgiving: "*gochisosama deshita*"—"It was a feast!" Cleanup then ensues, followed by recess. From start to finish, this daily ritual involves cooperation, patience, and goodwill on the part of students. Children mature through the experience of serving all members of the class, friend or not, equally and with empathy.[45]

Sometimes entire schools prepare and serve "vertical lunches" that bring together multiple grade levels. For example, at one elementary school, fifth graders planned and managed a vertical lunch to express gratitude to the graduating class of sixth graders. The first graders escorted sixth graders to special lunchtime classrooms where second and third graders presented specially prepared name tags and lunch placemats. Fourth graders created bingo games for everyone to enjoy. The school principal noted that while "children often tend to think only about themselves . . . vertical lunches provide a valuable opportunity for them to think about the concerns of

1.1 Students lead the class in a word of gratitude before the meal begins—
"*Itadakimasu!*" Credit: Nourishing Japan, LLC.

others."[46] At other times, students extend these unique lunch experiences to the broader community, sharing meals with nearby schools or senior centers.

OBJECTIVE IV: FURTHER APPRECIATION OF THE GIFTS OF NATURE THAT SUPPORT US, FOSTER RESPECT FOR LIFE AND NATURE, AND ENCOURAGE A SPIRIT OF ENVIRONMENTAL CONSERVATION

Cultivating an appreciation of nature is encouraged across the curriculum in Japanese schools, and school lunch is no exception. National elementary school curriculum guidelines require students to care for plants and animals at school, and even in crowded urban areas, nearly every school has a small garden plot where students grow some of the food they eat.[47]

Students are encouraged to grapple with the cycle of life and death and their responsibility to the natural world. Every year, an elementary school teacher in Tsuruoka City reads to her second-grade class the picture book *Partaking of Life: The Day Little Mii Became Meat*. Centered around the inherent conflict of killing a beloved pet cow for food, this book explores the turmoil that many people—even meat producers—feel in relation to killing and consuming animals. The story inspires a sense of gratitude toward animal life. In Joetsu, Niigata Prefecture, a class of fifth graders recently devoted an entire curriculum to learning about meat and where it comes from, including the delicate subject of end of life. Students watched a film to learn how cows and pigs "arrive at the table," and a staff member from a wholesale meat processing plant visited students to discuss his work. Students had an opportunity to cut, grill, and compare various cuts of meat, and they later visited a wholesale meat market.[48] One child reflected: "It was shocking to learn how a pig is killed. From now on I will try to eat mindfully and not have any leftovers." Another student stated: "I learned that I live through the lives of others. I want to eat with gratitude."

Students also acquire greater respect for the natural world by learning about, and working to mitigate, food waste. In 2019, the government passed a law to reduce the estimated six million tons of food waste generated every year.[49] Some schools have daily "weigh-ins" of leftovers or competitions for the least wasteful class,[50] while others shortened the lunchtime distribution time to ensure more time for eating. At the same time, educators strive not to pressure students to eat when they are not hungry. School lunch providers also note which meals or ingredients go uneaten and adjust recipes to make meals more appetizing.[51]

Student-led environmental committees implement other sustainable ecological practices such as recycling, conserving electricity, and using both sides of paper.[52] One of the most important school-wide initiatives is recycling empty milk cartons from lunch. Children unfold, rinse, and dry the cartons, which many schools exchange for toilet paper from a local supplier. The environmental committee at one school in Saitama Prefecture awards special school currency called "camphor trees" to students in exchange for each notable environmental deed they complete. They can use the "trees" to make purchases at the school environmental fairs. Recently, the fair featured morning glory seedlings raised by first graders who harvested the seeds the year before and sunflower seedlings sprouted from Fukushima sunflower seeds, whose purchase supported those impacted by the March 11, 2011, earthquake and tsunami.[53]

OBJECTIVE V: ACKNOWLEDGE HOW THE FOOD INDUSTRY IS SUPPORTED BY THE ACTIVITIES OF MANY PEOPLE AND RESPECT THEIR HARD WORK

Students begin learning about the food industry at an early age, often in preschool, through visits to farms, factories, kitchens, and school lunch centers. When students from one school visited a school lunch center, a staff member quizzed students about the various people who were involved in producing their meals, from administrators to the delivery staff. As part of the exercise, students were asked to guess how many employees were included in each category. At the end of the activity, on learning that eighty-four people were responsible for the center's daily work, the young students let out a cry of amazement. Their surprise and newfound appreciation found their way into follow-up letters to food industry workers. "Thank you for the warm rice and delicious bread! The *koshihikari* rice from Maizuru was very delicious!" wrote one student to the school lunch cooking staff. "Thank you for waking up every day at five in the morning to deliver our milk," wrote another to the milk delivery man.[54] One student wrote in an essay, "When I visited the school lunch center, I came to understand something I hadn't before: that so many people are working so hard to make school lunch every day. I'm sorry that I dreaded lunch [and all the vegetables I didn't like]. From now on, I'll be sure to eat all of my lunch to become big and strong. Thank you for always making our meals."[55]

Schools invite farmers, fishers, and other producers to share with students the nature of their work. One vegetable farmer likes to talk about the importance of soil to the success of his crops.[56] Another explains how colder weather makes certain types of vegetables sweeter. Personal interactions like these deepen the understanding of food for students. After these visits, students often remark that they feel grateful and find it easier to eat previously disliked vegetables.[57] Gratitude can also promote greater enjoyment of eating and thereby reduce food waste.[58]

Schools in urban settings throughout the country partner with agricultural communities to develop unique educational experiences for school-age children, from harvesting crops to cooking. Since 2009, students from Tokyo's Haketa Elementary School have taken a three-hour train ride to visit Sanjo City, in rural Niigata Prefecture, one of the country's largest producers of rice. In 2017, thirty-eight fourth- and fifth-grade students who visited Sanjo City worked with volunteers to harvest rice by hand using a sickle.[59] No matter where students live, by the time they finish elementary school, they understand where their school lunch comes from and know that many people work to make it possible. This reinforces their connection to the community and country and helps the producers, in turn, to feel supported.[60]

OBJECTIVE VI: FURTHER UNDERSTANDING OF NATIONAL AND LOCAL TRADITIONAL CUISINE

School lunch is considered an important means of preserving and celebrating Japanese culture, and the judging criteria for the National School Lunch Tournament, which began in 2006, reflects that value, favoring regional products that highlight local culinary traditions. In 2019, out of some 1,400 applicants, the winning meal came from the Tamba-Sasayama School Lunch Center in Hyogo Prefecture. The menu included *kuromame* rice using black soybeans, which urban third graders grew, harvested, and cooked, as well as mackerel topped with locally grown *Dekansho* leeks.[61] The soup contained wild boar and local root vegetables, including Amo-chi Taro, an heirloom variety that was once a local specialty but has declined in recent years. City fourth graders grew the taro in partnership with the community, helping to revitalize and protect it.[62]

Similar stories of school lunch contributing to the local community's food culture are widespread. In Hachijojima, an island off the coast near Tokyo, members of the Hachijojima Fisheries Cooperative were surprised to learn that island fish were not included in local school lunches. "Children who live on the islands should be able to eat island fish," stated one of the cooperative members. They partnered with the local school lunch center to develop a recipe featuring local fish,[63] simultaneously expanding the fishermen's market while helping children experience their local heritage. Similar examples exist across the country, as school lunch providers work to support regional specialties and culinary traditions.

School lunch also provides an opportunity for students to experience seasonal flavors and cuisines associated with both nationwide and regional annual observances. Cooking traditional or seasonal foods may prove challenging to some families or guardians due to unfamiliarity with cooking methods, lack of time, or the high cost of ingredients. School lunch becomes a reliable way for children to participate in the country's seasonal and cultural cuisine. For example, on Children's Day, May 5th, many school lunches feature traditional bamboo shoots. Autumn flavors may include favorites like chestnuts, sweet potatoes, and mushrooms. Even foreign foods and traditions have entered the seasonal rotation with a Japanese twist, including Halloween, Christmas, and Valentine's Day. It is not uncommon for kabocha pumpkin to appear on the menu on Halloween and fried chicken on Christmas, foods now associated with these holidays in Japan.[64]

OBJECTIVE VII: FOSTER AN UNDERSTANDING OF THE MECHANISMS OF FOOD PRODUCTION, TRANSPORTATION, AND CONSUMPTION

As school lunch programs orient children to national and local concerns, they also enable the exploration of issues like trade, food safety, and transportation networks that can be international in scope. The country's self-sufficiency rate (i.e., capacity to meet its own food needs from domestic production) decreased from 79 percent in 1960 to 40 percent in 2003. In 2020, Japan had one of the lowest food self-sufficiency rates among developed countries,[65] importing 7.19 trillion yen ($69 billion USD) of food.[66] School lunch is not exempt from these trends. On average, 27 percent of school lunch ingredients are imported, and the highest import rate per product is wheat (66 percent), fruit (40 percent), fish (40 percent), and dairy (40 percent).[67] As children learn about how food travels through supply networks and onto their lunch trays, educators hope that they will become consumers who prioritize domestic produce and contribute to the nation's economic vitality. Figure 1.2[68] illustrates a simple learning tool demonstrating how school lunch is produced, adapted from the Federation of Prefectural School Lunch Associations of Japan.

As in other countries, the COVID-19 pandemic highlighted structural weaknesses within Japanese food production and procurement systems. When schools closed in the spring of 2020, news reports showed vegetables ordered for school lunch rotting in the fields, dairies with school lunch milk with nowhere to go, and parents struggling to juggle work while also providing midday meals for their children. When schools eventually began

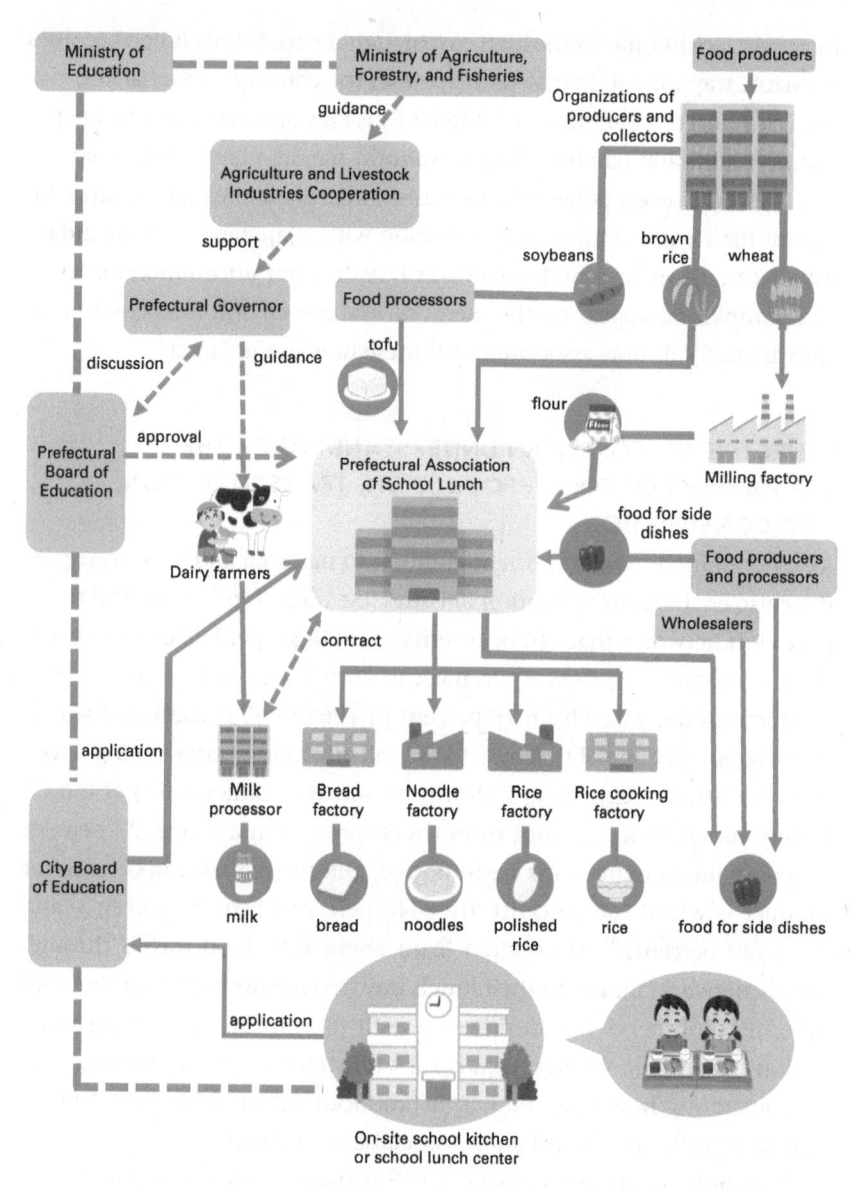

1.2 A flowchart of school lunch from producers to children. Clip art credit Irasutoya.

to reopen in August 2020, the country breathed a collective sigh of relief, and citizens felt a renewed sense of gratitude for this valuable public service. Today, school lunches have assumed an even greater symbolic value than before, suggesting resiliency, recovery, and a return to normalcy.

THE FUTURE OF SCHOOL LUNCH

In Japan, school lunch is a national priority. Yet, as school communities come together to provide meaningful experiences and wholesome nutrition to their students, they still face challenges. One concern is the increase of food-based allergies and anaphylaxis among children. Government-issued food allergy manuals and guidelines for production[69] may be inadequate for addressing the individualized nature of this health threat. School lunch producers are finding ways to adapt.

One nursery school has changed their meals to exclude egg, wheat, or dairy products altogether.[70] A school lunch center in Yamagata City has begun preparing supplementary meals without allergens like egg and milk, served to affected students in individual containers so they can still participate in classroom lunchtime activities.[71] Yet this special treatment for children with allergies may be considered stigmatizing, and some communities are still searching for a long-term solution to this issue. Streamlining and adapting to food allergies will take time and ingenuity across various sectors.

School lunch centers have become increasingly popular over the last few decades, and currently 52 percent of meals are produced at centers, while 47 percent are still prepared at on-site school kitchens.[72] Although centers are convenient, the increasing use of these facilities presents new challenges: maintenance, upkeep, and staffing. Moreover, the jobs available through contracted, privatized lunch production tend to be less stable than those offered through public government-run school lunch programs, which come with certain protections and benefits. Yet, in both the private and public sector, the country's ongoing labor shortage contributes to high turnover and overreliance on part-time workers. Despite food education's emphasis on valuing labor and the people who make school lunches possible, the growth of school lunch centers and contracted meals may reduce professional career paths in the sector and yield more part-time jobs.

Ultimately, the future of school lunch in Japan depends on the country's ability to make significant structural changes to the school lunch system as Japan's population ages and shrinks. One report estimates that more than one-third of the school lunch centers currently being developed would be underutilized in the latter half of the lives of the facilities.[73] Moreover, population decline may gradually diminish tax revenues and available funding for school meals. Maintaining high-quality equipment is an expensive but critical endeavor. Outdated equipment has already led to insects or even bits of metal showing up in school meals. Safe sanitation is another crucial expense. In 1996, there was a wide-spread outbreak of the pathogen Escherichia coli O-157 in school lunches.[74] National standards for hygiene management were adopted the following year and updated in 2008, but with funding shortages, food safety could be a risk again.

As these challenges unfold, the country's commitment to local control may prove insufficient to maintain a relatively uniform national system. The Basic Law on Food Education relies on *promotion* rather than enforcement of objectives. As a result, the success of school lunch depends on the commitment and capacity of local stakeholders. Against budgetary pressures, the law's flexible design may yield uneven and unreliable implementation of food education and reduce the quality of food served in Japanese schools.

Yet there is hope. In the past thirty years, Japanese school lunch has greatly improved and attracted significant public interest. School lunch's far-reaching integration into daily life is now a remarkable source of national pride and a unique rallying point for engaging communities in food politics. One meal at a time, school lunch nourishes the bodies of children, contributes to local and national enterprise, and supports public health. Ultimately, the Basic Law on Food Education and the School Lunch Act are an investment in the future, strengthening the social fabric of Japanese society. The current system ensures that lunchtime provides students with education, nourishment, and an opportunity to cultivate a sense of mindfulness. By comprehensively meeting the needs of each child through school lunch, the meals transcend nutrition and become a pervasive positive force in society.

Although advocacy groups remain limited in size and influence, more citizens are helping to play a part in shaping their food future. At the local level, in Samukawa Town, Kanagawa Prefecture, for example, citizens' input helped structure the new school lunch center's public management.[75] Families and guardians have also maintained pressure on local governments to ensure proper radiation testing of school lunch ingredients in the months following the 2011 Great East Japan Earthquake and Fukushima nuclear plant meltdown.[76] In some communities, the public has increasingly called for free universal school lunches. Although the implementation of free-for-all meals appears unlikely in the near-term, such advocacy work highlights the growing organization of Japanese citizens. School lunch has blossomed because of its connection to the community, and it is this connection that will help society address future challenges. The community connections represent an integrated systems-based approach to harnessing the potential of school lunch. This potential is ignited by recognizing the right of all people to consume nutritious food at school and to receive a robust education about food systems.

NOTES

1. MEXT, "Ryō wa 3-nendo gakkō kyūshoku jisshi jōkyō-tō chōsa no kekka o oshirase shimasu, Gakkō Kyūshoku Jisshi Jōkyō-Tō Chōsa," 2021, https://www.mext.go.jp/content/20230125-mxt-kenshoku-100012603-1.pdf.

2. MEXT, "Ryō wa 3-nendo."

3. MEXT, "Gakkō Kyūshoku-Hi Heikin Getsugaku: Gakkō Kyūshoku Jisshi Jōkyō-Tō Chōsa (Heisei 28-Nendo Chōsa Kekka)," 2016, https://www.mext.go.jp/b_menu/toukei/chousa05/kyuushoku/kekka/k_detail/__icsFiles/afieldfile/2019/02/26/1413836_001_002.pdf; National Institute for Education Policy Research, "School Lunch Program in Japan," National Institute for Education Policy Research, 2013, https://www.nier.go.jp/English/educationjapan/pdf/201303SLP.pdf.

4. More than 90 percent of students in Tomigusuku-city, Okinawa answered that school lunch was delicious. About 60 percent of the girls and 70 percent of the boys at elementary school liked school lunch in Miki-city, Hyogo, 2021, https://www.city.miki.lg.jp/uploaded/attachment/22629.pdf and https://www.city.tomigusuku.lg.jp/userfiles/TM020/files/anke-tohonpen.pdf.

5. Tsuruoka City, "Gakkō Kyūshoku No Rekishi—Tsuruoka No Kyūshoku," June 14, 2016, https://www.city.tsuruoka.lg.jp/kyoiku/gakko/kyūshoku/kyusyokunorekisi.html.

6. Astri Andresen and Kari Tove Elybakken, "From Poor Law Society to the Welfare State: School Meals in Norway 1890s–1950s," *Journal of Epidemiology and Community Health* 61, no. 5 (2007): 374–377.

7. National Institute for Education Policy Research, "School Lunch Program in Japan."

8. Michael Conlon, "Japan Agricultural Situation: The History of U.S. Exports of Wheat to Japan," USDA Foreign Agricultural Service GAIN Report, June 29, 2009, https://www.usdajapan.org/wpusda/wp-content/uploads/2016/04/History-of-US-Exports-Wheat-to-Japan.pdf.

9. National Institute for Education Policy Research, "School Lunch Program in Japan."

10. Masayo Kaneda and Shigeru Yamamoto, "The Japanese School Lunch and Its Contribution to Health," *Nutrition Today* 50, no. 6 (December 2015): 268–272.

11. National Institute for Education Policy Research, "School Lunch Program in Japan."

12. "Gakkō Kyūshoku Hō Shikō Rei: Cabinet Order 212," E-Gov Law Search, 1954, https://elaws.e-gov.go.jp/document?lawid=329CO0000000212.

13. Hiromi Ishida, "The History, Current Status, and Future Directions of the School Lunch Program in Japan," *The Japanese Journal of Nutrition and Dietetics* 76 (2018): S2–S11, https://doi.org/10.5264/eiyogakuzashi.76.S2.

14. Related legislation includes the following: School Meals in Part-time Night Courses of High School Education (1956) and the Law concerning School Lunches in Special-needs Schools of Pre-Primary and Upper Secondary Stages (1957).

15. House of Representatives, Japan, "Nihon Gakkō Kyūshoku-Kai-Hō," 1954, http://www.shugiin.go.jp/internet/itdb_housei.nsf/html/houritsu/02219550808148.html.

16. Masayo Kaneda and Shigeru Yamamoto, "The Japanese School Lunch and Its Contribution to Health."

17. Nobuko Iwamura, "Why Rice Is Vanishing from Japanese Tables," *Nippon*, August 22, 2012, https://www.nippon.com/en/currents/d00046/.

18. James Elliott, "The 1981 Administrative Reform in Japan," *Asian Survey* 23, no. 6 (1983): 765–779, https://doi.org/10.2307/2644390.

19. Hiroshi Shinmura, "Gakkō Kyūshoku-Hō Ni Okeru Gakkō Kyūshoku Un'ei No Chokuei Gensoku" Ni Tsuite No Ronshō," accessed May 18, 2021, https://core.ac.uk/download/pdf/230919686.pdf.

20. Alice Gordenker, "Can Our Kids Get a Healthy Meal for Less?" *Japan Times*, April 10, 2003, https://www.japantimes.co.jp/life/2003/04/10/lifestyle/can-our-kids-get-a-healthy-meal-for-less/.

21. *Chisan Chisho* is an abbreviation of *Chiiki seisan chiiki shōhi*.

22. Aya Kimura and Mima Nishiyama, "The Chisan-Chisho Movement: Japanese Local Food Movement and Its Challenges," *Agriculture and Human Values* 25 (January 1, 2008): 49–64, https://doi.org/10.1007/s10460-007-9077-x; Barbara Greene, "Moyashimon and Agrarian Nationalism: The Transition from Policy to Pop Culture," *Tokyo International University* 18, no. 2 (September 8, 2018), http://www.japanesestudies.org.uk/ejcjs/vol18/iss2/greene.html.

23. Nishiyama, Kimura Mima, and Aya Hirata, "Alternative Agro-Food Movement in Contemporary Japan," *Chiba University, Horticultural Department Bulletin* 59 (2005), https://core.ac.uk/download/pdf/96956504.pdf.

24. Ministry of Agriculture, Forestry, and Fisheries (MAFF), "Shokuryō Sangyō 6 Jisangyō-Ka Kōfu-Kin No Uchi Chiiki de No Shokuiku No Suishin," 2021, https://www.maff.go.jp/j/syokuiku/attach/pdf/torikumi-226.pdf.

25. Japanese Law Translation, "Basic Act on Shokuiku (Food and Nutrition Education)," June 17, 2005, http://www.japaneselawtranslation.go.jp/law/detail/?id=3419&vm=04&re=02.

26. Ministry of Agriculture, Forestry, and Fisheries (MAFF), "What Is Shokuiku (Food Education)?" accessed November 12, 2020, https://www.maff.go.jp/e/pdf/shokuiku.pdf.

27. For background on this legislative and legal approach, see Eugen Ehrlich's essays on "Living Law," in *Living Law: Reconsidering Eugen Ehrlich*, ed. Marc Hertogh (Sydney: Bloomsbury, 2008).

28. Nobuko Tanaka and Miki Miyoshi, "School Lunch Program for Health Promotion among Children in Japan," *Asia Pacific Journal of Clinical Nutrition* 21, no. 1 (2012): 155–158.

29. OECD, *OECD Reviews of Public Health: Japan: A Healthier Tomorrow* (Paris: OECD Publishing, 2019), https://www.oecd.org/japan/oecd-reviews-of-public-health-japan-9789264311602-en.ht.

30. National Association of School Lunch, "Gakko Kyushoku no Mokuhyo," accessed March 29, 2023, https://www.zenkyuren.jp/lunch/aim.html.

31. MHLW, "2019-Nen Kokumin Seikatsu Kiso Chōsa No Gaikyō," 2019, https://www.mhlw.go.jp/toukei/saikin/hw/k-tyosa/k-tyosa19/dl/14.pdf.

32. Chieko Yamashita, "Natsuyasumi Ni Yaseru Kodomo-Tachi e Fūdobanku de Hirogaru Shien," July 26, 2019, https://www.asahi.com/articles/ASM7963HCM79UTIL04J.html.

33. Keiko Asakura and SatoshiSasaki, "School Lunches in Japan: Their Contribution to Healthier Nutrient Intake among Elementary-School and Junior High-School Children," *Public Health Nutrition* 20, no. 9 (June 2017): 1523–1533, https://doi.org/10.1017/S1368980017000374.

34. MEXT, "Gakkō Kyūshoku Jisshi Kijun No Ichibu Kaisei Ni Tsuite (Tsūchi)," 2018, https://www.mext.go.jp/content/20210212-mxt_kenshoku-100003357_1.pdf.

35. MEXT, "Gakkō Kyūshoku Jisshi Kijun No Ichibu Kaisei Ni Tsuite: Monbu Kagaku Shō," July 31, 2018, https://www.mext.go.jp/a_menu/sports/syokuiku/1407704.html.

36. MEXT, "Gakkō Kyūshoku Jisshi Kijun No Ichibu Kaisei Ni Tsuite: Monbu Kagaku Shō"; World Health Organization, Regional Office for South-East Asia, "Japan Health System Review," *Health Systems in Transition* 8, no. 1 (2018), https://apps.who.int/iris/bitstream/handle/10665/259941/9789290226260-eng.pdf.

37. Shinbun Sankei, "Hirogaru Gakkō Kyūshoku No 'gen'en' Usuaji de Shōrai No Seikatsushūkanbyō Yobō," February 1, 2017, https://www.sankei.com/article/20170201-A5A6JOIL5BNBJEJP2A2BPHPYOY/.

38. For a weekly sample kondate translated into English see the ancillary materials for this book. Matsueshiritsu Shimane Gakkō kyūshoku sentā, "12gatsu Gakkō Kyūshoku

Kondate Hyō," December 2020, http://www1.city.matsue.shimane.jp/kyouiku/gakkou/kyusyoku/shimane_joho/shimane-kondatehyo.data/R2.12_shimane_kondatehyou.pdf.

39. MEXT, "Eiyō Kyōyu No Haichi Sokushin Ni Tsuite (Irai) (Heisei 21-Nen 4-Gatsu 28-Nichi Zuke 21 Monka Su Dai 6261-Gō)," April 28, 2009, https://www.mext.go.jp/a_menu/shotou/Eiyō/1279734.html.

40. MEXT, "Eiyō Kyōyu No Haichi Jōkyō (Heisei 28-Nendo)," January 15, 2021, https://www.mext.go.jp/content/20210115-mxt_kenshoku-100003340_1.pdf.

41. MAFF (Ministry of Agriculture, Forestry, and Fisheries), "Gakkō Kyūshoku Ni Okeru Dentō-Tekina Shoku Bunka Wo Keishō Shita Kondate No Katsuyō," May 17, 2016, https://www.maff.go.jp/j/syokuiku/wpaper/h27/h27_h/book/part2/chap6/b2_c6_2_01.html.

42. Yoshiaki Kawai, "Kyūshoku No Rekishi—Dasshifun'nyū Kara Age Pan, Sofuto Men e," Yomiuri Shimbun, October 30, 2017, https://www.yomiuri.co.jp/fukayomi/20171030-OYT8T50149/2/.

43. MEXT, "Shōgakusei You Shokuiku Kyōzai 'tanoshii Shokuji Tsunagaru Shokuiku'"; Jidō-Yō (Teigakunen)," accessed November 13, 2020, https://www.mext.go.jp/component/a_menu/education/detail/__icsFiles/afieldfile/2016/12/13/1367897_2.pdf.

44. MEXT, "Shōgakusei You Shokuiku Kyōzai 'Tanoshii Shokuji Tsunagaru Shokuiku'; Jidō-Yō/(Kōgakunen)," accessed November 13, 2020, https://www.mext.go.jp/component/a_menu/education/detail/__icsFiles/afieldfile/2016/03/10/1367897_4.pdf.

45. Elinor Ochs and Carolina Izquierdo, "Responsibility in Childhood: Three Developmental Trajectories," *Ethos* 37 (December 1, 2009): 391–413, https://doi.org/10.1111/j.1548-1352.2009.01066.x.

46. "Katsushika Kanamachi-Shō de `tate-Wari Kyūshoku-Kai'- i Gakunen to Mitsu Ni Kōryū, Sotsugyō Iwau," Katsushika Keizai, March 3, 2015, https://katsushika.keizai.biz/headline/1227/.

47. MEXT, "Shōgakkō Gakushū Shidō Yōryō (Heisei 29-Nen Kokuji) Kaisetsu," 2017, https://www.mext.go.jp/component/a_menu/education/micro_detail/__icsFiles/afieldfile/2019/03/18/1387017_006.pdf.

48. "Inochi Wo Itadakimasu!," Jōetsu Myōko Town Jōhō, March 12, 2019, https://www.joetsu.ne.jp/74450.

49. "Japan Enacts Legislation to Tackle Nation's Food Waste," Xinhua News, May 24, 2019, http://www.xinhuanet.com/english/2019-05/24/c_138086356.html.

50. Consumer Affairs Agency Consumer Education Promotion Division, "Shokuhin Rosu Sakugen Kankei Sankō Shiryō—Shōhishachō," February 12, 2020, https://www.caa.go.jp/policies/policy/consumer_policy/information/food_loss/efforts/pdf/efforts_200214_0001.pdf.

51. Uji City, Kyoto Prefecture Garbage Reduction Promotion Division, "Reduce the Tabenokoshi—Shōgakkō de No 10 No Torikumi to Sono Kōka," 2017, https://www.env.go.jp/recycle/%E3%80%90%E5%AE%87%E6%B2%BB%E5%B8%82%E3%80%

91%EF%BC%A829%E5%AD%A6%E6%A0%A1%E7%B5%A6%E9%A3%9F%E5%A0%B1%E5%91%8A%E4%BC%9A%EF%BC%88%E6%8A%95%E5%BD%B1%E7%94%A8%E8%B3%87%E6%96%99%EF%BC%89.pdf.

52. "Kankyō Iinkai Ga Chūshin to Natta Katsudō Wo Rei Ni Shita 'Gakkō-Ban Kankyō ISO' No Torikumi-Kata," Sasebo City, accessed November 17, 2020, https://www.city.sasebo.lg.jp/kankyo/kansei/documents/torikumi.pdf.

53. "Ekomāketto Daiseikō!," Kawaguchi Angyō Elementary School Blog, June 26, 2019, https://bit.ly/3tYO6sT.

54. Zenkoku gakkō kyūshoku Kōshien (National School Lunch Competition), "14-Kai Taikai Kesshō Taikai Shutsujō Hyōgo Tanbasasayama Shiritsu Seibu Gakkō Kyūshoku Sentā," 2019, https://kyusyoku-kosien.net/2019final_detail_hyogo/.

55. Reo Nakano, "Kyūshoku Sentā Wo Kengaku Shite," Kyūshoku Hiroba National School Lunch Memories Writing Contest, 2019, http://www.jcfs.or.jp/news/pdf/191119/sakuhin09.pdf.

56. *Nourishing Japan*, directed by Alexis Agliano Sanborn (2020; United States-Japan Foundation and Independent Filmmaker Project / The Gotham).

57. MAFF (Ministry of Agriculture, Forestry, and Fisheries), "Shokuryō Jikyū-Ryoku Jikyū-Ritsu No Kōjō Ni Muketa Torikumi u Chisanchishō No Suishin Jōkyō," accessed November 15, 2020, https://www.maff.go.jp/j/wpaper/w_maff/h20_h/trend/part1/chap2/t1_06.html.

58. Rie Akamatsu et al., "Gratitude for Food May Help to Decrease Food Dislikes in Children," *Journal of Nutrition Education and Behavior* 51, no. 7 (July 1, 2019): S110, https://doi.org/10.1016/j.jneb.2019.05.548; Betty Izumi, Rie Akamatsu, Carmen Byker Shanks, and Kahori Fujisaki, "Exploring Factors That Minimize School Lunch Waste in Tokyo Elementary Schools," *Journal of Nutrition Education and Behavior* 51, no. 7 (July 1, 2019), https://doi.org/10.1016/j.jneb.2019.05.318.

59. "Tōkyō no shōgakusei ga kyūshoku de tabete iru kome ga seisan sarete iru Sanjō de inekari," September 18, 2017, http://www.kenoh.com/2017/09/18_haketa.html.

60. Zenkoku gakkō kyūshoku Kōshien (National School Lunch Competition), "Nihon'no Gakkō Kyūshoku Dai 2-Kai Oishikute Eiyō Baransu No Toreta 'gakkō Kyūshoku' No Kondate-Dzukuri to Chōri," Kyusyoku Kosien, April 30, 2016, https://bit.ly/3w7BeRY.

61. "Jidō Sodateta Dentō Sakumotsu Tsukai, Kyūshoku Chōten 'metcha Ureshii' Chiiki to Issho Ni Saibai, PR Mo," Tanba Shinbun, last revised June 13, 2020, https://bit.ly/3gHUjWl.

62. Zenkoku gakkō kyūshoku Kōshien (National School Lunch Competition), "14-Kai Taikai Kesshō Taikai Shutsujō Hyōgo Tanbasasayama Shiritsu Seibu Gakkō Kyūshoku Sentā," 2019, https://kyusyoku-kosien.net/2019final_detail_hyogo/.

63. Ministry of Agriculture, Forestry, and Fisheries (MAFF), "Furusato Kyūshoku Jiman, Tōkyōto, Murobushi Gohan," 2008, https://www.maff.go.jp/j/pr/aff/2008/food01.html.

64. See J. T. Quigley, "A Kentucky Fried Christmas in Japan," *The Diplomat*, December 11, 2013, http://thediplomat.com/2013/12/a-kentucky-fried-christmas-in-japan/.

65. "Japan's Food Self-Sufficiency Rate Hits Its Lowest Level in 25 Years Due to Wheat Production," *Japan Times*, August 6, 2019, https://www.japantimes.co.jp/news/2019/08/06/national/japans-food-self-sufficiency-rate-hits-lowest-level-25-years-due-drop-wheat-production/.

66. "Import Value of Foodstuffs to Japan 2010 to 2019," Statista, 2020, https://www.statista.com/statistics/649071/japan-import-value-foodstuff/.

67. "Yunyū Shokuhin to Gakkō Kyūshoku," *Gakkō Kyūshoku Nyusu* 166 (November 2014), http://gakkyu-news.net/data/2014-11.pdf.

68. Figure 1.2 created by the authors using information provided by the Japan Association for Promotion of School lunch. Zenkoku gakkō kyūshoku-kai rengō-kai, "Seisansha Kara Kodomotachi Eno Gakkō Kyūshoku No Nagare," accessed December 10, 2020, https://www.zenkyuren.jp/pdf/leaf_03.pdf.

69. MEXT, "Gakkō Kyūshoku Ni Okeru Shokumotsu Arerugī Taiō Ni Tsuite," 2015, https://www.mext.go.jp/a_menu/sports/syokuiku/1355536.htm.

70. Nipponham, "Shokumotsu Arerugī Taiō No Zen'in Kyūshoku Wo Jitsugen Shita Ichikawa Hoikuen Vol. 1," accessed May 17, 2021, https://www.food-allergy.jp/use/scene/interview/detail/id=831.

71. "Arerugī Taiō-Shoku No Teikyō Ni Tsuite," Yamagata City, accessed April 13, 2021, https://www.city.yamagata-yamagata.lg.jp/shimin/sub6/kyusyoku/4b725pd1125133726.html.

72. MEXT, "Heisei 30-Nendo Gakkō Kyūshoku Jisshi Jōkyō-Tō Chōsa No Kekka Ni Tsuite," February 26, 2019, https://www.mext.go.jp/content/1413836_001_001.pdf.

73. MUFG, "Korekara No Gakkō Kyūshoku Sentā Seibi Ni Okeru Kadai to Kanōsei," August 3, 2015, https://www.murc.jp/report/rc/column/search_now/sn150803/.

74. Mie Prefecture Headquarters, "Kiseikaikaku No Ken-Shō—Gakkō Kyūshoku Chōri Gyōmu No Minkan Itaku Ni Taisuru Kōsatsu," accessed May 18, 2021, https://www.jichiro.gr.jp/jichiken_kako/report/rep_okinawa31/jichiken31/1/1_2_j_10/1_2_j_10.htm.

75. Samukawa Town, "Oishiī Min'na No Gakkō Kyūshoku -Reiwa 5-Nen 9 Gatsu Kyūshoku Sentā Ōpun," September 27, 2020, http://www.town.samukawa.kanagawa.jp/chosei/koho/kouhoushi/koho_backnumber/2020/20201001/20201001_1/10908.html.

76. Hiroko Tabuchi, "Angry Parents in Japan Confront Government over Radiation Levels," *New York Times*, May 25, 2011. See also: "Radiation Testing on School Lunches Issues," Education in Japan Community Blog, https://educationinjapan.wordpress.com/edu-news/radiation-testing-on-school-lunches-issues/.

2

CENTERING CHILDREN, HEALTH, AND JUSTICE IN CANADIAN SCHOOL FOOD PROGRAMS

Jennifer Black, Sinikka Elliott, Rachel Engler-Stringer, Debbie Field, Brent Mansfield, Stephanie Segave, and Thibaud Liné

According to UNICEF's 2020 report on the state of children and youth, compared to other affluent countries, Canada spends among the lowest proportion of its gross domestic product on services supporting children's well-being.[1] There is now ample evidence that both Canadian children's dietary quality and available public supports warrant major improvements to reduce nutritional inequities, bolster well-being, and lower chronic disease risk into adulthood.[2] UNICEF Canada's 2020 report recommended that Canada should "ensure that every child gets a healthy meal at school,"[3] echoing calls for federal-level support for a national school meal program heralded by several groups including the Coalition for Healthy School Food (CHSF), Canada's largest school food–focused advocacy organization. In 2023, CHSF membership included 240 organizations from every province and territory.[4]

While Canadian health policy documents frequently reference social justice and equity, Canada remains one of the few affluent countries with no nationally funded school lunch program (SFP).[5] In 2019, the federal government expressed support for developing a nationwide approach, but as of this writing, no funding has been committed.[6] Moreover, no consensus exists affirming the essential goals around which to build a future Canadian SFP. Public health scholars argue that inadequate articulation of core values and goals may mask the social forces that underlie health promotion efforts.[7] We argue that this gap in vision and mission leaves well-intended advocates unmoored and trapped debating finer details of SFP design, lacking agreement about the purpose or full societal potential of what a national program could accomplish. In this chapter, we take a step back to delve into core goals and guiding principles that we believe will drive progress and unite disparate stakeholders aiming to transform Canadian school food programming.

Canadian SFPs exist through a combination of programs run by local school districts, individual schools, nonprofit organizations, or local initiatives spearheaded by parents or parent associations.[8] Unfortunately, no comprehensive data exists describing the prevalence or variation in SFP models, and there are few reliable estimates documenting how many children receive a meal regularly at school, be it purchased at full price (for school fundraising purposes or run by for-profit or in-house catering services), partially subsidized, or offered at no cost (funded variably through combinations of charitable donations, grant funding from government or nongovernment sources, or through cost-sharing models). Many elementary schools offer no food programs or sales at all. A 2009/2010 national survey of administrators from 407 schools suggested that 47 percent of schools had no cafeteria, though the majority of schools offered some onsite food retailing (75 percent) or a vending machine selling soda, juice, or milk (70 percent).[9] Nationally representative dietary surveys suggest that few Canadian students venture home or off campus for lunch; fewer than one in ten students eat lunch provided by their school, and the majority of students (73 percent) rely on a home-packed lunch.[10]

Canada's current ad hoc system operates through a patchwork of funders and heavy reliance on charitable donors. No single level of government or specific ministry is charged with planning or overseeing SFPs, and little systematic evaluation or knowledge of children's needs, values, or experiences currently informs policymaking. Without a clear guiding framework confirming the goals of meal programs and evaluating whether programs achieve them, future programs will be susceptible to undue influence from partisan powers and biases driven by funders and their mandates, rather than being guided by a holistic and evidence-based vision of what SFPs could and should achieve. Recent examples point to pressures on ministries of education to focus narrowly on the educational benefits of school food, whereas ministries of health are pressured to focus on disease prevention. Meanwhile, charitable funders are beholden to organizational missions and donors. We fear that with programs developed with only narrow, siloed goals in mind, emerging models will become locked into approaches that limit the transformative potential that school meals have been shown to offer in other countries.[11]

In this chapter, we seek to move beyond tensions regarding the creation of a national SFP by articulating three core goals that our research, practice, and advocacy have revealed as critical in designing an effective national SFP, which center around: (1) children, (2) well-being, and (3) justice. A Canada-wide framework that explicitly affirms these goals can contribute to meaningful progress, making it easier to facilitate inter-ministerial and multisector collaboration.

This chapter brings together insights from empirical studies on school food and interviews with and writing contributions from four school food practitioners, named as authors, from across Canada. All authors are school food researchers or practitioners. The community-based contributors reflect geographical and SFP organizational diversity. We have all participated in long-standing debates about what and who SFPs are for and reflected on the varied arguments about why SFPs should focus on supporting vulnerable children, mitigating chronic disease risks, meeting sustainability targets, enhancing educational targets, reducing family burdens, or a combination of these things.[12] Other contentions include which program models eliminate or reduce stigma, what universality means in practice, who should pay for SFPs, what aspects of programs are most critical, and how much local versus central control should be built into a national program.

We began the process of writing this chapter intending to examine these major areas of contention. The academic contributors invited the community-based contributors to be interviewed about their thoughts on these tensions. Rachel conducted an initial analysis of their responses and shared them with Jennifer and Sinikka. Through the process of analyzing the interviews and integrating findings with our own work and that of others, we identified three common strands related to conceptions of children, health, and well-being running throughout. Together with the chapter's community-based collaborators, we developed the chapter's argument that focusing on three core aims of school food programming would cut through these tensions and transform school food politics in Canada. Such an approach would ensure that program designers and evaluators listen to children and center their perspectives in any programs designed for them and move toward models that can address our most pressing societal needs in terms of health and justice for all. In what follows, we develop a case for a clear articulation of the vision and values for how SFPs should address childhood, well-being, and justice as we move toward expanding SFPs in Canada.

CENTERING A VISION FOR CHILDHOOD AS A CORE GOAL

Students are essential stakeholders in SFPs, yet Canadian students' daily experiences and voices are typically overlooked in research on and advocacy around SFPs, even though successful programs rely on their participation. Drawing on insights from our previous research with children about school food programming, our aim here is to demonstrate the value of incorporating children's perspectives through a vision of childhood that positions children as competent social actors.[13]

The depiction of childhood underlying much research and activism around SFPs is one of vulnerable, at-risk children. In this view, SFPs protect children from hunger and set them up for good eating habits and a healthy future.[14] While children should, of course, be afforded sufficient and nutritious foods, this construction emphasizes their risk and vulnerability as beings who are in formation toward becoming adults. This approach to childhood is used to garner support for SFPs: no one wants to be responsible for children going hungry. The notion of hungry children is highly evocative and suggests a moral failing on the part of adults to properly care for children. Alternatively, the idea that SFPs will cultivate well-fed children who will become productive, healthy adults appeals to policymakers with the power to open purse strings. For example, the National School Lunch Program (NSLP) in the United States (US) was originally conceived in part as a program to help grow healthy soldiers fit for war.[15]

Treating children like adults-in-the-making, "becomings," rather than (or along with) beings in their own right, encourages an "adults know best" stance that risks disregarding children's social worlds and subjectivities. Framing children as becomings can also be stressful for children and adults alike when it comes to navigating eating relationships. Research with mothers who embrace the idea that children must be inculcated with good eating habits, for instance, finds that this approach leads to stress and anxiety around food and meals for mothers and children.[16] We argue that SFPs should not simply be seen as *for* children, based on a desire to ameliorate future health risks, but rather conceived, designed, and run *with* meaningful input from children. Adults often assume they know best what children need and do not consult children when designing programs meant to serve them. Consequently, these programs may not resonate with children who may exert their agency by opting out. We learn much by allying with children so that they can meaningfully take part in and shape programs that affect them. Next we detail two insights that come from viewing children as competent social actors who actively navigate and give meaning to their social worlds.

First, taking children seriously as competent social actors means understanding that food, far from being just a form of sustenance, is layered with social and symbolic meanings.[17] Children are not immune to or separate from wider meanings of food in a society, but they do not simply adopt adult perspectives and food cultures. Children have their "own cultural imperatives,"[18] which they create "in concert with their peers, as they collectively experience the world."[19] Children form ideas about food through relations with others, including peers, family members, and authority figures.[20] What it means to eat well, be hungry, or receive school food can take on vastly different meanings in different contexts, as children, together with peers but also parents, communities, and schools, collaboratively form these meanings. Thus, to understand SFPs, we need to look not only at the food itself but also beyond the food to the meanings students assign to school food experiences.

In a 2019 study of one school district's effort to transition to a new meal program model, researchers, including Sinikka and Jennifer, documented what happened during lunch through ethnographic fieldwork during twenty-six lunchtime visits to two elementary schools and one middle school.[21] These visits, which included informal interviews with children, underscored how profoundly students' eating was informed by their peers, including ideas about what constituted a good lunch and how they actually ate their food. Students knew a lot about what and how their classmates ate, often telling fieldworkers what their classmates liked to eat and who typically ate what, including whether a classmate participated in the SFP. Students also marked out their identities vis-à-vis food by, for example, declaring foods they liked and disliked, describing their eating styles, and displaying knowledge about food. As Allison Pugh observes, "Children collect or confer dignity among themselves, according to their (shifting) consensus about what sorts of objects or experiences are supposed to count for it."[22] The meanings children give to food should not be overlooked because those meanings are central to how children approach and feel about food at lunchtime. Collective meanings around food also shape interpersonal dynamics at lunch. In line with other research, we observed that children experienced and actively tried to avoid bullying and stigma for what they ate.[23]

Students in classes together often shared similar sentiments about the school's lunch program, revealing how their perceptions were informed by interactions with peers. In one class, despite being asked for their individual impressions, students described food from the new program as "airplane food," meaning it was made by an anonymous for-profit company that churned out identical, portable meals. (The SFP was run by an outside catering company, which delivered food that families ordered online to the schools at lunchtime each day.) Yet students in another classroom in the same school did not use the term "airplane food" at all. That children in different classes can form very different opinions of the same food points to their creativity and the social and shifting meanings of food. It also indicates that providing nutritious meals is a necessary but not sufficient role for SFPs. SFPs must collaborate with children to imbue food with meanings that resonate with children and support their enthusiasm and participation.

The meanings of food were also inextricably wrapped up with children's narratives about care. Students' perceptions of school meals were shaped by ideas about the caring labor that went into the meals.[24] For example, a student said now that the school district had "replaced the cook. It's [the new catered food] less homemade." Yet the catered meals involved more scratch cooking and fewer prepackaged foods than the food made by the lunch staff in the old program. In viewing the catered food as "less homemade," the student was responding less to what was on the menu and more to the relationships behind the food. The lunch worker who used to make their brown bag lunches was widely known and liked by students. The meaning of food changed for them when they didn't view it as part of the school's caring web of support and instead saw it as coming from an unknown company.

A second major lesson learned from listening to children is that children's lives are bound up in interdependent care relations. In their research, Jennifer and Sinikka found that children placed much value on knowing who made lunch and appreciated the work that went into preparing and serving school lunch when they could connect it with a caring adult. During classroom visits, students routinely noted who prepared their lunches and considered their food needs. When a fieldworker commented on how thin and uniform the apple slices were in one elementary school student's lunch, she said her dad had cut them the way she liked them done. Another told us, "My stepmom got me this thermos, so now I get hot lunch with bread." The caring work of lunch mattered to students, and some also expressed not feeling cared for because their food preferences were not considered by the adults making their lunches.

Students didn't just see themselves as depending on others for care during lunch; they also extended care to others. Students were observed sharing and trading food with classmates as they collaborated to meet their own and their classmates' food desires. Similarly, during a presentation about the new catered program, a student asked if they could bring leftovers home for family members to eat. Officially, the answer was no. Food safety rules prohibited storing unrefrigerated leftovers. Yet unofficially, we observed students saving leftovers and eating them the next day. We were not at school when students left at the end of the day, so we don't know whether some students took leftovers home, but research demonstrates that children in food-insecure households actively engage in food provisioning.[25] Children are not just passive recipients of the caring labor of lunch; like adults, they consider others' food needs and may even provide care themselves through food. Official program rules may be bent or ignored by students who find creative ways to secure and achieve desired ends with food.

In addition to talking about the caring work that students themselves or family members did to make daily lunches, students also highlighted the care work of the lunch staff who oversaw the former program.[26] Students in two schools with lunch workers whose positions were eliminated with the transition to the new program run by an outside caterer expressed how much they missed the lunch staff, even if they had not participated in the former program themselves. Although our research had not paid much attention to the lunch staff prior to their positions being eliminated, reflecting the way their work is often invisible, it quickly became clear that lunch workers had played a central role in caring for students.[27] For example, a fieldworker spoke with a group of middle school students, including one with no lunch, after the new program had been implemented and wrote:

I don't see this student with any lunch, and he and his fellow students start talking about how challenging it is for students who don't have a strong support network. They say, "Some kids don't have any food." These students were supported by the old program and felt like they could always go to [the former lunch staff] if they didn't have time (or their parents didn't have time) to pack a lunch. "Now you just have to starve." (middle school, visit #6)

This vignette points to the appreciation students had for adults who prepared meals, looked out for their food needs, and provided care at school and at home. It also shows how caring relationships between children and lunch staff created informal means by which children could secure needed food in a way that maintained their dignity. Students recognized that sometimes a student won't have lunch and will need help. When that happened, in the former program, they knew who to turn to and how they would be treated. Yet, in contrast to students' views, the former program was largely viewed by school district administrators as stigmatizing, and reducing stigma and improving access to healthy food were the main rationales for shifting to the new catered program. The differing views between students and administrators shows the value of including children's perspectives in understandings of SFPs.

The work involved in preparing, serving, and cleaning up after children's meals is often part of the "invisible care work" carried out by school lunch staff.[28] In the US, this work is most often done by low-paid lunch workers.[29] In Canada, the labor of lunch is so invisible that there is no research about the people charged with ensuring a safe, caring environment for children to eat, socialize, and learn during lunch. Yet they, and their caring efforts, are clearly visible to children. As Brent, a teacher and former director of a sustainable food systems advocacy organization stated, referring to a survey done in a school where he works: "When they did the survey of the entire school, who they [students] felt most connected to . . . It was the lunch lady . . . most frequently reported as who students felt connected to. But what's the value of that? When we have data that this carework enhances mental health and enhances academia, what's that worth?"

It is hard to estimate the value of care, but clearly care is central to children's experiences of and perspectives on school food.[30] It can be especially difficult to determine care's worth when it is being done in ad hoc ways, typically without federal or provincial support, as is the case in Canadian schools. A recent survey of British Columbia teachers found that 40 percent of teachers bring food to school for students who are hungry, spending an average of $29 per month, an estimated $4 million per year.[31] Practitioners tell us that the caring work of lunch is happening on the margins, carried out by parent volunteers and school staff who are often unacknowledged and are typically women. Conceiving of children as interdependent beings—requiring and participating in care—supports the need for and value of care workers in SFPs who are on the ground connecting with and to children through food. It also helps to acknowledge the role children themselves play in the caring labor of lunch. Children, like adults, give and receive care.

We stand to learn much by consulting children in the development of a national SFP and considering children as stakeholders. The goal of centering children's perspectives is amplified by a vision that positions children as competent social actors. This notion of childhood is needed to underpin an approach that prioritizes children, not based on adult conceptions of what's best for them but from children's own experiences and meaning making, recognizing that children are part of the broader social and cultural world they inhabit. Yet they also occupy an important vantage point from which to understand this world and to gauge whether programs designed for them are hitting the mark.

AFFIRMING AN INCLUSIVE VISION OF HEALTH AND BEING WELL AS A CORE GOAL

SFP advocates frequently posit that improved access to nutritious school meals is needed to improve Canadian children's suboptimal dietary quality and to reduce nutrition-related chronic disease risks in adulthood.[32] In a recent review of SFPs in Canada since 1970 (although most were from the last decade), Everitt and colleagues reported that *all* twenty-three programs overtly aimed to improve students' diets.[33] In this section, we argue for the need to explicitly affirm that health is a core SFP goal, given that when asked, school food administrators often prioritize food access for marginalized students over health benefits for all students.[34] We further propose an inclusive vision for health-promoting SFPs that embody the concept of "being well." We draw on Indigenous perspectives that conceptualize health as "achieved through relationships to other people, to the land and creation, and to our ancestors in the spiritual realm" along with ensuring access to fresh and healthy foods that are physiologically nourishing.[35]

Although there is consensus that expanded SFPs should be "healthy," there remain diverse definitions and values imbued in targets of what nourishing meals should strive for. At present, there are no national nutritional criteria for school food, although across Canada, provinces have created guidelines for school food, many of which share similar underlying nutritional principles drawing on national dietary guidance and Canada's food guides.[36] While we agree that defining and ensuring a high nutritional standard for school meals across the country is an important mandate for a national program, meaningful benefits will be lost if only narrowly defined nutritional improvements are posed as the primary measures of a healthy SFP. Limited nutrient-focused goals risk succumbing to challenges experienced in the United Kingdom and the US with "nutritionism."[37] In nutritionism, nutrient intakes and specific quantitative targets become the key measures of a meal program's success, whereas the overall quality, taste, appeal, cultural, social, and environmental value of the foods and meal experiences are largely overlooked and devalued.

Meal programs that focus exclusively on nutrient-based standards (e.g., specific limits on sodium or saturated fat or ensuring minimum levels of nutrients or food groups) can be co-opted by food industries with a vested interest in profiting by selling heavily processed or nutrient-fortified items to meet quantitative requirements at low costs.[38] Our key informants highlighted the overemphasis on nutrient targets or narrowly defined food targets (such as fruit/vegetable intake alone) as a potential pitfall. They argued that by framing broader concepts of nutrition and health within the recommendations in Canada's latest Food Guide (CFG),[39] meal programs could have more meaningful benefits. Accompanying the new CFG is a visual representation of a plate covered half in vegetables and fruit, one-quarter protein foods (emphasizing more plant-based proteins) and one-quarter grains (emphasizing whole grains).[40]

The guide places explicit emphasis on reducing consumption of highly processed foods, increasing consumption of a variety of health-promoting foods, and shifting diets toward including more plant proteins. It also promotes eating as a social and conscious act, the value of eating with others and cooking while involving others in meal planning and the cultural importance of food traditions. "Healthy eating is more than the foods you eat," according to the CFG, "it is also about where, when, why and how you eat."[41] The CFG may offer a more holistic and socially embedded model of food and eating to support a broader vision of food-related well-being if incorporated into formal and informal curricula.

Indigenous perspectives related to health and being well are crucial to foreground in SFPs to, among other things, connect pedagogically the ways food is grown and served with stewardship of the land, care, and connection. Indigenous notions of health and being well acknowledge "physical, emotional, spiritual, and intellectual aspects" of food and complex relationships between food, people, and land as described by Dennis and Robin.[42] By embracing Indigenous ways of conceptualizing health, the nourishing potential of SFPs can be expanded beyond physiological nutrient requirements to more comprehensively nourish community, the public provision of care for children, the land and water used to grow foods, and the people across the food system. It is important to acknowledge, however, that schools themselves and the government agencies that shape their programming are colonial institutions.[43] While some Indigenous communities have retaken control over their educational systems, the history and current contexts of Canadian school systems are indelibly marked by colonial processes and legacies.[44] There remains much work to be done in the process of moving forward in decolonizing the school context and decolonizing food and nutrition.[45]

There are also many strong arguments for expanding the health mission of SFPs to include environmental health and sustainability.[46] For example, the CHSF advocates for "comprehensive" best practices to bolster food literacy education and curricular connections between the food served and food system learning. And previous Canadian action-research such as the Think&EatGreen@School project have developed frameworks for weaving health, nutrition, and sustainability challenges into SFPs and educational strategies.[47]

Some Canadian schools have already integrated environmental health into their school food and nutrition philosophies.[48] The growing integration of school gardens, food preparation and composting activities, and hands-on food education also serve as entry points for schools to integrate food systems teaching and learning.[49] Our work documenting a new lunch program in a suburban school district also found that environmental concerns, while not the main priority for parents' decisions about ordering school meals, was a meaningful consideration. When parents were surveyed about their perceptions about the new program, 40 percent agreed or strongly agreed that they would order more often if "there was less packaging waste," and several parents wanted the meal program to model environmental sustainability values. As one parent noted, "Biodegradable packaging would set an example-reduce greenhouse gas emissions, lower carbon footprint, be sustainable with our choices. The kids will see that and grow to expect life cycle stewardship rather than single-use." With climate change posing one of the world's greatest challenges, future meal programs would be remiss to neglect the opportunity to affirm planetary health as part of the core mission.

Overall, our work finds growing examples of Canadian SFPs that are successfully integrating broader notions of health that foster physical, mental, social, spiritual, and environmental health. But to reap these benefits, health targets must explicitly acknowledge the value of food beyond its nutritive value.

IMPROVING JUSTICE, FAIRNESS, AND EQUITY AS CORE GOALS

Justice is a broad concept, but here, we consider fairness and equity, and how considerations of stigma must be central to conceptualizing both.[50] Fairness is the idea of equal treatment between groups. But fairness can mean treating people unequally to rectify harms that have disproportionately impacted groups.[51] Equity is closely related to fairness and focuses on removing avoidable inequalities between people.[52] Finally, stigma is defined as labeling, stereotyping, status loss, and discrimination in contexts where power is exercised and is an important aspect of both equity and fairness, but neither can be achieved when stigma exists.[53] Critically, there is compelling evidence that people who experience food insecurity also experience significant stigma (described as "targets" of stigma), and also face misconceptions and prejudicial assumptions made by people in positions of power (described as "perceivers" of stigma).[54]

Historically, most national SFPs have shared the expressed goal and dominant framing focused on reducing food insecurity and its consequences.[55] Many existing SFPs in Canada were established in response to child hunger with healthy eating as a secondary goal.[56] There is evidence that SFPs have narrowed gaps in food security and nutrition-related health outcomes for low-income children in countries such as the US.[57] However, given the narrow reach of Canada's current SFPs and vastly insufficient social safety nets more broadly, inadequate and unstable access to food affects over one in six Canadian children.[58] Beyond the physical and mental health consequences, food-insecure children on average report slightly lower dietary quality during school hours and are twice as likely to report eating no lunch on school days in national surveys.[59]

The practitioner authors explained that equity and stigma need to be considered when framing meal programs as broadly serving population health goals. Yet, previous Canadian SFPs typically targeted the needs of low-income, food-insecure or otherwise vulnerable students. Their developers sought ways to solve perceived problems: namely that some children were bringing no lunches, inadequate lunches, or were not coming back to school after the lunch period.[60] This deficit framing by "perceivers," people in positions of power, in this case community organizations or school administrations, contributes to stigma experienced by "targets," in this case children and caregivers perceived as not bringing "adequate" lunches to school.[61]

Paradoxically, there is reason to believe that targeting meal programs at more vulnerable students is likely to weaken the potential benefits of SFPs for those very students. Evidence suggests that framing programs around food insecurity alone, ignoring the lived experiences of children and broader conceptions of well-being described in the previous sections, leads to targeted programs that are stigmatizing to users and resisted by parents who fear stigmatization.[62] These notions were raised during interviews with all community-based practitioner authors. Emphasizing the food security mission also risks overlooking food quality, as program planners aim to get (any) food into bellies but have less incentive (and sometimes more barriers) to ensure high standards for nutrition (and other facets of well-being described earlier, including taste and environmental sustainability). These concerns have been well documented in the US NSLP, where, without the ongoing advocacy of affluent parents who are less likely to participate in programs framed as targeted for needy children, the nutritional quality and overall meal experience for program users (including the experience of stigma) suffers as programs aim to keep costs low while meeting minimum nutrient standards.[63]

In our 2019 study of a new program designed so "no child goes hungry and all children eat healthy," parents requesting financial subsidies were asked to indicate financial need such that they "struggle to provide a healthy meal for their child(ren)."[64] Requiring parents to attest to struggling to feed their children before accessing the subsidy was described by parents and school staff as stigmatizing. Food provisioning is a key aspect of what families are expected to do and are held morally accountable for.[65] Yet key school district staff, while worried about stigma, also feared that some parents might "undeservedly" get a free ride if there was not some stigma attached to applying for subsidies. This is an example of staff playing the role of "perceivers." As one program planner put it: "The challenge is always, the program has to be fiscally sustainable, so you can't have people subscribe for a subsidy that don't need a subsidy, and just want to get a free lunch. Yet you don't want to create so much stigma that people don't apply."

There is also evidence that participation by the wider school community (beyond students who are labeled as vulnerable/at risk) is needed to mobilize and advocate for better quality services for all students. As Thibaud, who leads an organization that runs school lunch programs across Montreal, stated:

Our approach has been to make it available, all the food programs available to everyone . . . but making sure that it's economically and culturally accessible for the most vulnerable people. And that's the idea of universality. I mean, we're very anti-targeted programs. They're bad. Not only are they bad because of stigmatization, but also, when your goal is to promote healthy food, the main goal is to promote healthy eating, it's not necessarily the most vulnerable people that eat badly.

If we consider the ideas presented in this quote in relation to the concepts of justice, equity, and stigma, we see each at play. There is clearly an intention to avoid overemphasizing group differences (equity approach) and to have special considerations ensuring food is appealing and accessible for those most marginalized (fairness). Both aims may in turn reduce stigma. In fact, Canadian data agree that suboptimal dietary intake is a nearly universal problem among children, regardless of socioeconomic status.[66] Stigma carried out by "perceivers" in their focus on "vulnerable" or otherwise marginalized children overlooks evidence that most children could benefit from a nutritious meal at school and that increased participation by a broader array of children (if the program is well designed) could reduce stigma.

Another problem with targeted approaches is establishing a definition of which children are viewed as "needy" versus "deserving" and how to identify them. The stakes are high for some parents to admit that they need help feeding their children a healthy lunch. Indigenous, Black, racialized, and other marginalized families worry about losing custody of their children if an authority figure believes they cannot feed them adequately.[67] A British Columbia Provincial report found parents "fearful of having their children taken away, because they are struggling to afford healthy food."[68] Families may be uncomfortable applying for subsidies, and the language of "struggl[ing] to provide a healthy meal" can activate feelings of parental inadequacy and possibly stigma.

This leads to questions about alternatives to targeted programs, which are described in the literature as "universal."[69] The term universal is broad and used in different ways. Debbie, the coordinator of the Coalition for Healthy School Food, who is retired from decades of running a large community organization in Toronto that established hundreds of SFPs, addressed this when she said: "I . . . have made the distinction that has stuck, between the two words universality and universal. So, what I think we are doing is looking for universality in the catchment area to reduce stigma on our way to a universal program. It will take four or five years to phase in." Her distinction is between offering a program to everyone (universality) and one where everyone participates (universal). Moreover, she argued that a program can be universal (all children participating) without being free. Japan, France, and Italy are countries with (near) universal participation, but where most parents pay a portion of the cost. Only two affluent countries have universally free programs (Finland and Sweden).[70] As discussed in this volume, there are also less affluent countries with universal free programs (e.g., Brazil and India). Other than the five affluent countries mentioned already with near-universal participation—two free for parents, three where parents pay a portion—there is much less than near-universal participation in most SFPs (ranging from ~10–60 percent). In most affluent countries, most parents pay all or part of the cost, with some parents (deemed neediest) paying nothing.

Another issue of justice relates to care work and whether SFPs should alleviate some of the burdens families shoulder for feeding children. While schools are responsible for caring for children during school hours, in Canada, food provisioning is still largely seen as a private responsibility.[71] The majority of that burden still falls to mothers, who now often do "double duty," commonly working in the paid labor force but also on average performing more hours of housework and childcare than men.[72] COVID-19 has revealed these gender inequities starkly as mothers lost jobs at faster rates and also shouldered more burden juggling family life, home schooling, and food preparation than fathers.[73] And while there is some recent evidence that Canadian fathers have increased participation in housework and childcare, supporting public provisioning of food is a collective way to share the load across society, freeing a small slice of time and cognitive load for mothers and other caregivers.[74]

The Canadian state is built on colonial displacement, forced assimilation, and ignorance of the rights of Indigenous peoples.[75] It would be a significant omission to consider an SFP for Canada without addressing justice related to the sovereignty of Indigenous nations and the rights of people considered Aboriginal (First Nations, Inuit, and Métis) under the Canadian Constitution.[76] We argue that this is an important opportunity to get a program "right" by centering Indigenous rights from the very inception of any national program. When speaking about a model for a national program, Thibaud stated:

> To me, the local control piece is not just about engagement, but to me, that's the only way that the cultural and especially Indigenous piece can come in. There needs to be [a] governance piece. I think the federal standards could be parameters . . . It could be quite loose, and then give that over. And I think especially, probably how it's handled with Indigenous communities, it's going to need to be quite different even [than] in how we look at urban culturally diverse populations.

He is bringing up an important issue that falls within the purview of justice: the balancing of central versus local control. There was considerable consensus among informants that the role of the federal government is to create a framework (including nutritional and other standards) and funding, but that control over all other aspects of the program should be in the hands of local communities. When it comes to Indigenous community programs, this is particularly critical. The Canadian government has an extensive history of undermining Indigenous sovereignty, and this may be far more difficult to address than it seems. One way forward may be the development and rollout of a national program that starts with Indigenous communities, with funding and other resources provided (an equity approach). This is challenging because more than half of Indigenous people are urban residents, yet they must be a priority.[77]

The final justice issue we will address is the importance of including what Gaddis calls "real jobs" in a future national SFP.[78] Paid employment opportunities that provide a living wage, fair working conditions, autonomy, and job satisfaction are important justice concerns. Bringing up the issue of good jobs in school food, Brent, who is a teacher, stated: "There's a tension to me about how much of it is public and unionized, and how much of it is not, that I don't know the answer to, but it actually worries me a little bit." Ultimately, difficult funding decisions will be needed to ensure adequate and stable resources to enact labor standards that honor the justice goals articulated here. But as a starting point, we argue that justice must be ratified as a core goal of a Canadian SFP, and that the broad goal of justice cannot be achieved without ensuring: equity of access for all who serve to benefit (which we argue includes all children and families who want to participate), programs delivered without stigma, the sovereignty of Indigenous peoples, and a fair distribution of economic benefits across workers and communities.

CONCLUSION

In this chapter, we argue for a foundational vision of the transformational potential of school food in Canada by articulating three broad and interrelated goals for Canadian SFPs. There is now a need for collective support around such goals given the national policy reckoning transpiring following the COVID-19 pandemic. While we have presented each of these three goals related to centering children, health, and justice separately, we argue that these are intersecting and mutually dependent aims. Choosing or valuing one over the others will weaken the power and potential of achieving any of them. Without centering the experiences of children, we can't know how program designs exacerbate injustice or stigma for children; without centering justice, we may leave out children, workers, and communities who stand to gain, and without centering broad conceptions of health, programs could provide nutrient-rich food products but still fail to nourish the relationships, land, and bodies they intend to serve while reproducing past social and nutritional inequities.

CHSF and its members are currently mobilizing efforts across the country and asking provincial leaders and ministers of education to begin immediate negotiations with the federal government on a plan to implement the school food program proposed in the 2019 Food Policy for Canada and Federal Budget. The coalition's priorities come from members' views about the need for universal, non-stigmatizing school food programs that focus on healthy food, and through research partnerships, the coalition seeks to learn from global best practices. Its priorities are continuously refined in conversations with members and academic partners that include nonprofit organizations, Indigenous leaders, and national health, education, and philanthropic organizations from all provinces and territories with the endorsement of 123 government bodies and other nonprofit organizations. But it is time to come together to ratify a vision that embraces the full transformational potential of a national SFP. This will require future program designers and advocates to center the voices and perspectives of children, strive for a holistic understanding of health, and commit to enhancing justice by ensuring universal access, equitable distribution of economic and social benefits across families, food-system workers, and communities, and commit to an actively decolonizing approach.

NOTES

1. "UNICEF Report Card 16," UNICEF Canada: For Every Child (UNICEF Canada, n.d.), https://www.unicef.ca/en/unicef-report-card-16.

2. "UNICEF Report Card 16"; Claire N. Tugault-Lafleur, Susan I. Barr, and Jennifer L. Black, "Examining Differences in School Hour and School Day Dietary Quality among Canadian Children between 2004 and 2015," *Public Health Nutrition* 22, no. 16 (November 2019): 3051–3062, https://doi.org/10.1017/S1368980019000788.

3. "UNICEF Report Card 16."

4. "UNICEF Report Card 16."

5. "UNICEF Report Card 16"; Tugault-Lafleur, Barr, and Black, "Examining Differences"; Claire N. Tugault-Lafleur and Jennifer L. Black, "Lunch on School Days in Canada: Examining Contributions to Nutrient and Food Group Intake and Differences across Eating Locations," *Journal of the Academy of Nutrition and Dietetics* 120, no. 9 (September 2020): 1484–1497, https://doi.org/10.1016/j.jand.2020.01.011.

6. "Coalition for Healthy School Food: Canada," Coalition for Healthy School Food (Coalition for Healthy School Food, 2020), https://www.healthyschoolfood.ca.

7. Dennis Raphael, "A Discourse Analysis of the Social Determinants of Health," *Critical Public Health* 21, no. 2 (June 1, 2011): 221–236, https://doi.org/10.1080/09581596.2010.485606.

8. Mustafa Koc and Japji A. Bas, "Canada's Action Plan for Food Security: The Interactions between Civil Society and the State to Advance to Advance Food Security in Canada," in *Health and Sustainability in the Canadian Food System: Advocacy and Opportunity for Civil Society*, ed. Rod MacRae and Elisabeth Abergel (Vancouver, BC: UBC Press, 2012), 173–203; Clare Harper, Lesley Wood, and Claire Mitchell, "The Provision of School Food in 18 Countries," *School Food Trust, UK*, 2008, 52.

9. "Chapter 4: Delivering Real Change," Budget 2019 (Government of Canada, March 19, 2019), https://www.budget.canada.ca/2019/docs/plan/chap-04-en.html.

10. Dennis Raphael and Toba Bryant, "The Limitations of Population Health as a Model for a New Public Health," *Health Promotion International* 17 (July 1, 2002): 189–199, https://doi.org/10.1093/heapro/17.2.189.

11. Kimberley Hernandez et al., "The Case for a Canadian National School Food Program," *Canadian Food Studies / La Revue Canadienne Des Études Sur l'alimentation* 5, no. 3 (September 30, 2018): 208–229, https://doi.org/10.15353/cfs-rcea.v5i3.260.

12. Koc and Bas, "Canada's Action Plan for Food Security."

13. Tracy Everitt, Rachel Engler-Stringer, and Wanda Martin, "Determining Promising Practices for Canadian School Food Programs: A Scoping Review," *Journal of Hunger & Environmental Nutrition* 17, no. 6 (September 18, 2020): 743–762, https://doi.org/10.1080/19320248.2020.1823925.

14. H. Frances Browning, Rachel E. Laxer, and Ian Janssen, "Food and Eating Environments: In Canadian Schools," *Canadian Journal of Dietetic Practice and Research* 74, no. 4 (2013): 160–166, https://doi.org/10.3148/74.4.2013.160.

15. Hernandez et al., "The Case for a Canadian National School Food Program."

16. Claire N. Tugault-Lafleur, Jennifer L. Black, and Susan I. Barr, "Lunch-Time Food Source Is Associated with School Hour and School Day Diet Quality among Canadian Children," *Journal of Human Nutrition and Dietetics: The Official Journal of the British Dietetic Association* 31, no. 1 (February 2018): 96–107, https://doi.org/10.1111/jhn.12500; Marije Oostindjer et al., "Are School Meals a Viable and Sustainable Tool to Improve the Healthiness and Sustainability of Children's Diet and Food Consumption? A Cross-National Comparative Perspective," *Critical Reviews in Food Science and Nutrition* 57, no. 18 (December 12, 2017): 3942–3958, https://doi.org/10.1080/10408398.2016.1197180; Jennifer L. Black et al., "SD40 School Nourishment Program 2018–2019 Report Insights about School Lunch Experiences from Three Schools with Pre-Existing Lunch Programs During the 2019 Transition to the Fuel Up! School Nourishment Program in New Westminster," 2020, 40, https://lfs-jblack.sites.olt.ubc.ca/files/2020/10/BC-School-Lunch-Program-Full-Report-June-2020.pdf.

17. Oostindjer et al., "Are School Meals a Viable and Sustainable Tool."; Kristina E. Gibson and Sarah E. Dempsey, "Make Good Choices, Kid: Biopolitics of Children's Bodies and School Lunch Reform in Jamie Oliver's Food Revolution," *Children's Geographies* 13, no. 1 (January 2, 2015): 44–58, https://doi.org/10.1080/14733285.2013.827875.

18. Gibson and Dempsey, "Make Good Choices, Kid."

19. Jennifer Patico, *The Trouble with Snack Time: Children's Food and the Politics of Parenting* (New York: NYU Press, 2020), 206.

20. Gibson and Dempsey, "Make Good Choices, Kid."; Joslyn Brenton, "The Limits of Intensive Feeding: Maternal Foodwork at the Intersections of Race, Class, and Gender," *Sociology of Health & Illness* 39, no. 6 (July 2017): 863–877, https://doi.org/10.1111/1467-9566.12547.

21. Tracy Everitt, Rachel Engler-Stringer, and Wanda Martin. "Determining Promising Practices for Canadian School Food Programs: A Scoping Review." *Journal of Hunger & Environmental Nutrition* 17 (2020): 743–762.

22. Allison Pugh, *Longing and Belonging: Parents, Children, and Consumer Culture* (Oakland: University of California Press, 2009), 7.

23. Gibson and Dempsey, "Make Good Choices, Kid."; Brenton, "The Limits of Intensive Feeding."; Best, *Fast-Food Kids*; Pugh, *Longing and Belonging*.

24. Patricia A. Adler and Peter Adler, *Peer Power: Preadolescent Culture and Identity* (New Brunswick, NJ: Rutgers University Press, 1998).

25. Brenton, "The Limits of Intensive Feeding"; Kate Cairns, "Relational Foodwork: Young People and Food Insecurity," *Children & Society* 32, no. 3 (May 1, 2018): 174–184, https://doi.org/10.1111/chso.12259.

26. Adler and Adler, *Peer Power*.

27. Adler and Adler, *Peer Power*; Anna Ludvigsen and Sara Scott, "Real Kids Don't Eat Quiche: What Food Means to Children," *Food, Culture and Society: An International Journal of Multidisciplinary Research* 12 (December 1, 2009): 417–436, https://doi.org/10.2752/175174409X456728.

28. Adler and Adler, *Peer Power*; Jennifer E. Gaddis, *The Labor of Lunch: Why We Need Real Food and Real Jobs in American Public Schools*, vol. 70 (Oakland: University of California Press, 2019); Ludvigsen and Scott, "Real Kids Don't Eat Quiche.".

29. Ludvigsen and Scott, "Real Kids Don't Eat Quiche."

30. Oliver W. Edwards and Gordon E. Taub, "Children and Youth Perceptions of Family Food Insecurity and Bullying," *School Mental Health* 9, no. 3 (September 1, 2017): 263–272, https://doi.org/10.1007/s12310-017-9213-8.

31. Gaddis, *The Labor of Lunch*.

32. Maryah Stella Fram et al., "Children Are Aware of Food Insecurity and Take Responsibility for Managing Food Resources," *Journal of Nutrition* 141, no. 6 (June 2011): 1114–1119, https://doi.org/10.3945/jn.110.135988; Jennifer Gaddis, "Mobilizing to Re-Value and Re-Skill Foodservice Labor in U.S. School Lunchrooms: A Pathway to Community-Level Food Sovereignty?," *Radical Teacher* 98 (February 27, 2014), https://doi.org/10.5195/rt.2014.67.

33. Harper, Wood, and Mitchell, "The Provision of School Food in 18 Countries."

34. Paula England, "Emerging Theories of Care Work," *Review of Sociology* 31, no. 1 (July 10, 2005): 381-399. doi: 10.1146/ANNUREV.SOC.31.041304.122317.

35. BC Teachers' Federation, "Hungry Students in BC Public Schools and the Adequacy of School Meal Programs to Support Them. Poverty and Education Survey: A Teacher's Perspective," 2015, 4.

36. Senate Canada, "Obesity in Canada: A Whole of Society Approach for a Healthier Canada" (Standing Senate Committee on Social Affairs, Science and Technology, March 2016), https://sencanada.ca/content/sen/committee/421/SOCI/Reports/2016-02-25_Revised_report_Obesity_in_Canada_e.pdf.

37. Barbara Parker and Mario Koeppel, "Beyond Health & Nutrition: Re-Framing School Food Programs through Integrated Food Pedagogies," *Canadian Food Studies/La Revue Canadienne Des Études Sur l'alimentation* 7, no. 2 (November 16, 2020): 48–71, https://doi.org/10.15353/cfs-rcea.v7i2.371.

38. Adler and Adler, *Peer Power*; Mary Kate Dennis and Tabitha Robin, "Healthy on Our Own Terms: Indigenous Wellbeing and the Colonized Food System," *Critical Dietetics* 5, no. 1 (May 14, 2020): 4–11, https://doi.org/10.32920/cd.v5i1.1333.

39. Government of Canada, "Canada's Food Guide" (Ottawa, 2019), https://food-guide.canada.ca/en/food-guide-snapshot/.

40. Ministry of Citizens' Services, "Ministry of Education—Province of British Columbia" (Province of British Columbia, 2010), https://www2.gov.bc.ca/gov/content/governments/organizational-structure/ministries-organizations/ministries/education.

41. "Health Canada," Government of Canada (Government of Canada, 2019), https://www.canada.ca/en/health-canada.html.

42. Dennis and Robin, "Healthy on Our Own Terms."

43. Gyorgy Scrinis, *Nutritionism: The Science and Politics of Dietary Advice* (New York: Columbia University Press, 2015).

44. Janet Poppendieck, *Free for All: Fixing School Food in America* (Oakland: University of California Press, 2011); "Health Canada."

45. The Standing Senate Committee on Aboriginal Peoples, "How Did We Get Here? A Concise, Unvarnished Account of the History of the Relationship between Indigenous Peoples and Canada"(Ottawa, 2019), 64.

46. Koc and Bas, "Canada's Action Plan for Food Security"; England, "Emerging Theories of Care Work."

47. Ian Mosby and Tracey Galloway, "'Hunger Was Never Absent': How Residential School Diets Shaped Current Patterns of Diabetes among Indigenous Peoples in Canada," *Histoire Sociale/Social History* 46 (August 14, 2017), https://doi.org/10.1503/cmaj.170448.

48. England, "Emerging Theories of Care Work"; Mosby and Galloway, "'Hunger Was Never Absent.'"

49. Ian Mosby, "Administering Colonial Science: Nutrition Research and Human Biomedical Experimentation in Aboriginal Communities and Residential Schools, 1942–1952," *Histoire Sociale/Social History* 46, no. 1 (2013): 145–172, https://doi.org/10.1353/his.2013.0015.

50. Craig A Hassel et al., "Decolonizing Nutrition Science," *Current Developments in Nutrition* 3 (August 1, 2019): 3–11, https://doi.org/10.1093/cdn/nzy095; Alejandro Rojas et al., "Insights from the Think&EatGreen@School Project: How a Community-Based Action Research Project Contributed to Healthy and Sustainable School Food Systems in Vancouver," *Canadian Food Studies /La Revue Canadienne Des Études Sur l'alimentation* 4, no. 2 (December 22, 2017): 25–46, https://doi.org/10.15353/cfs-rcea.v4i2.225.

51. Hassel et al., "Decolonizing Nutrition Science."

52. Alejandro Rojas, Elena Orrego, and Stephanie Shulhan, "Community-Based Action Research in Vancouver Public Schools: Improving the Quality of Children's Lives through Secure and Sustainable School Food Systems and Experiential Learning,"

Engaged Scholar Journal: Community-Engaged Research, Teaching, and Learning 1, no. 2 (2015): 17–35, https://doi.org/10.15402/esj.v1i2.98.

53. Margot Hurlbert, *Pursuing Justice: An Introduction to Justice Studies, Second Edition* (Fernwood Publishing Company, 2018); Rojas et al., "Insights from the Think&Eat Green@School Project."

54. Rojas et al., "Insights from the Think&EatGreen@School Project."

55. Valerie Earnshaw and Allison Karpyn, "Understanding Stigma and Food Inequity: A Conceptual Framework to Inform Research, Intervention, and Policy," *Translational Behavioral Medicine* 10 (2021): 1350–1357, https://doi.org/10.1093/tbm/ibaa087.

56. Paula England, "Emerging Theories of Care Work."

57. "World Health Organization," World Health Organization (World Health Organization, 2021), https://www.who.int.

58. Bruce G. Link and Jo C. Phelan, "Conceptualizing Stigma," *Annual Review of Sociology* 27, no. 1 (2001): 363–385, https://doi.org/10.1146/annurev.soc.27.1.363.

59. Gaddis, "Mobilizing to Re-Value and Re-Skill Foodservice Labor in U.S. School Lunchrooms."

60. Oostindjer et al., "Are School Meals a Viable and Sustainable Tool."; Craig Gundersen, "Food Assistance Programs and Child Health," *Future of Children* 25, no. 1 (2015): 91–109; Valerie Tarasuk and Andy Mitchell, "Household Food Insecurity in Canada, 2017–2018. Toronto: Research to Identify Policy Options to Reduce Food Insecurity (PROOF).," PROOF: Food Insecurity Policy Research, 2020, https://proof.utoronto.ca/.

61. Rojas et al., "Insights from the Think&EatGreen@School Project."

62. Gundersen, "Food Assistance Programs and Child Health"; Tarasuk and Mitchell, "Household Food Insecurity in Canada, 2017–2018. Toronto: Research to Identify Policy Options to Reduce Food Insecurity (PROOF)"; Patricia L. Williams et al., "The 'Wonderfulness' of Children's Feeding Programs," *Health Promotion International* 18, no. 2 (June 2003): 163–170, https://doi.org/10.1093/heapro/18.2.163.

63. Adler and Adler, *Peer Power*; Dennis and Robin, "Healthy on Our Own Terms."

64. Everitt, Engler-Stringer, and Martin, "Determining Promising Practices for Canadian School Food Programs: A Scoping Review."

65. Adler and Adler, *Peer Power*; Lynn McIntyre and Jutta B. Dayle, "Exploratory Analysis of Children's Nutrition Programs in Canada," *Social Science & Medicine (1982)* 35, no. 9 (November 1992): 1123–1129, https://doi.org/10.1016/0277-9536(92)90224-e; Oostindjer et al., "Are School Meals a Viable and Sustainable Tool"; Tugault-Lafleur, Black, and Barr, "Lunch-Time Food Source Is Associated with School Hour and School Day Diet Quality among Canadian Children".

66. Lynn McIntyre, Kim Travers, and Jutta B. Dayle, "Children's Feeding Programs in Atlantic Canada: Reducing or Reproducing Inequities?," *Canadian Journal of Public Health* 90 (1999): 196–200, https://doi.org/10.1007/BF03404506.

67. McIntyre and Dayle, "Exploratory Analysis of Children's Nutrition Programs in Canada."

68. Government of British Columbia, "What We Heard about Poverty in B.C." (Province of British Columbia, Vancouver, BC, 2018), 31, https://www2.gov.bc.ca/assets/gov/british-columbians-our-governments/initiatives-plans-strategies/poverty-reduction-strategy/what-we-heard.pdf; Kim Raine, Lynn McIntyre, and Jutta Dayle, "The Failure of Charitable School-and Community-Based Nutrition Programmes to Feed Hungry Children," *Critical Public Health* 13 (June 1, 2003): 155–169, https://doi.org/10.1080/09581590302768.

69. Sinikka Elliott and Sarah Bowen, "Defending Motherhood: Morality, Responsibility, and Double Binds in Feeding Children: Defending Motherhood," *Journal of Marriage and Family* 80 (February 1, 2018): 499–520, https://doi.org/10.1111/jomf.12465.

70. Government of British Columbia, "What We Heard About Poverty in B.C."; Claire N. Tugault-Lafleur, Jennifer L. Black, and Susan I. Barr, "Examining School-Day Dietary Intakes among Canadian Children," *Applied Physiology, Nutrition, and Metabolism* 42, no. 10 (October 2017): 1064–1072, https://doi.org/10.1139/apnm-2017-0125.

71. Oostindjer et al., "Are School Meals a Viable and Sustainable Tool."

72. Tina Moffat and Danielle Gendron, "Cooking up the 'Gastro-Citizen' through School Meal Programs in France and Japan," *Food, Culture & Society* 22 (2019): 63–77, https://doi.org/10.1080/15528014.2018.1547587.

73. Harper, Wood, and Mitchell, "The Provision of School Food in 18 Countries."

74. Moffat and Gendron, "Cooking up the 'Gastro-Citizen' through School Meal Programs in France and Japan."

75. Scrinis, *Nutritionism: The Science and Politics of Dietary Advice.*

76. Poppendieck, *Free for All: Fixing School Food in America.*

77. Jeffrey Neilson and Maria Stanfors, "It's About Time! Gender, Parenthood, and Household Divisions of Labor Under Different Welfare Regimes," *Journal of Family Issues* 35, no. 8 (June 1, 2014): 1066–1088, https://doi.org/10.1177/0192513X14522240.

78. Adler and Adler, *Peer Power*; Gaddis, *The Labor of Lunch.*

3

SCHOOL FOOD POLITICS, IDENTITY, AND INDIGENEITY IN THE PERUVIAN AMAZON

Emmanuelle Ricaud Oneto

May 22, 2017, in a Maijuna village in the northwest Amazon, Peru.

It is a foggy morning. Romana[1] gets up before dawn. It is her turn to prepare snacks and lunch for school children. This little village counts twenty-two elementary students, including her nine-year-old daughter. She walks from her house to the canteen, a little house on stilts made of wood and crowned with a thatched leaf roof next to the concrete school building. At the back of the canteen, in the kitchen, there is some wood and a bucket of water her husband brought the evening before. She lights the fire. The teacher, Noe, climbs the few steps of the canteen, reaches the storage area, and with his key unlocks the heavy chain. He shows me the foodstuff from Peru's National School Feeding Program, *Qali Warma*, which means "vigorous child" in Quechua.[2] Among the tuna, sardine, and chicken cans, the pasta, rice, lentils, powdered eggs, and canned milk, he selects some ingredients based on the suggested menus sent by Qali Warma for Romana to prepare.

The menu of the day? For breakfast: porridge with milk, oats, and sugar, with quinoa cookies. For lunch: tuna, pasta, rice, and split peas. In a large metal pot, Romana pours the milk and lets it cook with the oats and sugar until it has the consistency of porridge (*mazamorra*, or *jùrù* in Máíjɨ̀kì, Maijuna language). She serves one cup for each child; meanwhile, the teacher distributes cookies wrapped in plastic. At 7 a.m., children dressed in colorful and fluorescent clothes—usually football T-shirts and shorts for boys, shades of pink T-shirts and shorts or skirts for girls, and shoes—sit on the bench at the table to eat.[3] The smaller ones eat on the floor as they do not reach the table. Once breakfast is finished, they go to school. Later, Romana prepares lunch. Since she fished the day before, she prepares *sudado de pescado* (stewed fish) and puts the tuna cans aside. She adds some condiments: garlic she bought at the little village bodega, sweet pepper, turmeric, and coriander from her garden. When the meal is ready (stewed fish with split peas mash, rice, and pasta), she serves it generously in individual plates. The children eat a part of it at the canteen and save the rest to take home on plates they brought from home.[4] Members of their families share the food later. Romana brings home the unopened cans of tuna she set aside, in case her household runs out of game or fish.

This extract from my fieldwork notes describes how a mother inhabiting a Maijuna village has both applied and deviated from Qali Warma to realize her own vision of what school meals should be and to allot herself a compensation for her collaboration: the canned tuna. During twelve months of ethnographic fieldwork conducted from 2013 to 2017 in the lowlands of the northwest Amazon,[5] I witnessed many mothers adapting the program to their needs in similar ways. I was working in six different villages in northeastern Peru, officially and locally called Native communities.[6]

Four were Maijuna villages, and two were Napuruna villages in the lower Napo River Basin. Located in the Loreto department, they lie in various degrees of remoteness from the city of Iquitos, from five hours to a full day of travel by boat. After receiving official authorization from local representatives and community assemblies, I collected data using ethnographic methods such as participant observation and semi-structured and informal interviews. In this chapter, I draw on that material to analyze the implementation of Qali Warma at the local level, focusing especially on the role of the mothers who almost always cook school meals.[7] They are the last intermediaries between what the state provides and what ends up on children's plates. Within that limited space for maneuver, caregivers[8] both concretize and transform the school food program that has been designed by state policies.[9] They engage in a complex negotiation with

3.1 A Napuruna mother prepares sardines, rice, and plantains for a school meal. Students harvested the plantains. Credit: Emmanuelle Ricaud Oneto.

the Peruvian government as they grapple with the constraints of the program and deploy strategies to adapt it to their own agendas.

I use the term negotiation to emphasize the active process deployed by mothers, which does not involve actual, verbal discussion between government representatives and beneficiaries. Rather, mothers "negotiate" by preparing some supplied foods while expressing concern, or altogether avoiding others; substituting local ingredients; and spreading rumors about the nature of government-provided food and its risks. I understand these discrete resistances as the "infrapolitics of subaltern groups," that is, "political acts that are disguised or offstage [that] help us to map a realm of possible dissent."[10]

Despite their concerns, both groups seem to embrace the program because, like school itself, it allows their children to acquire a *mestizo* socialization. In general, *mestizo* is a Spanish word that refers to anyone who adopts a behavior related to modernity, technology, or urbanity. It is also used as an adjective to indicate industrial or urban-style food (*comida mestiza*). Caregivers believe that learning how to be mestizo, by adopting their cultural habits and eating the food, will open up possibilities for children, fostering less discriminatory and more egalitarian relationships with the mestizo and providing easier access to job opportunities in the mestizo world. The motivation behind appropriating these cultural habits is that, in the long term, it might serve the community's best interests.

All this happens within what scholar Antonella Tassinari, writing about Indigenous schools, calls a *frontier*.[11] Rather than seeing schools as merely imposed on from the top-down or appropriated or resisted from the bottom-up, Tassinari writes, we should understand them as "an area of contact and exchange between peoples, with translatable space, as creative situation in which knowledge and traditions are rethought, sometimes reinforced, sometimes rejected, in which ethnic differences both emerge and are built."[12] I argue that school meals constitute a similar space of exchange, interrelation, and negotiation between non-Indigenous and Indigenous worlds.

REGIONAL CONTEXT

Mothers' school food negotiations and the contours of the frontier that they shape are influenced by local geographies, histories, and cultures. The Napuruna are settled on the Napo River, a large commercial shipping lane that connects the Andean Region in Ecuador to the Peruvian Amazon. They call themselves both *Kichwa del Napo* [of the Napo River] and Napuruna, number around 7,600 individuals, and speak Kichwa and Spanish.[13] The approximately five hundred Maijuna inhabit the more remote banks of the tributaries of the Napo and Algodón Rivers. Maijuna is their self-determined name, and they speak Máíjìkì and Spanish.

Both groups have a long history of colonial exploitation, discrimination, and disregard from external actors (colonial settlers to, more recently, the Peruvian government and extractive companies).[14] However, their respective locations have contributed to diverging historical relationships with the mestizo. Napuruna are inclined to exchange, trade with, and marry into other ethnic groups and with mestizo people.[15] In contrast, the Maijuna, who have inhabited harder-to-reach interfluvial areas, have maintained more distant relationships with the mestizo. According to historical records, during the colonial and missionary period from the sixteenth century to the end of the twentieth century, their ancestors, the *Payagua*, were generally depicted by missionaries and explorers as rebellious, unstable, and insubordinate.[16] In the last few decades, however, the Maijuna have begun to establish more connections with mestizos in nearby towns.

Both the Maijuna and the Napuruna compose their meals from their large gardens where they grow a great diversity of crops and tubers; with bushmeat and gathered fruits from the forest; with fish from rivers and lagoons; and, more recently, with industrial food purchased in cities or local bodegas. Forest resources are drawn from their Native communities' territories and from the 391,000-hectare regional conservation area Maijuna-Kichwa, decreed in 2015 for their sustenance. Their dietary diversity can be attributed to specific cultural knowledge of the area's wide variety of species prepared using many culinary techniques that expand the array of meals.[17] Both groups present some noticeable food systems' differences, but from a broad perspective, their daily meals contain boiled, grilled, smoked, or steamed fish or game with plantains and cassava, the staple food. Women also prepare juices and fermented drinks with cassava and other plants. These shared traditions, as well as each group's regional interethnic relationships, shape how they have received and transformed Qali Warma, a recent national policy that stems from a longer history of Peruvian school food politics.

OVERVIEW OF SCHOOL MEALS PROGRAMS IN PERU

During the 1950s, the newly founded US Agency for International Development (USAID) began routing agricultural surpluses to developing countries, which meant the poorer sections of Peruvian society began receiving some food assistance.[18] By the 1980s, as Peru emerged from twelve years of military rule (1968–1980), it underwent a profound political, social, and economic crisis marked by market liberalization and economic adjustment policies. Like other Latin American countries, Peru could no longer borrow from foreign countries and implemented austerity policies to pay extant debts. To try to mitigate the effects of rising poverty, grassroots women's associations, first in Lima and eventually across the country, created *comedores populares* (community kitchens) that significantly increased food aid to poor families, as well as informal glasses of milk programs for children and pregnant women. The kitchens were funded primarily by the USAID but also by international organizations, channeling food donations through local private agencies like Christian organizations and NGOs.[19]

In a clientelist maneuver, or an exchange of public goods for political support, the mayor of Lima announced the creation of *Programa Vaso de Leche* (Glass of Milk Program) for the city in 1984. The following year, the Peruvian president expanded the program to the national scale, morphing into the first national food program. Through successive national governments, several programs succeeded one another until passage of the 1992 *Programa Nacional de Asistencia Alimentaria*, PRONAA (National Food Assistance Program),[20] which provided nutritional supplements for infants and pregnant women as well as school lunches for children in poor areas. PRONAA was, however, an inefficient and controversial program due to a combination of inadequate funding, poor organization, and corruption.[21]

In 2012, the newly elected president Ollanta Humala terminated PRONAA and launched a new package of social policies, including a Mother Allowances Program, old-age pensions, and the National School Food Program Qali Warma, which aims to provide meals for all children in state nursery schools and elementary schools, and seeks to increase school attendance and food security by delivering "a sustainable and healthy quality food service, adapted to local eating habits, co-managed by the community."[22]

Before 2014, when Qali Warma extended to Indigenous communities in the Amazon, children tended to eat before or after class, returning home for meals during a school-day break. On days schools were open, elementary-aged children received both a breakfast snack (usually porridge with cookies) and lunch. Secondary schools did not receive Qali Warma food. Some students still returned home during breaks to eat with their families, and the ones living at boarding schools, since secondary school was far away from their families' village, cooked dishes from ingredients provided by their parents.

Since 2014, Qali Warma was expanded for students in the Amazonian region to include lunch for elementary students (in addition to breakfast) and extended to middle and high school students. In that year, the federal government conferred[23] the status of "extreme poverty"[24] on inhabitants of Amazonian Native communities, thus automatically expanding Qali Warma's reach. By 2017, there were 1.2 million children in state nurseries (from three to five years old) and 2.6 million children in elementary schools (from six to eleven years old).[25] Approximately 3.5 million rations were distributed every school day throughout the country.[26] Qali Warma reaches 330,000 Indigenous students from Peru's fifty-five officially recognized Indigenous peoples.[27]

Qali Warma recipients at times must demonstrate that they meet various requirements. More specifically, their mothers must show proof of, for example, birth control use, infant and children health controls and vaccinations, and ensure that children attend school until the age of fourteen. In some Napuruna villages, mothers who do not come to prepare school meals on their assigned days have to pay a fine of around 10 soles (US$3), which is used later for condiments. Teachers, nurses, and state representatives have all been found to demand informal "shadow conditions."[28] For example, some teachers threaten to suspend food allocations if children do not wear school uniforms, despite it not being mandatory for students to wear them. As scholars of Peru, and Latin America generally, have pointed out, antipoverty social policies that promote co-responsibility mean, in practice, that the "burden of responsibility"[29] falls on mothers' shoulders.[30]

Qali Warma's structure reflects the global context of neoliberal governance, specifically the principle of co-responsibility with systems of co-management and cooperation with local actors. This model replaces direct social assistance from the central government, which policymakers argue creates dependency on state welfare.[31] As in other Latin American countries, new participatory committees oversee the local implementation of national government programs. The School Food Committee (CAE), composed of parents and teachers, is responsible for receiving the food, controlling its quantity and quality, and cooking it. The Purchasing Committee (CC), composed of parent and teacher representatives working with local governments, organizes the purchase of food to comply with menus sent from the Ministry of Development and Social Inclusion (MIDIS). Although the program's guidelines state that MIDIS should source the products from within Peru, giving preference to local suppliers,[32] small and family farms rarely meet the required industrial standards regarding production, packaging, and transport.[33] Thus, as MIDIS goes through rounds of public bidding,[34] they source most food from large national and sometimes international agro-industrial companies.[35]

Even though Indigenous communities—who hunt, fish, collect and cultivate fresh, nutritious food—provide large quantities of food to city-dwellers, they do not meet the government hygienic and logistical requirements to qualify as suppliers for Qali Warma. Neither are they involved or consulted[36] in policymaking decisions that deeply impact their communities; despite policies stipulating participatory committees, Indigenous stakeholders are still excluded from the policy process. The provision of fresh products sourced from beyond the region to Amazonian villages is logistically challenging, so the government provides industrial canned or packaged food to the Maijuna and the Napuruna once a month by boat, the primary mode of transport in the region.

In villages, local leaders, family farmers, and caregivers have complained both formally and informally about the quality of the food from national producers.[37] Some parents complained about allergies their children had when exposed to some products, usually canned food, and about low-quality food with a lot of fat and outdated expiration labels. In 2018, the Interethnic Association for the Development of the Peruvian Jungle (AIDESEP) published the Indigenous Women of the Amazon Agenda to

3.2 A Maijuna girl playing with school meal ingredients. Credit: Emmanuelle Ricaud Oneto.

continue this demand for fresh, healthy, culturally responsive, and sustainable school food: "To influence MIDIS so that social programs aimed at Native communities, such as *Qali Warma* and *Cuna Más*, acquire local products and prepare food in accordance with the cultural consumption of Indigenous peoples.[38] Though the Peruvian government has not changed its policies, the Maijuna and the Napuruna enact their communities' Indigenous logics to rework the goals and implementation of Qali Warma at the local level to further their own aims for their children's learning: to embody and become mestizo by eating school meals.

EATING MESTIZO, BECOMING MESTIZO: AMAZONIAN INDIGENOUS LOGICS RELATED TO THE PURPOSE OF SCHOOLING

For the Maijuna and Napuruna people, schooling is understood as highly important for children's futures. When I asked parents why they want their children to study in the schools, they answered that by studying they can get a salaried job, which most parents do not have. For instance, an old man who had adopted his grandchild told me:

I do not want him to sweat in the garden. He should have a position, like working for the State and they give him a salary. Nowadays, children should study to be able to earn a salary. Because, if he does not study, he will marry, go [to the garden] with his ax, his basket. For me, this is not good. I want him to complete his education (*superar su educación*). Working as a secretary, with computers, all of that, with papers. It seems to me that it is better. But living and gardening, no. He will suffer a lot.

Most of my interlocutors stressed that they would like their children to become professionals who, after pursuing secondary education, would return to their villages to support their communities. When I asked Lucía what she expected for her daughter's future, she responded, "I would like her to be what God wants: a nurse, maybe an engineer, a nurse. I would like that my children move forward, that they study." I asked if she wanted her daughter to stay in the village, and she explained, "No. I would like her to work first to learn how it is to be a nurse, what pills should be used for what disease. And when she can return here, she might serve people." Like other Amazonian Indigenous groups, the Maijuna and Napuruna seemed to see school not as an essentially colonizing institution but as something to instrumentalize to meet communities' needs and expectations.[39]

School physically and symbolically is a non-Indigenous arena within the community. While the local houses are made of wood, the school is a concrete building. Inside, children learn mestizo knowledge and mestizo behaviors, from clothing, language, and posture to food habits. At school, they have notebooks and pencils; they wear shoes, uniforms, or new clothes, and girls tie their hair. After school, they change into used clothes, take off their shoes, and untie their hair. Parents insist on the importance of this knowing in order "not to be fooled." Many of the adults in these villages have suffered discrimination in cities when they needed hospital attention or asked for government support, and mestizo retailers who sell Maijuna products have ripped them off. Parents hope that, if their children learn about mestizo behavior, they will be able to anticipate and avoid similar discriminations and injustices and they will pursue secondary or higher education or find work in different locales.

School food is a cornerstone of this process of becoming mestizo. Schoolchildren perform mestizo ways of eating, but they also embody mestizo identity and take a non-Indigenous point of view when they eat mestizo food. As Viveiros de Castro has written, "food and cooking regimes in Amazonia" have a "symbolic importance," such that "the set of habits and processes that constitute bodies is precisely the location from which identity and difference emerge."[40] My Maijuna and Napuruna interlocutors revealed this too: when I asked them about what eating a specific food or diet means for them, their answers involved identity. For instance, a Maijuna man, Felipe, explained to me what kind of food he does not eat and why:

FELIPE: Salad, chopped leaf, I do not eat.

Do you not like it?

FELIPE: Do I eat leaves?! In Iquitos, I remove leaves, I am not a *motelo* (yellow-footed tortoise, *Chelonoidis denticulata*) that eats leaves! [...] And, another meal, ceviche. I also do not like ceviche. Ceviche you eat raw raw, with mere chili. It burns the meat of the *paiche* (a fish, *Arapaima gigas*). I am not a jaguar that eats that!

In both Maijuna and Napuruna cosmologies, the difference between beings does not lie in their bodies, understood as substance or physiology, but rather in their behavior and food ethos—a concept Viveiros de Castro calls "perspectivism."[41] Thus, eating the food that a certain animal eats or performing its habits means becoming this animal, adopting its point of view.[42] For instance, the Maijuna and Napuruna people do not drink water from the river like other Amazonian Indigenous groups because, as they say, it is an animal habit.[43] For most Amazonian groups, the Maijuna and Napuruna included, food behaviors mark the bodily differences between humans and animals, as well as distinct human groups such as mestizo and Indigenous.[44] Regarding mestizo food, Lucía, a Maijuna woman, said:

LUCÍA: Mestizo food is motelo stew, of meat, of chicken. Mestizo food is made of chicken. They eat it in Iquitos.

Do you eat chicken?

LUCÍA: Yes, I do. I am also mestiza!

Similarly, in a Napuruna village, when I was eating with María and her children in the kitchen, she said that we were eating as *wiracocha*, white or mestizo people. She referred to the fact that we were seated on a bench in front of a table covered with a white tablecloth, eating our fish soup with cassava flour on plates, with forks and spoons. The following day, she told me that she wanted to eat as a *Nativa* (Indigenous). Seated on the floor, we used our hands to eat boiled fish and cassava from one *bijao* leaf (*Calathea sp.*) placed on the ground between us. Ingredients themselves transform according to how they are cooked and served. When Romana added local river fish to the school lunch described at the start of this chapter, she cooked it *sudado de pescado*, as a mestizo meal, and it was thus perceived as mestizo or prepared food. Similarly, when Maijuna and Napuruna mothers add to school meals local fresh ingredients from their garden—such as sweet pepper, *cocona*, a local tropical fruit, or *sacha culantro* (local coriander)—they are considered mestizo food, used in mestizo cuisine.

Like other Amazonian Indigenous people, the Maijuna and the Napuruna do not just perform identity; they embody it. Enacting the school meal program, then, children who learn mestizo eating habits are also becoming mestizo.[45] This allows them to experience social (state) policies not as interactive, not unidirectional. Although a few elders expressed concerns that children in school might learn to deny or depreciate their origins and their own culture, most of the parents with whom I spoke did not see the process of acquiring mestizo knowledge, norms, and behaviors as a way of forgetting or denying their own culture; rather, they presented it as a useful addition. Nevertheless, rumors about school food that circulated throughout the villages reflected real concerns and fears about both mestizo eating and, more broadly, the possible long-term consequences of becoming mestizo.

NEGOTIATING SCHOOL FOOD: NUANCING LOGICS AND STRATEGIES

The Maijuna and Napuruna people value the food schools receive from the government for its role in the process of becoming mestizo, for the variety it adds to school menus, and for its economic and practical benefits. When parents are working in the garden or in the forest, or when local resources are scarce, children can still be fed at school. But the status of the food provided differs from one product to another. Overall, caregivers tend to value their own food resources over industrial or mestizo products, some of which—particularly canned food—they mistrust or altogether reject. They explain their judgment in terms of values, allergies observed after ingestion, and a general distrust of the government. Even though Maijuna or Kichwa caregivers are not consulted and cannot become official Qali Warma suppliers, they develop strategies to participate, adapt, and transform the program according to their Indigenous views and values.

For example, caregivers mostly appreciated white rice from Peru or other countries, which replaces plantains or cassava to accompany game or fish. White rice is often eaten during community gatherings when the hosts can afford it, providing dietary variety and a sense of prestige to the hosts. However, caregivers and some elders criticize the quantity of white rice children are getting used to eating, noting that it should not be consumed every day. A Maijuna man explained to me that eating natural food, not rice and sugar, should be the rule: "You are not going to eat every day just that [rice and sugar], you should eat your natural food. When you are tired, you eat something else. Varied, varied that is how one should eat."

"Natural food" is the phrase both the Napuruna and the Maijuna use to refer to their normal diets, contrasting rainforest or garden food with the urban industrial food they pejoratively call *comida química* ("chemical food"). For instance, artificial flavors are considered chemicals and therefore make food unhealthy. Lucía, a Maijuna woman, told me that she carefully limits the doses of *ajino*[46] (monosodium glutamate) in her soups: "I put a little bit of ajino in the food. I do not put a lot. If you put a lot, it gives you disease in your body. Some like it, they put half of it [the sachet]. I take care of myself, of my children." When I asked her what chemical food signifies, she said that it refers to "what food causes disease," which contrasts with the health value inherent in natural food.

Chemical/natural dichotomies within Indigenous food logics shape how Qali Warma is perceived and negotiated at the village level. For example, the people I spoke with during fieldwork pointed to health concerns around the canned tuna provided by the government. Canned tuna is generally despised by adults and most children. Although it is kept in school kitchens in case of need, in practice, mothers either replace it with game, fish, or eggs when they collaborate or they tell their children to eat only the rest of the meal, usually rice. Almost all the mothers told me that students have suffered from allergies when they ate canned tuna. I have noticed several children with the symptoms they described as signs of allergies: white spots, hives, itching, and diarrhea, symptoms that are likely due to preservatives, additives, other chemical substances, or expired tuna. The Maijuna and the Napuruna I spoke to added that eating canned food when they are sick risks aggravating their symptoms, an extension and adaptation of similar cultural knowledge regarding not eating the meat of specific animals when sick.

These examples illustrate how caregivers set limits to the introduction of mestizo school food into their children's diets. Paradoxically, even as they value consuming a variety of "natural" food from gardens, forests, and rivers, they do not encourage their children to orient their lives to obtain it: they prefer their children to find salaried jobs instead of working in gardens, and they hope that a carefully managed mestizo diet will help them achieve that goal.

QALI WARMA AND INDUSTRIAL FOOD AS AFASI MIKUNA FOR NAPURUNA

Many Napuruna consider industrial products like canned fish *afasi mikuna* (lazy food) as opposed to the more coveted game or fish, called prey, without which an Amazonian meal is considered an incomplete "naked dish." Only when no prey is available do the Napuruna choose to eat canned fish. In these cases, despite being disliked, canned fish is a food security device that allows women to prepare a "real meal." When I asked a Napuruna man if he eats canned food, he answered, embarrassed:

If you cannot find any game, it is our afasi mikuna, afasi mikuna. Cans, rice, pasta and oil, and the meal is done. When you have nothing left in your kitchen, it is afasi mikuna, it is made with products from the bodega.

The Napuruna value system places a high value on *sinzhi* (strength) and hard work whether in Indigenous locales or the mestizo world of cities.[47] Men are expected to provide game and money for their families, and women are expected to work hard in the gardens, *chacras*, for the same ends. Caregivers endeavor to "throw away the laziness" of children by holding macerated tobacco or chili close to children's eyes, nostrils, or mouth, which causes vomiting, urinating, or defecating.[48] Such practice is believed to evacuate a phlegm that causes laziness; they use the same method to improve dogs' hunting abilities. Another practice is to give children liquids to drink with plants considered "strong," such as *chuchuwasha* (Maytenus laevis), early in the morning. Some Napuruna feared that Qali Warma's canned, "lazy food" might make their children become lazy or fragile. For instance, a father criticized the nonchalance of schoolchildren who do "as they please" while parents must labor hard.

To limit this transformation, caregivers maintain the local moral framework at schools, and encourage children's autonomy in kind. At the canteen, for instance, older schoolchildren can gain some prestige when they bring fish for lunch. One day, a twelve-year-old boy told me proudly, in the presence of the male teacher and two mothers who were there to cook, that he was used to fishing early and bringing his catch to school. Usually, he only had enough fish for himself, but on this day, he brought two fish, one for him, the second for the teacher, who thanked and praised him, as did the mothers. All three caregivers were balancing the school feeding program's work to help children become mestizo with their own Indigenous values and practices.

RUMORS AS INFRAPOLITICAL DISCOURSES AMONG MAIJUNA

In general, when I asked Maijuna and Napuruna people why they participate in the Qali Warma program, they gave the same reasons as state representatives. They mentioned the risks of undernourished and anemic children as well as situations where parents are not able to prepare breakfast. Mealtimes are flexible, as it depends on the availability of fish and game; parents usually eat around 9–10 a.m., but school begins at 7 a.m.

Yet many Maijuna, mostly mothers, expressed skepticism about Qali Warma, saying that they do not know the true reason the government has in providing the food. For instance, a young mother, Lucila, told me that: "We do not know. For education, that is what they say, but we do not know why." After several months in Maijuna communities, during which there was an increased number of state agents present, I heard mothers worrying and disseminating rumors about both the Qali Warma program and the broader set of social policies.

These stories tended to follow one of two narratives. In the first, the state will kidnap their children, kill them, and return them to the village in tuna cans. The indefinable content of canned food and meat under vacuum—which is either minced meat or fish but not easily recognizable as such—sparks many rumors.[49] In the initial years of the program, the Napuruna and the Maijuna told me they threw away all the cans because they thought it was Indigenous people's flesh. Health controls for children, such as measuring their weight and height, are sometimes seen as a check of their fatness and suitability for the cannibalistic end of becoming canned tuna. Another study with the Maijuna details a rumor that "cans of tuna or sardines in oil are the favorite food of the whites in the forest because they contain Indian meat."[50] Similar rumors have been in circulation for the last few centuries in the Andes and Amazon about the *pishtaco*, an outsider figure—sometimes a colonial settler, sometimes a boss, sometimes a government or NGO agent—who threatens Andean or Amazonian Indigenous lands.[51] In this case, the pishtaco is a cannibalistic outsider threatening their children and, by extension, their social reproduction and way of life.

According to a second set of rumors, drawing on the Bible,[52] the government conspires with merchants and bankers, and people who receive government support (family allowances or food) will be marked by the devil or the Beast. When the Apocalypse comes, all marked people will be killed.[53] These rumors previously circulated among the Napuruna and are still shared among the Maijuna. However, the Maijuna do not seem to fully believe these accounts: in some cases, Maijuna women were laughing when recounting the story, while others seemed quite worried or suspicious. Each story can be understood as "a proposition for belief,"[54] rumors that reflect real fear felt by women for their children, and real distrust, suspicion, and resistance vis-à-vis government institutions and actors.[55] Andean and Amazonian Indigenous communities have understood Qali Warma and other co-responsibility programs not under the promoted logic of rights and duties, but rather as gifts "around which an exchange relationship is created and renewed with a powerful external actor: the Peruvian state."[56] Under this logic of reciprocity, the gifts, supports, or aid of food and money can only be maintained by meeting official requirements, seen as compulsory and coercive.

One of those perceived requirements seems to be eating the school meals. For example, a Maijuna woman said: "We have to eat what the State gives, otherwise it will not send anymore [food supplies]." Another is the required maternal health controls to receive social policy supports: women usually do not feel comfortable in mestizo health institutions. A third are school requirements, even those that are not official, such as the threat that a teacher might suspend their allowances if their children do not wear a uniform. Within this understanding, state agents such as Qali Warma officials, nurses, or teachers appear as intrusive and coercive actors,[57] and the mothers are self-policing by respecting the main program guidelines and providing unpaid work at the canteen. At the same time, rumors indicate a form of resistance.[58]

Such stories bring to light mothers' concerns for the future of their children in the mestizo world. Rumors that the state will kidnap children might be interpreted as mothers' expressions or feelings about losing their children to the mestizo world, and more broadly, the loss of Indigenous knowledge and ways of being. Mothers want their children to study and find work but fear that they might continue to live far from their villages, forget their culture, or even reject their origins. Although the Maijuna and Napuruna don't expect school to be the place where Indigenous knowledge and behaviors are transmitted, some of them, mostly elders, do criticize children for failing to respect their Indigenous heritage. Taken as a whole, rumors[59] about school food reveal the power dynamics, questions, and struggles between mothers and government agents involved in the program.

CONCLUSION

In both Maijuna and Napuruna villages where this research was completed, most families seem not to directly question the provision of school food from the government: they openly ask for food supplies and sometimes even request larger quantities. They understand school food as providing sustenance and helping students pursue what they see as the main objective of schooling: becoming mestizo. Nevertheless, mothers circumscribe this process with precise limits to prevent unwanted effects of school food that their sociocultural values warn against.

Through the introduction of local food to provide more variety in daily meals, Indigenous peoples support the resilience of their own diets and traditions, and by extension, their identities. They transform school food at the "frontier" between Maijuna and Napuruna and mestizo relational social categories. Their informal acts also push back against the bureaucratic apparatus that excludes Indigenous peoples as potential school food suppliers. At the same time, rumors, as infra-political discourses, express skepticism and doubt about the process of becoming mestizo and the ways that the program's constraints risk preventing mothers from providing for their family and supporting their community. In other words, even as these villagers try to follow the basic contours of the program, beneficiaries feel threatened by, and resistant to, the dominant figure of the Peruvian state.

NOTES

1. All names are pseudonyms.
2. This is one of the dominant and Indigenous languages in Peru, but it is not the language of the Maijuna or the Napuruna.
3. Most school children also have national uniforms that parents purchase. They wear them only on Mondays in this village as it is considered a more formal school day.

4. Qali Warma provides cooking and eating utensils, but because the children bring food home, they use their own utensils and dishes.

5. Master's fieldwork was conducted in 2013 with funding from the Research Institute for Development. From 2015 to 2017, doctoral research received financial support from the Interdisciplinary Institute of Contemporary Anthropology; two grants from the Lelong Legacy associated with the French National Center for Scientific Research; the Institute of the Americas' grant; the French Ministry of Foreign Affairs' Aires Culturelles Grant; Île-de-France Regional Council's International Mobility Aid; and the French Institute of Andean Studies Grant. I thank Matthias Teeuwen for his insightful suggestions on this chapter.

6. "Ley de Comunidades Nativas y de Desarrollo Agrario de la Selva y de Ceja de Selva" (Decreto-Ley No. 20653, Peru, 1974).

7. During the survey, only one Napuruna man told me he prepared school meals because he was a cook in the National Army. Similarly, in Maijuna villages, no man cooks at the canteen, including a widower and single father who relies on women in the community to cook.

8. Instead of parents, this term points to all individuals involved in childcare.

9. As Weaver-Hightower and Robert argue, "School Food [. . .] Is Deeply Political on Every Level." See Sarah A. Robert and Marcus B. Weaver-Hightower, *School Food Politics: The Complex Ecology of Hunger and Feeding in Schools around the World* (New York: Peter Lang Publishing, 2011), 6. Guidelines and rules are not followed in the local context the way they were meant to be followed as envisioned and introduced by state officials, illustrating the "deviations" (dérives) that Olivier de Sardan's calls "the recurrent gap between expected behavior and real behavior." See Jean-Pierre Oliver de Sardan, *Anthropology and Development: Understanding Contemporary Social Change* (London-New York: Zed Books, 2005), 28.

10. James C. Scott, *Domination and the Arts of Resistance: Hidden Transcripts* (New Haven, CT: Yale University Press, 1990), 20.

11. Antonella Tassinari, "Escola Indígena: Novos Horizontes Teóricos, Novas Fronteiras de Educação," in *Antropologia, História e Educação: A Questão Indígena e a Escola*, orgs. Aracy Lopes da Silva, and Mariana Ferreira (Sao Paulo: Global, 2001).

12. Tassinari, "Escola Indígena," 68; Antonella Tassinari and Clarice Cohn, "'Opening to the Other': Schooling among the Karipuna and Mebengokré-Xikrin of Brazil." *Anthropology & Education Quarterly* 40, no. 2 (2009): 150–169.

13. Irène Bellier, *El temblor y la luna: ensayo sobre las relaciones entre las mujeres y los hombres mai huna* (Lima: Instituto Francés de Estudios Andinos, 1991); INEI, "Censos nacionales 2017: XII de Población, VII de Vivienda y III de Comunidades Nativas y Comunidades Campesinas" (Lima, 2017).

14. Anne Taylor, "The Western Margins of Amazonia from the Early Sixteenth to the Early Nineteenth Century," in *The Cambridge History of the Native Peoples of the Americas: Volume 3: South America*, ed. Frank Salomon and Stuart B. Schwartz, vol. 3, (Cambridge: Cambridge University Press, 1999), 188–256, https://doi.org/10.1017

/CHOL9780521630764.005; Bellier, *El temblor y la luna: Ensayo sobre las relaciones entre las mujeres y los hombres mai huna*.

15. Taylor, "The Western Margins of Amazonia"; Michael Uzendoski and Norman Whitten Jr., "From 'Acculturated Indians' to 'Dynamic Amazonian Quichua-Speaking Peoples,'" *Tipití: Journal of the Society for the Anthropology of Lowland South America* 12, no. 1 (July 26, 2014): 1–13.

16. Bellier, *El temblor y la luna*.

17. Emmanuelle Ricaud Oneto, "Dynamiques de Changement d'un Système Alimentaire Autochtone. Le Cas Des Maijuna En Amazonie Péruvienne" (master's thesis, National Museum of Natural History, Paris, 2013).

18. United States Agency for International Development, "30 Años, Programa de Alimentos Para La Paz" (Folleto del Servicio Cultural e Informativo de Estados Unidos, Washington, DC,1985).

19. Cecilia Blondet and Carmen Montero, *Hoy: Menú popular: Los comedores en Lima* (Lima: Instituto de Estudios Peruanos and UNICEF, 1995), 41, https://repositorio.iep.org.pe/handle/IEP/617.

20. Decreto Supremo N° 020–92-PCM.

21. Food and Agriculture Organization (FAO), *Alimentación Escolar y Las Posibilidades de Compra Directa de La Agricultura Familiar* (Cooperación Brasil-FAO, 2013), https://www.fao.org/family-farming/detail/en/c/1041702/.

22. Decreto Supremo No 008–2012-MIDIS.

23. Resolución Ministerial No 227–2014-MIDIS.

24. The Household Targeting System (*Sistema de Focalización de Hogares*—SISFOH) defines this status to decide the granting of social programs. It refers to a range of criteria such as the household income, socioeconomic situation, and so on. In the decree mentioned, it is based only on a geographical and identity (Indigenous) criteria.

25. "Estadísticas De Educación," Perú Instituto Nacional de Estadística e Informática (INEI), Instituto Nacional de Estadística e Informática (INEI), accessed April 12, 2023, https://www.inei.gob.pe/estadisticas/indice-tematico/education/.

26. https://plataformacelac.org/programa/185.

27. Instituto Nacional de Estadística e Informática , "Censos Nacionales 2007: XI de Población y Vivienda. Resultados Definitivos de Las Comunidades Indígenas" (Lima: Government of Peru, 2009).

28. Tara Patricia Cookson, "Peruvian Mothers Contending with Conditional Aid and Its Selective Inattention to the Conditions of Rural Life," in *Money from the Government in Latin America*, ed. Maria Elisa Balen and Martin Fotta (New York: Routledge, 2019), 69.

29. Cookson, "Peruvian Mothers," 73.

30. Sarah Bradshaw and Ana Quiros, "Women Beneficiaries or Women Bearing the Cost? A Gendered Analysis of the Red de Protección Social in Nicaragua," *Development*

and Change 39 (October 28, 2008): 823–844, https://doi.org/10.1111/j.1467-7660.2008.00507.x; Sylvia Chant, "The 'Feminisation of Poverty' and the 'Feminisation' of Anti-Poverty Programmes: Room for Revision?," *Journal of Development Studies* 44, no. 2 (February 1, 2008): 165–197, https://doi.org/10.1080/00220380701789810; Cookson, "Peruvian Mothers"; Nora Nagels, "Les Représentations Des Rapports Sociaux de Sexe Au Sein Des Politiques de Lutte Contre La Pauvreté Au Pérou," *Recherches Féministes* 24, no. 2 (January 1, 2011): 115–134, https://doi.org/10.7202/1007755ar.

31. Food and Agriculture Organization (FAO), *Alimentación Escolar y Las Posibilidades de Compra Directa de La Agricultura Familiar: Estudio de Caso en Ocho Países* (Rome, Italy, 2013), 58–59, https://www.fao.org/3/i3413s/i3413s.pdf.

32. Law No. 27767 (2002) established the norms to regulate the compulsory purchase of national food products of agricultural and hydrobiological origin by the Food Support and Social Compensation Programs and all state agencies that use public resources. Law No. 29367 (2009) added, "All government agencies purchase local and regional products directly from peasants, Natives, individual or organized producers, and agro-industrial micro-enterprises in the region that use locally produced inputs, at more favorable prices and quality conditions" (Peru), Article 2.

33. Moreover, the use of pesticides, plastic or metal packaging, food additives, and preservatives are not mentioned in purchasing guidelines. "School Menu Planning Guidelines," Resolución Jefatural No. 001–2013, No. 001–2013, Lima.

34. FAO, "Alimentación Escolar y Las Posibilidades de Compra Directa de La Agricultura Familiar".

35. FAO, "Alimentación Escolar y Las Posibilidades de Compra Directa de La Agricultura Familiar".

36. I refer to the right of Indigenous peoples to free, prior, and informed consent according to the International Labor Organization Convention (ILO) promulgated in 1989 and ratified by Peru in 1993 (Legislative Resolution No. 26253).

37. See Redacción EC, "Qali Warma, una historia de escándalos y denuncias," *El Comercio*, March 21, 2014, https://elcomercio.pe/peru/ica/qali-warma-historia-escandalos-denuncias-303593-noticia/.

38. Asociación Interétnica de Desarrollo de la Selva Peruana, "Agenda de las mujeres indígenas de la Amazonía" (Peru, 2018), 5.

39. Raphaël Colliaux, "De l'emprise à la prise de l'école. Usages de la scolarisation et expérience de la 'communauté'chez les Matsigenka (Amazonie péruvienne)" (PhD dissertation, École des hautes études en sciences sociales, Paris, 2019), https://theses.fr/2019EHES0001; Peter Gow, *Of Mixed Blood: Kinship and History in Peruvian Amazonia* (Oxford, UK: Clarendon Press, 1991); Laura M. Rival, *Trekking through History: The Huaorani of Amazonian Ecuador* (New York: Columbia University Press, 2002).

40. Eduardo Viveiros de Castro, "Cosmological Deixis and Amerindian Perspectivism," *Journal of the Royal Anthropological Institute* 4, no. 3 (1998): 479–480, https://doi.org/10.2307/3034157.

41. Viveiros de Castro, "Cosmological Deixis."

42. Viveiros de Castro, "Cosmological Deixis;" See also, Aparecida Vilaca, "Devenir Autre: Chamanisme et Contact Interethnique En Amazonie Brésilienne," *Journal de La Société Des Américanistes* 85 (1999): 239–260; Aparecida Vilaça, "Chronically Unstable Bodies: Reflections on Amazonian Corporalities," *Journal of the Royal Anthropological Institute* 11, no. 3 (2005): 445–464; Fernando Santos-Granero, "Hybrid Bodyscapes: A Visual History of Yanesha Patterns of Cultural Change," *Current Anthropology* 50, no. 4 (August 1, 2009): 477–512, https://doi.org/10.1086/604708.

43. For example, P. Descola, *La nature domestique. Symbolisme et praxis dans l'écologie des Achuar* (Paris: Foundation Singer-Polignac et Editions de la Maison des Sciences de l'Homme, 1986), 52, https://www.erudit.org/en/journals/as/1990-v14-n3-as786/015150ar/.

44. Vilaca, "Devenir Autre," 245.

45. Mestizo should not be confused with the process of mestizaje, which in Latin American countries refers to an ideology related to the construction of nation-states that promotes the fusion of Indigenous and European colonizers into "mestizos." In contrast, becoming mestizo in the situations described coincide with a "hybridity" rather than a fusion of different ethnic identities. For example, José Antonio Kelly, *About Anti-Mestizaje* (Species—Núcleo de Antropologia Especulativa, Desterro [Florianópolis]: Cultura e Barbárie, 2016); Fernando Santos-Granero, "Hybrid Bodyscapes: A Visual History of Yanesha Patterns of Cultural Change," *Current Anthropology* 50, no. 4 (August 1, 2009): 477–512, https://doi.org/10.1086/604708.

46. Monosodium glutamate sold by the Japanese brand *Ajinomoto*.

47. Michael Uzendoski, *The Napo Runa of Amazonian Ecuador* (Urbana: University of Illinois Press, 2005).

48. This practice, *tabaquear*, is also applied to dogs for being good hunters.

49. In contrast, sardine is interpreted as a more valued product than tuna as the fish is seen in its entirety.

50. Irène Bellier, *El temblor y la luna: Ensayo sobre las relaciones entre las mujeres y los hombres mai huna* (Lima: Instituto Francés de Estudios Andinos, 1991).

51. Ludwig Huber et al., "Programa Juntos: Certezas y malentendidos en torno a las transferencias condicionadas, estudio de caso de seis distritos rurales del Perú," UNICEF–*Instituto de Estudios Peruanos*, 2009, https://repositorio.iep.org.pe/handle/IEP/723; Emmanuelle Piccoli, "«Dicen que los cien soles son del Diablo»: L'interprétation apocalyptique et mythique du Programa Juntos dans les communautés andines de Cajamarca (Pérou) et la critique populaire des programmes sociaux," *Social Compass* 61 (September 1, 2014): 328–347, https://doi.org/10.1177/0037768614535701; Norma Correa, Terry Roopnaraine, and Amy Margolies, "Conditional Cash Transfer Program Implementation and Effects in Peruvian Indigenous Contexts," in *Cash Transfers in Context: An Anthropological Perspective*, ed. Jean-Pierre Olivier de Sardan and E. Piccoli (New York-Oxford: Berghahn Books, 2018), https://doi.org/10.2307/j.ctvw04jbv.9. Irène Bellier and Anne Marie Hocquenghem, "De Los Andes a La Amazonia: Una Representacion Evolutiva Del 'Otro,'" *Bulletin de l'Institut Francais d'Etudes Andines* 20, no. 1 (1991): 41–59.

52. The Napuruna are mainly Catholic, and the Maijuna have been Christianized by evangelists in recent decades—currently, few are evangelicals though they usually maintain connections with evangelists.

53. This rumor takes up parts of the Revelation of St. John (Rev. 13, 1–17) and reflects Emmanuelle Piccoli, "«Dicen que los cien soles son del Diablo»."

54. Julien Bonhomme, *The Sex Thieves: The Anthropology of a Rumor* (Chicago: University of Chicago Press/Hau Books, 2016), 119; Robert H. Knapp, "A Psychology of Rumor," *The Public Opinion Quarterly* 8, no. 1 (1944): 22.

55. Emmanuelle Piccoli, "«Dicen Que Los Cien Soles Son Del Diablo»"; Fernando Santos-Granero and Frederica Barclay, "Bundles, Stampers, and Flying Gringos: Native Perceptions of Capitalist Violence in Peruvian Amazonia," *Journal of Latin American and Caribbean Anthropology* 16, no. 1 (April 2011): 143–167, https://doi.org/10.1111/j.1935-4940.2011.01128.x; Scott, *Domination*, 4.

56. Correa, Roopnaraine, and Margolies, "Conditional Cash Transfer Program," 42.

57. Michel Foucault, *Surveiller et punir: Naissance de la prison* (Paris: Editions Gallimard, 1975).

58. Scott, *Domination*, 198.

59. Julien Bonhomme, *The Sex Thieves: The Anthropology of a Rumor*; Emmanuelle Piccoli, "«Dicen Que Los Cien Soles Son Del Diablo»"; Scott, *Domination*.; Michael T. Taussig, *The Devil and Commodity Fetishism in South America* (Chapel Hill: University of North Carolina Press, 1980).

II

CLAIMING SPACE FOR YOUTH AND WORKER VOICES

Jennifer E. Gaddis and Sarah A. Robert

Feeding students during the school day involves the work of many different stakeholder groups, but only a select few (mostly policy elites) see themselves as doing "political" work and claim power in the policymaking process. For the social organization of school meals to reflect and advance a feminist politics of food and education, youth and the workers who feed them need to assert real decision-making power over who feeds whom, what, how, when, and for what purpose. The four chapters in part II illuminate the potential for transformation when educators, school nutrition workers (i.e., school caterers), youth, school transportation staff, and community supporters answer these critical questions for themselves and ensure that school meals are educational, nourishing, and responsive to community needs.

In chapter 4, "Sustainable Food Education in Finnish Schools through Collaborative Pedagogy," we learn how home economics teachers and school catering staff can engage in parallel reproductive labor—educating, feeding, and caring for students—which when intertwined can translate to a curriculum that engages young people in building more sustainable futures through their own policy protagonism in relation to school meals. Located in another national context, chapter 5, "Rebel Ventures and Youth-Led Food Initiatives in the United States," offers a first-person account of young people who have used their situated knowledge, leadership potential, and other assets to change food systems in their schools and broader communities.

The next two chapters, both cowritten by academics and practitioners, further demonstrate how overlooked stakeholders can transform school food systems at local and national scales. Chapter 6, "Creating a Mobile Method to Nourish Children in the United States with the 'Yum-Yum Bus,'" details the policy protagonism of school nutrition workers concerned with providing summer meals to rural students. This pre-pandemic initiative was responsible for the creation of mobile infrastructure, internal processes, and collaborations that were vital for ensuring students continued to receive the multitude of care-based support that schools provided throughout the pandemic. Chapter 7, "Local and National Responses to the COVID-19 Pandemic in the United States," then discusses a variety of ways in which essential workers continued to feed students during the COVID-19 school closures and the national policy changes that empowered communities to provide universal free school meals and exercise a greater degree of self-determination.

The COVID-19 pandemic underscored the centrality of schools within the infrastructure of daily life—particularly the role of schools in meeting children's needs for education, food, and care. It also disrupted supply chains due to the fragility of large-scale corporate food systems. The chapters in this section remind us that youth, educators, food chain workers, and other community stakeholders can play an important role in rebuilding school food systems that are more resilient and ecologically sustainable.

4

SUSTAINABLE FOOD EDUCATION IN FINNISH SCHOOLS THROUGH COLLABORATIVE PEDAGOGY

Kristiina Janhonen, Marjaana Manninen, and Karin Hjälmeskog

Every school day, approximately nine hundred thousand Finnish public school students, ranging from one to eighteen years old, consume a tax-funded school meal. For students, the mealtime is embedded into the structure of their daily school experience.[1] Students make their way from the classroom to the dining room, queue for food, and select their meals. The food and mealtime are guided by national recommendations,[2] which state that mealtimes should last at least thirty minutes and should be organized with consideration of students' daily rhythms. A prepared plate and a visual guide showing a recommended meal composition are often placed at the start of the food line.[3] In many schools, these guides are also discussed with students in the classroom, especially as a part of home economics education.[4]

Moving through the food line, students typically serve themselves a variety of dishes, usually a casserole or soup, vegetables and/or salad, bread, spreads (e.g., margarine), and beverages (milk, sour milk, and water). Children in early childhood education and primary levels typically receive help from adults to pick food and carry their plates, while older students (e.g., those in secondary level) have more independence during the lunch break.[5] Full plate in hand, students then pour into the dining room. They cluster together at tables with their friends and school staff, eating and relaxing during the break from class. As the meal ends, students take plates, cutlery, and any leftover food to a collection point. Often, they enjoy a short recess before returning to class for their next lesson.

According to the current curriculum and recommendations, school mealtimes in Finland support students' well-being and nutritional intake. They are a long-term investment in learning and sustainability.[6] School meals aim to provide one-third of a student's daily energy intake. In addition to lunch, some schools provide free breakfast, while others offer snacks for purchase. Employees that work in school-based kitchens or in municipal central kitchens are typically employed by private for-profit companies (which means that they have a different employer than, for example, teaching staff). These companies are required to serve school food according to nutritional recommendations as a prerequisite for receiving state subsidies.

Throughout its development, the nationwide school meal system has been a Finnish social innovation, promoting equality and learning opportunities for all students regardless of background. However, Finnish society has changed significantly since the school meal system was established and refined in the first half of the twentieth century.[7] Education around school meals has changed considerably too[8] as the environmental movement encouraged more focus on sustainability. Recent studies emphasize the importance of combining eating and learning that is participatory, experimental, and collaborative, which, in turn, has influenced the nation's school meal policies.[9]

The Finnish school meal program is often held up as an international model. Yet it is also a realm of tensions and untapped potential. Understanding the current implementation framework and how the school meal program has been shaped by key historic milestones can facilitate more creative and sustainable forms of school mealtimes and food. We build on the promotion of sustainability in the Finnish school meal system to examine how collaborations between home economics and food services can be strengthened to support students' food-related learning for sustainable outcomes, including awareness of food choices and the environmental impact of food production (e.g., water and energy use) as well as food waste reduction. To develop these arguments, we use *pragmatist learning theory* and the term *food sense* to conceptualize food-related learning outcomes focused on sustainability.[10] We suggest that these frameworks can help build collaborations across professional spheres for students and school staff to participate in the co-development of sustainable school food practices. Such collaborations could become the platforms for transforming school food politics in the lunchroom and classroom by engaging the stakeholders most affected by mealtimes: students, their teachers, and the school catering staff.[11]

THE CURRENT FRAMEWORK OF SCHOOL MEALTIMES IN FINLAND

At a legislative level, the Finnish Law on Compulsory Education[12] outlines that school meals should be appropriately organized and nutritionally balanced. The intent of this law, specifically the requirement of an appropriately organized mealtime, is translated by the Finnish National Agency for Education into the national core curriculum for basic education, which states that school mealtimes have both recreational and educational aims, including themes such as sustainable living, cultural competence, and manners.[13] Additionally, the school meal recommendations of the Finnish National Nutrition Council emphasize collective learning during mealtimes.[14] These recommendations constitute a key political document that frames the organization of school meals. The nutritional recommendations are linked to state subsidies received by school food caterers.

Both the core curriculum and the school meal recommendations appoint all in-school adults, including teachers, healthcare staff, and food services staff, with the task of providing guidance and education during the lunch period.[15] The national recommendations suggest that school meals offer wide-ranging learning opportunities and that food-related content can be readily integrated into many school subjects, such as home economics, health education, environmental studies, and biology. In recent years, Finnish policy has given more attention to student participation, handling the topic in a more versatile manner and also providing practical ideas for implementation. These ideas include the implementation of yearly projects to develop school mealtime experiences together with the students. The national core curriculum for basic education is a binding document, and schools are required to encourage students to participate in planning, delivering, and evaluating school meals. In practice, though, municipalities, schools, and teachers have flexibility in how they execute these requirements, leading to varying levels of student participation in school mealtime organization. Furthermore, the varying topics and extent of professional training about school mealtimes and food education of these different in-school adults can create tensions.[16]

Additionally, at an operative level, school meals are organized by municipalities, so implementation models and services differ across the country. In each municipality, school meals are included in the overall education budget. Schools of different sizes and locations incur different total costs for school mealtimes. The school meal budget covers fluctuating costs for food, staff, accommodation for students not living within municipal boundaries, transportation of supplies, and food service property maintenance. To manage and plan budgets, local data on costs are analyzed by food providers and municipalities. Information about implementation is gathered regularly at local and national levels. Authorities monitor students' school meal participation, food choices, nutritional intake, and food waste volume.[17] The school meal recommendations strongly advise against selling sodas, juice, and food items with high levels of added sugar, salt, or saturated fat on school premises.[18] Although delivery contracts, and overall budgets, are negotiated separately by municipalities, the quality of school meals is still defined by binding national legislation and nutritional guidelines for schools.

THE ROAD TOWARD SUSTAINABILITY—SIGNIFICANT MILESTONES AND INITIATIVES OF SCHOOL MEALTIMES

As Finnish society changed, nutrition and food education initiatives also have changed. The foundations of the Finnish school meal system were established in the last decades of the nineteenth century and first decades of the twentieth century.[19] During this time frame, Finland was a poor country with an agriculture-based economy.[20] Many children lacked sufficient food and clothing to remain healthy enough to regularly attend school,[21] and 40 percent of children under fifteen years of age were illiterate. The initial aim of school meals was to support good health and boost attendance.[22] During this time frame, the organization of school meals was scattered and relied on the active participation of private associations, teachers, and parents. Food shortages during World War I, however, highlighted the importance of school meals for children's well-being and expedited the formalization of the national system.[23]

In 1921, the law of compulsory education defined the arrangement of school mealtimes as a municipal responsibility. This law also affected elementary school funding: the state was now officially responsible for funding two-thirds of the costs of meals for students of limited means.[24] World War II brought a new round of difficulties in accessing sufficient healthy foods, and many people were displaced from their homes. After the experience of acute food shortages (1890–1930) came a period of managing the food supply through rationing and regulation (1940–1950). In 1943, the government extended the law to include a free meal for all schoolchildren every school day. Students were required to participate in food production and distribution, bringing milk and bread from home to supplement the school meal.[25] Finnish municipalities were given a five-year transition period to implement the program.[26] In 1948, Finland became the first country in the world to require a tax-funded school meal system.

During the 1960s and 1970s, school lunch programs sought to address nutritional challenges caused by overconsumption of unhealthy foods.[27] The 1980s and 1990s, characterized by a culture of flexibility, led to the need for school meal guidelines to acknowledge the various factors that influence people's daily food choices. Additionally, scientific studies revealed that the provision of health information on its own is not enough to change an individual's food behavior.[28]

During the 2000s and 2010s, the range and number of professionals interested in addressing food education issues increased. In 2004, reflecting the growing interest in "food education" (*ruokakasvatus*) in Finnish public and scientific discussions, school mealtimes became part of the Finnish national core curriculum, strengthening their role in student welfare and coursework.[4] Early childhood programs were among the first in the education field to incorporate food-related teaching by using the term "food education." These programs emphasized experiential, sensory (e.g., taste, touch), and emotional (e.g., joy) aspects of eating.[29] The availability of food education resources also expanded to allow for people-centered, context-dependent, and functional approaches. School mealtime shifts in Finland at the beginning of the 2020s included the development of approaches that consider sustainability, for example, examining food choices not only at the individual level but also at societal and production levels.[30]

Sustainability, albeit not labeled as such, has been a guiding aim of the Finnish school meal system since its inception. Table 4.1 provides a historical overview of how school mealtime developments are connected to the four dimensions of sustainability: social, cultural, economic, and ecological.[31] We understand the social dimension of sustainability as concerning poverty reduction, social investment, and the building of safe and caring communities. The cultural dimension relates to the maintenance of cultural beliefs, practices, and heritage, and attempts to determine the future existence of any current culture. The economic dimension concerns the organization's impacts on the economic conditions of its stakeholders and on the economic systems at local, national, and global levels. Sustainability in relation to ecology means ensuring that climate and the environment are safeguarded worldwide.

Today, sustainability is written into policies, directing the meal program to promote social, economic, cultural, and, increasingly, environmental sustainability. The current Finnish nutritional recommendations, the national core curriculum, and the recommendations for school mealtimes all discuss sustainable development.[32] The Finnish government promotes sustainable choices in public procurement,[33] and the promotion of nutritionally recommended food consumption is a central environmental and political measure.[34] Opportunities for increasing sustainability in public meal provision include serving more plant-based foods, decreasing meat consumption, reducing water and energy use, minimizing food waste,[35] and using seasonal, local, or organic foods. Organic products can be challenging to obtain due to limited availability and high prices.[36] A 2017 Finnish government decision (MMM/2017/93) tried to alleviate some of this difficulty by allocating funding to pay producers for providing organic school meal ingredients to the EU's school food delivery system (e.g., an increase of .18 euros per liter for organic milk products and a 10 percent increase allotted to the purchase of organic produce).

Yet mealtimes involve more than just procuring food to serve. We suggest that collaboration of multiple school-based stakeholders can widen sustainability learning aims. In this respect, the Finnish school system

Table 4.1 Sustainability and Finnish school meals in broader historical and societal context

Years	National food and dietary priorities	Emphasizing the four dimensions of sustainability through school meals
1890–1930	Preventing nutritional deficiencies and caring for economically disadvantaged populations.	*Social*: reducing poverty and malnourishment among children. *Economic*: encouraging school attendance.
1940–1950	Securing versatile diets and solving food shortages, followed by a focus on vitamins and minerals.	*Economic*: establishing and implementing the national system. *Cultural*: providing a unifying cultural experience for students during mealtimes.
1960–1970	Tackling the consequences of abundance and excess, followed by a focus on reducing consumption of salt and saturated fats.	*Social*: teaching proper table manners and broadening students' palates. *Economic*: economizing resources and processes for school meal preparation.
1980–1990	Reacting to a changing landscape of food availability while recognizing the sociocultural factors that influence food choices.	*Ecological*: examining global environmental issues in schools. *Social*: cultivating greater awareness of different food cultures.
2000–2010	Expanding forms of expertise and incorporating new perspectives; emphasizing active, people-oriented, and grassroots approaches to food education.	*Cultural*: deepening the aims for learning during and through school mealtimes. *Social*: integrating mealtimes and their learning aims more clearly into the educational work of schools.
2020–	Acknowledging the multilevel nature of change processes (e.g., food system, institutions, daily practices); strengthening collective, experimental, and participatory approaches to food education.	*Ecological*: incorporating ecological concerns into nutrition recommendations and national school meal guidelines. *Social*: fostering safe and caring communities through increased student voice and co-development of school meals.

has room to improve and can do so from within the supportive set of policy guidelines outlined above. Food education themes are already part of home economics teachers' university programs and in the content descriptions of school subjects in the national core curriculum. However, university-based teacher education for all teachers, especially for the elementary level, should include instruction in food education. Also, pedagogical training of school food service staff is crucial to increasing in-school adult participation in students' food learning.[37] In recent years, school-level initiatives and structures, such as school meal committees, have been increasingly supported in Finnish schools.[38] The members of these committees—typically representatives from the teaching staff, food catering staff, and the student body—develop the mealtime plans for their school (e.g., how to serve food, what menu items to offer, how to structure the mealtime, and so on). This is a positive trend and a form of collaboration that—together with classroom-based teaching and food education in the cafeteria—could accelerate the development of sustainable food practices in school communities.

FOOD EDUCATION ACROSS THE CLASSROOM-MEALTIME DIVIDE THROUGH PRAGMATISM AND FOOD SENSE

The Finnish national core curriculum for basic education states that school mealtimes have both recreational purposes and educational aims. There can be tensions between these two goals—to relax and socialize, and to learn.[39] Previous research has shown that students generally regard school mealtimes as personal time to hang out with friends, which might make them reluctant to engage with formal learning during mealtimes.[40] Previous studies have also shown that lunch periods are often not integrated into school educational activities, due in part to practical constraints such as a tight time frame.[41] Therefore, it is important to identify creative ways to support students' food-related learning. Expanding food education collaborations between food catering staff and teachers provides an excellent opportunity to advance this aim. Such collaborations should draw on the different roles and strengths of both stakeholder groups. Food-related learning should focus not just on increasing individual students' health or nutrition knowledge[42] but also on increasing students' opportunities to influence food issues that affect them daily in school. Ultimately, students working together with teachers and staff is the only way to develop broad and sustainable collaborative school-level practices.

In Finland, policy supports these open-ended and bottom-up aims. However, there is currently a lack of practical tools to aid school-level practitioners in their implementation. To outline a framework for this potential school food educator collaboration, we draw inspiration both from Dewey's pragmatist theorizations of learning and from the concept of food sense. Dewey's pragmatism promotes active learning, often described as "learning-by-doing."[43] Van Poeck et al., explain that Dewey does not promote a linear process of learning "the right thing" but emphasizes, instead, the importance of learning through experience, experiment, and inquiry while focusing on the consequences of doing.[44] Thus, pragmatism provides tools—such as increased awareness and conflict resolution—for real-life problem-solving.[45] Dewey understands learning as dependent on context, both social and cultural.[46] Interactions, or transactions, between people and their environments are at the core of this theory. Learning from experience involves interaction and continuity, emphasizing that people and their environments are mutually interdependent and "transform continuously and reciprocally."[47]

The concept of food sense builds on pragmatist aims of using tensions as opportunities to create further change.[48] Janhonen et al., define food sense as the ability to understand, apply, and potentially redefine the everyday routines and habits of food practices.[55] The framework allows tensions (e.g., frictions, conflicts, contradictions, disagreements, dissatisfactions, and so on) that arise to be the starting point for codeveloping school food practices. This approach supports students' sense that they are able to influence matters important to them and their development of skills for engaging in participatory processes. Consequently, the framework suggests a shift in aims and power structures for food education, wherein the role of the learner is not as a passive recipient of predefined (e.g., health, nutrition) knowledge but as an active, collaborative change agent. Supporting youth empowerment is crucial for transformative school food politics and for recognizing students as important social and political actors.

When planning, executing, and evaluating participatory learning processes in schools, it is useful to examine the different levels of food sense. Accordingly, figure 4.1 presents food education and collaborations with

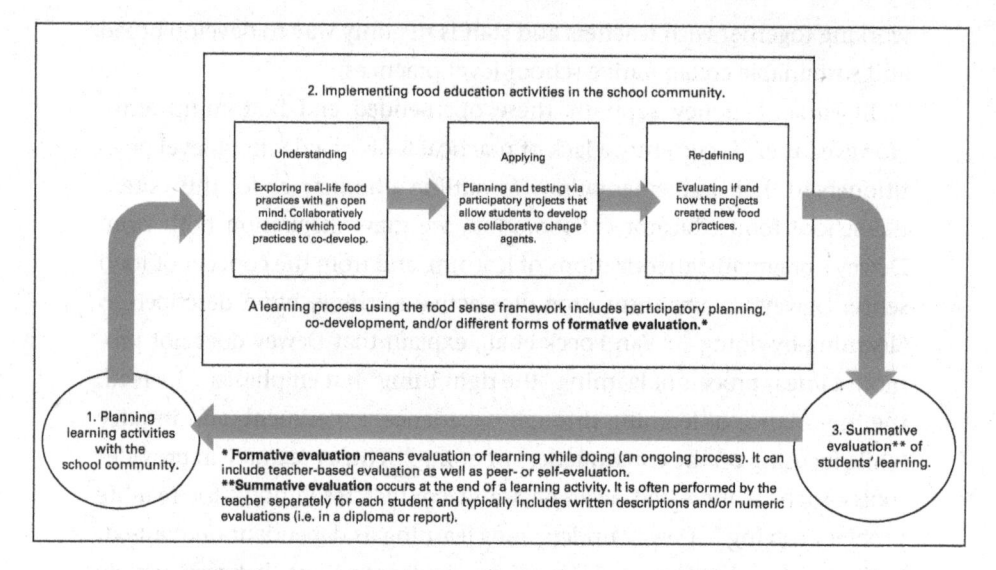

```
                    2. Implementing food education activities in the school community.

         ┌─────────────────┐     ┌─────────────────┐     ┌─────────────────┐
         │  Understanding  │ ──▶ │    Applying     │ ──▶ │   Re-defining   │
         │                 │     │                 │     │                 │
         │ Exploring real-life│   │ Planning and testing via│ │ Evaluating if and │
         │ food practices with│   │ participatory projects that│ │ how the projects │
         │ an open mind.     │   │ allow students to develop│ │ created new food │
         │ Collaboratively   │   │ as collaborative change │ │ practices.        │
         │ deciding which food│   │ agents.                │ │                   │
         │ practices to co-develop.│ │                     │ │                   │
         └─────────────────┘     └─────────────────┘     └─────────────────┘

   A learning process using the food sense framework includes participatory planning,
          co-development, and/or different forms of formative evaluation.*
```

(1. Planning learning activities with the school community.) ← ... → (3. Summative evaluation** of students' learning.)

* **Formative evaluation** means evaluation of learning while doing (an ongoing process). It can include teacher-based evaluation as well as peer- or self-evaluation.
****Summative evaluation** occurs at the end of a learning activity. It is often performed by the teacher separately for each student and typically includes written descriptions and/or numeric evaluations (i.e. in a diploma or report).

4.1 Integrating the food sense framework into a school community.

food services as practices that are fully integrated into teachers' work and throughout the school year.

The aim of this framework is to provide tools that promote continuity, perseverance, and a comprehensive acknowledgement of the educational potential of school mealtimes. The overall purpose is to cooperatively develop real-life practices using participatory methods. The teacher's role in this process is to serve as a facilitator who creates optimal settings for student learning.[49] While this approach can be applied to many examples, we focus below on the design of a course for home economics that addresses sustainability through practice-based learning in collaboration with food catering.

PRACTICAL EXAMPLE: DESIGNING A COURSE FOR SUSTAINABILITY TRANSFORMATION

Using the food sense framework, we have created an example for a home economics curriculum called "Sustainability transformations in our school" (table 4.2). This school subject has been selected based on our own professional backgrounds and the current inclusion of food, eating, and cooking, or "food competence and food culture" as one of the three key focus areas in the national core curriculum. We have designed this for grades 7 to 9. Its purpose is to promote sustainable food education through collaboration of home economics programs and food catering.

The curriculum could be implemented in a variety of ways. For example, sustainable food choices[50] could be the focus of activities and evaluations, which are informed by school-level and national curricula. However, students' interests and the school mealtime structure should inform learning activities and assignments. Table 4.2 demonstrates how the three components of food sense (understanding, applying, and redefining) could be used as sequential building blocks for the co-development of the course.

The three building blocks together can help promote sustainability transformation and active learning in schools. Alternatively, practitioners who are in the early phase of integrating forms of collaboration into their work could initially test one or two building blocks and then slowly broaden the scope. The transformative process illustrated through these three steps could be expanded to also introduce collaboration into several courses or class grades. In any execution, learning activities should be directed toward identifying and codeveloping existing tensions and practices within the school and with students.

Such a framework both compliments and expands on existing platforms that allow students to speak and be heard in school settings, such as student councils and school food councils. These platforms are typically built on the idea of representative participation; the councils typically include a limited number of democratically elected students. This framework could engage larger groups of students in participatory projects, students who could then understand themselves as agents of, and collaborators for, active change in their communities.

CONCLUSION

This chapter has highlighted the potential for collaboration between different stakeholders at the school level to support the aim of providing students with increased opportunities to influence and be part of changing food issues that affect and interest them. The framework outlined in this chapter aims to support such bottom-up and participatory development work, as well as to empower students as active change agents. Reorganization of

Table 4.2 Sequential building blocks for the course "Sustainability transformations in our school" using the food sense framework

Understanding	Applying	Redefining
Examples of learning activities for building a shared understanding of project goals: • Observe behavior of oneself and/or students in the school dining area (e.g., taking notes or photographs). • Interview food catering staff, teachers, health service professionals, guardians, and other stakeholders. • Conduct school-level surveys (e.g., attitudes toward and baseline knowledge of school mealtimes). • Review data collected by food services (e.g., number of people served, production records, waste). • Co-plan an evaluation.	Examples of learning activities for formulating and testing a change management action plan: • Apply practical exercises in the home economics classroom (e.g., codeveloping school meal dishes and/or cooking assignments for food waste reduction or higher vegetable intake, emphasizing the social and cultural dimensions of food and eating). • Execute practice-based campaigns or other school-level initiatives with students. • Influence broader structures and decision-makers outside the local school environment (e.g., writing letters or organizing events). • Collect concise data that meets jointly agreed evaluation targets.	Examples of collaborative analysis of a codeveloped project for changing practices: • Consider future steps and involve food catering and school administration. • Present and discuss results and future steps at school assemblies. • Involve guardians by presenting results at parent-teacher events. • Instituting collective problem-solving to identify ways to involve and motivate the whole school community; begin with one course then broaden the perspective. • Evaluate project goals (e.g., decreasing waste production, increasing vegetable consumption) and the students' broader learning processes, including the social and cultural aspects of learning.

resources, through creative use of teaching time, more support for student participation, and multi-professional alliances, can aid the process of shifting students from the role of passive recipient of knowledge to the role of partner in processes that seek to solve real-world problems together with adults. In this work, teachers need action models like the one presented in this chapter, as well as tools for evaluation that help them justify integrating innovative activities into their teaching.[51] The practical examples presented in this chapter approach school mealtimes as a context for experiential and active learning—a novel view grounded in ongoing Finnish education reform and its movement toward student participation and co-development. Further research and development work should strive toward providing real-life examples of student participation in sustainable food education, as well as examples of how these projects have failed or succeeded in practice. In addition to creative reorganization of resources at the school level, it is crucial that collaborative initiatives for sustainable food education integrating student participation are also recognized as important at municipal and other governance levels, and that adequate resources are provided to schools for this work. Although student participation and collaborative endeavors within food education and school mealtimes are encouraged at the policy level in Finland, providing more extensive professional and in-service training in these areas to all potential school food educators will be key to creating real change in schools.

NOTES

1. Kristiina Janhonen and Johanna Mäkelä, "To Connect and Be Heard: Informal Dimension of School Mealtimes Represented by Students' Self-Initiated YouTube Videos," *YOUNG*, June 18, 2021, https://doi.org/10.1177/11033088211015802.

2. For more information about the Finnish education system and organization of school mealtimes, see Katri Pellikka, Marjaana Manninen, and Sanna-Liisa Taivalmaa, *School Meals for All: School Feeding: Investment in Effective Learning—Case Finland* (Ministry for Foreign Affairs of Finland and Finnish National Agency for Education (EDUFI), June 2019), https://www.oph.fi/en/statistics-and-publications/publications/school-meals-all.

3. National Nutrition Council (NNC), *Syödään Ja Opitaan Yhdessä—Kouluruokailusuositus [Eating and learning together—Recommendations for school meals]* (Helsinki, Finland: National Nutrition Council and National Institute for Health and Welfare, 2017), https://www.julkari.fi/bitstream/handle/10024/134867/URN_ISBN_978-952-302-844-9.pdf?sequence=1&isAllowed=y.

4. Home economics begins in grades 7–9 (thirteen-to-sixteen-year-olds) and in 2014 became an optional subject for grades 1–6 (six-to-twelve-year-olds). The EDUFI, "Perusopetuksen opetussuunnitelman perusteet," Opetushallitus, 2014, https://www.oph.fi/fi/koulutus-ja-tutkinnot/perusopetuksen-opetussuunnitelman-perusteet.

5. See Kristiina Henrietta Janhonen, Johanna Mäkelä, and Päivi Palojoki, "Adolescents' School Lunch Practices as an Educational Resource," *Health Education* 116, no. 3 (January 1, 2016a): 292–309, https://doi.org/10.1108/HE-10-2014-0090.

6. We define the key aim of sustainability as progress that meets current requirements without compromising the ability of future generations to meet their own needs—see World Commission on Environment and Development (WCED), *Our Common Future (The Brundtland Report)* (Oxford: Oxford University Press, 1987). Sustainability themes are acknowledged also in the Finnish National Curriculum for Basic Education and National school meal recommendations.

7. Seija Lintukangas, "Kouluruokailuhenkilöstö matkalla kasvattajaksi," November 20, 2009, https://helda.helsinki.fi/handle/10138/20045; Katri Pellikka, Marjaana Manninen, and Sanna-Liisa Taivalmaa, *School Meals for All: School feeding: Investment in Effective Learning—Case Finland*; Ritva Prattala, "North European Meals: Observations from Denmark, Finland, Norway and Sweden," in *Dimensions of the Meal: The Science, Culture, Business and Art of Eating*, ed. Herbert L. Meiselman (Gaithersburg, MD: Aspen Publishers, 2000), 191–201; Susanna Raulio, Eva Roos, and Ritva Prättälä, "School and Workplace Meals Promote Healthy Food Habits," *Public Health Nutrition* 13, no. 6A (June 2010): 987–992, https://doi.org/10.1017/S1368980010001199.

8. Janhonen, Mäkelä, and Palojoki, "Adolescents' School Lunch Practices," 292–309; Kristiina Janhonen, Johanna Mäkelä, and Päivi Palojoki, "Food Education: From Normative Models to Promoting Agency," in *Learning, Food, and Sustainability*, ed. Jennifer Sumner (New York: Palgrave Macmillan, 2016), 93–110, https://doi.org/10.1057/978-1-137-53904-5_6.

9. Lintukangas, "Kouluruokailuhenkilöstö matkalla kasvattajaksi"; Minna Kaljonen, Taru Peltola, Marja Salo, and Eeva Furman, "Attentive, Speculative Experimental Research for Sustainability Transitions: An Exploration in Sustainable Eating," *Journal of Cleaner Production* 206 (January 1, 2019): 365–373, https://doi.org/10.1016/j.jclepro.2018.09.206.

10. John Dewey, *Democracy and Education: An Introduction to the Philosophy of Education* (New York: Macmillan, 1916); John Dewey, *Experience and Education* (New York: Macmillan, 1938); Janhonen, Mäkelä, and Palojoki, "Food Education"; Kristiina Janhonen, Kaisa Torkkeli, and Johanna Mäkelä, "Informal Learning and Food Sense in Home Cooking," *Appetite* 130 (November 1, 2018): 190–198, https://doi.org/10.1016/j.appet.2018.08.019.

11. The Finnish term *ruokapalveluhenkilöstö* would directly translate into "food service personnel." However, some academics/school meal advocates have argued that this translation undermines the professionalism of these employees because of its connotations to the terms "servant" or "maid." Because of this, we have opted to use the term school food caterer.

12. Law on Compulsory Education 628/1998, 31§.

13. EDUFI, "Perusopetuksen opetussuunnitelman perusteet."

14. NNC, *Syödään Ja Opitaan Yhdessä*.

15. EDUFI, "Perusopetuksen opetussuunnitelman perusteet"; NNC, *Syodaan Ja Opitaan Yhdessa*.

16. Lintukangas, "Kouluruokailuhenkilöstö matkalla kasvattajaksi," https://helda.helsinki.fi/handle/10138/20045; Kristiina Janhonen and Bente Elkjaer, "Exploring

Sustainable Food Education as Multiprofessional Collaboration between Home Economics and School Food Catering," *Journal of Education for Sustainable Development* 16, no. 1–2 (2022): 19–41, https://doi.org/10.1177/09734082221120101.

17. The Finnish Institute for Health and Welfare (FIHW), "School Health Promotion Study," 2019, https://thl.fi/en/web/thlfi-en/research-and-development/research-and-projects/school-health-promotion-study; The Finnish Institute for Health and Welfare (FIHW), "TEAviisari—Benchmarking System of Health Promotion Capacity Building in Municipalities," 2020, http://teaviisari.fi/teaviisari/en/index.

18. NNC, *Syödään Ja Opitaan Yhdessä*, 40.

19. Lintukangas, "Kouluruokailuhenkilöstö matkalla kasvattajaksi."

20. Katri Pellikka, Marjaana Manninen, and Sanna-Liisa Taivalmaa, *School Meals for All: School feeding: Investment in Effective Learning—Case Finland*, https://www.oph.fi/en/statistics-and-publications/publications/school-meals-all.

21. Pellikka, Manninen, Taivalmaa, *School Meals for All*.

22. EDUFI, "Perusopetuksen opetussuunnitelman perusteet."

23. Kaija Rautavirta, "Petusta pitsaan: Ruokahuollon järjestelyt kriisiaikojen Suomessa" (doctoral diss., University of Helsinki, June 11, 2010), https://helda.helsinki.fi/handle/10138/20862.

24. Pellikka, Manninen, and Taivalmaa, *School Meals for All*.

25. Pellikka, Manninen, and Taivalmaa, *School Meals for All*.

26. Lintukangas, "Kouluruokailuhenkilöstö matkalla kasvattajaksi"; R. Prattala, "North European Meals: Observations from Denmark, Finland, Norway and Sweden"; Raulio, Roos, and Prättälä, "School and Workplace Meals Promote Healthy Food Habits."

27. Kristiina Janhonen, Johanna Mäkelä, and Päivi Palojoki, "Perusopetuksen Ruokakasvatus Ravintotiedosta Ruokatajuun [Food Education in the Basic Education Context—from Nutrition Knowledge to Food Sense]," in *Luova Ja Vastuullinen Kotitalousopetus, Kotitalous- Ja Käsityötieteiden Julkaisuja* 38 (Helsinki: Kirjoittajat, 2015), 107–121; see also Kaija Rautavirta, "Petusta pitsaan."

28. Mäkelä Janhonen and Päivi Palojoki, "Perusopetuksen Ruokakasvatus Ravintotiedosta Ruokatajuun" [Food education in the basic education context—From nutrition knowledge to food sense]; Janhonen, Mäkelä, and Palojoki, "Food Education."

29. A. Koistinen and L. Ruhanen, eds., "Aistien Avulla Ruokamaailmaan. Sapere-Menetelmä Päivähoidon Ravitsemus Ja Ruokakasvatuksen Tukena" [Entering the world of food through the senses. The Sapere-Method as a support in the nutrition and food education in the daycare context] (Jyväskylän kaupungin sosiaali-ja terveyspalvelukeskuksen raportteja, 2009), http://www.sitra.fi/julkaisut/muut/Sapere_tyokirja.pdf.

30. For example, see Minna Kaljonen et al., "From Isolated Labels and Nudges to Sustained Tinkering: Assessing Long-Term Changes in Sustainable Eating at a Lunch Restaurant," *British Food Journal* 122, no. 11 (January 1, 2020): 3313–3329, https://doi.org/10.1108/BFJ-10-2019-0816; Taru Peltola, Minna Kaljonen, and Marita Kettunen, "Embodied Public Experiments on Sustainable Eating: Demonstrating

Alternative Proteins in Finnish Schools," *Sustainability: Science, Practice and Policy* 16, no. 1 (December 10, 2020): 184–196, https://doi.org/10.1080/15487733.2020.1789268.

31. WCED, *Our Common Future*.

32. National Nutrition Council (NNC), *Terveyttä Ruoasta—Suomalaiset Ravitsemussuositukset 2014 [Health from Food—Finnish Nutrition Recommendations 2014]* (Helsinki: VRN, 2014); NNC, *Syödään Ja Opitaan Yhdessä*; EDUFI, "Perusopetuksen opetussuunnitelman perusteet."

33. Government's Principle Decision (GPD), "Valtioneuvoston Periaatepäätös Kestävien Valintojen Edistämisestä Julkisissa Hankinnoissa" [Governments principle decision about promoting sustainable choices in public procurement], 2009, http://www.ymparisto.fi/download.asp?contetid=101162&lan=en; Ministry of Social Affairs and Health (MASH), "Joukkoruokailun kehittäminen: Joukkoruokailun seuranta-ja kehittämistyöryhmän toimenpidesuositus" [Developing food services: Guidelines for implemetation from the working group for monitoring and developing of food services] (Sosiaali-ja terveysministeriö, 2009), https://julkaisut.valtioneuvosto.fi/handle/10024/73291.

34. Ministry of the Environment, Helinski (MTE), *Valtioneuvoston selonteko keskipitkän aikavälin ilmastopolitiikan suunnitelmasta vuoteen 2030—Kohti ilmastoviisasta arkea [Governments' report of plan for environment politics to the year 2030—Towards climatewise daily life]* (Helsinki: Ympäristöministeriö, September 25, 2017), https://julkaisut.valtioneuvosto.fi/handle/10024/80703.

35. Government's Principle Decision (GPD), "Valtioneuvoston Periaatepäätös Kestävien Valintojen Edistämisestä Julkisissa Hankinnoissa [Governments Principle Decision about Promoting Sustainable Choices in Public Procurement]"; Kristiina Aalto and Eva Heiskanen, *Kestävä ruokalautanen joukkoruokailun kestävän kehityksen edistäjänä* (Kuluttajatutkimuskeskus, 2011), https://helda.helsinki.fi/handle/10138/152350.

36. Aalto and Heiskanen, *Kestävä ruokalautanen joukkoruokailun kestävän kehityksen edistäjänä*.

37. Seija Lintukangas, "Kouluruokailuhenkilöstö matkalla kasvattajaksi."

38. EDUFI, "Perusopetuksen opetussuunnitelman perusteet."

39. Janhonen, Mäkelä, and Palojoki, "Adolescents' School Lunch Practices"; Janhonen and Mäkelä, "To Connect and Be Heard."

40. See, for example, Paul Daniel and Ulla Gustafsson, "School Lunches: Children's Services or Children's Spaces?," *Children's Geographies* 8, no. 3 (August 1, 2010): 265–274, https://doi.org/10.1080/14733285.2010.494865; Eva Neely, Mat Walton, and Christine Stephens, "Young People's Food Practices and Social Relationships. A Thematic Synthesis," *Appetite* 82, no. 1 (November 2014): 50–60, https://doi.org/10.1016/j.appet.2014.07.005; EDUFI, "Perusopetuksen opetussuunnitelman perusteet"; Janhonen and Mäkelä, "To Connect and Be Heard."

41. Linda Berggren, "'It's Not Really about the Food, It's about Everything Else': Pupil, Teacher and Head Teacher Experiences of School Lunch in Sweden" (doctoral diss., Umeå University, 2020), http://urn.kb.se/resolve?urn=urn:nbn:se:umu:diva-179401; Linda Berggren et al., "Between Good Intentions and Practical Constraints: Swedish Teachers' Perceptions of School Lunch," *Cambridge Journal of Education* 51, no. 2 (2020): 247–261, https://doi.org/10.1080/0305764X.2020.1826406.

42. Janhonen, Mäkelä, and Palojoki, "Food Education."; Janhonen, Torkkeli, and Mäkelä, "Informal Learning."

43. Dewey, *Democracy and Education*.

44. Katrien Van Poeck, Leif Östman, and Thomas Block, "Opening up the Black Box of Learning-by-Doing in Sustainability Transitions," *Environmental Innovation and Societal Transitions* 34 (March 1, 2020): 305, https://doi.org/10.1016/j.eist.2018.12.006.

45. Bente Elkjaer, "Pragmatism: A Learning Theory for the Future," in *Contemporary Theories of Learning: Learning Theorists—In Their Own Words*, ed. Knud Illeris (London: Routledge, 2008), 74–89; Kaljonen et al., "Attentive, Speculative Experimental Research"; Van Poeck, Östman, and Block, "Opening up the Black Box."

46. Dewey, *Democracy and Education*.

47. Van Poeck, Östman, and Block, "Opening up the Black Box." 306.

48. Janhonen, Torkkeli, and Mäkelä, "Informal Learning."

49. Dewey, *Democracy and Education*; Atli Harðarson, "The Teacher Is a Learner: Dewey on Aims in Education," *Educational Philosophy and Theory* 50, no. 5 (2017): 538–547, https://doi.org/10.1080/00131857.2017.1395735.

50. Anna-Liisa Elorinne, Noriko Arai, and Minna Maarit Autio, "Pedagogics in Home Economics Meet Everyday Life: Crossing Boundaries and Developing Insight in Finland and Japan," in *Reforming Teaching and Teacher Education*, ed. Eija Kimonen and Raimo Nevalainen (Rotterdam: Sense Publishers, 2017), 145–168; Lolita Gelinder, "Smak för hållbar mat?: Undervisning för hållbar matkonsumtion i Hem- och konsumentkunskap," (doctoral diss., Uppsala University, 2020), http://urn.kb.se/resolve?urn=urn:nbn:se:uu:diva-407876; Emmalee Gisslevik, "Education for Sustainable Food Consumption in Home and Consumer Studies" (doctoral thesis, University of Gothenburg, 2018), https://gupea.ub.gu.se/handle/2077/54558; Karin Hoijer and Karin Hjalmeskog, eds., *Didaktik för hem- och konsumentkunskap* (Malmo: Gleerups, 2019), http://www.gleerups.se/universitet-och-hogskola/universitet-och-hogskola-lararutbildning-pedagogik/lararutbildning-och-pedagogik-didaktik-och-pedagogik/didaktik-for-hem-och-konsumentkunskap-p51100463.

51. Höijer and Hjalmeskog, *Didaktik för hem- och konsumentkunskap*.

5

REBEL VENTURES AND YOUTH-LED FOOD INITIATIVES IN THE UNITED STATES

Raven Lewis with Jarrett Stein

My name is Raven Lewis. At the time of writing this, I am a senior at the Philadelphia High School for Creative and Performing Arts in Philadelphia, Pennsylvania. I was in middle school when, in 2017, I ate my first Rebel Crumble, a delicious fruit and grain snack invented, tested, produced, and sold by Rebel Ventures in Philadelphia public school cafeterias. I learned that Rebel Ventures was a youth-led nonprofit organization dedicated to feeding the students of Philadelphia healthy food that we will enjoy. Three years later, I applied for a job through their website. My mom had been berating me about getting some work experience, but I had a lot of anxiety about customer service or waitressing jobs. One of my friends was working at Rebel Ventures, so I knew they were big on teen representation in the workplace and learning through experience. I was hired to join their crew in March 2020.

Initially, I had taken only editing jobs within my work at Rebel because that was my main role in the team: cinematographer and editor. I wanted to stick with what I knew, media arts. But at one meeting, our co-executive director, Jarrett Stein, presented us with an opportunity, writing this chapter, to strengthen our communication skills and write about Rebel's mission. I decided I was up to the task. This led to me reading grants, meeting key people, and conducting interviews with our high school social media manager Tiguida Kaba, entrepreneurship mentor Kevin Dixon, co-executive

5.1 Raven testing recipes in Rebel Ventures' commercial kitchen in 2020. Credit: Rebel Ventures.

director Trecia Gibson, co-executive director Jarrett Stein, Amy Virus of the School District of Philadelphia Division of Food Services, board member Jane Kauer, and Rebel Ventures alum Tim Scott. As I learned about their experiences and the history of our organization, I also did a little introspection about my own experiences.

A REBEL STORY

The origins of Rebel Ventures can be traced back to Pepper Middle School in Southwest Philly. According to Tim, the neighborhood was tough on the city's youth, and street life seemed like the only option for many adolescents. As a student, he wanted to stay out of trouble and participated in many sports so he could stay on a positive path. But he worried about his peers and their overall well-being. At the time, it was common to see students walking through the hallways with chips and candy bars from convenience stores rather than the healthier, free meals that the district offered for breakfast and lunch. He was in eighth grade when he met Pepper's nutrition class teacher Jarrett Stein (now Rebel's advisor and the University-Assisted Community Schools director of health partnerships and social ventures for Penn's Netter Center), in 2009, and found that they both wanted to improve their school food environment.

With the help of Pepper's science teacher Ms. Siegler, Tim and Jarrett gathered a group of ten eighth graders who were dedicated to working cooperatively to make a change in the middle school. They started making and selling healthy snacks to their peers. Jarrett describes the experience in greater detail: "We were in the basement of Pepper Middle School. Myself, as a teacher who knew nothing, with a small group of eighth graders who had a ton of energy . . . making [snacks in] a little classroom with ingredients stored in bins in our closet and trying to partner with the cafeteria manager to let us use the oven and then going upstairs to another classroom after they were cooked to package them in plastic wrap and then go and sell them in this hallway."

The first product the students at Pepper made were Far Bars, with the tagline "It takes you farther!" These bars were made with granola and dried fruit and sold at an accessible price of fifty cents. When Tim and his fellow Far Bar makers walked around after school trying to sell them to their peers, they were met with a lot of questions and skepticism. It was also difficult because many students were focused on trying to get on the bus. Still, they got some sales, teachers were very supportive, and Tim and his classmates were excited to work on the project.

In 2013, a few years after the first Far Bar was made, the School District of Philadelphia decided to close Pepper Middle School along with twenty-three other public schools.[1] Jarrett worked to secure funding from his employer, the Barbara & Edward Netter Center for Community Partnerships at the University of Pennsylvania, to hire Pepper graduates to continue the Far Bar project as an after-school job training program. The students decided to call themselves Rebel Ventures and started working afternoons in the basement kitchen of the People's Emergency Center in West Philadelphia. The crew soon moved to the Center for Culinary Enterprises, a commercial incubator kitchen, where we continue to work today. Far Bars became Rebel Bars, hundreds of which were handmade, packaged, and sold by the crew to local schools through Netter Center after-school programs.

To expand the reach of Rebel Bars, the crew reached out to the School District of Philadelphia Division of Food Services. Manager of food services Amy Virus explained how working with Rebel Ventures was different from her experience with other food vendors: "There are people who want to sell us something every single day . . . so the difference here was helping us to understand that this was not just a Rebel Crumble, or one product. This is an experience for students, something that's going to fund a nonprofit that will ultimately give job skills and other opportunities to our students . . . Once we understood that, then it was a no brainer."

The school district supported Rebel Ventures' ideas but explained that to get on the school breakfast menu, they had to create a product that contained one-half cup of fruit and thirty-two grams of grain (at least sixteen grams of whole grain) per serving. They also need to supply fifty thousand units at a time and do so for about 50 cents per product. Because Rebel Bars didn't fit these requirements, the team got straight to work on recipes that included healthy ingredients like bananas, sweet potatoes, and applesauce, assembled into a snack whose name evolved with its transformation

5.2 Students giving feedback on Rebel Crumbles' packaging designs in 2016. Credit: Rebel Ventures.

to the current one, Rebel Crumbles. They also did public taste tests at local K–12 schools through the Netter Center's University-Assisted Community Schools programming, visiting hundreds of classrooms and public events to get a consensus on things that the children liked.

They provided samples of different versions of the Crumbles and asked tasters to fill out a paper survey with smiley faces and sad faces to measure how much they liked the Crumbles and the packaging design, and a space to write in any suggestions for improvement. Our crew later entered this data into a spreadsheet to compare flavors and make adjustments based on the feedback.

During the Crumbles development process, the school district introduced us to Michel's Bakery in Philadelphia, who had the capacity to help us manufacture our new product in the quantity the school district needed. By January of 2017, the first Rebel Crumbles were being served in over three hundred schools. Since then, more than one million Crumbles have been distributed citywide in district schools.

OUR ORGANIZATION

In 2016, Rebel Ventures, while still actively partnering with Penn, evolved into an independent nonprofit with a mission of increasing access to healthy nutritious foods and developing youth entrepreneurs. The high school crew has continued to power the organization, as I learned when I joined in 2020. We continue to get support from the Netter Center and engage Penn undergraduates, graduate students, staff, and faculty as mentors and co-learners. Over the years, we have also formed partnerships with the School District of Philadelphia, through the offices of Food Services, Student Leadership, School Climate, and Nutrition Education, as well as principals, teachers, and staff in K–12 schools. We partner with nonprofits such as The Food Trust, Philabundance, and The Enterprise Center as well as government (Philadelphia Health and Commerce Departments) and industry partners (Michel's Bakery, Bimbo Bakeries, High Street Hospitality, Dechert Law Firm) to support our crew's learning and organizational growth.

Currently, the crew of high schoolers making up Rebel Ventures work nine to twelve hours per week during the school year and twenty to twenty-five hours per week in the summer. These Rebels develop healthy food products and educational activities that reach thousands of students, create videos and marketing campaigns, track budgets, steward partnerships, speak at conferences, fill out IRS 990 forms, take business trips, and learn through each experience. The high school Rebel crew, a group ranging from five to fifteen students, is supported by a group of mentors, including paid part-time and full-time staff mentors as well as college and graduate students and professional volunteers. Our goal is to have a balance of high school students and adults in the crew. We are also overseen by a board of directors who share a commitment to Rebel's mission and values. As of 2022, the board has eight members, but it can change size over time with crew input.

To ensure that youth have meaningful leadership positions, Rebel Ventures also has a high school student co-executive director. Our first teen co-exec, Tre'Cia Gibson, described her experience this way:

In my 11th grade year, I went from being a high school team member to high school co-executive director. At that time, I was taking on a lot of responsibilities because 11th grade is the most important year in high school because colleges look at it. It took a lot of effort, but I was able to manage. Being in high school and managing high school students was a challenge, this is wholeheartedly true. I would not change anything and being at Rebel helped me achieve. The experience was amazing and if I had the chance to bring every high school student on I would.

MISSION AND VALUES

The Philadelphia School District is made up of almost two hundred thousand students, most of whom are Black and / or African American.[2] All students in Philadelphia public schools are eligible for free breakfast and lunch.[3] But a research study conducted in 2016–2017 found that student breakfast participation across the School District of Philadelphia averaged 42 percent.[4] Based on my experience, reasons for low participation include the difficulty some students have getting to school early, the "outside-of-school" competition from fast-food and corner stores, as well as the stigma around school food not being good.

As students, the Rebel crew identifies these issues and actively works to create change. We were created to empower youth to speak out about what we believe in and to create a better school food environment. Today, youth power is a core feature of our approach to transforming school food politics. We live in a time when adults are primarily in charge of what students consume daily at school,[5] but students have valuable perspectives and capabilities too. The youth at Rebel Ventures understand modern school food communities, and we believe that school food will be better if the people eating that food have control over what is being purchased, produced, and served.

We believe that students want to be healthy but don't always enjoy the food they're told they need to eat to reach their goals. To solve that problem, we promote "healthy deliciousness," a phrase developed by Rebel youth leaders to reflect the idea that fresh food should be good *for* you as well as good *to* you, so that staying healthy does not mean sacrificing taste or flavor. In our entrepreneurship mentor Kevin Dixon's words, "Rebel Crumbles is telling you that it's healthy deliciousness. It's right there. It's health in your face and it's tasting so good."

Youth power extends beyond having youth envision the product they want to create and consume. It is the core value that guides our actions.

5.3 Rebel crew member Lauren testing new recipes in 2020. Credit: Rebel Ventures.

Youth power doesn't just mean providing teens with jobs and leadership positions. Youth power means high school students taking real-world responsibility to run our nonprofit. Our predecessors at Pepper Middle School set Rebel's values: kids can grow into the young entrepreneurs and leaders we know we are capable of being.

Since we are our own target audience, we have a unique drive and determination to improve our community. When asked about the importance of youth power, manager of food services Amy Virus explained: "It's informing. [Rebel] helps make pathways for other students to do more work within the district and remind the district that, you know, we are the students. We need a voice. We want to be heard. We want to be seen." This is how our organization grew to be what it is today. Power is in the hands of the food consumer. With this control, we have created a model for how youth power can be directly applied to the school cafeteria.

IMPACT AND CHALLENGES

As the first youth-created product served in all Philadelphia public schools, Rebel Crumbles has a special place in the heart of the community. Rebel board member Jane Kauer speaks to the impact of these snacks: "As an anthropologist, to me, we have a cultural artifact that is something that people interact with in this very physical way because you're eating it. This is hugely powerful and the fact that kids are making the decisions that lead to that getting into schools or into stores is amazing." Jane also elaborates on Rebel's status as a social enterprise that engages students in running a business: "Kids are too infrequently associated with ... commerce.... They're out there and they're repeatedly showing up in the community and people are interacting with them, eating the Crumbles, reading the packaging, and hopefully going back and looking at social media and all these other things. In terms of Rebel Crumbles, I think that itself is hugely powerful."

My personal experience shows how youth perspectives on school food have changed since Crumbles was created. I remember my middle school cafeteria being livelier than ever on Crumble day. And, as I later came to appreciate, healthy deliciousness was making it possible. My friends and I say that Rebel Crumbles remind us of fresh baked goods. As co-exec Tre'Cia Gibson put it: "Crumbles remind me of a cake fresh out the oven, even when they're reheated. It's a burst of flavors."

We also impact the lives of the students on our crew. While working with Rebel, teens learn life lessons including cooking, time management, and leadership skills. High school student and Rebel crew member Tiguida Kaba says that working with us has helped her with her struggles with stepping out of her comfort zone: "One challenge is forcing yourself to be comfortable doing things you're usually uncomfortable with. Presenting at an event by yourself, it's like, 'You expect me to go out into all these people by myself?' It's gotten to a point where I'm comfortable doing that. Sometimes I get nervous a few seconds before I have to do it. In terms of getting prepared, practice makes perfect. You get better at it the more you do it."

I relate to this a lot. Coming into the crew, I planned on staying behind the scenes. It was only about a month later that I found myself leading an hour-long workshop at our annual Youth Entrepreneurship Expo. The audience for the workshop was high school students across Philadelphia, and the topic was planning and organization. In the moment, I was incredibly anxious and sweating profusely, but when the event was over and I had a moment to process everything, I felt this amazing sense of accomplishment. The impact of working at Rebel comes after we overcome our challenges.

I, and many of my peers, decided to work for Rebel when we saw how different it was from your typical first job or after-school activity. This wasn't a fast-food job that would pay us the bare minimum for hard labor. This was an opportunity to better the community and ourselves in the process. Our work has inspired us, as individuals, to speak out on other issues that are important to us. For example, Tim Scott started his own nonprofit organization after his work with Rebel: Project Pledge Philly, an initiative dedicated to providing students with the resources to excel academically.

WHAT'S NEXT

While I write this, we are in the middle of a life-changing pandemic. People are losing their jobs, their homes, and access to food. At Rebel, we knew we could help solve at least one of those problems with the help of the school district. When the Coronavirus struck, a lot of Philadelphia's youth were either going hungry or spending their money on junk food without realizing that there was healthier food accessible to them at no cost. The School District of Philadelphia was providing free grab-and-go meals for students at sixty-three different district sites, but far fewer kids retrieved these meals than those who were eating school food prior to the pandemic. The Division of Food Services realized that they needed help getting the word out, and asked their formal partner, Rebel Ventures, to improve communication between the district and its students. Starting in May 2020, the Rebel Team created social media posts and videos telling people where to get their grab-and-go meals and how to spice them up in true Rebel fashion. There is more to Rebel Ventures than making and selling our own products.

Prior to the pandemic, we had been designing and testing a new program, the Rebel Market, which we plan to restart when it is safe. The afterschool-based Rebel Market is run by students in schools with the goal of providing healthy and delicious snack options, which are "sold" for coupon incentives called "Rebel Bucks." Students earn Rebel Bucks in school for good behavior and completing tasks. Product offerings will include fruit smoothies, whole fruits, Rebel Crumbles, Rebel Nachos (whole grain chips with lentil barbacoa and vegan carrot/potato "cheez" sauce), and other fruit- and veggie-centric snacks. Unlike Crumbles, which are manufactured by Michel's Bakery, products served at the Rebel Market will be made off-site by the Rebel Crew and delivered by Rebel staff to the schools. The market will employ high school students as entrepreneurs running school-based stores that provide students with access to healthy, delicious, affordable, kid-desired foods right in school.

Rebel Ventures is part of a community, in Philadelphia and around the country, of youth-led organizations focused on building healthier food systems. Since our founding, we have been influenced and inspired by the work of others. The Agatston Urban Nutrition Initiative in Philadelphia (a program of Penn's Netter Center) has for many years engaged high school students in building gardens, growing food, running fruit stands, farmer's market entrepreneurship, and cafeteria interventions—all of which inspired Rebel Ventures' approach. Across the country there are organizations such as Food Empowerment Education Sustainability Team (FEEST) in Seattle, Washington, and the Food and Finance High School in New York City that directly engage young people in advocating for and creating healthy school food. Moving forward, we plan to continue our youth-powered school food work and collaborate and learn from these organizations and others.

We also hope to increase youth power with new connections between the school curriculum and the school cafeteria. For example, Philadelphia has a category of school called Career and Technical Education (CTE), which offers courses in specific, practical, and professional skills. The school I attend is CAPA HS, where I'm majoring in media design and television. Other schools include majors such as culinary arts, food processing science, and horticulture. We see great potential in having students use and refine those skill sets to help transform school food. For example, CTE culinary arts students can be responsible for creating their school's cafeteria menus, and the meal itself. CTE horticulture students can grow the produce used in school meals. And CTE media students like me can participate and make commercials and designs to promote school food. Here at Rebel, we truly believe in food justice, and we actively work to engage youth in creating healthier schools.

NOTES

1. James Jack and John Sludden, "School Closings in Philadelphia," *PennGSE Perspectives on Urban Education* 10, no. 1 (2013): 1–7.

2. "Fast Facts," The School District of Philadelphia, last modified January 20, 2023, https://www.philasd.org/fast-facts/.

3. Kevin McCorry, "Let Them Eat Lunch: All Philly Students Now Eligible for Free School Meals," WHYY, September 4, 2014, https://whyy.org/articles/let-them-eat-lunch-all-philly-students-now-eligible-for-free-meals/.

4. "School Breakfast Participation," The School District of Philadelphia, last modified June 30, 2021, https://www.philasd.org/research/programsservices/projects/school-breakfast-participation/.

5. For a similar argument at a national scale, see chapter 2 in this volume.

6

CREATING A MOBILE METHOD TO NOURISH CHILDREN IN THE UNITED STATES WITH THE "YUM-YUM BUS"

Rebecca A. Davis, A. Brooks Bowden, and Lisa Altmann

It is so rewarding to see the smiles on students' faces as they see the bus arrive. The [Rowan-Salisbury School Nutrition] staff have worked over time to build relationships with students so that they feel cared for and connected to the school system over the summer months. When you collaborate across departments to meet the nutritional needs as well as the educational needs of students, magic happens!
—Jason Gardner, assistant superintendent of curriculum and instruction, Rowan-Salisbury School District

ORIGINS OF THE YUM YUM BUS

During a typical school year, US school food programs provide important meals to students, helping to combat poverty and making it easier for families to meet their nutritional needs. During the summer, however, schools in most areas close, this source of nutrition dries up, and food insecurity among households with school-age children increases.[1] Some districts offer summer meal programs at sites such as schools or parks, but numerous barriers associated with these programs, including traveling to and from the site, make them insufficient for many families.[2] Federally funded summer meal programs only reach about 10 percent of the number of children served during the school year.[3] One school district in the state of North Carolina addressed this challenge within its own community by creating a summer meal program that brings the food directly to the children's homes.

The Rowan-Salisbury School (RSS) System's "Yum Yum Bus (YYB)" is the brainchild of a group of school nutrition workers who were granted autonomy and flexibility by district leadership to help address summer food insecurity, particularly among rural community members. Staff collectively set a goal to increase the number of meals served in the summer months by 10 percent but ended up far exceeding this goal, eventually increasing the number of meals served by over 50 percent. By adapting to the needs of the community and incorporating ideas of school food and transportation workers, this summer nutrition program efficiently repurposed resources and tailored services to improve access and uptake of summer meals, and in the process expanded stakeholder engagement. While the structure of this program was highly determined by the US federal summer meal program's rules and regulations, the basic design is relevant to rural and suburban communities both within the US and internationally in areas where school is closed for prolonged periods (e.g., summers or other extended school holidays).

BACKGROUND CONTEXT

As authors, we draw on a combination of practical experience with, and analysis of, school food programs. Altmann, the school nutrition services director for RSS and a cofounder of the YYB program, has worked in the district for twenty years and was previously the site-level kitchen manager. During the academic year, Altmann's work involves coordinating the logistics and operation of the YYB program, while in the summer she typically goes out on the bus herself to help serve food to students and families. Davis and Bowden are researchers who focus on school food programs. They have spent three years working closely with RSS. During that time, they collected data on the YYB program through site visits, document analysis, and interviews.[4]

Located about forty-five minutes northeast of Charlotte, North Carolina, RSS includes the small city of Salisbury and surrounding rural towns and communities. The district enrolls nearly twenty thousand students across K–12 grade levels in thirty-four schools, where 65 percent of students are eligible for free and reduced-price meals and 15 percent come from a home where the primary spoken language is Spanish.[5] To understand the lived experiences and needs of students living in poverty, the district synthesizes observations and information from a variety of sources, including families, school social workers, teachers, and bus drivers. Together, they make clear that many of the students in the district experience periods of deep poverty and housing insecurity. Some students' families do not have stable access to kitchen facilities. Some students live in inadequate housing, are hypermobile with frequent moves to different homes, or live with other families in overcrowded single homes or apartments. Some do not have consistent access to necessities such as laundry, phone or internet, or hygiene facilities.

When Dr. Lynn Moody became superintendent in 2013, she began to push for innovation across the district to better meet student needs. As part of those efforts, she gave the nutrition team a new level of autonomy to rethink school food and its role within the education system. The school nutrition department is housed in the district's main office and comprises employees who were promoted to their leadership roles from school kitchens throughout the district. They have developed three principles to guide their work: they seek to engage the communities of families that they serve and the community of employees on their teams; they are improvement-oriented and prioritize innovation; and they are focused on the well-being and humanity of the children and families in the district.

To rise to their new challenge in 2013, they collaborated with other parts of the district. For example, they worked with the technology team to envision how the district's new 1:1 technology access program (e.g., one laptop for each student) would change the spaces students needed to work and relax within the school. Eventually, they converted typical self-contained cafeterias into flexible spaces throughout school buildings with café tables and space for outdoor meals. In an interview with the authors, Superintendent Moody recalled thinking that the school nutrition department would be the least likely to be able to innovate, given that their programs are substantially influenced by tight federal restrictions, but she was surprised to see how much they accomplished.

In 2018, the state granted the district "renewal status." This designation allows it to use state funding and develop the curriculum with more flexibility and autonomy than other North Carolina districts, akin to how charter schools function in other parts of the US. For example, the district is not limited to teaching only courses listed in the state catalog. It offers a variety of courses and programs such as trauma-informed yoga programming for students and a substantial apprenticeship program for high schoolers. This flexibility has also allowed for innovative staffing practices, which helped to facilitate collaboration across departments, and provides autonomy to district-level leaders, including the school nutrition department.

DESIGNING THE YUM YUM BUS

RSS had an existing site-based summer meal program in partnership with community organizations, churches, affordable housing developments, and summer camps to offer US Department of Agriculture (USDA) reimbursable meals to children, sometimes with supplemental funding from outside sources.[6] Food was prepared in school kitchens and delivered to these sites where a trained staff member—sometimes a volunteer and sometimes an employee of the hosting organization—supervised the distribution. At the time, federal school meal regulations included a "congregate feeding" requirement, which meant that students could not pick up the food to go or have it dropped off to them using standard vehicles. Instead, they had to consume meals under the supervision of an adult, at a site that featured shelter, trash facilities, hand sanitizer or hand washing facilities, and a place for the children to sit and eat.

Such site-based programs tend to best serve children who live close to meal sites, have access to transportation, or both. By contrast, RSS observed that students in households experiencing poverty, students living in more rural areas, students with transportation barriers, and students who did not attend camps or community center programs seemed less likely to participate in the summer meals program. Guided by their goals of improving student well-being and increasing innovation, the district leadership team identified lagging summer meal participation as a priority. In 2014, the RSS nutrition team responded by beginning to develop a mobile food program that would allow them to bring summer meals directly to the students who could not otherwise access food served at existing meal sites. To comply with the USDA's "congregate feeding" regulations, they decided to design a cafeteria on wheels: the Yum Yum Bus.

The RSS team shared the concept plan for the YYB with staff of all ranks and solicited their input to ensure that the program was designed to meaningfully address the needs of both children in the district and school food staff. Staff buy-in for a mobile cafeteria was also critical because working conditions in the summer months are difficult in North Carolina, where temperatures regularly exceed 90 to 100 degrees Fahrenheit. To facilitate inter-department collaboration and encourage buy-in, district-level nutrition leaders worked alongside staff during the summer, a practice that they continue to this day.

The YYB program development was an interdepartmental effort. Principals shared their knowledge of neighborhoods in the district where the mobile cafeteria would be beneficial. The technicians who manage the district's bus fleet contributed design ideas and supported the logistics and outfitting of the bus program. School-level kitchen staff proposed a book distribution component and organized drives to collect books so that they could share them with the children along the routes once the program was launched. The curriculum department was also engaged to help with the literacy component of the program by seeking further donations of books and texts that were likely to engage students with a wide range of interests and at a variety of reading levels.

RSS applied for—and won—a grant to fund the retrofitting of a specially designed bus to serve as a meal site. The mobile cafeteria design involved a traditional yellow school bus, but the similarity stopped there. The transportation department[7] contributed a retired school bus that would fit the bill and got to work. They began by removing the typical bus seats and installed cafeteria-style tables where the bus seats once were. In the back of the bus, food coolers and warmers were installed to keep the food at safe temperatures. Using elbow grease and readily available cafeteria furniture, the bus was transformed into a space for up to thirty students to eat lunch. To fund the program itself, RSS drew on both the federal dollars and community contributions that were already funding the site-based meal program.

6.1 School nutrition staff serving lunch to children on the YYB. Credit: Rowan-Salisbury Schools.

Regulations do not allow the school bus to run without a driver in the seat, yet the program design relied on the driver to help assist the food service worker in handling the food and connecting with students and families. This meant that the buses could not idle in park, running their built-in air conditioners. Given the high temperatures of North Carolina summers, it quickly became apparent that just opening the windows on a summer's day was insufficient, so an auxiliary air conditioner was installed along with a generator to power it. A staff member designed a mural for the buses, and a local business donated a colorful "wrap" or decal that covers the entire bus in cartoon pictures of foods, setting it apart from a typical yellow bus. In June 2015, the first "Yum Yum Bus" was ready and it began to deliver food to children across the district (figure 6.1).

On a typical summer day, the YYB begins by heading to a central school-based kitchen to pick up meals prepared by a team of food service workers. A food service worker from one of the local schools that serves children along the route joins the bus driver so that the children served are likely to see a familiar food service worker from their school. This intentional staffing decision aims to strengthen the relationship between the schools and the children and families in the community and provides extended employment options to food service workers in the summer months when hours were previously limited.

The bus rolls every weekday during the summer on a predetermined route. Any child under eighteen is eligible to receive food from the YYB. Participating families do not need to demonstrate financial need or citizenship status to receive a meal. The structure of the rural areas in Rowan County partially facilitates the effectiveness of the YYB. There are a number of informal clusters of mobile homes and camps, allowing the bus to stop in a single location and reach many students. The routes include a mixture of larger groups of homes, smaller clusters, and the occasional single family.

The bus stays at each stop for twenty to thirty minutes. Children climb on to eat and converse with other children and the staff members; family members, who are also permitted on, join in the conversations as connections are forged and deepened. On the bus, the food service worker and the bus driver discuss the food with the children and the families to find out what they like and don't like. This informal process is occasionally supplemented with "tastings" where children can sample new options and provide feedback that is incorporated into subsequent menu planning. For example, when the program began, cold options such as sandwiches were frequently offered. However, it became clear from formal and informal feedback on the bus that there was a strong preference for warm foods. As a result, the menu was converted to mainly hot options. The menu on the YYB follows the same food quality goals used during the school year and prioritizes fresh fruit and vegetables, sourced locally when possible. The department prioritizes scratch cooking and baking, and even foods that in other cafeterias are often prepared in a heat-and-serve style, such as pizzas, soups, pastas, and meats, are often made from scratch. This is facilitated in part by a set of heat-sealing machines that allow food such as baked ziti to be safely packaged for transit. The coolers and heated containers on the bus maintain the food temperature of hot and cold items during the day.

When it is time to go, children are permitted to pick one fruit or grain to take off the bus for later. Children are also invited to pick a book from a box that the curriculum department stocks to meet a range of student reading levels and interests. Access to books helps all children, but is especially important for housing-insecure families, who have shared with the district that they often cannot pack books when they need to move quickly or unexpectedly. Children are allowed to keep the books, but many families bring the books back when they are done with them so others can read them as well.

TAILORING IMPLEMENTATION AND CULTIVATING TRUST

During the first few weeks of the bus's operation, staff noted that some families, particularly in Spanish-speaking communities, were hesitant to participate. To better serve these constituents, RSS knew it needed to build trust with Spanish-speaking families. The team promoted Carolina Hernández, a native Spanish speaker, into a leadership role in the bus program. Hernández reached out to Spanish-speaking communities in person to describe the program. The nutrition department already employed multiple native Spanish speakers, and they promoted these staff members from within to ensure that a Spanish speaking staff member was on the bus every day. As the program expanded to multiple buses, this practice continued. These intentional considerations led to greater participation rates among Hispanic/Latin American communities. After addressing these issues, the program was able to reach two hundred children a day across different communities throughout the district.

While the YYB is a school meal program by name, its effect goes far beyond simply providing nutrition. By design, the program aims to provide students from low-income households with consistent and dependable access not just to food but also to educators during the summer. In an interview with the authors, Superintendent Moody explained that many teachers in the district do not fully understand generational poverty and thus impose cultural norms in their classrooms that leave children of poverty disconnected. While the district works on reforming in-classroom practices to be more inclusive, the YYB literally and figuratively meets the families where they are. The bus drivers and the food workers that staff the bus serve as representatives of the school system and are specifically trained not to judge students but instead to offer consistent warmth and connection with families that may be disenfranchised or otherwise alienated from the system. Altmann and the rest of the leadership team identify staff members that are particularly strong at building relationships with students and prioritize their involvement on the bus team and provide opportunities for newer employees to work with these employees so that they can observe their practices. Altmann notes that over time this process of encouraging staff to go beyond simply serving students food to having meaningful conversations with the children and families leads to a high level of excitement among the children when the bus arrives each day. Superintendent Moody recalled a time when she rode the bus and offered to help a young child open her milk. The child rejected the offer of help and took it instead to the driver who opened the milk and explained that they have a routine: every day, he said, "she counts on me."

While the YYB program was motivated by the goal to increase summer meal participation by 10 percent, participation in the first year increased by over 50 percent, increasing from 68,030 summer meals in 2014 to 102,329 in 2015. The first YYB was replicated in 2018, using a similar combination of community contributions, federal reimbursements, and district resources. The second bus purchase was financed by a donation from a private citizen. The expansion of the program allowed more neighborhoods to be served, and by 2019, the bus program was serving 145 stops a day, five days a week during the summer.

IN-DISTRICT SUPPORT

A main reason for the success of the YYB program has been the priority placed on earning the support from hourly staff by engaging them in decision-making and creating a culture where feedback and ideas are encouraged. The directors and supervisors work to create a culture where all staff can develop new ideas and identify areas for growth. For example, staff members frequently develop new recipes, while a team of staff works to develop new methods for efficiently transporting warm food, and all relay feedback from their direct observations of the program and children's and families' reactions to it.

Staff are promoted from within the organization, and there is a substantial effort to train kitchen workers on the job and to pay for certification courses and off-site training so that they can be promoted to managers and leaders. All current school- and district-level school nutrition managers were promoted directly from kitchen staff. Further, the YYB program allows hourly school workers, such as bus drivers, kitchen staff, and teacher's assistants, the opportunity to expand their employment beyond the school year to work in the summer weeks for at least thirty hours a week. While the school nutrition leadership does not have the ability to make compensation decisions, they advocate for higher wages for these workers, who are typically the lowest paid in the district and/or who have ten-month contracts and do not typically have access to summer employment through their district jobs. The support of the transportation department is integral to the program. The staff at the transportation department built and now maintain the buses and work closely with the nutrition department to dream up new ideas and find innovative ways to purchase or acquire resources at low cost. For example, the transportation employees scoured classified ads for vehicles, generators, and air conditioners to find affordable options. During the academic year, the bus drivers identify neighborhoods that may be experiencing hardship and would benefit from summer nutrition delivery. They do this via their observations when driving, along with their conversations with children and families. Occasionally when typical staff are out, mechanics from the transportation department step in to drive the buses.

This foundational support from district employees working in the garages, in the kitchens, and on the buses is supplemented with "top-down" buy-in from district leaders. Every principal and member of the district leadership has ridden a YYB. School leaders commented that riding along on the bus helped them better understand the true extent of the need in their communities. Additionally, after riding alongside the bus driver and food service workers, the school leaders often develop a new level of appreciation and awareness about the importance of the work done by these teams. Kelly Withers, a current associate superintendent and prior school principal in the RSS district, shared via email: "Riding the Yum Yum Bus as a principal was one of the most moving experiences of my career. The dedication of our school food service staff to meeting the needs of all children in our community inspired me to open discussions in our school about how we could help and contribute to giving back through our programs in the schools. The bus is seen as a source of sustenance but most importantly it is a source of hope and partnership between our schools and our families."

Additional partnerships such as one with the curricular department to promote literacy via book distribution further cement the program as an essential part of the school system. This interconnectedness and support from school leaders makes future operation and expansion of the program possible.

COMMUNITY PARTNERSHIPS

Partnerships both within the school district and within the larger community are essential to the YYB program. Outside of the summer months, the buses are used for special events. For example, the buses have been set up at community centers during WIC[8] enrollment and immunization drives so that when families come to get services, their children can get a meal and a book. The buses also go out during the holidays with bags of food donated by a local grocery store along with donated gifts for the children.

The meals are funded by the USDA summer meals program; only individuals eighteen and under can take food. While children are permitted to take fruit or a grain home with them, USDA rules state that perishable food must be discarded at the end of the meal. This policy has led to food waste and has the potential to erode trust with communities where food can be scarce, putting school food workers in a difficult position. They work to mitigate this tension by making sure the permissible take-home foods are available and clearly offered.

To help expand food access for the whole family, the program also partners with Bread Riot, a local nonprofit. Bread Riot seeks to mitigate food insecurity and food waste simultaneously by using grant funding to buy surplus produce that is leftover after local farmers markets as well as directly from farmers. This produce is packed onto a truck that follows the buses. Several times a week during the summer, families, including both children and adults, can select produce from the truck to take home, free of charge.

The YYB also occasionally travels to fundraising events. The local Realtor's Association holds an annual golf tournament to support the YYB program and is supporting current efforts to outfit the buses with Wi-Fi.

Participation in such events helps to raise awareness among multiply privileged communities of the need within their changing communities.

COVID-19 AND BEYOND

The COVID-19 pandemic led RSS to shut down on Friday, March 13, 2020. The nutrition and transportation departments sprang into action immediately. The USDA waived several requirements, including the congregate feeding requirement, so that any vehicle—not just a cafeteria-style bus—could participate in the COVID emergency feeding program. Yet RSS staff attribute their own rapid response to the pandemic to the important lessons learned from five years of operating the YYB program. On Tuesday, March 17, after just a single school day of downtime, they began dispatching regular yellow school buses, now stocked with packs of meals for students and families, on their normal routes. Teachers, bus drivers, custodians, and school food workers rallied to staff the bus for food distribution. In conversations with teachers who joined the ranks, Altmann heard repeatedly that they had a new level of appreciation for the important jobs that school food workers do.

In the early days of the pandemic, food shortages and last-minute changes in delivery schedules made menu planning particularly challenging, but staff were able to adapt the menu and offer nutrition continuity despite the disruptions. One team took charge of recipe modifications to adjust meals for portion size and reheating. Another team worked on efficient packaging solutions. A third, bilingual, team worked to create "at-a-glance" sheets that families could refer to for nutrition information, allergens, and reheating instructions. Lastly, the school nutrition leadership team sewed masks for staff who participated in the distribution efforts.

In the fall of 2020, schools partially reopened, and six grab-and-go meal site hubs were created where families could go pick up bundles of meals for days when their children were in virtual school. With the typical school operations still substantially curtailed, the bus drivers' hours were cut, jeopardizing their access to benefits. The nutrition department quickly found work for transportation staff packaging and serving food so that those employees' benefits were protected. As a result, any school transportation or nutrition staff member who wanted to retain their regular hours could do so.

The staff knew transportation would be a barrier to participation in the meal hubs, just as it is for families in the summer, so the district also dispatched the YYB to deliver bundles including five breakfasts, lunches, and suppers to several thousand students per week. Each meal was packaged and included directions for reheating in both Spanish and English. As of 2021, the district planned to keep a virtual school option available past the end of the COVID-19 pandemic. Under this scenario, the RSS nutrition team planned to maintain some version of this meal delivery program to serve students who were not attending school in person and who would not have access to school meals as a result.

Even before COVID-19, work had begun in partnership with the local Association of Realtors to outfit the buses with wireless internet so they could serve as access points for communities with limited broadband access. The idea was that the bus could go out several times a week during the school year with snacks and with a certified teacher or teacher's assistant who could help with homework or other academic support. Once the social distancing requirements of COVID-19 eased, the program planned to allow students back on the YYB to access these Wi-Fi connections and to connect with a teacher or teacher's aide for support with virtual learning.

The YYB team continuously seeks ways to better reach underserved community members, including working with community and church leaders to identify future areas of improvement. The primary barrier to expansion and further program improvement is funding; despite the grant funding and the creative program design, it will take more funding to expand the program. While the program's day-to-day operations are sustainable using USDA reimbursements, the startup costs, including the purchase and retrofitting of the bus, require extra funds. Additional barriers include finding and identifying areas, getting opt in from neighborhoods, overcoming issues of stigma and pride, and navigating areas that may be unsafe for employees to visit.

Yet staff are proud that the YYB seems to have passed the test that COVID-19 has presented. It was unclear if the community-based nature of the program could endure with limited direct contact between students, families, and school staff in the mobile dining rooms. However, it seems that these connections are enduring, and families remained excited to see the buses even though the program was altered to keep all participants safe (e.g., meal drop-off only). By knowing where the communities were that were most likely to experience food insecurity, and having pre-established connections pre-pandemic, the district was able to continue to provide high-quality nutrition throughout the closures.

INGREDIENTS TO BUILD THE YUM YUM BUS

The process of creating the YYB depended on the organization of a set of complex resources to build and run the program. In table 6.1, we document and quantify these "ingredients" in the hope that it will enable other organizations to develop similar programs in their own contexts.[9] The purpose of this method is to capture all ingredients used in providing educational programming—whether reallocated from other sources, donated, or otherwise procured—so that the costs reflect the true economic value of the approach, regardless of how various components were financed.

We matched US average market prices to estimate the value of these ingredients using constant 2019 US dollars to estimate an approximate price per meal served.[10] This matching process was based on qualitative data descriptions and observations. We find that the cost per delivered meal was about seven dollars, including the cost of food. This estimate includes all costs to various funders, including community partners, donors, and the federal government, and does not reflect district expenditures.

Our findings indicate that the YYB, an intensive approach that is tailored to the needs of the community, is nevertheless achievable. Two concepts, economies of scale and cost sharing, help to make this program financially feasible. First, economies of scale, or the ability to save money by serving a larger number of people, allow for greater efficiency. By offering an expansive summer meal program, both via the existing sites and the YYB, the district stretches scarce funding further. This leveraging of economies of scale manifests as benefits to the program and the community, for example by being able to hire employees full time or to save on high-quality locally sourced foods by ordering in bulk. Should the district

Table 6.1 Mobile cafeteria ingredients list

Ingredient	Description	Quantity
Personnel[11]		
Food service workers	Prepare and serve food	540 hours
Food service worker training	Food safety training	2 courses
Bus driver	Drives the bus and helps serve	225 hours
Central office admin	Responsible for the majority of the program's functionality, along with the nutrition supervisor	50 hours
District nutrition supervisor	Responsible for the majority of the program's functionality, along with the nutrition supervisor	30 hours
District nutrition director	Oversees all nutrition programs, assists with bus program	16 hours
Facilities		
Converted school bus	Converted retired school bus with mural	1 unit
Bus mileage	Mileage for meal delivery	1,440 miles
Bus maintenance	Routine maintenance	3 months
Food coolers	Keeps food and milk cold	4 units
Ice packs	Freezable ice packs	12 units
Food warmers	Keeps food warm	2 units
Heat packs	Keeps hot food warm	4 units
Generator	Runs A/C after parking	1 unit
A/C units	Keeps the bus cool while students eat	2 units
Tables with seats	Cafeteria-style tables with attached seats	4 units
Materials		
Food	Federally reimbursable summer meals	5,000 units
Books	Available for students to take home	35 books
Uniforms	Worn by drivers and food service workers	6 units

Note: The above list represents a single bus, serving 110 children for forty-five days.

have chosen to run a smaller-scale program, they may not have been able to leverage resources to the same degree and would likely have served fewer children yet at a higher per-participant cost. That is not to say that economies of scale are not available to smaller agencies or school systems; the unique needs and circumstances of a given community will dictate the best mode of operation.

Second, by leveraging multiple funding opportunities, the costs of the program are shared across groups, making the program more feasible and affordable for each group. In this case, the bulk of the program is funded by federal funds that are widely available to schools across the US. Additional funds from grants, donations, and partnerships with local nonprofits further help share the burden, leaving the school district with relatively low costs to support the administration of the program and the routine bus maintenance. In the case of the YYB, the original startup costs were covered mainly from community contributions and grants, while day-to-day operation of the program is largely sustained by USDA reimbursements with district funds supporting a modest share of the administrative and organizational overhead.

CONCLUSION

US school food systems are substantially restricted by strict federal rules and regulations, making innovation difficult but not impossible. Changes or a relaxation of federal summer meal regulations might allow the YYB program to be more flexibly or efficiently run. Yet even within existing constraints, the program has been remarkably successful. That success comes, in part, because the school nutrition department, as well as school food and transportation workers, have been empowered to innovate. It also reflects the fact that the YYB program is inherently community based. Without connections within the school nutrition department, within the school district, and in the greater community, the program would be unlikely to thrive as well as it has. Community outreach was integral to the program's success and engagement of the Spanish-speaking community was essential. Once established, the program began to also play a community-building role by serving as a positive bridge between the school system and families and between the end of one school year and the start of the next. Today, the YYB program continues to build awareness among community members, educators, and leaders outside of the school nutrition community of both the deep need within their communities and the efforts of school food workers.

NOTES

1. Mark Nord and Kathleen Romig, "Hunger in the Summer: Seasonal Food Insecurity and the National School Lunch and Summer Food Service Programs," *Journal of Children and Poverty* 12, no. 2 (2007): 141–158, https://doi.org/10.1080/10796120600879582.

2. Kim Caldwell et al., "Summer Meals Transportation Barriers and Solutions: Opportunities and Practices for Promising Partnerships and Recommendations for Stakeholders," No Kid Hungry Share Our Strength Center for Best Practices, 2015, https://www.worldhunger.org/wp-content/uploads/2016/04/summer_meals_study.docx; Kathryn Hill, "Summer Meals for NYC Students: Understanding the Perspectives and Experiences of Families. Equity, Access & Diversity," Research Alliance for New York City Schools, 2021, https://steinhardt.nyu.edu/sites/default/files/2021-05/Summer%20Meals%20for%20NYC%20Students%20in%20Layout%205.7.21%20FINAL.pdf.

3. United States Department of Agriculture, "Summer Food Service Program," last modified December 22, 2022, https://www.ers.usda.gov/topics/food-nutrition-assistance/child-nutrition-programs/summer-food-service-program.aspx.

4. The resource use analysis presented in this chapter was originally conducted as a part of a cost analysis to document the costs borne at the grassroots school and district levels to combat food insecurity in North Carolina and was used in a report to the court on the Leandro Case, a long-running constitutional lawsuit asserting the right of North Carolina students to a "sound basic education." A. Brooks Bowden and Rebecca A. Davis, "Addressing Leandro: Supporting Student Learning by Mitigating Student Hunger," *Center for Benefit-Cost Studies of Education* 3 (2019): 22, https://repository.upenn.edu/cbcse/3/. WestEd Learning Policy Institute, and Friday Institute for Education Innovation at North Carolina State University, *Sound Basic Education for All: An Action Plan for North Carolina* (San Francisco, CA: WestEd, 2019).

5. Institute of Education Sciences, "Education Demographic and Geographic Estimates. ACS-ED District Demographic Dashboard 2017–21: Rowan-Salisbury Schools North Carolina" (United States National Center for Education Statistics, Washington, DC, n.d.), accessed September 8, 2023, https://nces.ed.gov/Programs/Edge/ACSDashboard/3704050.

6. Both the Yum Yum Bus and the site-based meal programs described in this chapter use funding from the USDA. To receive summer funding, districts work with the state to apply to serve summer meals based on demonstrated poverty rates and school meal programming during the academic year. The federal policy requires a sheltered and supervised meal site and allows all children who come to get a meal. Funding for the program is then reimbursed based on participation.

7. The district owns its bus fleet and directly employs the staff members that drive and maintain the buses.

8. The Special Supplemental Nutrition Program for Women, Infants, and Children (WIC) provides supplemental foods, health care referrals, and nutrition education for low-income pregnant, breastfeeding, and non-breastfeeding postpartum women, and to infants and children up to age 5 who are at nutritional risk. USDA, "Special Supplemental Nutrition Program for Women, Infants, and Children (WIC)," (Washington, DC, July 31, 2023), accessed November 27, 2023, https://www.fns.usda.gov/wic.

9. Henry M. Levin et al., *Economic Evaluation in Education: Cost-Effectiveness and Benefit-Cost Analysis* (Los Angeles: SAGE Publications, 2018). For a full analysis, see: Bowden and Davis, "Addressing Leandro."

10. United States Department of Labor. "U.S. Bureau of Labor Statistics," 2019, https://www.bls.gov/.

11. These prices were retrieved from representative sources, such as national restaurant and food services supply stores, the Bureau of Labor Statistics, and school transportation management sources; for a complete list, see Bowden and Davis, "Addressing Leandro," 22.

7

LOCAL AND NATIONAL RESPONSES TO THE COVID-19 PANDEMIC IN THE UNITED STATES

Margaret Read, Anne Moertel, Courtney Smith, and Jennifer LeBarre

As the COVID-19 pandemic began to sweep across the US, California was one of the first states to issue government orders to prevent the spread of the virus. In San Francisco, for example, residents were instructed to shelter in place beginning March 17, 2020, and schools were shuttered. That same day, the San Francisco Unified School District (SFUSD) started distributing school meals from the doors of school buildings. As the largest meal provider in San Francisco, SFUSD typically serves 7.5 million meals per year to fifty-six thousand students at 136 schools across the city. During the shelter-in-place order, providing the breakfast, lunch, and after-school meals students had relied on during the school day was deemed an "essential service."

As the shutdown continued, the US Department of Agriculture (USDA) Food and Nutrition Service (FNS) issued a series of waivers that gave school food programs across the country flexibility in the preparation and delivery of meals for students. Thanks in part to these policy changes, SFUSD was able to create three new service models. Grab-and-go sites were established at schools to distribute meals from walk-up windows fashioned with plexiglass in the door of school buildings. To expand the district's reach, community organizations began distributing grab-and-go meals from their facilities as well. Lastly, custom meal boxes were home-delivered to students with disabilities and special dietary needs. By the end of 2020, as

San Francisco schools remained shut down, SFUSD's grab-and-go program had provided over four million meals; its community-based partners had provided 240,000 meals, and the home delivery program provided more than one million meals.[1]

SFUSD's efforts are just one example of how local school districts joined a nationwide push to reduce the crisis of child hunger brought on by the COVID-19 pandemic. But throughout this chapter we return to SFUSD to illustrate how the federal government's policy response to the COVID-19 pandemic shaped on-the-ground practice and how local circumstances shaped the implementation of federal policy.

THE US NATIONAL SCHOOL MEAL PROGRAMS

Federally funded school meal programs contribute significantly to the social safety net for families, ensuring that students have access to the nutrition they need. When school buildings closed across the country in March of 2020 and families sheltered in place, school nutrition staff and their allies successfully advocated for program flexibilities and funding that allowed them to develop innovative ways to continue to provide meals to students. As the pandemic continued, the long-term implications for school food programs in the US were not yet known. But it was clear that large numbers of students and their families depended on school meal programs to remain healthy, particularly since the Healthy, Hunger-Free Kids Act (HHFKA Public Law 111–296) became law in 2010. As a result of this landmark legislation, the USDA updated nutrition standards for school meals and Smart Snacks for the first time in fifteen years. Smart Snacks are the national nutritional standards for foods and beverages sold outside of school meals. The HHFKA has significantly improved school meals,[2] and ensured that students consume more fruits and vegetables, and less total fat, saturated fat, and sodium than before.[3] The stronger nutrition standards also increased student participation in school breakfast and lunch and therefore, increased food service revenue for school districts.[4]

In addition to setting the nutritional standards for meals, the FNS administers fifteen federal nutrition assistance programs that include the School Breakfast Program (SBP), the National School Lunch Program (NSLP), the Summer Food Service Program (SFSP), the Seamless Summer

Option (SSO), and the Child and Adult Care Feeding Program. FNS provides school meal programs with cash reimbursements for each qualifying meal. The reimbursement rates for each program depend on a variety of factors, primarily whether the child qualifies for free or reduced-price meals. Students in households that make less than 130 percent of the federal poverty level or participate in certain federal benefit programs are eligible for a free meal, while students from families with income between 130 and 185 percent of the federal poverty level qualify for a reduced-price meal. Federal reimbursements and local funds (including student payments) are the primary sources of school meal funding, with some states choosing to provide supplemental funding.[5] School meal programs are administered at the state level by state child nutrition agencies and at the local level by School Food Authorities (SFAs). SFAs and schools have discretion in how they administer the programs within federal and state guidelines. During a regular school year, these agencies provide school meals to thirty-five million children a day.[6]

But the coronavirus pandemic upended the way school meal programs had been designed to work, requiring major changes at the federal, state, and local levels. In late February 2020, the first US public school shut down due to the spread of the virus.[7] By the end of March, almost one hundred thousand schools serving more than fifty million students had closed. The impact on school nutrition departments was enormous. Collectively, schools would have served almost forty-four million school meals each day during regular operations, in addition to snacks and suppers served after school hours and fresh fruits and vegetables served in some elementary schools.[8] Instead, schools began operating the largest emergency food program in modern American history.

CONGRESS RESPONDS TO THE CORONAVIRUS PANDEMIC

The sudden loss of access to school meals put millions of children at risk for food insecurity. In May 2020, more than one in five adults living with children (21.8 percent) reported that their households experienced food insecurity during the prior thirty days. Racial and ethnic disparities were pronounced: 27.1 percent of Hispanic adults' households and 27.0 percent of Black adults' households experienced food insecurity compared to

13.5 percent of white adults' households.[9] The pandemic quickly became a hunger crisis, requiring urgent national policy solutions to address food insecurity. National organizations like Share Our Strength, the Food Research and Action Center, the Center for Science in the Public Interest, the Urban School Food Alliance, and many others pushed Congress to act. The federal government responded in three ways: (1) allowing for greater flexibility in federal nutrition programs, (2) providing funds directly to families with school-aged children who were missing regular meals at school, and (3) approving funding for states to support pandemic school meal programs.

Congress passed the Families First Coronavirus Response Act of 2020 on March 18, which provided nationwide waiver authority for school meal programs, specific meal pattern waiver authority, and authority to issue waivers that increase federal costs. The USDA used its congressional authority to issue waivers and guidance memoranda that permitted states, school districts, and sponsors to operate modified school meal service programs. The USDA granted seventy waivers and guidance memoranda between March 18, 2020, and December 1, 2020, and more than twenty additional waivers and guidance memoranda since then. The waivers have helped school districts to adapt their meal programs to meet the challenges of the pandemic and address hunger in their communities (table 7.1). They have allowed all children under the age of eighteen to eat for free, outside of the traditional group mealtime settings; allowed parents to pick up meals with or without the child's presence; and allowed school districts to send home multiple days of meals at a time or to drop off food directly at the homes of students who continued to learn virtually part- or full-time. School districts were also able to get waivers around the meal program requirements, a necessary relief given the supply chain issues during the pandemic.

On March 27, President Trump signed into law the Coronavirus Aid, Relief, and Economic Security (CARES) Act that allocated billions of dollars in emergency relief funds to cover costs associated with the pandemic. Funds from the CARES Act permitted schools to purchase personal protective equipment (PPE) for school nutrition staff, reinforce school nutrition budgets that were exhausted due to added service costs, cover costs associated with school meal delivery, and hire additional staff to expand or maintain operations when current staff were sick or unavailable.

Table 7.1 Selected USDA waivers

Waiver	Programs	Release date	Description
1. SFSP and SSO operations	CACFP, NSLP, SBP, SFSP, SSO	August 31, 2020	Programs may continue to operate under SFSP and SSO.
2. Meal service time flexibility	CACFP, NSLP, SBP, SFSP, SSO	March 20, 2020	Meals and snacks can be provided at times that best meet the needs of the communities, even if the times are outside of federal guidelines.
3. Non-congregate feeding	CACFP, NSLP, SBP, SFSP, SSO	March 20, 2020	All meals and snacks may be taken to consume off site.
4. Meal pattern flexibility	CACFP, NSLP, SBP, SFSP, SSO	March 25, 2020	Meal pattern flexibility is granted across all child nutrition programs, allowing programs to serve meals based on foods available.
5. Parent/guardian meal pick-up	CACFP, NSLP, SBP, SFSP, SSO	March 25, 2020	Parents/guardians are allowed to pick up meals for children without them being present.
6. Area eligibility flexibility for closed enrolled sites	SFSP, SSO	April 21, 2020	Closed enrolled SFSP and SSO sites may determine site eligibility through area eligibility in lieu of collecting income eligibility applications.

The CARES Act also established the Pandemic Electronic Benefit Transfer (P-EBT) program that provided students with debit cards, with which they could purchase their own food. Eligible students included those approved for free or reduced-price meals, those directly certified for free meals through eligible public benefit programs such as the Supplemental Nutrition Assistance Program (SNAP), and those attending a school participating in a federal provision allowing all students to receive free meals without applications (Community Eligibility Provision, Provision 2, or Provision 3). In some states, children enrolled in pre-kindergarten or Head Start (a federal program for children ages zero to five from low-income families) were also eligible. The P-EBT cards contained funds equal to the amount of school meal benefits recipients would have received were schools open. Depending on the number of days school buildings were closed and the federal school meal reimbursement rate in their state, students could receive $250–$458 each to replace benefits for the period of March through June 2020. Funds could be used at grocery stores, farmers markets, and some online grocery retailers, following the same method and guidelines as SNAP benefits. Families who received EBT cards could still participate in grab-and-go school meal programs: the benefits were not mutually exclusive.[10] However, families faced up to five months of delays in accessing these initial P-EBT benefits and when continued P-EBT funding was provided by the American Rescue Plan (ARP) Act, many students did not receive benefits covering the 2020–2021 school year in the summer of 2021.

SCHOOL FOOD SYSTEM RESPONSE

In the weeks that followed initial school closures, as the USDA began to roll out child nutrition waivers and provide guidance to state agencies, schools continued to adapt their school meal service to better meet demand and the needs of students and families. USDA waivers allowed schools to serve meals through multiple federal meal programs. Many schools chose to operate programs originally aimed at feeding kids during the summer or unanticipated periods of school closure such as a snowstorm: the Summer Food Service Program (SFSP) and the Seamless Summer Option (SSO). This helped schools serve their wider communities, including younger siblings not enrolled in school and neighborhood children who did not attend their school, and provide all meals free of charge. More than half of school meals served nationally in April and May 2020 were served through the SFSP. While the SFSP provides higher reimbursement rates, additional paperwork is required. As a result, many districts opted for SSO in the summer.

Some schools utilized multiple programs to maximize the number of meals they could serve to children. For example, schools could provide three meals per day if they continued to operate the Child and Adult Care Feeding Program (CACFP) At-Risk Afterschool Meals program in addition to lunch and breakfast programs. The Dallas Independent School District took that route, distributing breakfast, lunch, dinner, and a snack for each school day. Many other school districts, daunted by the complexities of running the CACFP during a pandemic, did not provide suppers, at least initially. In those cases, nonprofit partners could help supplement school meal programs. For example, Monroe Public Schools in rural Michigan provided students breakfast and lunch, while the Monroe Family YMCA stepped in to serve supper and a snack.[11]

Although state agencies could waive meal pattern requirements due to food supply disruption, most schools continued to provide meals that met federal nutrition standards for the summer meals program. In April 2020, many school districts switched from serving meals daily to providing children with multiple days' worth of meals at a time. This schedule could reduce the burden on families, who no longer had to travel to the school each day. It also facilitated social distancing for staff and volunteers. However, school nutrition departments had to overhaul their food preparation and menus to provide the sheer volume of meals served at one time. School nutrition directors reported that they used a variety of meal options, most commonly shelf-stable meals and entrées or side dishes that could be reheated at home. Some continued to serve hot meals, and others provided bulk food such as gallons of milk or loaves of bread. Schools often included reheating instructions and recipe ideas for at-home preparation of school meals. Some districts even put together meal kits with ingredients and instructions for preparing multiple meals.

School nutrition departments also had to rethink their staffing models, altering when, where, and for how long staff worked. Many districts provided hazard pay to their employees, often using the federal funding provided by the March and December 2020 relief bills. Operations were

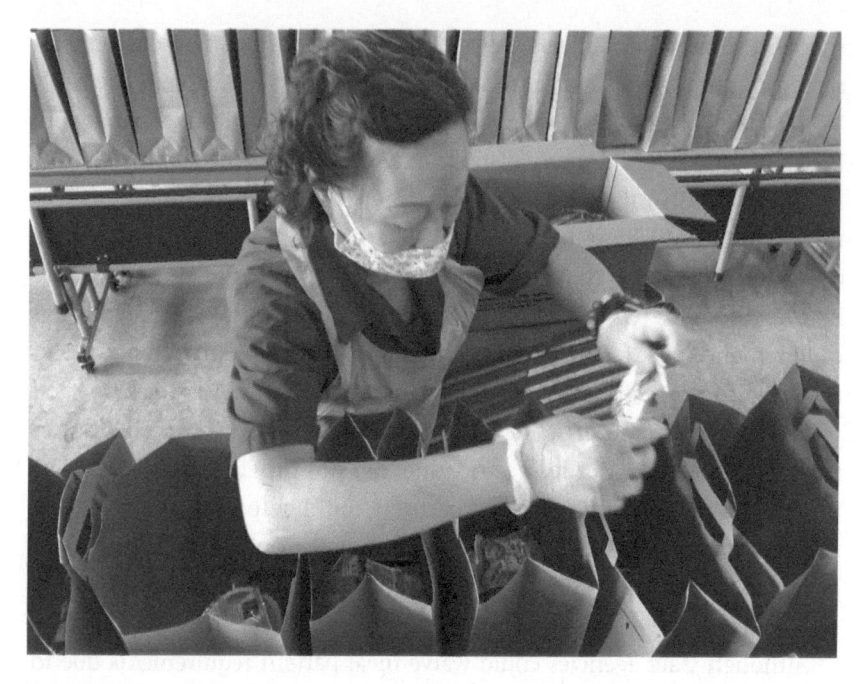

7.1 School nutrition staff prepare bags of "grab-and-go" meals for children in San Francisco. Credit: San Francisco Unified School District.

sometimes hampered by a staffing shortage with staff furloughed, quarantined, or unable to come to work because they had to care for young children whose daycare or school was closed. Others did not feel comfortable coming to work because they were at risk due to age, underlying medical conditions, or had family members who were at high risk for severe illness due to COVID-19. As a result, many schools relied on community volunteers or school staff who could assist with meal distribution.

Employees who were furloughed or unable to work due to these circumstances qualified for up to twelve weeks of paid leave as part of the Families First Coronavirus Response Act (FFCRA), which was passed in March 2020 but expired in December 2020. Any employee who could not work beyond that time had to apply for leave under the Family Medical Leave Act (FMLA). This allowed for an additional twelve weeks of unpaid, job-protected leave. For many that meant that this protection expired before access to coronavirus vaccines. For school district employees, their future employment status would be dependent on collective bargaining agreements and state laws. In California, Governor Newsom made state funding commitments to districts with the condition that they not lay off any employees, which included food service departments.

School districts responded to disrupted school meal service with innovative strategies to safely continue to provide meals by changing when, where, and how meals could be accessed. This could not have been accomplished without the dedicated school nutrition staff who stepped up to serve children in a time of crisis. By the end of April 2020, schools were using four primary meal service models: walk-up distribution, drive-thru or curbside distribution, home delivery, or delivery via school bus routes. In surveys of school nutrition directors, drive-thru or curbside distribution was the most common model used, followed by walk-up distribution.[12]

Many schools employed multiple models to reach diverse student populations. To ensure that students and their families knew how to access meals, school districts often posted maps of meal sites and service hours online and used social media to communicate service changes, holiday schedules, and menus. School districts also relied on media outlets and elected officials to share information about the availability of school meals. Nonprofit organizations ran hotlines, texting services, or meal-finder websites that helped connect families with school meals.[13]

WALK-UP, DRIVE-THRU, AND CURBSIDE DELIVERY

Virtually overnight after school buildings closed, even before many of the program waivers were in place, schools began distributing meals to students outside school buildings. While drive-thru and curbside models were most common across the country, urban school districts were more likely to implement walk-up models than rural or suburban schools. Outside distribution allowed for social distancing among staff, volunteers, and families but also posed challenges. Schools had to implement creative solutions for moving food from the cafeteria to outdoor settings, establish food safety protocols, and determine how to package meals so that families could easily carry them away. Staff in some districts faced inclement weather, serving in the rain, snow, heat, or poor air quality due to wildfires. At the same time, school nutrition directors had to ensure their staff could continue to work safely. Schools scrambled to secure masks and other PPE, and school cafeterias and gymnasiums became home to enormous meal packaging operations where staff could follow social distancing guidelines. Many schools implemented other procedures to minimize the risk of contracting the virus, such as placing meals in the trunk of a car or installing plexiglass barriers and serving meals through a small window. Despite these efforts, the limited supply of PPE and a myriad of infrastructure challenges made it difficult for some school nutrition departments to follow recommended safety protocols, putting their staff at risk.

Every school district that opted to continue serving school meals was tasked with figuring out how to do so in their communities. The San Francisco Unified School District was able to pivot from the cafeteria to grab-and-go meals quickly in large part due to an existing partnership with a meal vendor that was well suited for this model. Before the pandemic, SFUSD had contracted with Revolution Foods, a school meal vendor that prepares individually wrapped meals in a San Lorenzo, California, facility and delivers them to schools daily. During the 2018–2019 school year, 114 out of 136 schools served Revolution Foods meals. These school kitchen facilities included only warming ovens to heat meals and refrigerators to store milk. Other schools with additional kitchen equipment were able to freshly prepare school meals before the pandemic. The existing partnership with Revolution Foods allowed SFUSD to continue serving the same meals via grab-and-go bags with an at-home heating guide included. Parents remarked that their children seemed to benefit from the routine of walking to pick up meals at school, seeing the familiar faces of staff each week, and eating the same meals they had grown accustomed to at school.

Each grab-and-go bag consisted of multiple days' worth of meals, including breakfast, lunch, supper, fresh fruits and vegetables, and milk. To reduce packaging and offer local California produce, the district opted to include whole fruits and vegetables. This helped SFUSD not just feed families but also continue to follow the Good Food Purchasing Program. In 2016, SFUSD became the second school district in the country to adopt this framework, which directs buying power toward suppliers that value five interconnected domains: local economies, environmental sustainability, workforce, animal welfare, and nutrition. By purchasing from local small businesses, SFUSD stayed committed to the health and equity of students and the food system. The district distributed locally grown strawberries, melons, plums, cucumbers, and even pumpkins. Recipes, preparation videos, and nutritional information were shared on social media to provide families with ideas for how to prepare the produce at home.

Despite the limits of the district's kitchen facilities and staffing, SFUSD was able to expand its footprint by leveraging community-based organizations as additional distribution sites. By mapping the address data of SFUSD students eligible for free or reduced-price school meals, the district was able to strategically place additional grab-and-go meal sites at community-based organizations that could serve children with the greatest need. Revolution Foods delivered food to the community-based organizations, and the organization's volunteers packed and distributed bags of school meals.

Hope Williams, a family liaison at SFUSD and eleven-year resident of Treasure Island, a small island off San Francisco with a population of three thousand, advocated for an SFUSD meal site to serve the Treasure Island community. The district partnered with the Ship Shape Community Center to open a site on the island staffed by community volunteers. She said, "Without this program, at least 300 children, including preschoolers, would go without meals. Children would go hungry, and families would struggle to feed their children. It has been a vital resource for parents. I don't know if they could make it through COVID recovery without it. This program shows a commitment that their voices are being heard." Williams also coordinated with families to deliver meals directly to their homes.

BUS ROUTES

In addition to serving meals at school sites, some districts provided meal delivery along school bus routes. Surveys suggest that approximately 30–40 percent of schools used this method to some degree, although it was not typically the primary model employed.[14] Rural districts, which often serve fewer students spread over a large geographical area, were more likely to serve along bus routes than urban schools. For example, Grandview School District in the Yakima Valley, Washington, delivered meals along bus routes every day to maintain regular interactions with students and to provide fresh food to families who often did not have refrigeration or storage space to accommodate bulk meal delivery. Other districts supplemented school pick-up models with bus delivery to reach students who were not able to access meal sites. The DeKalb County School District in metro Atlanta began serving meals via school bus after receiving calls from parents reporting that they did not have transportation to pick up meals.

Schools often relied on volunteers or reassigned school staff to serve meals along bus routes. Teachers and aides at Morgan County Schools in eastern Tennessee helped school nutrition staff pack meals and rode buses to help hand out food to students every day. Commerce City Schools in Georgia staffed bus routes with volunteers, allowing school nutrition staff to focus on meal preparation.

HOME DELIVERY

For most school districts, home delivery was not the primary method for meal service, but supplemented other models. Schools in rural districts and small towns were more likely to deliver directly to students' homes than schools in urban and suburban areas. In the Necedah Area School District in rural Wisconsin, staff felt that home delivery was the only option to reach students, as many families lacked transportation. Social workers at Wake County Public Schools in North Carolina delivered meals to hotels serving as temporary housing for families. In New York City, a partnership with the online food delivery platform DoorDash brought meals to medically fragile students and students who lacked the mobility to access meals at the distribution centers.[15]

Home delivery was typically a more targeted approach than distributing meals along bus routes, serving a subset of students and their families. Some school districts reached out to their community to determine who would most benefit from home meal delivery. Students attending Ithaca School Districts in New York could fill out a form each week requesting meal delivery.[16] Williamsburg Community Food District in Iowa surveyed families weekly to determine which families needed meals delivered.[17] In San Francisco, home delivery was used to serve students with disabilities and special dietary needs—a population that could become especially vulnerable to food insecurity during a crisis as special diet ingredients become more expensive or harder to source.

Five months before the pandemic hit San Francisco, SFUSD had opened its first full cooking kitchen, the McAteer Culinary Center. This new facility, complete with a culinary team, cooking equipment, and allergen-free prep spaces, provided the opportunity to prepare special meals for these students. Staff planned menus according to each dietary need, prepared food in the new facility, and packed five days' worth of meals in boxes labeled for each student. Boxes were delivered to each student's home weekly. Because student address data could not be shared with an outside vendor or volunteers, SFUSD employees volunteered as delivery drivers, and SFUSD transportation staff (trained to create bus routes) provided driving routes from March to December 2020. In January 2021, after months of preparation, the district began using an outside vendor, Food Connect, to manage meal delivery and logistics. This allowed SFUSD to expand home delivery to serve more students. Students without special dietary needs were provided with meal boxes prepacked by Revolution Foods, while staff at the McAteer Culinary Center continued to prepare meal boxes for students with special dietary needs.

In addition to providing meals, home delivery offered an opportunity for school staff to visit students, assess how they were coping with the crisis, and identify other support needed. Staff at Williamsburg Schools in eastern Iowa used home delivery as an opportunity to check on students and relay any concerns to school administrators. Similarly, the child nutrition director of Pleasants County Schools in West Virginia trained her staff and a group of volunteers to conduct socially distant home visits, "the porch visit," during meal delivery.[18]

PAIRING MEALS WITH OTHER ESSENTIAL GOODS

As food insecurity and unemployment continued to sharply rise in the spring of 2020, school nutrition directors sought to expand meal service to family members or supplement meals with other critical supplies. As a trusted space for the community, schools became access points for families to address other needs. Although federal school nutrition programs only provide reimbursements for meals served to children eighteen and under, schools forged strategic partnerships and secured additional funds to expand their service to family members. For example, nonprofit organizations Martha's Table and DC Central Kitchen partnered with D.C. Public Schools to offer grocery distribution at meal sites. New York City schools leveraged

Federal Emergency Management Agency (FEMA) funding to offer free meals to adults regardless of whether they had children.[19] Oakland Unified School District partnered with the Alameda County Community Food Bank to distribute bags of groceries at schools where adults were picking up school meals. School meal sites also provided diapers, feminine hygiene products, pet food, children's books, art supplies, plants, homework packets, and promotional materials for the 2020 Census.[20]

SFSUD partnered with its local food bank to distribute produce and pantry items during school meal pickup. A local nonprofit distributed bags of free children's books. School nurses distributed thermometers for families to track coronavirus symptoms and free dental kits for children. City agencies provided census outreach, on-site voter registration, and hospice information for elderly family members. The SFUSD enrollment office was also able to utilize the grab-and-go sites during the district's open enrollment period. The point-of-sale system at each site was set up to alert school nutrition staff to provide an enrollment packet to students who had not yet completed the enrollment process for the next school year.

PROMOTING FREE MEAL SITES

FALL 2020: PROVIDING SCHOOL MEALS DURING HYBRID LEARNING

The start of the 2020–2021 school year brought a host of new challenges to school nutrition departments. Whereas nearly every public school had closed in spring 2020, school districts started the next school year with a variety of in-person, virtual, and hybrid learning models that often changed throughout the school year in response to changing rates of community infection, contracts with teachers' unions, political pressure, and local sentiment. The number of districts operating full in-person learning decreased throughout the fall as COVID-19 cases increased, but districts began to move to in-person learning again in the spring. By March 29, 2021, 51 percent of public school districts in the United States were offering hybrid learning, 42 percent were providing in-person learning (though students could opt out), and 7 percent remained fully remote. Throughout the school year, the most common model across districts was hybrid learning. Decisions were made at the local level, and it was not uncommon for schools within the same district to employ different models.[21]

For students in full- or part-time distance learning, school nutrition departments continued to provide meals through many of the delivery and distribution models described previously. But school nutrition departments also had to develop new staffing and service models to accommodate hybrid models of at-school and at-home learning. And no matter where students were attending school, staff had to implement social distancing and safety protocols that altered the way they served school meals.

The experience of Burke County Public Schools in rural Georgia illustrates the complexities that many schools across the country faced. During the spring and summer of 2020, Burke County school nutrition staff delivered breakfast, lunch, and supper every weekday at nine hundred bus stops along thirty bus routes. When school buildings reopened in the fall, half of the students opted to remain in distance learning, and half opted to participate in hybrid learning. The students in hybrid learning were divided into two groups: group A attended school on Mondays and Wednesdays, and group B attended on Tuesdays and Thursdays. All students participated virtually on Fridays. The school nutrition department established a new schedule, menu, and serving model. Students who attended in-person received a hot breakfast and lunch at school and received a bagged breakfast, lunch, and supper to have at home the following day. For students who were fully virtual, staff prepared boxes that included five days' worth of breakfasts, lunches, and dinners each Friday for families to pick up each week. In accordance with safety guidelines, students ate breakfast in their classrooms rather than the cafeteria. For lunch, half of the students ate lunch in the cafeteria while half ate in the classrooms. Staff delivered meals to classrooms on newly purchased carts, and teachers distributed milk.[22] Students who ate in their classroom had the same menus as those eating in the cafeteria.

ONGOING POLICY RESPONSE

School nutrition professionals were hailed as heroes by the media and graced the April 2020 cover of *Time* magazine, an edition dedicated to essential workers keeping the economy afloat. Some school nutrition directors reported closer communication with superintendents and inclusion in back-to-school planning for the first time. School nutrition staff across the county joined Facebook groups sharing best practices, advice, concerns, and success stories with each other. Operating during the crisis, however, took a toll on staff, as they worked long hours under stressful conditions, suffered changing schedules and reduced work hours, or were furloughed. More than a quarter of US school districts reported reducing work hours, and almost half reported reassigning staff to different roles or work sites.[23]

Despite helpful waivers from the USDA and enormous efforts on behalf of school nutrition staff across the country, schools served far fewer meals during the pandemic than before. Between March and April 2020, school closures caused a drop of almost four hundred million meals served compared to the previous year. Schools served on average 30 percent fewer meals in the first nine months of the pandemic.[24] The loss of reimbursement from lower meal counts, lost revenue from catering and a la carte items, combined with the increased costs of PPE and the equipment and supplies needed to deliver, package, and prepare meals, has had an enormous impact on school nutrition budgets. In May 2020, the Urban School Food Alliance, an association of twelve school districts in large urban areas, estimated their districts were losing $38.9 million in revenue each week.[25] An analysis of data from March through November 2020 indicates that school nutrition revenue was down more than $2.1 billion compared to the same period in 2019.[26]

After a year of the pandemic, it became clear that many of the meal programs and flexibilities needed to continue to meet the needs of students and their families. In April 2021, the USDA extended universal free school meals through the 2021–2022 school year. In March 2021, the American Recovery Act extended P-EBT to be available to children during both school and summer months during the public health emergency, and in August 2021, the USDA released guidance for issuing P-EBT during the 2021–2022 school year. In December 2021, the Biden-Harris administration provided up to $1.5 billion to states and school districts to support school meal program operators with the challenges of supply chain disruptions.

In the pandemic's third year, although most school operations have stabilized, school meal programs continue to struggle with unprecedented challenges. School nutrition departments face ongoing supply chain disruptions, soaring food costs due to rising inflation, and sustained staffing shortages.[27] In June 2022, Congress passed the Keep Kids Fed Act of 2022, which increased federal reimbursements for school meals and extended no-cost waivers including flexibilities for schools unable to meet nutrition standards due to supply chain disruptions. President Biden followed by announcing that the USDA would provide nearly $1 billion in funding to schools to support the purchase of American-grown foods for school meal programs. However, the pandemic policy of serving all students, regardless of eligibility, free school meals ended in June 2022.

For the 2022–2023 school year, five states implemented universal school meals to continue providing free meals despite the end of the federal policy. California and Maine passed permanent legislation, while Massachusetts, Nevada, and Vermont passed legislation permitting the policy for one school year. In November 2022, Colorado became the third state to pass permanent legislation via a ballot measure. While a state-by-state approach will not improve nutrition equity for all students in the US, these state campaigns showcase the potential of universal school meals and provide momentum to achieve this policy nationwide.

CONCLUSION

Throughout the coronavirus pandemic, school and pandemic meals have continued to play a vital role in combating child hunger and stabilizing families, a role that is expected to continue to grow. In September 2022, the Biden-Harris administration hosted the first White House Conference on Hunger, Nutrition, and Health in more than fifty years following the release of a national strategy. A key component of the administration's national strategy to end hunger is advancing a pathway to free healthy school meals for all: "A 'healthy meals for all' approach would reorient the school meal programs from an ancillary service to an integral component of the school day. Elevating school meals is a key strategy to improve our nation's health and would benefit all children—importantly, it would significantly strengthen the school meals program for those children who rely upon it the most."[28]

While school nutrition professionals already knew how crucial school meals were for their students, the coronavirus pandemic cast a spotlight on the critical role these programs play in supporting student health, well-being, and success. During a crisis, there is no "one-size-fits-all" approach to allowing schools to continue providing the meals that students rely on. Swift, flexible policies like those implemented during the coronavirus pandemic allowed schools to tailor their programs and ensured more students were fed. These lessons should influence future federal policy, recognizing the value of school meals and school nutrition professionals nationwide.

NOTES

1. San Francisco Unified School District, "San Francisco Unified Provides 1 Million Meals and Counting During COVID-19 Crisis," (May 15, 2020), last updated July 10, 2020, https://www.sfusd.edu/1-million-meals-and-counting.

2. Megan Lott, Lindsey Miller, Mary Story, and Kirsten Arm, *Rapid Health Impact Assessment on USDA Proposed Changes to School Nutrition Standards* (Durham, NC: Healthy Eating Research, 2020), https://healthyeatingresearch.org/wp-content/uploads/2020/03/her-hia-report-final-1.pdf.

3. Junxiu Liu et al., "Trends in Food Sources and Diet Quality among US Children and Adults, 2003–2018," *JAMA Network Open* 4, no. 4 (April 1, 2021), https://doi.org/10.1001/jamanetworkopen.2021.5262.

4. Food and Nutrition Service, "School Nutrition and Meal Cost Study," United States Department of Agriculture, April 2019, last modified October 19, 2021, https://www.fns.usda.gov/school-nutrition-and-meal-cost-study.

5. Food Research & Action Center (FRAC), "School Meals and Legislation and Funding by State," last modified February 2021, https://frac.org/wp-content/uploads/state_leg_table_scorecard.pdf.

6. Economic Research Service, "Child Nutrition Programs," United States Department of Agriculture, last modified August 3, 2022, https://www.ers.usda.gov/topics/food-nutrition-assistance/child-nutrition-programs/.

7. "The Coronavirus Spring: The Historic Closing of U.S. Schools (A Timeline)," *Education Week*, July 1, 2021, https://www.edweek.org/leadership/the-coronavirus-spring-the-historic-closing-of-u-s-schools-a-timeline/2020/07.

8. Food and Nutrition Service, "Child Nutrition Tables," United States Department of Agriculture, last modified April 14, 2023, https://www.fns.usda.gov/pd/child-nutrition-tables.

9. Elaine Waxman, Poonam Gupta, and Michael Karpman, "More Than One in Six Adults Were Food Insecure Two Months into the COVID-19 Recession," Urban Institute, July 18, 2020, https://www.urban.org/research/publication/more-one-six-adults-were-food-insecure-two-months-covid-19-recession.

10. Kone Consulting, "Pandemic EBT Implementation Documentation Project," Center on Budget and Policy Priorities & Food Research and Action Center, September 2020, https://www.cbpp.org/sites/default/files/atoms/files/10-7-20fa-kone.pdf.

11. No Kid Hungry | Center for Best Practices, "Back-to-School Meal Service Webinar: How Out-of-School Time Providers Are Supporting Schools & Communities," No Kid Hungry, September 24, 2020, http://bestpractices.nokidhungry.org/resource/back-school-meal-service-webinar-how-out-school-time-providers-are-supporting-schools.

12. No Kid Hungry | Center for Best Practices, "Innovations in Child Nutrition Programs During COVID-19 and Beyond," No Kid Hungry, 2020, http://bestpractices.nokidhungry.org/resource/innovations-child-nutrition-programs-during-covid-19-and-beyond.

13. Gabriella M. McLoughlin et al., "Feeding Students During COVID-19-Related School Closures: A Nationwide Assessment of Initial Responses," *Journal of Nutrition Education and Behavior* 52, no. 12 (December 2020): 1120–1130, https://doi.org/10.1016/j.jneb.2020.09.018; "Return to Learn Tracker (R2L)," 2021, https://www.returntolearntracker.net/.

14. School Nutrition Association, "Impact of COVID-19 on School Nutrition Programs: Part 2," https://schoolnutrition.org/uploadedFiles/11COVID-19/3_Webinar_Series_and_Other_Resources/COVID-19-Impact-on-School-Nutrition-Programs-Part2.pdf; No Kid Hungry | Center for Best Practices, "Feeding Kids During COVID-19: A Survey of Organizations Serving Kids," No Kid Hungry, 2020, http://bestpractices.nokidhungry.org/resource/feeding-kids-during-covid-19-survey-organizations-serving-kids.

15. Bettina Elias Sigel, "Door Dash Reaching NYC's Most Vulnerable Children, Plus More COVID School Meal Updates," *The Lunch Tray* (blog), March 26, 2020, https://thelunchtray.com/door-dash-reaching-nycs-most-vulnerable-children-plus-more-covid-school-meal-updates/.

16. WENY News, "Ithaca City School District Moves to Only Home Delivery for School," March 21, 2020, https://www.weny.com/story/41923808/ithaca-city-school-district-moves-to-only-home-delivery-for-school-meals.

17. No Kid Hungry | Center for Best Practices, "Innovations in Child Nutrition Programs During COVID-19 and Beyond."

18. No Kid Hungry | Center for Best Practices.

19. The City of New York, "Feeding New York: The Plan for Keeping Our City Fed During the COVID-19 Public Health Crisis," n.d., https://www1.nyc.gov/assets/home/downloads/pdf/reports/2020/Feeding-New-York.pdf.

20. Oakland Unified School District Fact Sheet, "Meals for Kids / Food Support / Food & Resource Distribution Fast Facts," accessed August 16, 2020, https://www.ousd.org/Page/http%3A%2F%2Fwww.ousd.org%2Fsite%2Fdefault.aspx%3FPageID%3D19434.

21. "Return to Learn Tracker (R2L)."

22. No Kid Hungry | Center for Best Practices, "Back-to-School Meal Service: Feeding Kids During the 2020–2021 School Year—Part 2," August 31, 2020, http://bestpractices.nokidhungry.org/webinars/back-school-meal-service-feeding-kids-during-2020-2021-school-year-part-2.

23. School Nutrition Association, "Impact of COVID-19 On School Nutrition Programs: Back to School 2020. A Summary of Survey Results," October 2020, https://schoolnutrition.org/uploadedFiles/6_News_Publications_and_Research/8_SNA

_Research/Impact-of-Covid-19-on-School-Nutrition-Programs-Back-to-School-2020.pdf.

24. Food and Nutrition Service, "November 2020 Keydata Report," United States Department of Agriculture, March 12, 2021, https://www.fns.usda.gov/data/november-2020-keydata-report.

25. Daphne Duret, "Coronavirus: School Lunch Programs Going Broke Because of Kids' Hunger," USA Today, May 31, 2020, https://www.usatoday.com/story/news/education/2020/05/31/coronavirus-school-lunch-programs-going-broke-because-kids-hunger/3101507001/.

26. School Nutrition Association, "School Nutrition Meals Served and Reimbursements During the COVID-19 Pandemic," June 2021, https://schoolnutrition.org/uploadedFiles/6_News_Publications_and_Research/8_SNA_Research/School-Nutrition-Meals-Served-and-Reimbursements-During-the-Pandemic-June2021-Data.pdf.

27. School Nutrition Association, School Nutrition Foundation, and No Kid Hungry, "Staying Afloat in a Perfect Storm," July 2022, https://schoolnutrition.org/wp-content/uploads/2022/07/Jul22-SupplyChainReport.pdf.

28. The White House, "Biden-Harris Administration National Strategy on Hunger, Nutrition, and Health," September 2022, https://www.whitehouse.gov/wp-content/uploads/2022/09/White-House-National-Strategy-on-Hunger-Nutrition-and-Health-FINAL.pdf.

III

STRUGGLING FOR JUST SCHOOL FOOD ECONOMIES

Jennifer E. Gaddis and Sarah A. Robert

The chapters in this section feature three countries—Brazil, India, and South Korea—that operate universal free school meal programs and use school food policy to create economic opportunities for marginalized groups in their societies. The authors provide examples of civil society organizations and grassroots policy protagonists who are demanding that the rights of children and farmers be respected and supported by a just school food system.

Chapter 8, "Civil Society Activism and Government Partnerships in India," invokes what political theorist Joan Tronto describes as "the larger structural questions of thinking about which institutions, people and practices should be used to accomplish concrete and real caring tasks" and to what ends.[1] From the Right to Food campaign, which helped secure Indian children's right to a free midday school meal, to current clashes over outsourcing school meal preparation, to powerful NGOs that manage large centralized kitchens, this chapter takes a critical look at how civil society organizations can help, and in some cases hinder, community self-determination over how school meals are provided. In doing so, it reveals the political tensions behind the seemingly simple question: Who should cook school meals and for whom?

The next three chapters shift the focus to another critical question: Who should produce the food and for what purpose? In many countries around the world, school meals are made with ingredients that travel through complex commodity chains spanning countries or even continents. This globalized corporate food system prioritizes "cheapness" as a central value, often to the detriment of students' health, workers' livelihoods, and the natural environment. However, schools that practice a different type of "values-based" sourcing are redirecting billions of public food dollars away from the corporate food system toward small- and midsize producers who emphasize ecological sustainability, fair labor standards, and healthy food access.[2]

In Brazil, national law requires schools to engage in values-based sourcing, but the impact is mediated by state- and local-level translations of policy and cultural practices within diverse community contexts. Chapter 9, "Cooperative and Small-Scale Farming through Brazil's National Procurement Standards," shows how the intended population of historically disadvantaged producers and agroecological farmers engage in policy protagonism with local school districts and school leaders to ensure that their fresh produce and farm products are on the plates of children in their communities.

Then, in chapter 10, "Agroecology and Feminist Praxis in Brazilian School Food Politics," we see that gender impacts the experience of producers who sell to the school meal programs and that changing procurement policies does not guarantee an end to gender coloniality of land use or patriarchal power relationships within household economies. This chapter also teaches us to recognize non-economic motivations to produce food for school meals by highlighting how feminist agroecologists prefigure the transformations in eating, learning, and relationships with the natural environment they aim to create and sustain.

Finally, chapter 11, "Direct Urban-Rural Supply Chains for South Korean Communities," traces the Seoul metropolitan government's development of the Urban-Rural Coexistence Meal Service Program, which reflects the city's decision to join the Milan Urban Food Policy Pact. Through this international agreement, more than 250 cities around the world have rejected the economic logic of cheapness as synonymous with public value. Instead, they are working to "develop sustainable food systems that are inclusive, resilient, safe and diverse, that provide healthy and affordable food to all people in a human rights-based framework, that minimize waste and conserve biodiversity while adapting to and mitigating impacts of climate change."[3] Taken together, these chapters present promising strategies for fostering *community economies* in which all people are able to not only survive but also thrive and invest in the future by caring for one another and for our shared environmental and cultural commons.[4]

NOTES

1. Joan C. Tronto, *Caring Democracy: Markets, Equality, and Justice* (New York and London: New York University Press, 2013), 139.

2. For more on values-based supply chains, see UC Sustainable Agriculture Research and Education Program (UC SAREP), "Value-Based Supply Chains," UC Division of Agriculture and Natural Resources, accessed July 15, 2020, https://sarep.ucdavis.edu/sustainable-ag/values-based-supply-chains.

3. Milan Urban Food Policy Pact, "Milan Urban Food Policy Pact," 2015, https://www.milanurbanfoodpolicypact.org/the-milan-pact/.

4. Community Economies, "Community Economies Research and Practice," accessed April 23, 2023, https://www.communityeconomies.org/about/community-economies-research-and-practice.

8

CIVIL SOCIETY ACTIVISM AND GOVERNMENT PARTNERSHIPS IN INDIA

Prerna Rana

The Indian Supreme Court (SC) ordered government and government-aided schools to provide cooked food to children in 2001. The following year, when the deadline for implementation had passed unheeded in multiple states, civil society groups across the country called for a day of action on April 9. People from more than one thousand villages and slums in over one hundred districts of nine states took part. In Jharkhand, a local group named Bharat Gyan Vigyan Samiti organized an awareness campaign in the weeks before what the group called "Dhanbad appeal." It consisted of wall paintings, posters, leaflets, and street plays.[1] As a form of direct action, policy protagonists including several civil society bodies like the *Panchayats* (grassroots body of governance)[2], *Gram Sabha* (village assembly),[3] teachers, and the public, prepared a "people's school meal." Later, on July 11, 2002, hundreds of students marched to the chief minister's residence to present him with a petition. As government inaction continued, the group mobilized to raise awareness on government policy around the school lunch program. In November 2003, they prepared another people's school meal, held a children's parliament, and organized a sit-in at the Secretariat (central government office). Owing to the persistent public campaign, the government finally took heed of the citizens' demands, and midday meals were introduced in government schools starting in December 2003. This campaign is an example of the constant struggle by grassroots civil society actors to operationalize existing legislation and make the school lunch program in India a reality.

The school lunch program of India, popularly known as the midday meal scheme (MDMS), is aimed at improving the daily nutritional intake and overall educational outcomes of children. The MDMS also plays a key role in achieving the collective objectives of the Right to Food campaign, a civil society initiative that started in 2001, and the Right to Education Act,[4] passed in 2009. The scheme covers children studying in classes 1–8 in government and government-aided schools, Special Training Centers (STCs), and *Madrasas* and *Maktabs* under the government education program *Samagra Shiksha*. According to government data, nearly 2.6 million cook-cum-helpers served 91.1 million school children in 2018–2019, making it the largest school lunch program in the world.[5]

Several assessments and evaluations of the program have been conducted over the years, showing positive outcomes in educational advancement, child nutrition, and equity.[6] The program has led to a notable increase in the enrollment of children in primary schools. According to a survey conducted by the Center for Equity Studies, there was a 14.5 percent increase in enrollment in class one.[7] The results were even better for girls. In most studies, girls' enrollment was much higher than the overall increase in enrollment. There are gender disparities in the education sector especially in more rural and remote regions of the country. The provision of midday meals at school is an extra incentive for parents to send their children, regardless of gender, to school every day—and it helps students stay for the full day, too. Before the midday meal program came into being, many children would leave for their homes during lunch break to eat at home, and some who lived a few kilometers from the school premises would not come back for the remainder of the school day.

As long as the menus offer the recommended variety, the nutritional and health impact of MDMS is also positive.[8] One study provides evidence that the daily nutrient intake of the children participating in MDMS increased notably, and for a cost as low as 3 cents per child per school day, the daily protein deficiency was reduced by 100 percent.[9] Providing cooked meals at school also reduces the problem of "classroom hunger," which manifests as lower levels of energy and lack of attentiveness because the body demands nourishment. When children are fed, they are not only more likely to stay in school for the full day but also more engaged and able to learn while they are there.[10]

While these studies focus largely on measurable outcomes, there is limited discussion in academic and public discourse of the politics required for the program to become a reality: the role of civil society actors, the voices of community members, the accountability of state machinery, as well as the underlying factors that drive the final outcomes. The MDMS, in its present form, is the result of the active involvement of various civil society actors who continue to play a key role in influencing school food policy. These actors exist in a complex ecosystem of school food politics, supporting each other and, at times, coming into conflict over how best to achieve the shared goal of food security.

A HISTORY OF CIVIL SOCIETY ORGANIZING

On August 15, 1995, the country launched the MDMS, officially called the National Programme of Nutritional Support to Primary Education (NP-NSPE). The aim of this scheme was to enhance enrollment, retention, and attendance as well as improve nutrition among children. The assistance provided by the central government was twofold. They were to provide one hundred grams of food grains per child per school day, free of cost, to children studying in classes 1–5 in all government, local body, and government-aided primary schools. They were also to provide a subsidy on transportation of food grains up to a maximum of Rs. 50 per quintal (per 100 kg). Two other major expenses, the cost of cooking and provision of essential infrastructure, were to be provided by the state government/local bodies. The cost of cooking was to include cost of ingredients, cost of fuel, and wages/remuneration payable to cooking personnel, whereas the infrastructure needed was a kitchen-cum-store,[11] adequate water supply, cooking devices, utensils, and containers for storage. The state governments were given two years to put these systems in place to provide cooked meals. However, even after six years, many states were only providing students with the dry government rations to be cooked at home, rather than using them as part of a cooked meal service in school as required.

Consequently, on November 28, 2001, the Supreme Court (the top judicial body of the country) directed the state governments and union territories to implement the midday meal scheme in all government and government-assisted primary schools by providing prepared meals constituting a minimum of three hundred calories and eight to twelve grams of protein for every day of school for a minimum of two hundred days. The cooked meals were to be provided within three months, by February 28, 2002, in half of the districts of the state (based on poverty levels), with cooked meals provision extended to the rest of the state within another three months, by May 28, 2002.[12]

The 2001 Supreme Court order that directed significant nationwide changes to the midday meal scheme was brought about by the active push from civil society organizations involved in the Right to Food (RTF) campaign. The RTF campaign advocates for the recognition of the right to food as a necessary component to fulfill the fundamental right to life enshrined in Article 21 of the Indian Constitution.[13] As part of this campaign, in 2001, the People's Union for Civil Liberties (Rajasthan) approached the Supreme Court with public interest litigation regarding the "right to food." The catalyst for this litigation was the occurrence of starvation deaths in the state of Rajasthan.[14] These deaths occurred despite availability of excess grains in government *godowns* (government storage units), an event that highlighted the accessibility issues in food security schemes due to the country's inefficient food distribution system. This litigation was the start of an ongoing movement to improve government policies and ensure compliance by state and local governments through judicial intervention.

Even after the 2001 Supreme Court order and continued civil society pressure, some states failed to provide cooked meals to students. When the February 28, 2002, SC deadline for implementation of midday meals in half of the districts in states had passed unheeded, civil society groups continued their efforts. They organized an April 9 day of action that included midday meals prepared not just in the state of Jharkhand but in communities across the country, as a form of public demonstration. The meals were prepared at strategic locations to make a stronger statement: for example, in front of the tax collector's offices, the chief minister's residence, village schools, and public parks. In Patna, five thousand students participated in the midday meal prepared at Miller school. And in Bhopal, four hundred students took their meal to the chief minister's residence and demanded the implementation of the lunch program.[15] Apart from the central event held in Patna, all districts of Bihar participated in this campaign. In Dhanbad district, sixty villages participated. An important feature was that in many places, events were organized by the Gram Sabhas themselves to demand answers from the respective district governments. There were also other forms of mass demonstrations. Children in Bangalore protested by standing with empty plates at the prominent MG Road.

In 2002, the Supreme Court issued an interim order that explicitly defined the responsibilities of people and institutions to implement the SC orders regarding the MDMS, with specific lines of accountability and grievance procedures for various levels of governance. The court appointed two commissioners to monitor the implementation of these orders and empowered them to inquire into any violations of the interim orders and demand redress.[16]

An interim court order dated May 2, 2003, cited the states of Bihar, Jharkhand, and Uttar Pradesh for failing to even start the lunch program in any capacity. In a 2004 court order, the provisions of the 2001 court order were reiterated, and all states not implementing the scheme were given a final deadline of September 1, 2004, to fully implement the lunch program in all eligible schools. There were additional directives in this court order: schools in drought-affected regions were to provide midday meals even during summer vacations; hiring preference for cooks and helpers was to be given to Dalits, Scheduled Castes, and Scheduled Tribes; and it was suggested that the scheme be extended to cover students up to the tenth standard.

In 2005, the court-appointed commissioners prepared a report recommending that chief secretaries of the states that were not fully implementing the midday meal scheme be issued a notice that contempt proceedings could be instituted against them. The report further urged them to develop a time frame for full coverage of every child in every school and explain why they had failed to comply with the Supreme Court orders thus far. Several warnings later and with the consistent efforts of a nationwide civil society campaign, the coverage of MDMS grew and is now near universal, with many states and union territories registering a coverage of more than

90 percent.[17] The efforts of civil society activists in mobilizing public action coupled with routine judicial intervention ensured that state and central government stayed accountable to and upheld their responsibility to the citizens.

Civil society was involved in events that put pressure not just on state authorities to implement food security schemes but on district and local authorities as well. In Uttar Pradesh, Allahabad district and Jalaun district witnessed active community engagement. In forty villages around Jalaun, community members served midday meals to children and shared posters and pamphlets. A delegation met with the *tehsildar* (land revenue officer) with their demand to implement the scheme. The tehsildar expressed ignorance about the SC order in the absence of communication from the district authorities. On the other hand, in Shakargarh (Allahabad district), a public hearing on the right to food was organized. It was attended by laborers from neighboring villages as well as government functionaries from the district administration. The hearing uncovered several cases of corruption in food-related programs due to which poor households had not received food grains for years. The participants passed a resolution at the end of the hearing that included a list of demands to the district administration. One of these demands was the immediate introduction of the midday meal scheme in all primary schools.

These demonstrations were highlighted extensively in the media with press conferences being held in nine states that had regional coverage as well to reach a wider audience. This was complemented with the translation of the Supreme Court order in various regional languages and its distribution to engage a wider section of the community in dialogue. In 2005, the RTF campaign came out with a "Tools for Action" primer on the Supreme Court orders related to food security schemes. A section titled "What We Can Do" detailed ways in which the public could be involved in creating pressure necessary to implement the SC orders. The primer emphasized the importance of public engagement at various levels, from the villages up to the national capital, and the role that every individual can play in their capacity whether they are teachers, activists, parents, or simply concerned citizens. The primer provides several suggestions for public action like mobilizing local community institutions to conduct

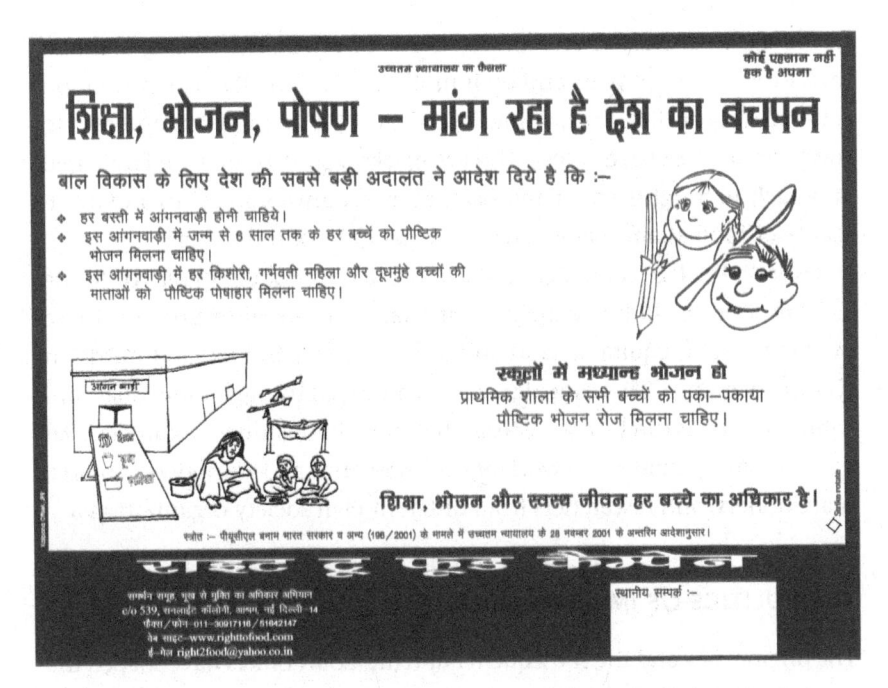

8.1 A poster prepared by the RTF campaign to create awareness. Credit: Right to Food campaign.

social audits or check corruption in government programs; filing a complaint with local authorities or making an appeal to the commissioners of the SC regarding shoddy implementation or non-implementation of the MDMS; seeking legal redress by filing an interim application in the SC or a petition in the High Court; or the role of media and research in advocacy.

Figure 8.1 specifically highlights the midday meal scheme and the right of children to a meal in their schools. The title of the poster translates to "The Country's Childhood Demands—Education, Food, Nutrition." It is one of many posters created about various issues like deaths by starvation, legal rights pertaining to employment guarantee, subsidized food grain provision, and so on. These posters were to be used in public spaces to spread awareness of the rights granted to all citizens and action that can be taken by them if these rights are not being met.

The campaign led to the National Food Security Act (2013), which includes several government programs like the Midday Meal Scheme, the Integrated Child Development Services scheme (covering children under the age of six years and their mothers), and the Public Distribution Scheme (responsible for distribution of essential food grains and fuel to the poor at subsidized rates). The act marks a shift from a welfare-based approach to a rights-based approach that recognizes access to and availability of food at affordable rates as a legal right of individuals.

Overall, the RTF campaign has taken up a range of topics related to the right to food, including employment guarantee, social security for those unable to work, equitable land and forest rights, and food and nutrition security demands. The campaign has been funded through individual contributions and is run by a secretariat that mostly constitutes volunteers. An advisory group guides the work of the secretariat and comprises activists, practitioners, and researchers from different civil society organizations.

THE POLITICS OF IMPLEMENTING THE MIDDAY MEAL SCHEME

The original law and the subsequent Supreme Court orders have shaped the requirements of the MDMS as it exists today. The midday meals are jointly funded by the central government and the respective state governments. The central government is responsible for providing food grains free of cost as well as transport allowance, and it also contributes Rs. 2.98 (US$ 0.041) and Rs. 4.47 (US$ 0.061) per child per day for cooking costs for primary and upper primary levels, respectively.[18] The central and state governments are supposed to share the cooking costs in a 60:40 ratio according to government guidelines, and the Ministry of Human Resource Development has revised the cooking cost frequently in the last few years. The cooking cost fixed by the government presents a minimum mandatory contribution from state governments, but states are free to contribute more if they so desire, and there are states who are contributing more than the minimum contribution. The difference in state contribution is reflected in the quality of meals that are provided in schools. Activists have noted that richer states like Tamil Nadu, Kerala, and Telangana are implementing the scheme well, but poorer states like Bihar and Uttar Pradesh continue to struggle and have not really made the scheme a political priority.[19]

The earliest guidelines on the midday meal program that came out in 2006 emphasized that the responsibility of cooking supply of the cooked midday meal should be assigned to local women's mother's self-help groups, local youth clubs, voluntary organizations, or personnel engaged directly by local bodies like the Parent Teacher Association (PTA), School Management and Development Committee, Village Education Committee (VEC), or Gram Panchayats (village councils).[20] The guidelines introduced the idea of centralized kitchens in urban areas that can provide cooked meals to a cluster of schools. And the cook and helper should be appointed with full community participation. Parents and other villagers are meant to elect VECs and PTAs, which then choose cooks and helpers from the community. The Supreme Court order dated April 20, 2004, states that preference should be given to "Dalits, Scheduled Castes and Scheduled Tribes" This was an attempt to mainstream vulnerable populations by providing them employment in a nationwide government program.

The MDMS has the potential to overcome deeply ingrained cultural prejudices and differences that are threats to communal living. It offers an opportunity to not only ensure better nutritional and educational outcomes for children but also to promote socialization by bringing children together to share a meal irrespective of their caste and class differences. Unfortunately, the program has had mixed success eroding these caste barriers. While there are cases in which communities have been able to effectively overcome their prejudices toward lower-caste individuals and have let go of discriminatory practices like keeping separate utensils, there are also cases where upper-caste parents adamantly resist the appointment of lower-caste cooks.[21] In the states of Chhattisgarh and Rajasthan, for example, most of the appointed lower-caste cooks were working in schools with no upper-caste children.[22]

Subtle forms of caste prejudice and social discrimination are prevalent. For example, upper-caste members have resisted the scheme because it encourages their children eating meals with children from lower-caste households. In such cases, they either send prepacked lunch with their children or children return home during lunch time to eat at home. Also, in a 2014 study across seven Indian states, it was found that Dalit children were given a significantly less amount of food compared to upper-caste children.[23] This discrimination was reinforced by differential treatment meted out to Dalit children in the form of separate seating for meals, separate meals being cooked and served for Dalit and non-Dalit children, higher-caste children eating first, and so on. The consequences of these discriminatory practices are that Dalit children were reportedly uninterested in attending school due to the discrimination they faced, and their attendance was irregular. These findings highlight that failing to create inclusive spaces for all children prevents the achievement of the midday meal scheme's objective of increasing educational outcomes for all. Such studies also shed light on the nuanced ways in which we need to understand the outcomes of government programs and policies. While several quantitative surveys have shown an overall increase in the enrollment and attendance of students due to the midday meal being offered at schools, focusing on the politics of implementation reveals the finer sociocultural context, which aids in expanding our knowledge by looking beyond simple metrics to personal experiences of individuals.

CURRENT ROLE OF CIVIL SOCIETY ORGANIZATIONS

With the enactment of the Right to Food Act and the rollout of the midday meal scheme nationwide, civil society organizations (CSOs) have changed the focus of their organizing to ensure that nutritious, hygienic, and timely meals are provided for all children, without exception. Nongovernmental organizations (NGOs) have been stepping in to fulfill the role of service delivery, and the government has encouraged their involvement to implement MDMS effectively and with reduced costs than might otherwise be possible. Yet there has been much confusion and indecisiveness regarding the role of NGOs and privatized bodies in preparing and distributing midday meals.

In 2010, the revised guidelines reiterated the importance of community participation in the effective implementation and monitoring of the midday meals at schools and the desirability of local community institutions being engaged to increase community ownership. There was also a more detailed mention of centralized kitchens that can be operated by NGOs under the public private partnership model. The role of centralized kitchens was deemed necessary for urban-area schools that might be struggling with space constraints.[24] In 2014, the Ministry of Human Resource Development asked states to not involve NGOs in implementing the midday meal scheme as it was anticipated that the involvement of NGOs would reduce opportunity for community participation.[25] While an NGO's mission can revolve around community development, in many cases, NGOs are not truly representative of the communities they work with. Many NGOs are not based in local communities and have development professionals, who are community outsiders, handle the operation side of community work. This setup hinders authentic community participation in which community members are at the forefront of planning, leading, and implementing action. According to the midday meal rules that came out in 2015, the central government restricted the role of NGOs more decisively by barring state governments from engaging NGOs in preparing meals in rural areas. In urban areas, NGOs were to be allowed to operate centralized kitchens only when schools did not have adequate kitchen and cooking components.[26]

The involvement of local CSOs/NGOs might be helpful to combat issues of hygiene. One of the major critiques of the midday meal scheme has been the quality of food being served at schools due to poor sanitation and hygiene conditions in school kitchens. There have been several reported instances of food poisoning and unpalatable food being served, leading to children being hospitalized and, in some cases, even dying. Having a centralized kitchen run by a CSO or NGO can in part help address this problem for schools that do not have adequate infrastructure for the preparation of meals in hygienic and healthy circumstances. According to revised guidelines that came out in 2017, states should constitute a committee to select CSOs or NGOs to supply cooked midday meals on a "no-profit" basis. The operation of the centralized kitchens as opposed to school-level kitchens will be entrusted to the selected CSO/NGO under the public private partnership model and only to such an organization that has "local presence and familiarity with the needs and culture of the State." This partnership will be formalized through a memorandum of understanding between the CSO/NGO and the respective state that clearly delineates the duration of the agreement, an evaluation system, stipulated food and nutrition norms, monthly reporting system, and so on.

At present, Akshaya Patra Foundation (APF), a philanthropic organization, runs centralized kitchens in twelve states and two union territories in the country that provide midday meals to more than nineteen thousand schools and approximately 1.8 million children.[27] APF's centralized kitchens have a sophisticated infrastructure that combines innovative technology and efficient management to prepare hygienic meals every day to be supplied to various schools. The preprocessing of vegetables, rice, and lentils is done with special attention to the cleaning process. Although much of the cooking process is automated and does not require close human contact, for whatever stages that workers come in touch with the food, very strict hygiene standards are in place with everyone dressed in clean overalls, gloves, head caps, and special footwear. In remote areas that APF is unable to reach directly, decentralized kitchens are set up and local women are trained as cooks.[28] These kitchens follow the hygiene and nutrition norms as set down by APF to ensure that there are no inconsistencies in the quality of food being served at schools. The food prepared in the centralized kitchen is packaged in large steel containers that are then dispatched to the schools through APF's vehicles every morning. Food is served to the children directly from these containers to their personal eating utensils, which are provided by the school.

The downside of the centralized kitchen model is that it has entrusted the implementation of midday meals to bigger foundations, thereby reducing community participation at the local level in decentralized school kitchens. The latest guidelines that came out in 2017 instructed that the centralized kitchen model can be used to supply cooked meals to identified rural areas as well. Still, community participation continues to be a key component of the midday meal program.[29] States are encouraged to roll out mass mobilization campaigns to involve students' mothers by giving preference to women for the roles of cook-cum-helpers, involving mothers in the supervision of the preparation of the meals, and including mothers in supervision committees to monitor the implementation of the program. While states are expected to take these steps, the centralized kitchen model can reduce opportunities for community participation with community members not being able to oversee the operations that do not take place in their local surroundings.

There is growing discontent among community members with the expansion of the centralized kitchen model. Some state governments and civil society actors prefer awarding MDMS contracts to grassroots organizations instead of large NGOs like APF. In Odisha, for example, the state government has consistently entrusted meal preparation to women's self-help groups (SHGs), which are made up of local women whose children might be studying in the schools for which they are preparing midday meals. In 2008, women's SHGs ran the MDMS in more than thirty-two thousand primary schools.[30] In 2019, the Odisha state government approved the guidelines for management of the scheme in schools by women's SHGs, thereby formalizing the role of grassroots civil society organizations in implementing the midday meal.[31]

Meanwhile, a growing number of women workers and members of left-leaning trade unions are protesting the privatization of the MDMS. In 2019, when the state of Assam outsourced the cooking and distribution of meals to nonprofit organizations in seventeen districts, midday meal workers protested this decision because they feared they might lose their jobs and believed that local school-based kitchens were a better alternative in rural areas.[32] Their apprehension is fueled by the fact that when APF was first contracted in Assam in 2010, they allegedly reduced the honorarium of existing cooks and helpers from Rs. 1,000 to Rs. 500.[33] Since government guidelines explain that the cook-cum-helpers are expected to perform all activities related to cooking, serving, and washing the utensils, in the event of a centralized kitchen preparing the meals, the honorarium of the existing cooks gets reduced since they are serving pre-cooked meals.[34] Monjura Begum, a midday meal worker in Morigaon district, shares that contracting the lunch program to bigger foundations can never replace the close relationship between the children and local community workers:

They (the children) lovingly call me *baideo* (elder sister) though I am not their teacher, and it is this respect and love that makes my back breaking work easy. Will any foundation be able to provide fresh and hot food like I do? Do they know their names or care for their likes/dislikes? The Government says we will not lose our jobs, but we will be kept only for food distribution. There will be a cut on our already meager pay, 500 rupees will go to the foundation and 500 rupees will be paid to us. But my main concern is for the children, what will be the food value in a meal cooked at dawn? And will my children eat the food they provide? Here, we use fresh vegetables sourced from the Matri Gut (mother's club) grown by the mothers in their kitchen gardens.[35]

Another recent criticism of the food prepared by APF is related to the religious beliefs of its parent organization, the International Society of Krishna Consciousness. APF does not include onion, garlic, and eggs in the meals it prepares, citing religious reasons.[36] In Karnataka, several activists including those from the RTF campaign and the Jan Swasthya Abhiyan (People's Health Movement) have criticized this policy of the foundation stating that "religious diktats cannot supersede the application of established principles of the right to food to midday meal schemes."[37] During a field visit in 2018, the Karnataka Food Commission found that children were not enjoying their meals and were eating less than they should as they found the food unpalatable. It was concluded that the exclusion of garlic and onion altered the taste of the meals being prepared, thereby not appealing to the students' taste buds. On being questioned by the state government on not following the state-prescribed menu, APF submitted necessary documents to prove that they are meeting all the nutritional requirements through their prepared meals and providing adequate substitutes for onion and garlic. The government sent these documents for review to the National Institute of Nutrition (NIN) and the Central Food Technological Research Institute (CFTRI). The NIN approved the APF's menu stating that it met the nutritional guidelines set forth by the Ministry of Human Resource Development. Following the NIN's decision, activists have expressed their dissatisfaction toward the unscientific evaluation of the foundation's menu but more importantly have highlighted the non-inclusion of testimonies from stakeholders, particularly the children eating the food. The main concern of activists is the nonrepresentation of the local food culture of the community in the midday meals being served, and since the aim of the scheme is to address hunger issues among children, a culturally appropriate meal that students enjoy should be given priority. From the government's perspective, this is not an easy decision to make since APF has the infrastructure to provide hygienic meals to a large population in the state. According to the principal secretary of education in Karnataka, "Who is going to serve such a huge number of children if we cancel this contract? There are logistical issues; overnight, we cannot build kitchens and hire cooks."[38] The case of APF in Karnataka brings forth the inherent tensions as well as challenges in a space that is populated by unique civil society actors. While national-level NGOs have the infrastructure to efficiently realize the objectives of the midday meal scheme, their inability to provide more local, culturally appropriate services has made other activists question whether they are fit for implementing this scheme.

At the grass roots, innovations by community members are strengthening midday meals in their own ways. Since the food grains for school meals are provided through a centralized structure, the vegetables for meals can be provided through more local means.[39] Creating kitchen gardens on school premises that are maintained by school-going children is an innovative way to not just diversify the diet but also ensure clean, pesticide-free food on one's plate. To augment the nutritional content of midday meals while creating awareness among children regarding healthy food habits, the central government of the country has come up with guidelines for setting up school nutrition (kitchen) gardens. The 2019 guidelines seek to create behavioral change among students by engaging them in meaningful activities that create awareness around issues of rapid urbanization as well as environmental needs. The guidelines also address children's malnutrition and micronutrient deficiencies by augmenting their consumption of freshly grown fruits and vegetables. The guidelines include practices that address the harmful effects of climate change with emphasis on using organic methods like composting to grow fresh produce and incorporating water management practices like drip irrigation to optimize the water consumption.

There are states in northeast India that are setting stellar examples. In Nagaland, school children in Viswema village decided to cultivate organic vegetables in a school kitchen garden to complement their lunch food.[40] This has not only helped them diversify the school menu but also encourages consumption of local foods like Naga lentils. Organic farming was introduced in the school's curriculum so that students are not just engaged firsthand in the process of cultivation but are also involved in holistic ecological practices like waste management. A similar endeavor is also underway in Mizoram where schools across the state are to demarcate 100 sq ft of land as a nutrition garden to provide fresh, local produce for the midday meals.[41] This idea is especially inspired by the accessibility issues faced by many smaller towns and villages. Instead of relying on shipments from nearby cities, the community could become self-reliant by growing their own organic produce. The latest government guidelines encourage the creation of kitchen gardens at the school level, which can lead to the institutionalization of this practice.[42] Decentralized decision-making and local sourcing of vegetables and grains is also being advocated by food activists belonging to various nonprofits. Local procurement has multiple benefits: contributing to the local economy by supporting livelihoods; increasing community participation and ownership; and providing safe and higher-quality food, a better alternative than the introduction of prepackaged fortified foods, a potential threat to the program.[43]

The current tensions among different civil society actors over the implementation of the midday meal program are indicative of the expansion of neoliberal ideals. Bigger civil society organizations are stepping in to replace grassroots community initiatives by promising higher levels of efficiency. This might come at the cost of thousands of local women losing their jobs and the community not being actively involved in preparing food for children they care both for and about. While initial guidelines had encouraged involvement of CSOs and NGOs to overcome the issues of shoddy infrastructure in urban schools, the expansion of such CSOs and NGOs to rural areas is a concern as it marginalizes community participation that is imperative to making such entitlement schemes successful. It took immense community efforts to make midday meals in schools a reality, and further community-organizing efforts are needed to keep India's lunch program a community-led initiative and to overcome deeply ingrained cultural prejudices and inequities.

NOTES

1. Jean Dreze, Vandana Bhatia, and Vandana Prasad, "Midday Meals: A Primer" (unpublished document of the Right to Food Campaign, New Delhi, India, 2005). Retrieve from https://www.righttofoodcampaign.in/campaign-material/primers.

2. Panchayats are institutions of self-governance constituted in rural areas under article 243B of the Indian Constitution.

3. The Gram Sabha consists of all the people above eighteen years old belonging to and registered in the electoral rolls of a village.

4. The RTE Act states that all children between the ages of six and fourteen have the right to free and compulsory education, and it is a fundamental right in the Indian constitution.

5. Tarun Krishna, "Mid-Day Meal Coverage Sees a Dip, Govt Says Students Are Shifting to Private Schools," *The Print*, December 12, 2019, https://theprint.in/india/mid-day

-meal-coverage-sees-a-dip-govt-says-students-are-shifting-to-private-schools/333210/; Global Nutrition Foundation, *State Survey of School Meal Programs: India 2020* (GNF, 2021), https://gcnf.org/wp-content/uploads/2021/05/State-Survey-of-School-Meal-Progr ams-in-India-Report-with-Annexes.pdf.

6. Jean Drèze and Aparajita Goyal, "Future of Mid-Day Meals," *Economic and Political Weekly* 38, no. 44 (2003): 4673–4683.

7. Drèze and Goyal, "Future of Mid-Day Meals."

8. Farzana Afridi, "Midday Meals in Two States: Comparing the Financial and Institutional Organisation of the Programme," *Economic and Political Weekly* 40, no. 15 (2005): 1528–1535.

9. Farzana Afridi, "Child Welfare Programs and Child Nutrition: Evidence from a Mandated School Meal Program in India," *Journal of Development Economics* 92, no. 2 (July 1, 2010): 152–165, https://doi.org/10.1016/j.jdeveco.2009.02.002.

10. Drèze and Goyal, "Future of Mid-Day Meals"; Rana Kumar, "The Possibilities of Mid-Day Meal Programme in West Bengal," paper presented at the workshop "West Bengal: Challenges and Choices," organized by the Centre for Social Services, Calcutta, July 27–28, 2004.

11. Kitchen-cum-store refers to a space on school premises that includes the kitchen and a storage area for food and other supplies necessary to prepare meals.

12. People's Union for Civil Liberties v. Union of India & Ors, In the Supreme Court of India, Civil Original Jurisdiction, Writ Petition (Civil) No.196 of 2001," ESCR-Net, accessed January 5, 2022, https://www.escr-net.org/caselaw/2006/peoples-union-civil-liberties-v-union-india-ors-supreme-court-india-civil-original.

13. As per Article 21 of the Indian Constitution, "No person shall be deprived of his life or personal liberty except according to procedure established by law."

14. See People's Union for Civil Liberties v. Union of India & Ors.

15. "Right to Food Campaign," Right to Food Campaign India, accessed April 22, 2023, https://www.righttofoodandnutrition.org/right-food-campaign-india.

16. See, Yamini Jaishankar and Jean Drèze, "Supreme Court Orders on the Right to Food: A Tool for Action," October 2005, https://www.corteidh.or.cr/tablas/27433.pdf.

17. Prema Ramachandran, "School Mid-Day Meal Programme in India: Past, Present, and Future," *The Indian Journal of Pediatrics* 86, no. 6 (January 2019): 542–547.

18. See Pradhan Mantri Poshan Shakti Nirman (PM POSHAN), "Meal Provision," Ministry of Education, Government of India, https://pmposhan.education.gov.in/Meal%20Provision.html.

19. The Wire Staff, "Budget for Mid-Day Meals Gets a Boost, but Still Lower than UPA's Allocations," *The Wire*, February 1, 2019, https://thewire.in/economy/interim-budget-2019-mid-day-meal-nda.

20. See Pradhan Mantri Poshan Shakti Nirman (PM POSHAN), "National Programme of Nutritional Support to Primary Education, 2006 [Mid-Day Meal Scheme]," Ministry of Education, Government of India, n.d., https://pmposhan.education.gov.in/Files/Guidelines/10.FINAL_Guidelines_MDM_19_sept.pdf.

21. Rhitu Chatterjee, "India's Free School Lunches Can Fight—or Reinforce—Caste Discrimination in India," *The World*, July 23, 2014, https://theworld.org/stories/2014-07-23/indias-free-school-lunches-can-fight-or-reinforce-caste-discrimination-india.

22. Drèze and Goyal, "Future of Mid-Day Meals."

23. Nidhi S Sabharwal et al., "Swallowing the Humiliation: The Mid-Day Meal and Excluded Groups," *Journal of Social Inclusion Studies* 1, no. 1 (December 1, 2014): 169–182, https://doi.org/10.1177/2394481120140111.

24. Ministry of Human Resource Development, Government of India and Department of School Education & Literacy Mid Day Meal Division, Government of India, "Guidelines for Engagement of Voluntary Organization/Non-Government Organizations (NGOs) under Mid Day Meal Scheme," September 8, 2010, https://pmposhan.education.gov.in/Files/Guidelines/3.MDM1%2021.09.2010.pdf.

25. "Centre to eliminate role of NGOs in mid-day meal scheme in rural areas," *Economic Times*, last updated October 9, 2015, https://economictimes.indiatimes.com/news/politics-and-nation/centre-to-eliminate-role-of-ngos-in-mid-day-meal-scheme-in-rural-areas/articleshow/49290693.cms.

26. Neelam Pandey, "NGOs Not to Prepare Mid-Day Meals in Rural Areas," *Hindustan Times*, October 10, 2015, https://www.hindustantimes.com/india/ngos-not-to-prepare-mid-day-meals-in-rural-areas/story-I2qfxxfkhYha5XQ5xQ7BiO.html.

27. Akshaya Patra Foundation, "Our Reach," accessed December 23, 2021, https://www.akshayapatra.org/our-reach.

28. Anuradha Parekh, "TBI Photo Essay: Akshaya Patra—How to Make 1.5 Million Meals in Less than 5 Hours," Text, *The Better India* (blog), September 14, 2012, https://www.thebetterindia.com/6048/tbi-photo-essay-akshaya-patra-how-to-make-1-5-million-meals-in-less-than-5-hours/.

29. Pradhan Mantri Poshan Shakti Nirman (PM POSHAN), "Community Participation," Ministry of Education, Government of India, accessed March 22, 2023, https://pmposhan.education.gov.in/.

30. Ashutosh Mishra, "Women SHGs Run Mid-Day Meal Schemes in Orissa Schools," *Down to Earth*, June 30, 2008, https://www.downtoearth.org.in/coverage/women-shgs-run-midday-meal-schemes-in-orissa-schools-4725.

31. Ommcom News, "Odisha Govt Ropes in SHGs for Midday Meals," *Ommcom News*, November 28, 2019, https://ommcomnews.com/odisha-news/odisha-govt-ropes-in-shgs-for-midday-meals.

32. Nasreen Habib, "Why Mid-Day Meal Workers Are Opposing Privatization in Assam," *CounterCurrents*, April 6, 2018, https://countercurrents.org/2018/04/why-mid-day-meal-workers-are-opposing-privatization-in-assam/.

33. Arunabh Saikia, "Why Mid-Day Meal Workers Have Been Protesting for Weeks in Assam," *Scroll.in*, November 19, 2019, https://scroll.in/article/943729/why-mid-day-meal-workers-have-been-protesting-for-weeks-in-assam.

34. Ministry of Human Resource Development, Government of India and Department of School Education & Literacy Mid Day Meal Division, Government of India, "Engagement of Cook-Cum-Helpers under Mid Day Meal Scheme," 2010. https://pmposhan.education.gov.in/Files/Guidelines/2014/Proportion_Cook_cum_helpers_dt-29-07-2010.pdf.

35. Habib, "Why Mid-Day Meal Workers Are Opposing Privatization in Assam."

36. Sylvia Karpagam and Vandana Prasad, "ISKCON-run NGO refuses to follow Karnataka order to include onion, garlic in mid-day meals," *Scroll.in*, December 12, 2018, https://scroll.in/pulse/905334/no-onion-no-garlic-akshaya-patra-opposes-karnataka-government-order-on-mid-day-meals

37. Scroll Staff, "Karnataka: Group of Citizens Asks Centre to Terminate Contract to ISKCON-Run NGO for Mid-Day Meals," *Scroll.in*, December 13, 2018, https://scroll.in/latest/905573/karnataka-group-of-citizens-asks-centre-to-terminate-contract-to-iskcon-run-ngo-for-mid-day-meals.

38. Archana Nathan, "Why Are Karnataka's Schoolchildren Unhappy with the Mid-Day Meal?" *The Hindu*, May 31, 2019, https://www.thehindu.com/news/national/karnataka/why-are-karnatakas-schoolchildren-unhappy-with-the-mid-day-meal/article27378176.ece.

39. The Food Corporation of India (FCI) is responsible for procuring from farmers food grains to supply states for various government food security schemes including the MDMS.

40. Sayantani Nath, "Nagaland School Kids Grow Organic Mid-Day Meals, Inspire Whole Village," *The Better India*, January 14, 2020, https://www.thebetterindia.com/209413/nagaland-school-students-organic-farming-vegetables-mid-day-meal-inspiring-say143/.

41. Rinchen Norbu Wangchuk, "'My School, My Farm': Mizoram IAS Officer Tackles Malnutrition with a Brilliant Idea," *The Better India*, July 25, 2019, https://www.thebetterindia.com/189687/ias-hero-mizoram-malnutrition-agriculture-lawngtlai/.

42. Ministry of Human Resource Development, Government of India, "School Nutrition (Kitchen) Garden Guidelines," Government of India, 2019, https://samagra.education.gov.in/docs/SNG_Guidelines.pdf.

43. Ananya Tewari, "Mandatory Fortification in Mid-Day Meal Bad for Local Food, Biodiversity, Livelihood," *Down to Earth*, July 6, 2018, https://www.downtoearth.org.in/news/health/mandatory-fortification-in-mid-day-meal-bad-for-local-food-biodiversity-livelihood-61043.

9

COOPERATIVE AND SMALL-SCALE FARMING THROUGH BRAZIL'S NATIONAL PROCUREMENT STANDARDS

José Arimatea Barros Bezerra and Ludmir dos Santos Gomes

Born to an agricultural family, Ana was raised farming in the Brazilian state of Ceará. However, she struggled in this challenging ecological region to produce enough to feed and financially support her family. João grew up in an urban environment. Despite this, he learned about rural life from visiting relatives in rural areas as a child and from his brother who introduced him to educational opportunities offered by the Landless Workers' Movement (MST).[1] These combined experiences led him to acquire land and to attempt to live from agricultural production. After taking very different paths to becoming farmers, Ana and João have found themselves in an unexpected alliance thanks to Brazil's National School Feeding Program (*Programa Nacional de Alimentação Escolar*; PNAE). In the Ceará state of northeast Brazil, Ana and João work together to grow food for local school meals.

Their stories are not so unusual. A 2009 federal law—which required 30 percent of the food served in the PNAE to be purchased from local producers—has increased family farmers' and small cooperatives' involvement in school lunch programs across Brazil. This turn toward smallholder farmer engagement and quality (i.e., fresh, local, culturally sustainable, and relevant) school foods has grown out of the sixty-six-year evolution of the PNAE, which began as an international "development" project reliant on foreign donations. In its present iteration, the PNAE represents the possibility of local sustainable development for communities, healthy and equitable food, reliable distribution to children, and broader social inclusion for farmers like Ana and João.

BRIEF HISTORY OF BRAZIL'S SCHOOL FEEDING: FROM WELFARISM TO SUSTAINABLE DEVELOPMENT (1955–2020)

Today's Brazilian National School Feeding Program (PNAE) was born from the Education Ministry's School Lunch Campaign (CME). Begun in 1955, the CME had an abstract goal to fight child malnutrition and poor student outcomes by improving eating habits and overall health. Within a year, the program was renamed the National School Feeding Campaign (CNAE), and it largely functioned as an international development project that provided food donations to first through fourth-grade students.

From 1956 to 1960, the United Nations Children's Fund (UNICEF) supported the program. Then from 1960 to 1973, the US Agency for International Development (USAID) and the Food and Agriculture Organization of the United Nations (FAO) took over. The donations were highly processed food products, mostly dry milk, which were not distributed regularly throughout the school year nor received by schools in the more distant northeast and Amazonian regions. Furthermore, the program often functioned as a political patronage system: program administrators focused more on gaining favor with certain political groups than on feeding students.[2] Foreign aid ended in 1973 during the "The Brazilian Miracle" (1964–1973), which was a period marked by strong national economic growth, fueled by nationalist ideology and a military dictatorship that consolidated power through violence, repressing political opponents, and rolling back individual and collective freedoms.

Without international (albeit unreliable) food donations and with distribution challenges but a desire to continue the CNAE, the national government made deals with domestic food industries. As a result, a Brazilian food industry subsector emerged that produced goods almost exclusively for the CNAE. As school food shifted from being internationally to domestically produced, school menus continued to feature highly processed prepared foods. The government also reduced operating costs (e.g., administrative structures and human resources).

When the military dictatorship ended in 1985, the principles of decentralization and community participation guided re-democratization of the country, and guided the CNAE.[3] The government allocated more funds to the program and attempted to decentralize school food acquisition through local purchasing in two hundred municipalities.[4] In 1993, the National School Feeding Campaign (CNAE) changed its name to the National School Feeding Program (PNAE) and continued attempts at decentralization so that school food could be managed locally. While at the beginning of 1993 only municipalities with greater than fifty thousand inhabitants were included in decentralization planning, all municipalities were invited to participate by 1994.[5] By the early 1990s, the CNAE's food reached 90 percent of urban schools and 85 percent of rural schools. However, the centralized management method and food distribution irregularities remained and so too did the disconnection between addressing food insecurity and poverty as an underlying root cause of hunger and malnutrition.

STRATEGIC POLICY SHIFT AND A PNAE TRANSFORMATION

Beginning in the twenty-first century with the presidency of Luiz Inácio Lula da Silva, a coordinated mobilization was intensified to combat hunger as a main effect of poverty. Stakeholders included universities, unions, land- and home-related (e.g., domestic laborers) social movements, and collectives of health, social assistance, nutritional, and food policy militants. They demanded a departure from the previous food distribution models that provided free food products, prioritized and privileged large and often transnational agribusiness, and were not concerned with addressing the root of hunger: poverty. Previous models also overlooked safe, nutritious, culturally and locally relevant fresh food and its agroecological production. Overcoming hunger, they asserted, required nutritious, safe, secure, and sovereign food systems linked to broader antipoverty strategies that produced stable and living-wage work, land access, and income.

In 2009, during the second Lula term as president, school food was universalized, codified in the Brazilian Constitution. The government was required to provide every student from kindergarten to high school, every day of the academic year, regardless of social condition, a free school meal. Also required was that students receive nutrition education as a part of the school curriculum.[6] Last, the 2009 law mandated community participation in controlling and monitoring the PNAE to reduce corrupt practices that previously proliferated under more centralized PNAE management.[7]

As of 2009, the PNAE aligns with the National Nutrition and Food Safety System (SISAM), which is responsible for ensuring adequate food to the population as a human right.[8] The PNAE became central to SISAM efforts to combat hunger, promote nutrition and food safety, and fulfill the human right to adequate food that must respect local food culture and traditions.[9]

Currently, all 5,540 municipalities within the twenty-six Brazilian states and the federal district participate in the PNAE. Each is responsible for managing local school food funds received from the federal government to plan menus, purchase foods, prepare, and distribute meals.[10] Each state and municipality also has a School Feeding Council (CAE)[11] to advise and monitor the local management of the PNAE.

BUYING SCHOOL FOOD FROM FAMILY FARMS

To facilitate compliance with the 30 percent minimum purchasing requirement from family farms, the 2009 school feeding law introduced an annual public call, in which family farmers compete against one another—but not against large farms—for annual contracts. This has increased inclusion of smallholder producers who were previously excluded from the benefits of a stable public policy program despite representing most of Brazil's population and food producers.[12]

PNAE-participating family farmers must be accredited, proving that they produce their products with family labor and are smallholder farmers. The term "farmers" is also applied to participants who are foresters, fish farmers, fishers, Indigenous peoples, *quilombolas*, land reform settlers, and foragers (e.g., harvesters of wild plants).[13] There are two accreditations available.[14] One is for individual family farms, and one is for farmer cooperatives. However, farmer collectives are prioritized in the public call to incentivize and strengthen cooperative models, which are considered to be more effective and reliable food suppliers.

A SUCCESSFUL COOPERATIVE FAMILY FARM EXPERIENCE

In the state of Ceará, in northeast Brazil, the National School Feeding Program has the potential to do immense good. The state's population is over nine million, and poverty levels are high, but so are levels of school attendance. A Human Development Index (HDI) of .682 ranks it seventeenth out of the twenty-six Brazilian states and the federal district in terms of HDI, and the state's poverty rate stood at 37.6 percent as of November 2020, compared to a 23.7 percent poverty rate for the national population.[15] Food insecurity is significant, yet access to universal elementary education is high. In 2019, 99.7 percent of children from six to fourteen years old were enrolled in primary and middle schools. Ceará is ranked third out of the twenty-six Brazilian states on the Basic Education Development Index (IDEB).[16]

Children in Ceará have access to regular, nutritious school food, but they are not the only ones who benefit. Family farmers in this semi-arid region[17] also benefit, however they labor in challenging ecological conditions in order to participate. We wanted to learn about farmers' lived experiences of the PNAE. Through a series of conversations and participant observation with PNAE family farmers in the Ceará region, we hoped to learn from them not as supposedly "neutral" researchers but with a spirit of solidarity.[18] Our search for a dialogical and nonhierarchical relation between ourselves and the farmers led us to Ana and João.

Ana grew up on her family's farm before starting her own operation. "I was born into agriculture, from a family of farmers. I've always worked as a farmer," she told us. She had lifelong experience in agricultural production: "First, planting corn and beans, which the local weather allows. Later I started to dedicate my work to vegetable gardening, such as coriander, scallion, bell pepper, and lettuce. The production was in nine rectangular seedbeds." Before working with João, she focused on selling her produce "to community people."

João grew up in a city. Before becoming a farmer, he worked with his father in a local print shop and spent weekends at his grandmother's place in the countryside. His urban-to-rural migration was the reverse of typical patterns in the region. It was his involvement in the Landless Workers' Movement (MST) that awakened a desire to live in the countryside because of the increased food security and safety he thought it could provide.

Ana and João began collaborating in 2016 out of mutual need. While João had experience in and preference for collective farm production developed through MST participation, Ana, on the other hand, preferred individual work. Like many Brazilians, she also had a bias against the MST.[19] However, they both saw an opportunity in the possibility of selling to the PNAE. Neither could become a PNAE food supplier individually because they could not meet the demands of the program. Forming a collective, a partnership, however, allowed each one to sign an individual sales contract with the PNAE, counting on the production of the other to complement or supply the food if the other's production was insufficient.

As they began to work together, João and Ana learned the benefits of their differences. João had internet skills, experience with collective production, and a connection to the MST—an organization that occupies public buildings, spaces, and unproductive estates and turns them into sustainable food production sites. Ana had experience with farming generally, and conventional vegetable gardening specifically, as well as selling to the local community. With MST resources, they developed a productive and sustainable farming system called the mandala.[20] "It was João who convinced me to make this [agroecological] change," Ana explained, "and I accepted the mandala."

THE MANDALA ENTERPRISE

Mandala technology is based on "an Indian philosophy characterized by a shared irrigation system based on seedbeds surrounding a water source, emulating the solar system."[21] Cultivated beds are laid out in concentric circles around the system's center, a water reservoir to irrigate plants and provide water for fish and poultry. A mandala can be constructed on small rural or urban properties of one to four hectares with adequate soil and a water source. It represents a viable technology for smallholder producers, as João explains:

I have learned garden cultivation with Ana. But working with mandala was a little different from what I did before, which was cultivating corn and beans. Even with Ana's knowledge, there were questions and difficulties about how to do some things inside the mandala. I looked for answers on the internet. But a lot of answers came from observing nature. We were observing, trying, and seeing what worked. To the current day, we [Ana and I] are watching and learning.

For example, there's a space in the mandala in which the scallion is smaller. The PNAE doesn't buy this smaller scallion, so we discarded it. But today we don't discard anymore; we use it to feed the poultry. Or for the composting. We learned to use everything. Nothing in the garden is wasted.

On both small land holdings, they created a round water reservoir that holds fifty thousand liters of water diverted from a nearby dam. In the tank, they raise fish and ducks. The ducks' feces help feed the fish, which also feed on small insects attracted by a light placed in the reservoir's center. The space between the water reservoir and the first ring of raised beds is used for raising and breeding poultry, usually chickens and turkeys. In the circles of cultivation beds around the tank, Ana and João grow coriander, scallion, bananas, papayas, sweet potatoes, pumpkins, cassava, cherry tomatoes, beans, cucumbers, and bell peppers. They also breed pigs.

Each mandala employs the owner and a total of five permanent workers. Ana's mandala system has two employees, while João's has three to help with planting, taking care of plants, harvesting, and delivering. All these phases are coordinated by Ana, with leadership skills she developed through daily practice. During the planting and harvesting periods, the need for labor increases to fifteen people. As João explains: "Daily, the following people work on my mandala: Careca, Bernardo, Bruna, Rosinha, Fábio e Cícero. They are always there and receive pay per day worked. But when it's papaya harvest time, we need many more people. At least fifteen people. So, we need help even from the neighbors."

By collaborating with each other and implementing the mandala, Ana and João strengthened their agricultural systems enough to become a sustainable, local source of both employment and food for schools. "The biggest farming difficulty for us, land reform settlers, is not the work, is not the water, is not the estate owning. The biggest difficulty is selling," according to João. "We don't have the customers to sell our produce. Because what I produce in my garden already feeds me and my family . . . selling to the PNAE, even with all the difficulties, helps me a lot."

When trying to sell on the open market, family farmers are subject to the whims of their buyers and shifting market and environmental conditions, making profits uncertain and variable. The setbacks and challenges of farming led Ana and João to participate in the PNAE. Once contracted to supply the PNAE with food, sales and thus profits are guaranteed. For

Ana and João, the stability it provides was worth enduring the challenges of becoming PNAE suppliers.

The first challenge Ana and João faced was the local city hall's rejection of their request to become PNAE-accredited suppliers. Ana and João were land reform settlers and collaborative producers, which should also prioritize their PNAE proposals. However, local officials did not believe they could meet contract demands. To solve this problem, the farmers carried out two actions. First, they and MST supporters occupied city hall for a week. Next, they called on the secretary of education, the local PNAE manager, to visit their production sites to prove their production capacity. Through this process, they revealed that city hall's resistance was linked to prejudice against the MST and land reform settlers, not related to their production capabilities.

The reluctance of public institutions to incorporate land reform settlers, quilombolas, and Indigenous peoples into the PNAE purchasing process can be attributed to "the lack of qualification of the involved servants, the organizational culture of the public institutions and the complexity of the decisions to be made by the procurement managers."[22] In spite of this bias, Ana and João won over the local PNAE management, who accepted them as suppliers.

Ana and João report that issues with the local PNAE did not end after securing a contract. The PNAE management asked the farmers to supply crops that are not regionally adapted nor part of the local food culture. They demanded, for example, the supply of tomatoes, which are neither locally produced nor consumed. At the same time, the food orders excluded locally produced and consumed produce including cucumbers, watermelons, pumpkins, and okra.

The 2009 school feeding law establishes that menus must be designed with consideration to local agricultural production. Exclusion of a significant amount of locally produced vegetables and fruits and inclusion of culturally inadequate or ultra-processed foods is considered an unsatisfactory preparation of local PNAE menus.[23] This arises from PNAE management and dieticians' lack of knowledge of local family farming production, including crop varieties, seasonal rotations, and quantities. What's more, family farmers lack knowledge of the legislation. If the farmers are unaware of program requirements, they cannot demand the managers' compliance.[24]

Farmers' knowledge of legislation and rules that regulate the PNAE food supply is necessary to empower them as policy protagonists.

The next struggle Ana and João faced was related to food delivery logistics. Local PNAE management required Ana and João to deliver their produce to a central warehouse in the closest municipality, forty-five kilometers away. The food then traveled those same forty-five kilometers back to the schools in town. While the food was initially fresh and of good quality, by the time schools received it at the end of its ninety-kilometer journey without refrigeration, the perishable items no longer met sanitation standards for consumption. The schools then had to reject the food, which had also become more expensive for the farmers due to the costs of the unnecessary transportation.

PNAE management's solution was to still require farmers to deliver their produce to the municipality warehouse and to only distribute the family-farmed produce to urban schools. Fresh, locally produced vegetables and fruits grown near rural schools would be substituted with processed food.[25] This violated the PNAE requirement to supply healthy and culturally adequate food to all schools. Perhaps the PNAE managers assumed that the rural population would be uneducated about their rights and would accept highly processed foods. They were wrong. Parents and farmers noticed that their children were eating industrially processed food products at school even though their families or neighbors were the producers.

According to Ana and João, teachers, students' parents, and farmers voiced complaints in meetings with the school principals who, in turn, communicated with the municipal managers. The farmers expressed to the managers that if the situation was not resolved, they would interrupt the food delivery to the urban schools by delivering only to the rural schools. The complaints or the possible interruption of the urban schools' fresh food supply led managers to remove the processed food from rural school menus. Today, the local PNAE runs more logically: producers deliver food to the schools closer to their farmland, with daily or weekly regularity. The supply chain has been shortened, thereby creating a deeper connection between the farmers and the eaters, reducing costs, and supplying healthy and fresh food for all students.

Ana and João's experiences show that direct food delivery from small farmers to schools creates an opportunity for new dialogue between PNAE stakeholders. The school professionals and the farmers now have a relationship, a bond. The acts of delivering, preparing, and consuming local food strengthen the ties between them, increasing trust in the products as well. The purchasing of school food from family farmers who deliver directly to local schools is an effective strategy for creating dialogue and understanding between education and agricultural stakeholders.

The local school workers we interviewed told us that the food they serve is produced both by conventional farmers and farmers like Ana and João with mandalas. The workers were initially skeptical that Ana and João could produce and deliver on time the quantities of food specified in the PNAE contract. But the mandala produced high yields of produce. Today, they praise Ana and João's work and the quality of foods they produce. Since the perishable food started to be delivered directly by the farmers to the school, there have been no issues with the school food supply. By successfully fulfilling their commitment and demanding changes to PNAE implementation, Ana and João have shifted the schools' perspectives about the value and capacities of local farmers.

The farmers also came to trust the schools. Previously, family farmers only engaged with schools as parents. Now, PNAE farmers have developed

9.1 Produce grown in the mandalas for school lunch. Credit: Jose Arimatea Bezerra and Ludmir dos Santos Gomes.

a broader multifaceted sense of belonging to the schools. They consider themselves a part of the institution with a duty to care for and defend it, as well as supply it with healthy food.

Ana and João have been personally and professionally changed by their PNAE work. Ana advanced professionally: she learned and integrated more innovative cultivation techniques that increased her agricultural productivity. However, she also improved the living standard of her family in terms of food quality and security and with increased ability to purchase consumer goods. "After I started to sell food to the PNAE, my life improved a lot," Ana shared. "My work changed a lot and changed for the better. The production increased. I had more opportunities. I bought a motorcycle, which I used every day for personal use and food delivery. And I also bought a lot of stuff, like furniture, home appliances and clothes. Thus, the income and even my family feeding got improved."

Ana is proud to be able to cover the costs of her daughter's university studies in the city of Fortaleza, making her the first family member to be admitted into a university. Ana's political perspectives have changed as well. She experienced firsthand and benefited from the efficacy of the MST's occupation of city hall. She also benefited from MST's promotion of the mandala system. She no longer distrusts the movement. Ana now personally understands how MST's collective strategies support socially excluded Brazilians' right to land, sustainable agricultural production, and improved farmer livelihoods.

One of the local teachers affirmed that Ana's achievements are not limited to income and purchase of material assets. According to him, with the mandala and the PNAE partnership, Ana has achieved not only better living conditions, in economic terms, but also attained something very important and exceptional: autonomy as a woman and as a family farmer.

As for João, he took a big risk when he made the opposite choice of many of his peers by migrating from the city to the countryside. While he had learned to do collective work on the MST settlement, it was due to the motivation of a potential PNAE contract that he formed a partnership with Ana. The mandala, the collaborative work with Ana, and supplying food to the PNAE impacted João's life. He saw his farm profits increase, which granted him stability and access to material assets. By delivering food to the schools, he became closer to the school managers, teachers, and students, which increased his connection and belonging in the rural community. Now, he and Ana are both more than family farmers. They are producers of food for their school, a role and relationship that gives them new value and purpose.

CONCLUDING REMARKS

There are hundreds of family farmers in the Ceará state like Ana and João who are improving their lives and overcoming poverty by selling food to the PNAE. Across Brazil, there are thousands more. With the more secure income they attain as PNAE suppliers, families with agricultural livelihoods can stay in the countryside, avoiding the rural exodus and improving the local economy.[26] At the same time, schools receive fresh local foods that contribute to ensuring the human right to adequate food, reinforce and stimulate the local food culture, and provide nutrition to all students.

From its origins in receiving foreign food aid to its 2009 shift to universalized school lunch, Brazil's National School Feeding Program has evolved significantly across its nearly seven-decade history to be able to better serve students and schools, family farmers, and local communities. However, gaps still exist between PNAE laws and objectives and their practical execution. Obstacles, both cultural and administrative in nature, hinder purchasing from family farmers, even though national law now specifies that their foods must make up at least 30 percent of PNAE supply. Due to lack of understanding of PNAE rules and personal prejudices, local managers often resist signing contracts with the land reform settler, Indigenous, and *quilombola* farmers whom they are legally obliged to prioritize. As a result, PNAE's declared objectives become watered down in reality.

Purchasing from family farms should be a regular, integrated, and uninterrupted PNAE practice. However, sometimes it becomes an area of dispute between farmers and managers. Like Ana and João, farmers have had to develop resistance strategies—occupation of public buildings, protests, and mobilization of school workers and students' families—to overcome the imposed barriers and finally become PNAE suppliers. In this way, they translate the idealized goals of the PNAE into reality.

Another approach to ensuring program implementation is by expanding farmer-university partnerships. The Federal University of Ceará (UFC) houses the Collaboration Center for School Food and Nutrition (CECANE) which operates through a partnership between the UFC and the National Fund of Education Development (FNDE).[27] CECANE's objective is to develop teaching, research, and extension services about school food. Since 2016, it has accompanied and monitored the PNAE's actions in the Ceará state. In 2019, CECANE started to develop educational programs for family farmers and managers of the PNAE from municipalities that spend less than 30 percent of their FNDE funds buying from family farms. As these educational actions align school food managers with local family farming and expand family farmers' knowledge about the PNAE, school food menus can better meet the needs of local students and farmers.

Farmers should not face the challenges that Ana and João shared with us. The PNAE is codified in the constitution. Clearly, laws and rules are not enough. To establish a connection between laws and their enactment on the ground, more effort needs to be committed to uprooting a government culture of favoring big food industries and exposing and eliminating prejudices against family farming. Such efforts could enable thousands more Brazilian family farmers to secure sustainable livelihoods and provide hundreds of thousands more students with fresh food grown by their neighbors.

NOTES

1. The Landless Workers' Movement (MST) is a rural social movement that aims to achieve land reform in Brazil, i.e. fair land distribution to rural people, and to improve life conditions of the rural population.

2. Marcos Coimbra, João Francisco Pereira de Meira, and Mônica Barros de Lima Starling, *Comer e aprender: Uma história da alimentação escolar no Brasil* (Belo Horizonte: MEC/INAE, 1982); José Arimatea Barros Bezerra, "Do Programa Nacional de Merenda Escolar (1954) ao Programa Fome Zero (2003): Rastros do itinerário da política de alimentação escolar no Brasil," in *Vários. Biografias, instituições, ideias, experiências e políticas educacionais* (Fortaleza: Editora UFC, 2003), 449–467; Albaneide Peixinho, "A trajetória do Programa Nacional de Alimentação Escolar no período de 2003–2020: Relato do gestor nacional," *Ciênc. saúde coletiva* 18, no. 4 (2013): 909–916.

3. Maria do Socorro Chagas Barreira, "A intervenção planejada e o discurso da participação," in *Vários. A Política da Escassez: Lutas Urbanas e Programas Sociais Governamentais* (Fortaleza: Fundação Demócrito Rocha, 1991), 77–110.

4. Francisco de Assis Guedes Vasconcelos, "Acumulação de capital, corrupção e fome," *Revista Saúde em Debate* 39 (1993): 48–52.

5. Mariza Abreu, "Experiências de 'municipalização' da merenda: Problemas e tendências atuais," *Em Aberto: Merenda escolar* 15, no. 67 (1995): 129–135.

6. Presidência da República do Brasil, Lei no. 11.947, June 16, 2009.

7. Presidência da República do Brasil, "Lei no. 11.947" (2009).

8. SISAM, Law no. 11.346, 2006.

9. Presidência da República do Brasil, Lei no. 11.947.

10. Presidência da República do Brasil, *LDB: Lei de Diretrizes e Bases da Educação Nacional*, 4th ed. (Brasília, DF: Senado Federal, Coordenação de Edições Técnicas, 2020).

11. Each CAE is composed of one representative appointed by the local leader (e.g., mayor), two education workers and/or students selected by local teacher and student unions, two student-parent representatives, and two representatives from civil society organizations.

12. Ministério da Educação do Brasil, *Aquisição de produtos da agricultura familiar para a alimentação escolar*, 3rd ed. (Brasília, DF: Fundo Nacional de Desenvolvimento da Educação, 2017).

13. Presidência da República do Brasil, Lei no. 11.326, July 24, 2006.

14. Aptitude Declaration for the Family Farming Strengthening National Program (DAP/PRONAF).

15. Vitor Hugo Miro C. Silva and Natália Carvalho Araújo, "Indicadores de renda e pobreza no Ceará em 2020: O que dizem os dados da PNAD Covid-19," *Desenvolvimento Econômico em Foco* (Universidade Federal do Ceará, Laboratório de Estudos da Pobreza: 2021), 4.

16. The Basic Education Development Index (IDEB) measures two indicators: the students' grades or performance and language and math tests.

17. The caatinga, a biome particular to Brazil, covers 88 percent of the Ceará territory, with the remaining 12 percent composed of mountain regions and the Cariri Valley, which is less affected by water shortages. Rains are irregular and during the long dry season, from July to December, water shortages require creative irrigation for agricultural production.

18. Paulo Freire, *Educação e mudança*, 31st ed., trans. Moacir Gadotti and Lilian Lopes Martins (Rio de Janeiro: Paz e Terra, 2008); Victor Vincent Valla, "Procurando compreender a fala das classes populares," in *Saúde e educação*, ed. Victor Vincent Valla (Rio de Janeiro: DP&A, 2000), 11–32.

19. Many Brazilians, taking cues from the press, politicians, conservative governments, and landowners, object to what they see as a threat of violence in the MST's tactics.

20. The mandala is a social technology that changes small pieces of land into productive food spaces, producing income and ameliorating poverty and hunger. Social technology is a concept that defines products, techniques, and/or methodologies developed through community interactions and that seek effective social change

solutions. Renato Peixoto Dagnino, "Tecnologia social: Base conceitual," *Ciência & Tecnologia Social* 1, no. 1, (2011): 1–12.

21. Renata Knychala Martins et al., "O sistema mandala de produção de alimentos: Uma estratégia para o desenvolvimento da agricultura familiar," Paper presentation, Anais do XXI Encontro de Geografia Agrária: Territórios em disputa: Os desafios da Geografia Agrária nas contradições do desenvolvimento Brasileiro, Universidade Federal de Uberlândia, October 15–19, 2012, 9.

22. Hugo Leonnardo Gomides do Couto and Francis Lee Ribeiro, "Objetivos e desafios da política de compras públicas sustentáveis no Brasil: A opinião dos especialistas," *Revista de Administração Pública—Rio de Janeiro* 50, no. 2 (March–April 2016): 337.

23. Ministério da Saúde do Brasil, *Guia alimentar para a população Brasileira*, 2nd ed. (Brasília, DF: Ministério da Saúde, Secretaria de Atenção à Saúde, Departamento de Atenção Básica, 2014).

24. Ludmir dos Santos Gomes and José Arimatea Barros Bezerra, "Alimentação escolar e desenvolvimento social local: O caso da aquisição de gêneros da agricultura familiar," *Educação & Formação* 4, no. 11 (May–August 2019): 114.

25. Ministério da Saúde do Brasil, *Guia alimentar para a população Brasileira*.

26. Pierre Bourdieu, *O poder simbólico*, trans. Fernando Tomaz (Rio de Janeiro: Bertrand Brasil, 1998).

27. Currently, there are seventeen Collaboration Centers for School Food and Nutrition, located in the different regions of Brazil. With the FNDE financial and technical support, these centers provide monitoring and advising for the PNAE, as well as research and educative actions.

10

AGROECOLOGY AND FEMINIST PRAXIS IN BRAZILIAN SCHOOL FOOD POLITICS

Sônia Fátima Schwendler, Cristiane Coradin, and Islandia Bezerra

"Agroecology will be carried forward, and it is being carried forward because it is something that women have embraced for themselves... for food sovereignty, for the matter of bringing healthy food to the family first." Through this statement, Violeta, a feminist agroecologist from the Contestado Settlement, explains why she and others work together to feed Brazil's children through Brazil's National School Feeding Program (*Programa Nacional de Alimentação Escolar*, PNAE).

In 2009, the PNAE was transformed by a requirement that at least 30 percent of the PNAE purchasing budget from the National Fund for Education Development (*Fundo Nacional de Desenvolvimento da Educação*, FNDE) must be invested in the direct purchase of food and food products from local and regional family farms.[1] This policy generated more inclusive processes of school food procurement and increased access to family farm–produced foods for school children across the country. It is also shifting local food systems across Brazil. As communities reconsider what is produced for and eaten in schools, agroecologists have become important public policy stakeholders.

Agroecology is a science, movement, and practice that is "a combination of bio-physical and socioeconomic elements grounded in the three pillars of sustainable development—the social, the economic and the environmental."[2] Agroecologists apply an ecological approach to farming, working with natural resources to produce nutritious, culturally relevant, and sustainable food while also striving to create locally focused, sustainable, and socially conscious approaches to food production including fair markets for smallholder farmers. Agroecology can help stimulate significant changes in local food systems.[3] The PNAE's procurement process prioritizes such shifts, specifically the purchase of food and/or products certified as organic or agroecological.[4] What's more, farmers from indigenous and *quilombola*[5] communities, as well as land reform settlers, are also supposed to be prioritized when annual PNAE contracts are awarded.

Many of the required 30 percent local PNAE providers are women agroecologists: land reform settlers who, having worked to transform food systems linked to their households, are extending that focus to local schools. They are often affiliated with the Brazilian Landless Workers' Movement (*Movimento dos Trabalhadores Rurais Sem Terra*, MST),[6] a social movement rooted in struggles for agrarian reform and rural social justice.[7] To understand more about their participation in the PNAE, we conducted field research in the Brazilian state of Paraná between 2017 and 2019.[8] We focused on two sites where agrarian reformers who are part of the MST live and work: the Emiliano Zapata Encampment, which for nearly twenty years has been occupied by families agroecologically cultivating their plots, kitchen gardens, and forests,[9] and the Contestado Settlement,[10] where about 50 percent of the 150 families who currently live in the area produce agroecologically. We recorded oral histories with forty-five agroecologists: thirty-nine women and six men.[11] Our sample is stratified by diversity (of gender, age, race/ethnicity, work experience, and leadership level) and for saturation.[12]

In addition to listening closely to our interviewees' perspectives, we analyzed their accounts to understand the connections between their agroecology work, their role as PNAE suppliers, and their agency as women. We complement the participant interviews with interviews and observations of agroecological farmers from settlements near Londrina, Cascavel, and Francisco Beltrão, who participate in annual learning spaces called Agroecology Journeys[13] in Paraná.

We found that the PNAE's most recent policy shifts have accelerated and expanded agroecological transitions in land reform territories associated with the MST. By producing, harvesting, processing, and marketing food for the PNAE using their agroecological farms, these women have increased their agency, asserted leadership capacities, and elevated their socioeconomic autonomy. Utilizing their role in the PNAE to advance the ethics of care integral to their agroecological operations, the women in our study promote a feminist decolonization of Brazil's food systems. They have helped transform schools into healthy food environments—spaces that promote access to and consumption of nourishing foods for all social groups.[14] Within the transformed PNAE framework, the school becomes a strategic environment to build new food cultures that promote self-care, care for the environment, and care for others.[15]

FEMINIST AGROECOLOGY AND THE PNAE

Much of Brazil's land is controlled by a domestic oligarchy and foreign-based multinational corporations, mainly from China and the US. The widespread industrial agriculture system tends to intensively exploit natural resources and labor to cultivate and export monoculture crops, using agrochemicals and genetically modified seeds, with intensive manual labor and heavy machinery. This rural development model, the result of centuries of Brazilian colonization, has bolstered patriarchal power and led to countless social and environmental injustices.[16] Rural Brazilian women have been excluded from basic social rights, such as land access and ownership and a retirement, affecting their capacity to farm, generate income, and gain autonomy.[17]

Despite these complementary forces, rural women have long been saving seeds, reproducing medicinal plant knowledge, and protecting biodiversity.[18] According to Copaíba (Contestado Settlement), women "historically already did agroecology. They just didn't call it that." The Landless Women had agroecologically cultivated fields, kitchen gardens, and orchards prior to their involvement in public procurement programs, not to generate profits but as an act of care for the health of land and family.[19]

Women in the MST who practice agroecology aim to transform both colonial food and oppressive gender systems, with profound implications for self and family as well. Their intimate understandings of care practices, traditionally assigned to women, have formed them into leaders of actions related to "biodiversity and food sovereignty and security, which are pillars of family autonomy."[20] Agroecology has become a site for swelling "feminist, decolonizing and anti-capitalist consciousness based on the observation of and work with nature for the production and distribution of food."[21]

Women's agroecological practices have been undervalued, but the 2009 mandate that the PNAE purchase at least 30 percent of food from local and regional suppliers is beginning to change that, allowing women to profit from—and earn respect for—their agroecological food production. There is still significant untapped potential. According to FNDE data, 36 percent of the local PNAE purchasing committees, known as Executing Entities (EEx), did not meet the minimum requirement of family farming purchasing in 2014. By 2017, with the PNAE serving 40.6 million students, the economic investment was R$3.9 billion. The PNAE may be falling short of its promises, but it is already creating real change in the lives of family farmers.

Coradin, Pereira, and Bezerra, when studying the PNAE in a *quilombola* territory,[22] found that to the community, "eating is a political act [that] reverberates in agriculture (planting and harvesting in an agroecological way), in cooking (preparing and processing food/ingredients) and finally in eating."[23] Perez-Cassarino, Bezerra, and Costa e Silva studied how the inclusion of agroecological foods in the PNAE connected to the human right to adequate food. Integrating family-farmed agroecological foods into school meals comes to fruition through collective community efforts driven "by dialogues, confrontations, and contradictions . . . (and) guided by principles and values of agroecology," which ultimately transform the lives of both producers and consumers.[24] Through the PNAE, the Landless Women in our study are initiating these efforts on their land, transforming their local schools and communities into spaces of care through daily practices of agroecology.

Copaíba reveals how PNAE policies boosted environmental sustainability in agrarian reform settlements and the economy.

I think that the PNAE, with it, [the settlement] discovered in production its true vocation, that is, the production of vegetables, of legumes. The PNAE had a differentiated price for agroecological products, at the same time it had to have a certification process. Families were included in this certification process. I think it was a great learning moment to advance agroecology.

In other words, the policy valued women's approach to caring for the land and producing food. Women were ready to seize the opportunity to become PNAE suppliers. As Imbuía (Contestado Settlement) stated, "We never thought that we could sell food to schools because historically, Brazil's [school food program], who supplied the schools, was not family farming, it was big business. (. . .) The women, they took over [supplying school food] in the beginning."

The women PNAE producers whose experiences we analyzed produced vegetables, fruits, legumes, and tubers: cassava, pumpkins, lettuce, cucumbers, beets, cabbage, green onions, parsley, spices, broccoli, cauliflower, carrots, tomatoes, oranges, and tangerines for schools.

However, for family farmers and smallholder producers, especially women, it is often not easy to access the certification mechanisms that operationalize the PNAE. To be qualified as a supplier for the PNAE, our interviewees told us, they must provide a document called Document of Aptitude (*Documento de Aptidão ao Programa Nacional de Fortalecimento da Agricultura Familiar*, DAP) proving that they are family farmers, land reform settlers, or quilombolas. In addition, they must prove that they formally participate in a cooperative. On approval of these documents, they may join the PNAE through their cooperative, which takes responsibility for the production, delivery, and flow of food. Women collectively define what, how much, how, and when they should produce and deliver to school communities.

Women who successfully navigated the certification processes earned a better income than they had previously. As income has increased, so too has the time devoted to agricultural labor and management, for as Hibiscus (Eli Vive Settlement) said, "The PNAE for us today is the only way to earn money a little easier." In interviews, the women mention incomes ranging between R$200.00 to R$2,000.00, dependent on varying productive capacities, for an average of R$800.00/R$1,000.00 per month per family. Some earnings are saved.[25] Others are used to support and expand operations. Rosa (Emiliano Zapata encampment) explains the effects of joining the PNAE: when "the cooperative opened for us, sales improved [. . .] We started earning and investing little by little, little by little." Margarida (Emiliano Zapata Encampment) tells us, "With this money that comes from [the PNAE] we are investing here, like buying seedlings, getting a tractor, tilling farmland, and such."

Participation in the PNAE has boosted women's self-esteem, confidence, and pocketbooks. Aroeira (Emiliano Zapata Encampment) says that on starting to sell to the PNAE, "[. . .] you learn to be more, to respect yourself more, and not let anyone step on you." For the Landless Women, the financial autonomy they derive from PNAE income is fundamental to their emancipation "because" as Violeta (Contestado Settlement) explains, "no woman is emancipated with an empty pocket." However, they also understand their value in terms that exceed finances: their own cultural and historical agricultural practices are helping them remake the dominant, neoliberal food regime, decreasing the PNAE's reliance on exploitive food systems. Dente de Leão testifies that women "have built an important counter-hegemonic culture. This proposal of agroecology owes a lot to our capacity to put this message of agroecology into the subjectivity of the processes [. . .] and this is thanks mostly to women" (Eli Vive Settlement). "Subjectivity" here refers to the expansion of women's agency, their increased capacity to effectively build agroecology in their home settlement and, thus, to elevate their social positions in the community, the MST, and the school food program, such that their voices command more respect.

However, the success women have found with PNAE participation has also produced tensions within the MST. As women start to gain monetary income and the empowerment that accompanies it, men start to show interest in running, and profiting from, spaces previously the domain of women, including kitchen gardens, fields around the home, and orchards.[26] Melissa (Contestado Settlement) attests, "interest in the gardens increased a lot after these programs when men saw that [women] earned an income."

Women see the entry of men into this activity in a positive way, as they identify that this process has taken place in conjunction with the maintenance of their female empowerment and the possibility of the transformation of patriarchal culture. However, they also identify tensions in this process and call attention to the need to continue the permanent "gender struggle within the struggle for land"[27] and agroecology as a framework for agricultural production.[28] The women affirm that the reproduction and reinforcement of gender coloniality if or when men engage in this activity can be countered. Their earlier training on gender equality provided by

MST and feminist social movements helps them assert agency in and over their fields. Copaíba (Contestado Settlement) explains that "it is a matter that women have to be aware of, but many women are in charge here on their plots, they are deciding what to do and how to do it." Iris (Walmir Motta Settlement) points out that the struggle for gender equity is "a constant struggle" when they are included in PNAE. She continues, "We want a woman to have a voice and a turn," and that is not simply "won."

FOOD SOVEREIGNTY AND CULTURALLY RELEVANT FOOD BECOMES PEDAGOGY

The PNAE represents a new direction for MST women seeking to change the intertwined systems of food and gender in rural Brazil: food sovereignty vis-à-vis school food. "No longer [is food] just a matter of eating, but of being 'sovereign' and being able to decide" our system of production based "on local, peasant, ecological, seasonal agriculture."[29] PNAE's commitment to local, sustainable sourcing that aligns with local food culture valorizes food sovereignty and, in doing so, also valorizes the Landless Women of our study. Their agroecological school food production makes food sovereignty possible for their communities, revalorizing their previously invisible and undervalued domestic work as political, a source of resistance to multiply intertwined oppressions.[30] As Violeta (Contestado Settlement) reflected in an interview: "So, this relationship of agroecological work, of work without the use of agrochemicals, fertilizers, begins in this small work that is developed with women and that is why I believe that agroecology will be carried forward, and it is being carried forward because it is something that women have embraced for themselves. And that today men [are contributing], but it was women [who fought] for the preservation of seeds, for cultivation on small scales, for food sovereignty, for the matter of bringing healthy food to the family first."

In these Agrarian Reform contexts especially, women's work with agroecology promotes their increased participation in spaces of sociopolitical action.[31] Through sociopolitical organization, women become the protagonists of their own constructions of agroecology. As they establish linkages between their diversified fields and school cafeterias, women suppliers to the PNAE carry the practice of food sovereignty beyond their direct family sphere.³² By constituting themselves as agroecologists, women claim and promote food sovereignty at home and in their community as a political and transformative act of care.

The declaration of healthy food as a right has been the most concrete achievement of the PNAE, especially since the implementation of mandatory food purchases from local family farms. In addition to food sovereignty, culturally relevant food is a priority, leading to the inclusion of locally produced and prepared foods on school menus. However, PNAE staff—especially the nutritionist technical responders (RT, *Resposta Técnica*)—assert certain menu requirements, which in turn requires producers to diversify what they grow.³³ This may seem like a challenge, a contradiction even, to the PNAE feminist agroecologists' food sovereignty and assertion of culturally relevant and sustaining food. However, there has been a give-and-take involved in learning from and teaching about diversified crop production. There was increased diversity and quality of feminist PNAE farmers' household food consumption that, in turn, potentially improved their nutrition: "People produce and eat," Ameixa from the Contestado Settlement shared. "So, we saw a lot of change here in the settlement in the way of eating based on agroecology, on food diversity. Because if people plant just for themselves, they won't plant 5, 10 kinds of things to eat. But if they're going to sell 5, 10 kinds of things, they're going to eat 5, 10 kinds of things. So, this changes food, changes health." (Ameixa, Contestado Settlement).

The introduction of more diverse agroecological food in schools increased student consumption of fresh and minimally processed foods and decreased consumption of ultra-processed foods. This has contributed to a more robust culturally relevant and sustainable food sovereignty.³⁴

As the women take part in school food networks as PNAE producers, they strengthen their agroecological movements and produce new meaning for agriculture and health that seeps into schools and beyond.³⁵ Specifically, the channeling of women's agency into PNAE production has proved essential for producing healthy, agroecological food spaces for eating and for learning in schools. The women have not stopped sharing their knowledge at the cafeteria. They also teach what they are learning to communities-at-large. Aroeira (Emiliano Zapata Settlement) highlights how she is reteaching consumers in street market interactions and transactions about the quality of her products. "I always share [. . .] a few words [of advice] too, because there are some people who have no notion [of agroecology]. You talk about what the product is like in the supermarket, right, and they say, wow, I didn't know that, and I used to get the most beautiful [produce]." Aroeira teaches, for example, that the tomato that has a few spots, which is uglier, had less chemicals, "so we become more aware." Additionally, by sharing agroecological knowledge in schools and in PNAE workshops, Rosa Vermelha (Contestado Settlement) explains that "for the first time our knowledge is validated for more people," which contributes to increased self-esteem and valuation of women's knowledge. Women are ensuring they are recognized and asserting themselves as knowledgeable of agroecological experiences and of a liberating feminist agroecological praxis based on food sovereignty and culturally relevant principles.[36]

A FEMINIST PEDAGOGY OF CARE FOR LIFE

From historical experiences in the struggle for land and gender equality, women farmers have contributed to the construction of feminist epistemology, through which they rework their own understandings of agroecology and build a pedagogy of care for life that is integrated into schools. While care should not be the exclusive role of women, the rural women of our study were often its sole practitioners. By expanding their care practices beyond the home to schools through PNAE participation, they were able to expand care networks and advocate through action for democratization of care.[37]

For the women, care implies building new forms of relationships with agriculture, nature, and human beings. Amora (Contestado Settlement) elaborates, "For me, the care for human beings is one of the main things in a [feminist] agroecology. How do you look at the people that are around you, how do you relate to them? And how do you give space to each one, each one really, you know?"

Through their ethics of care, the PNAE women producers seek socioecological transformations for all beings living in their communities. "We don't want things [just] for women. We are not a separate process; we are part of the process. We want to contribute to the quality of life in the settlements," shared Flor (Eli Vive Settlement).

PNAE participation is an opportunity to teach an ethics of care in their settlements that extends beyond the agroecological ethic of care for land or the economic impact of becoming a producer. "We must discover that it is not just thinking that doing agroecology makes money," shared Maravilha (Contestado Settlement). "It's not just about money; you have to know that you are protecting the environment, that you are producing life, health, all these things. That to sell to school lunch, where the children are going to eat, you have to send a quality product, not a poisoned product."

The integration of care begins with agroecological school food organized and supported by the productive capacity and active political agency of women agroecologists. Malva (Emiliano Zapata Encampment) says, "I practice this agriculture, because I'm aware of the harmful effects of chemicals. [...] I make a point of maintaining an agroecological garden because it's for schools."

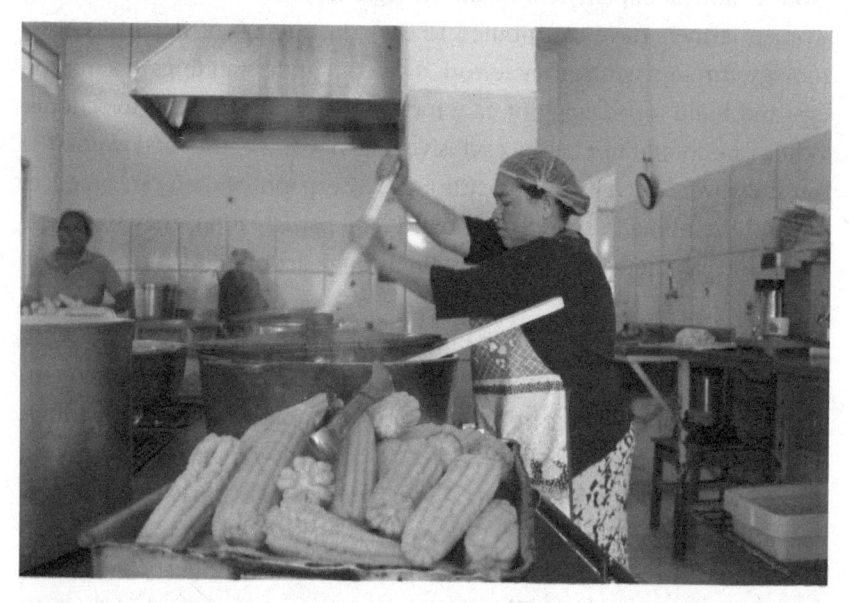

10.1 Cooks preparing lunch in the Latin American School of Agroecology, Contestado Settlement. Credit: Elisa Cordeiro Brito.

The women PNAE producers encourage school students, nutritionists, cooks, and teachers to question their eating habits and food values. For Margarida, a teacher (Contestado Settlement), "agroecology is a way of life that involves education, health. Health is already the result of good nutrition. There's no way the school cannot work on this issue [without agroecology], yeah?" She further shares that school can generate spaces for student reflection on the production of healthy food: "We did some experiments in a kitchen garden, in the forest garden, to try to show the children how we manage to produce some [crops]." School goers also learn about diversified food cultivation: "There's fruit trees there, there's native [trees], all planted on the same land. There's lettuce, there's beets."

Margarida's narrative demonstrates that an understanding of nonhierarchical socio-natural relationships is essential to propagating an agroecological ethics of care in education. "There are also other forms of relationships between people and nature, yeah? Of feeling part of nature and not superior to it, yeah?," she asks. "We have to teach these kids how to take care of our common home, which is the environment, the land, the forests, etc., because if not, in the future, what will become of this country?" Camélia, another teacher from the Contestado Settlement, further reveals the possibility of teaching agroecological awareness in early childhood education: "I take [agroecology practices into my classroom] . . . we always have a little fruit here at school, but I also ask them to bring what they have at home and then . . . we talk about the importance of eating healthy and so on, but they learn a lot more by doing it, showing it, and they go home talking about it."

FINAL CONSIDERATIONS

Agroecology and food sovereignty take center stage in contemporary discussions about promoting the health of people and environments. In Brazil, rural women are central to these discussions. In our study sites, MST-associated women maintained agroecological fields, kitchen gardens, and orchards to feed their families prior to their PNAE involvement. Then, they became PNAE producers and increased their incomes, increased and diversified their home's food production, increased healthy and nutritious food in schools, and created better living conditions for their families and communities.

These transformations impacted the women's self-esteem, which led them to assert and share their agroecological knowledge in school and community spaces. As women have become more vocal agents in local public school food systems, they are building and expanding on new meanings of the relationship of agroecology, food, and gender relations for their communities. The Landless Women of our study serve as an example for PNAE producers across Brazil of how to utilize school food policy to not only reshape the landscape of school food but also promote agroecological foodways, feminist women's agency, and care for life.

NOTES

1. See Brazil Law 11.947/2009.

2. Food and Agriculture Organization (FAO), "Agroecology Definitions," accessed April 20, 2023, https://www.fao.org/agroecology/knowledge/definitions/en/.

3. Gema Esmeraldo, "O Protagonismo político de mulheres rurais por seu reconhecimento econômico e social," in *Mulheres Camponesas: Trabalho produtivo e engajamentos políticos*, ed. Delma P. Neves and Leonilde S. de Medeiros (Niterói: Editora Alternativa, 2013), 237–256; Emma Siliprandi, "Mulheres agricultoras e a construção dos movimentos agroecológicos no Brasil," in *Mulheres Camponesas: Trabalho produtivo e engajamentos políticos*, ed. Delma P. Neves and Leonilde S. de Medeiros (Niterói: Editora Alternativa, 2013), 329–343; Liliam Telles, "Desvelando a economia invisível das agricultoras agroecológicas: A experiência das mulheres de Barra do Turvo, SP," (master's diss., Mestrado em Extensão Rural—Universidade Federal de Viçosa, 2018); Cristiane Coradin, "Entre buvas e flores vermelhas: Autorias das mulheres Sem Terra na ecologização da reforma Agrária no Paraná," (PhD diss., Programa de Pós-graduação em meio ambiente, UFPR, 2020).

4. According to Law no. 10.831 (2003).

5. Territories defined by land ownership, whose population is descended from African peoples who escaped slavery in Brazil.

6. This movement takes place in encampments comprising families who are still fighting for the right of access to productive land, and in settlements or territories on land expropriated from oligarchy families through federal agrarian reform.

7. Esmeraldo, "O Protagonismo."; Coradin, "Entre buvas e flores vermelhas."; Sônia Fátima Schwendler, "O processo pedagógico da luta de gênero na luta pela terra: O desafio de transformar práticas e relações sociais," *Educar em revista* 55 (March 2015): 87–109.

8. This study was partially funded by the Education Sector of the Federal University of Paraná MCTI/CNPQ/MEC/CAPES funding, edict no. 22/2014—Humanities and Social and Applied Social Sciences.

9. The Emiliano Zapata Encampment, located in Ponta Grossa, Paraná, was occupied in 2003 by about eighty families. See Coradin, "Entre buvas e flores vermelhas."

10. The Contestado Settlement is an agrarian reform territory started in 1999 in the municipality of Lapa, Paraná. The Settlement also hosts, since 2005, the first Latin American Technological School of Agroecology. See Sônia Fátima Schwendler, "'Sem feminismo não há agroecologia': A resistência camponesa com democracia de gênero," in *Conflitos agrários na perspectiva socioambiental*, coordinators Maria Cristina Vidotte Blanco Tárrega, Katya Regina Isaguirre-Torres e Gilda Diniz dos Santos (Goiânia: Editora da PUC Goiás, 2020), 131–154.

11. Although our study was based on the agroecological experiences of Landless Women, we included men who shared feminist perspectives as well. To maintain the anonymity of the interviewees, we will use as identification the popular names of trees, fruits, medicinal plants, and flowers, which in agroecology symbolize strength, resistance, resilience, flavor, beauty, and harmony.

12. Jacques Marre, "História de Vida e Método Biográfico," *Cadernos de Sociologia* 3, no. 3 (January/July 1991): 89–141.

13. Since 2002 in the state of Paraná, Agroecology Journeys are organized by rural social movements as learning spaces for Agrarian Reform—occupying families and settlers to promote agroecology in Agrarian Reform. See Coradin, "Entre buvas e flores vermelhas."

14. Karen F. Glanz et al., "Healthy Nutrition Environments: Concepts and Measures," *American Journal of Health Promotion* 19, no. 5 (May/June 2005): 330–333.

15. Joan C. Tronto, "Assistência democrática e democracias assistenciais," *Sociedade e Estado* 22, no. 2 (May/August 2007): 285–308; Joan C. Tronto, "Particularisme et responsabilité rellationelle em morale: Une autre aproche de l'Étique globale," in *Contre l'indifférence des privilégies: À quoi sert le care*, ed. Carol Gilligan, Arlie Hochschild and Joan C. Tronto (Paris: Payot, 2013), 99–137; Marie Garrau and Alice Le Goff, *Care, justice et dépendence: Introdutión aux théories du care* (Paris: Press Universitaires de France, 2010); Alícia Puleo, *Ecofeminismo para otro mundo es posible* (València, Spain: Universitat de València, 2013).

16. Carlos Walter Porto-Gonçalves, *A globalização da natureza e a natureza da globalização* (Rio de Janeiro: Civilização Brasileira, 2017).

17. Esmeraldo, "O Protagonismo."

18. Via Campesina, "Declaration of the Second International Assembly of Rural Women," June 13, 2004, https://viacampesina.org/en/declaration-of-the-second-international-assembly-of-rural-women/.

19. Sônia Fátima Schwendler, "'Sem feminismo não há agroecologia': A resistência camponesa com democracia de gênero"; Coradin, "Entre buvas e flores vermelhas."

20. Ceres Hadich and Tânia Mara de Bastiani, "As mulheres assentadas e a construção da agroecologia no Oeste Catarinense," in *Mulheres camponesas e agroecologia*, ed. Valdete Boni, Lucélia Peron, Siomara A. Marques, Naira Estela R. Mohr, and Tânia Mara de Bastiani (Curitiba: CRV, 2017), 139.

21. Peter Rosset et al., 2019. "Agroecology and La Via Campesina II. Peasant Agroecology Schools and the Formation of a Sociohistorical and Political Subject," *Agroecology and Sustainable Food Systems* 43, no. 7–8 (2019): 16, https://doi.org/10.1080/21683565.2019.1617222.

22. Remaining Quilombo Community (CRQ) of João Surá in the municipality of Adrianópolis/PR.

23. Cristiane Coradin, Carla Fernanda Galvão Pereira, and Islândia Bezerra, "Somos mulheres quilombolas: Resistindo e construindo autonomia em sistemas alimentares saudáveis" in *Agroecologia: Caminho de Preservação do Meio Ambiente 2*, org. Jessica Aparecida Prandel (São Paulo, Brasil: Atena Editora, 2020), 191.

24. Julian Perez-Cassarino, Islandia Bezerra, and Leticia Costa e Silva, "Alimentos ecológicos no Programa Nacional de Alimentação Escolar: Um caminho para a promoção do Direito Humano à Alimentação Adequada (DHAA)," in *Alimentação Escolar: Construindo interfaces entre saúde, educação e desenvolvimento*, ed. Carla Rosane Paz Arruda and Rozane Márcia Triches (Chapecó, SC: Argos Editora da Unochapecó, 2016), 138.

25. Coradin, "Entre buvas e flores vermelhas."

26. Emma Siliprandi, "Mulheres agricultoras e a construção dos movimentos agroecológicos no Brasil"; Maria Ignez Silveira Paulilo, *Mulheres rurais: Quatro décadas de diálogo* (Florianópolis: Editora da Universidade Federal de Santa Catarina, 2016).

27. Sônia Fátima Schwendler, "O processo pedagógico da luta de gênero na luta pela terra: O desafio de transformar práticas e relações sociais," 88.

28. Emma Siliprandi, *Mulheres e agroecologia: Transformando o campo, as florestas e as pessoas* (Rio de Janeiro: Editora da UFRJ, 2015).

29. MST women often organize with Via Campesina—an international peasant movement founded in 1993 and recognized worldwide as the main actor in food and agricultural debates and a strong advocate of food sovereignty. See Esther Vivas Esteve, *O negócio da comida: Quem controla a nossa alimentação?* (São Paulo: Expressão Popular, 2016), 73–74.

30. Bruna Vasconcellos, "Mulheres rurais, trabalho associado e agroecologia," in *Questão agrária, cooperação e agroecologia*, vol. 1, orgs. Henrique Tahan Novaes, Ângelo Diogo Mazin, and Lais Santos (São Paulo: Outras Expressões, 2015), 341–369.

31. Vasconcellos, "Mulheres rurais, trabalho associado e agroecologia."

32. Emma Siliprandi, *Mulheres e agroecologia: transformando o campo, as florestas e as pessoas*; Laeticia Medeiros Jalil, Gema Galgani Silveira Leite Esmeraldo, and Maria Socorro de Lima Oliveira, *Rede Feminismo e Agroecologia do Nordeste* (Recife: Rede Feminismo e Agroecologia do Nordeste, 2017); Bruna Vasconcellos, "Mulheres rurais, trabalho associado e agroecologia."

33. Islandia Bezerra and Sergio Schneider, "Produção e consumo de alimentos: O papel das políticas públicas na relação entre o plantar e o comer," *Revista Faz Ciência* 14, no. 19 (2012): 35–61.

34. Ministério da Saúde, Secretaria de Atenção à Saúde, Departamento de Atenção Básica, *Guia alimentar para a população brasileira*, 2nd ed. (Brasília: Ministério da Saúde, 2014).
35. Coradin, "Entre buvas e flores vermelhas."
36. Coradin, "Entre buvas e flores vermelhas."
37. Garrau and Le Goff, *Care, justice et dependence*; Puleo, *Ecofeminismo para otro mundo possible*; Tronto, "Assistência democrática e democracias assistenciais"; Tronto, "Particularisme et responsabilité rellationelle em morale: une autre aproche de l'Étique globale."

11

DIRECT URBAN-RURAL SUPPLY CHAINS FOR SOUTH KOREAN COMMUNITIES

Seulgi Son

A morning chill fills the air inside a district-level public meal center in Seoul, South Korea. Workers are preparing to ship fresh local produce, collected from rural towns overnight, to early childhood education centers in the city. Seoul has twenty-five such districts, and to date, twelve of them have public-meal centers like this one. Each one is partnered with a distinct rural town, where farmers—the majority of whom are small- and mid-sized or family farmers committed to sustainable agriculture practices—supply meat, vegetables, grains, fruits, dairy, and minimally processed foods to local food hubs, primarily supported by local governments. Each day, food is transported from these rural towns' hubs to the public meal centers in Seoul that serve as urban food distribution centers. Administrators at participating urban institutions place orders one week ahead of delivery based on a standardized meal plan shared with key actors in rural areas.

Seoul's public meal centers are the daily point of contact for rural producers and urban consumers, who work together to support the preparation of scratch-cooked meals for South Korean children and targeted urban institutions, including daycare centers, welfare facilities, hospitals, and government buildings. These meal centers were developed under the auspices of the Urban-rural Coexistence Public Meal Service Program (UCPM), a public food procurement program that emerged from the Universal, Free, and Eco-Friendly School Lunch Program (UFEF). Together, these programs are helping transform food systems in South Korea by re-localizing production, shortening agricultural food chains at the regional level, and expanding just and sustainable food economies.

Concentration of corporate power has created innumerable problems within food systems, with only a handful of transnational food businesses controlling over 40 percent of the global retail industry.[1] Profit-driven food systems contribute to biodiversity loss, disparities in healthy food access, exploitation of farmers and other food workers, and dietary diseases such as obesity and diabetes.[2] Alternative food movements have evolved globally over the last decades as various stakeholders have worked to challenge the dominant market-based system and build new models for food production and consumption.[3] The majority of these initiatives are supported by the private sector or nonprofit organizations. Few efforts to re-localize and shorten supply chains have been led by the public sector using mandatory, effective policy toolsets. A notable exception is the public food system in the Brazilian state of Belo Horizonte and Brazil's Programa Nacional de Alimentação Escolar (PNAE).[4]

Governments have mandates and regulations at their disposal, as well as considerable purchasing power, that they can use to re-embed local food systems that are attuned to environmental and sociocultural concerns.[5] Thus far, public procurement has played a limited role in affecting mainstream food policy,[6] but many countries are experimenting with new models such as voluntary values-based purchasing programs (e.g., the US-based Good Food Purchasing Program), state-sponsored purchasing subsidies (e.g., 10 Cents A Meal Program in Michigan, US), or innovating within the context of the United Nations Home Grown School Feeding Program. The case of South Korea's UCPM demonstrates that municipal-level governments can play an important role in reestablishing local food chains and reforming conventional food systems, beginning with school meals.

Cities provide fruitful sites for innovation when policies are designed to address the ecological and political dimensions of complex socioecological systems.[7] Global and local policymakers are increasingly recognizing the need to focus their efforts on food *systems* to solve both chronic and new food challenges such as food security, food safety, and food justice. Food systems encompass "the entire range of actors and their interlinked value-adding activities involved in the production, aggregation, processing, distribution, consumption, and disposal of food products that originate from agriculture, forestry, or fisheries, and parts of the broader economic, societal and natural environments in which they are embedded,"[8] as well as the ramifications for the environment, health, and society.[9] Thinking of food as a "system" requires shifting from thinking about structure to thinking about process, grasping interrelationships between components and agents within the system, and understanding the multiple foundations of knowledge construction.[10] Thus, applying systems thinking to food enables researchers, policymakers, and other stakeholders to take a holistic approach to addressing food issues by evaluating food practices as either a process or a result of interactions between multiple elements, especially local and regional actors, throughout the system.

Public-led food initiatives like Seoul's UFEF and UCPM suggest one way that public policy and public procurement can be leveraged to support alternative food economies and shortened supply chains through government-sponsored food programs. Seoul, the capital of South Korea, is one of the world's largest metropolises with a population of almost ten million. The city serves as the country's economic, political, and cultural hub. The annual budget of the Seoul Metropolitan Government is equivalent to more than 7 percent of the national government budget, demonstrating the importance of Seoul's weight in national policy formulation. According to the Seoul Food Master Plan 2020, the first comprehensive city-level food plan in Seoul, 1.83 million people eat a daily meal through the city's public food programs, accounting for 18.3 percent of the city's population. The number of students who benefit from the UFEF is 1.28 million (70 percent), while daycare centers and welfare facilities account for 490,000 consumers of publicly provided food (27 percent). The extent of public meal service in Seoul demonstrates the impact that urban food procurement policy can have on reshaping regional food systems, altering consumer behavior, and improving public health via its purchasing power and education programs. The nationwide UFEF and the Seoul Food Master Plan 2020 laid the basis for the UCPM to become a public food system that benefits a broad spectrum of food systems stakeholders across urban and rural areas.

ORIGINS OF SOUTH KOREA'S UNIVERSAL, FREE, ECO-FRIENDLY SCHOOL LUNCH PROGRAM

The origin of South Korea's public school food system stretches back to the 1950s, when foreign food aid expanded after the Korean War. Canada, the United Nations International Children's Emergency Fund (UNICEF), and the US Agency for International Development (USAID) donated milk powder, wheat flour, and corn flour, which the South Korean government used to manufacture porridge or bread for school lunches. Elementary school students received free school meals, which were mostly bread, for the following two decades, while the dictatorship curtailed the scope of national-level social welfare programs. When foreign food aid ended in 1972, the government shifted financial responsibility for school lunches to parents by requiring them to pay a portion of the cost of school bread. This school lunch program entirely ceased in 1977, however, after a massive outbreak of food poisoning caused a fatality.[11]

Following democratization in South Korea in the late 1980s, a self-governing local administrative system was established in 1995 in which the national government devolved much of its authority to local governments. The delegation of state power to local governments created a window for bottom-up initiatives to gain influence. Social movement activists pushed back against the influence of the General Agreement on Tariffs and Trade (GATT), the World Trade Organization (WTO), and other global actors on the South Koren food system; meanwhile, public demand for locally administered school food programs was increasing. In response, the fifth amendment of the National School Meals Act in 1996 authorized the establishment of *witak-geubsik*, which subcontracts the operation of school food canteens to private enterprises. During the presidency of Daejoong Kim (1998–2002), the government expanded its school lunch program to include elementary, middle, and high schools.

The prevalence of food poisoning and managerial corruption under *witak-geubsik* in the early 2000s prompted policy protagonists within the national school food movement to shift their focus from quantity to quality. For instance, the Nationwide School Lunch Network, one of the largest civic organizations committed to improving the public school food system, asserted that school lunches should "a) be school-managed, b) be available free to all students, and c) use organically grown local foods."[12] To enhance food safety and transparency of the school food system, an extensive reform of the National School Meals Act in 2006 mandated *jikyeoung-geubsik*, which features the direct operation and monitoring of school food canteens by schools. Overall, in response to bottom up initiatives, South Korea's school food policies evolved to stress both the nutritional and educational components of school lunch. The national- and local-level governments also increased administrative and financial support to expand school lunch programs.

Years of continuous grassroots campaigning led to a critical political realignment of the school food landscape in the early 2010s, with the progressive party winning numerous local elections. These politicians and superintendents of education[13] backed the broad expansion of universal, free, and eco-friendly school meal programs that had been spearheaded by certain local governments. For example, the city of Gwacheon launched the first universally free school meal program for elementary school students in 2001, and in 2003, the city of Naju passed the first local ordinance mandating local government assistance for the use of environmentally friendly local food. In 2010, Jeongseon County started the first universally free *and* eco-friendly school program for all students from kindergarten to high school. Drawing on a decade of local efforts, many municipalities have actively implemented universally free and eco-friendly school lunch programs since then. According to the Ministry of Education, 97.4 percent of the students in elementary, middle, high, and special-education schools benefited from free school meals (but not necessarily environment friendly yet) in South Korea as of March 2020.

Seoul has had the most impressive track record of implementing a universal, free, and eco-friendly school food program by rapidly expanding the UFEF at the municipal level. To demonstrate, Seongbuk District, one of Seoul's twenty-five districts, was the first in the city to launch its UFEF in 2010 by subsidizing the cost rather than relying on the funding model used by other municipalities. The Seoul Metropolitan Government approaches school food as a basic human right tied closely to the right to an education.[14] Since 2021, all public school students in the city have had access to free eco-friendly school meals. This expansion happened in three stages: (1) Phase 1 in 2011 for partial implementation in elementary schools, (2) Phase 2 from 2012 to 2014 for the entire elementary and middle school populations, and (3) Phase 3 from 2019 to 2021 for expanding the UFEF into high schools.[15] Seoul Metropolitan Office of Education, Seoul Metropolitan Government, and district-level local governments each contribute 50 percent, 30 percent, and 20 percent, respectively, of the total budget to operate the UFEF.[16]

By establishing alternative food distribution channels, Seoul's UFEF, like other UFEF initiatives in various municipalities, aims to boost local food economies as well as provide nutritious food to all students regardless of socioeconomic position. According to the Seoul Metropolitan Government, *Orbon*, a public-funded distribution hub for eco-friendly food founded by the Seoul Metropolitan Government, supplies ingredients to 75 percent of the city's schools.[17] As part of Seoul's efforts to localize and shorten supply chains and establish a more transparent school food system, *Orbon* was introduced in 2010 to help schools procure certified organic or sustainably grown foods via the shared distribution center.[18] By incentivizing public food purchases of environmentally friendly foods through *Orbon*, the municipal government aims to create short, direct distribution routes that will enable contract farming on local farms based on stable demand from urban schools, which will, in turn, help promote a transition to sustainable agriculture.

SEOUL FOOD MASTERPLAN 2020—A VISION TOWARD SUSTAINABLE URBAN FOOD SYSTEMS

In the late 2000s, South Korea was hit by a series of food scandals, including an amendment of the Free Trade Agreement with the US that obliged the country to open its agriculture and livestock industries. Concerns about failing domestic food systems, including dwindling rural economies, a high reliance on food imports, and the westernization of South Korean diets, were voiced by farmers and grassroots activists coordinating nationwide food sovereignty movements. The public's increased awareness of food safety and food security led to a substantial increase in the demand for organic food and interest in urban agriculture as a means of achieving self-sufficiency. As such, both the national government and local governments developed food policies to support and scale up alternative food initiatives.

In 2015, Seoul joined over one hundred other cities from around the world to sign the Milan Urban Food Policy Pact, a promise to create "sustainable food systems that are inclusive, resilient, safe and diverse, that provide healthy and affordable food to all people in a human rights-based framework."[19] Two years later, the Seoul Metropolitan Government launched the Seoul Food Master Plan 2020, its first comprehensive city-level food plan, with a particular emphasis on citizens' well-being, public health, social welfare, and the environment.[20] To incorporate diverse perspectives into the plan, feedback was gathered at both public hearings and at regular meetings of a task-force team made up of fifteen members across the city government and the civic sector.

The Seoul Food Master Plan 2020 focuses on five key areas: (1) healthy food, (2) food security, (3) urban-rural coexistence, (4) food safety, and (5) governance building. The first aim, for healthy food, will be advanced through educational programs and revised nutrition standards that can improve general knowledge about healthy diets and the urban food environment. The second aim, food security, concentrates on urban populations that are food insecure, such as seniors or children from low-income households. From 2013 to 2014, 5.1 percent of households in Seoul (approximately 180,000 households) reported having difficulty obtaining food on a regular or occasional basis due to their economic status.[21] The years-long expansion of the UFEF for students of all ages is part of Seoul's attempts to decrease gaps in access to healthy food via public meal service. The third aim, urban-rural coexistence, envisions an urban food system that can help revitalize shrinking rural communities and economies resulting from decades of depopulation, changes in industrial structure, and changes in South Korean diets (i.e., a decrease in rice consumption) by establishing a public food procurement system that directly connects urban consumers and rural producers. The fourth aim addresses public concerns about food safety by strengthening legislative measures such as testing residual agricultural chemicals, monitoring food facilities including school food canteens, and enhancing food labels. Finally, the aim of governance building involves cultivating collaborative food decision making and the enactment of a local ordinance protecting the human right to healthy food.

URBAN-RURAL COEXISTENCE PUBLIC MEAL SERVICE

One of the most important and influential projects under the Seoul Food Master Plan 2020's third aim, urban-rural coexistence, is the Urban-Rural Coexistence Public Meal Service Program (UCPM). It reflects the understanding that cities, particularly a metropolis like Seoul with its dense population, can play a critical role in reinvigorating local food economies by providing a consistent source of demand for locally produced goods. At the 2018 Mayors Summit, the UCPM was recognized with a Milan Urban Food Policy Pact Award for Winning Practices for its efforts to build a regional food supply and distribution system.

The UCPM's basic concept is to establish short, direct supply chains between twenty-five urban districts in Seoul and rural towns, which are paired one to one, so that public institutions (e.g., early childhood or regional education centers, welfare facilities, hospitals, and government buildings) can source fresh local food from small-scale and family farmers. As an outgrowth of the UFEF with a separate scope, the UCPM focuses primarily on early childhood education centers that are not included in the UFEF. While expenses for meal service at early childhood education centers (including daycare centers and preschools for children aged zero to five) are already covered by government subsidies, Seoul offers additional financial incentives to institutions that spend more than 60 percent of their monthly food budget through the UCPM system. When an urban district, which has autonomous political and legislative power as a sub-administrative unit of Seoul, decides to join the UCPM, a municipal-level selection committee composed of invited external members evaluates candidate rural towns based on the robustness of their local food system, administrative support, and regional capabilities, then matches a rural town with the urban district. As of March 2023, the UCPM had twelve pairs of urban districts and rural towns.

Each district needs to build a district-level public meal center that serves as an urban food hub connecting a partnered rural town and the district

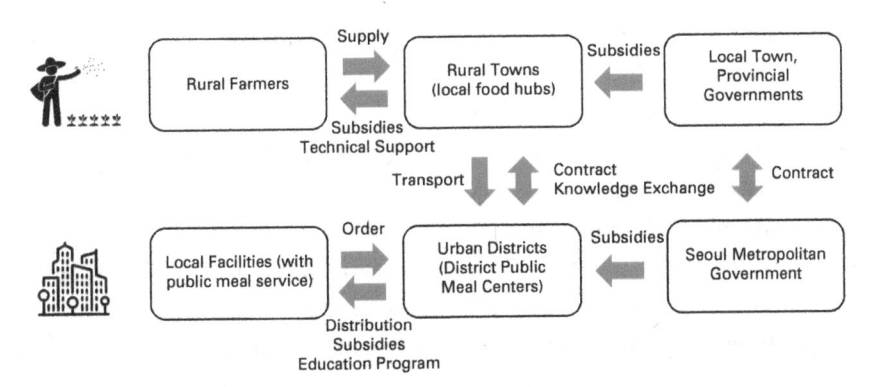

11.1 The partnership structure of the Urban-Rural Coexistence Public Meal Service.

in order to join the UCPM system. These public meal centers are distinct from *Orbon*, which is operated at the city level for the UFEF. New direct supply chains utilizing food hubs in rural towns and UCPM district-level public meal centers in Seoul (see figure 11.1) are expected to increase the availability and affordability of eco-friendly food for public meal services, while also expanding the market for small-scale sustainable farms. The UCPM requires the provision of "environmentally friendly" food products that include: (1) nationally certified *organic* produce grown without the use of agricultural chemicals (including pesticides, herbicides, and growth regulators), chemical fertilizers, and antibiotics and (2) nationally certified *non-pesticide* produce grown without the use of agriculture chemicals and with less than one-third of the recommended amount of chemical fertilizer. Several participating rural towns have developed independent local-level certificates to assist farmers in transitioning to sustainable farming by providing administrative and technical assistance, as obtaining a national certificate often requires an excessive amount of time and effort, which is particularly challenging for elderly farmers. The UCPM also accepts non-herbicide, non-GMO (non-genetically modified organisms), and radiation-free criteria to accommodate these local-level certificates, which frequently have lower standards than the national certificates and reduce entry barriers for farmers.

District-level public meal centers in Seoul and local food centers in rural towns are two pivotal players in the UCPM. These district-level public meal centers have been newly built for the UCPM with funds from district-level governments and the Seoul Metropolitan Government. Human resources, storage space, and delivery trucks are all part of the public meal centers, the operation of which is subsidized by the district- and city-level governments. District-level public meal centers not only serve as urban food hubs, gathering and transporting food to participating institutions, but they also regularly run extensive tests for residual agricultural chemicals and lead education programs about healthy eating and sustainable food systems for children and their parents. Local food centers in rural areas, which are typically founded and run by town- and/or provincial-level governments, aggregate and distribute locally produced food to schools and other institutions. They also function as umbrella organizations that set action plans and assist local farmers through various programs such as year-round farmers markets and support for agricultural cooperatives to foster sustainable farming practices.

What sets the UCPM apart from other global examples of innovative institutional food procurement is that the public sector has been actively involved in building the "infrastructure of the middle" to connect smallholder and family farmers in rural areas with metropolitan public institutions.[22] The concept of infrastructure of the middle indicates both hard infrastructures (food hubs, warehouses, and transportation) and soft infrastructures (networks, subsidies, and education).[23] By using public purchasing power to connect small- and mid-scale farmers with consumers, the infrastructure of the middle constructed through the UCPM mobilizes "the resources, facilities, and networks that create a critical mass, enabling alternative food producers to meet the needs of high-volume, high-profile food service clients."[24] This particular form of infrastructure of the middle within the UCPM, which binds an urban area and a rural town in a pair as an exclusive food chain via anchor institutions in the city, was made possible by the UFEF's successful implementation since 2010. In Seoul, and South Korea more broadly, the UFEF helped pave the way for further government investments in alternative supply chains. Policy language within the UFEF to encourage the use of sustainably grown local produce enabled the conception of the UCPM as a city-led initiative, which focuses on more direct actions to strengthen shrinking rural economies by empowering smallholders and family farms.

CONCLUSION: OPPORTUNITIES AND CHALLENGES OF PUBLIC FOOD PROCUREMENT

The evolution of Seoul's public food procurement (see table 11.1) illustrates the government's commitment to enhancing the sustainability and equity of food systems across urban and rural areas. According to an interim evaluation report, the sourcing capacity of participating rural towns meets about 73 percent of the total demands from urban institutions in Seoul.[25] The number of people sourcing food for the UCPM (excluding the UFEF) increased more than five times since the beginning of the program as of June 2019 (from 7,844 to 44,328). The percentage of eco-friendly ingredients used for meal service at participating institutions increased from 22 percent (March 2016, before the program) to 67 percent (December 2017, after the program) to 85 percent (June 2019). This matters for the livelihoods of rural farmers since they keep up to 95 percent of the cost of food sold through the UCPM supply chain, in comparison with 61.5 percent or less than the cost of food sold through conventional wholesale markets.

Table 11.1 Major timeline of public food procurement programs in Seoul

Year	Major milestones
2011	Launch of the UFEF in public primary schools in the Seoul metropolitan area.
2014	Expansion of the UFEF to middle schools (public and private).
2015	Formulation of the Seoul Master Plan begins.
2017	Six districts join the UCPM: Gang-dong, Geum-cheon, Do-bong, Seong-buk, No-won, and Gang-buk.
2018	Four districts join the UCPM: Seo-daemon, Dong-jak, Eun-pyeong, and Joong-rang.
2021	Expansion of the UFEF to private primary schools and high schools (private and public).
2022	More districts join the UCPM, bringing the total to twenty-five districts.

Note: The UCPM program was to be fully implemented by 2022. However, logistical challenges, budgetary constraints, and the unexpected obstacle of COVID-19 have resulted in delays.

While the UCPM has had some success in increasing the quality of public food services and the livelihoods of rural farmers, this public food procurement model is still in the early stages of development. An evaluation report of the Seoul Food Master Plan 2020, released in March 2021, exposed some concerns related to the UCPM including insufficient public funding, insecurity of policy continuity, and failures in cross-departmental coordination. It also pointed out that the current plan as a whole, which is largely focused on food distribution, food security, and food safety, ignores issues with food production and food waste disposal.[26] Problems such as backlash from conventional food markets, which are arguably losing market share due to the government intervention, and the potential for co-opting grassroots food initiatives that had already been committed to alternative supply chains for childcare centers have also been raised by grassroots stakeholders. In attaining long-term shared visions, ambiguous definitions of "local" and inconsistent interpretations of "eco-friendly" food could be barriers. For instance, the questions of what a local food system should look like, what standards for eco-friendly food in public meal service should be, and whether the exclusive consumption of *organic* food is conducive to encouraging sustainable farming in the long run remain controversial and unresolved. Finally, the COVID-19 pandemic-related shutdowns of public institutions, such as schools and childcare centers, put additional strain on these alternative supply chains by halting public food sourcing. To offset food systems disruptions during the pandemic, the national and local governments in South Korea attempted to redirect foods reserved for public sourcing to individual-level consumers and group purchasing by other public institutions.[27]

To grapple with these problems and others, the Seoul Metropolitan Government is now crafting the first part of the Seoul Food Master Plan 2030, building on insights from the execution and evaluation of the 2020 version. Different departments with expertise in lifelong education, public health, and social welfare are working together on this revised plan, and the Seoul Food Civic Council has helped collect public feedback from various interest groups such as consumer cooperatives, producers, and grassroots stakeholders. To achieve a comprehensive municipal-level food master plan, it will be necessary to negotiate and integrate conflicting perspectives and priorities into shared goals—for example, food safety must not come at the expense of food justice—and to develop a mechanism to ensure policy continuity based on the long-term vision.

To date, though, South Korea's UCPM already suggests a possible path in which city-level initiatives to expand public food procurement can contribute to re-localizing regional food systems by rebuilding the middle of supply chains. The UCPM's governance structure and logistics enable stakeholders from both urban and rural areas to partner together in a transformative effort to create more sustainable local food systems. It is critical for planners and policymakers to understand the fundamental issues underlying contemporary food systems as public goods and the local context of food politics to achieve collaborative partnerships across different sectors and geographies. The UCPM, as a government-led initiative to develop a place-based public food procurement system that stemmed from the UFEF school lunch program, demonstrates how transforming school food politics can lead the way to broader changes in regional food systems that benefit both rural producers and urban consumers. Ultimately, lessons from South Korea's UFEF school lunch program and Seoul's UCPM will help policymakers, practitioners, and academics in many worldwide cities who are looking for a transformative instrument to establish sustainable local food supply chains using the power of public food procurement.

NOTES

1. Beth Hoffman, *Behind the Brands: Food Justice and the 'Big 10' Food and Beverage Companies*, vol. 166 (Oxford, UK: Oxfam, 2013); Lanka Elvira Horstink, "A Global Food Polity: Ecological-Democratic Quality of the Twenty-First Century Political Economy of Food" (diss., Universidade de Lisboa, Portugal, 2017).

2. Jennifer Clapp, "Mega-Mergers on the Menu: Corporate Concentration and the Politics of Sustainability in the Global Food System," *Global Environmental Politics* 18, no. 2 (2018): 12–33; Jennifer Clapp, "The Problem with Growing Corporate Concentration and Power in the Global Food System," *Nature Food* 2, no. 6 (2021): 404–408; Jennifer Clapp and Doris A. Fuchs, *Corporate Power in Global Agrifood Governance* (Cambridge, MA: MIT Press, 2009); Corinna Hawkes, "Linking Agricultural Policies with Obesity and Noncommunicable Diseases: A New Perspective for a Globalising World," *Food Policy* 37, no. 3 (2012): 343–353, https://doi.org/10.1016/j.foodpol.2012.02.011; Barry M. Popkin et al., "Global Nutrition Transition and the Pandemic of Obesity in Developing Countries," *Nutrition Reviews* 70, no. 1 (2012): 3–21, https://doi.org/10.1111/j.1753-4887.2011.00456.x; Thomas Reardon, "Agrifood Industry Transformation and Small Farmers in Developing Countries," *World*

Development 37, no. 11 (2009): 1717–1727, https://doi.org/10.1016/j.worlddev.2008.08.023.

3. Lesli Hoey et al., "'Put Your Own Mask on Before Helping Someone Else': The Capacity of Food Hubs to Build Equitable Food Access," *Journal of Agriculture, Food Systems, and Community Development* 8, no. 3 (2018): 41–60; Betty T. Izumi et al., "Farm to School Programs: Exploring the Role of Regionally-Based Food Distributors in Alternative Agrifood Networks," *Agriculture and Human Values* 27, no. 3 (2010): 335–350; James Matson and Jeremiah Thayer, "The Role of Food Hubs in Food Supply Chains," *Journal of Agriculture, Food Systems, and Community Development* 3, no. 4 (2013): 43–47; Sarah A. Robert and Marcus B. Weaver-Hightower, *School Food Politics: The Complex Ecology of Hunger and Feeding in Schools around the World. Global Studies in Education, Volume 6* (New York: Peter Lang, 2011); Mark Vallianatos et al., "Farm-to-School: Strategies for Urban Health, Combating Sprawl, and Establishing a Community Food Systems Approach," *Journal of Planning Education and Research* 23, no. 4 (2004): 414–423; Gerda R. Wekerle, "Food Justice Movements: Policy, Planning, and Networks," *Journal of Planning Education and Research* 23, no. 4 (2004): 378–386.

4. See chapters 9 and 10, this volume. See also Emilie Sidaner et al., "The Brazilian School Feeding Programme: An Example of an Integrated Programme in Support of Food and Nutrition Security," *Public Health Nutrition* 16, no. 6 (2013): 989–994; Hannah Wittman and Jennifer Blesh, "Food Sovereignty and *Fome Zero*: Connecting Public Food Procurement Programmes to Sustainable Rural Development in Brazil," *Journal of Agrarian Change* 17, no. 1 (2017): 81–105.

5. Roberta Sonnino and Susannah McWilliam, "Food Waste, Catering Practices and Public Procurement: A Case Study of Hospital Food Systems in Wales," *Food Policy* 36, no. 6 (2011): 823–829.

6. Kevin Morgan, "The Politics of the Public Plate: School Food and Sustainability," *International Journal of Sociology of Agriculture and Food* 21, no. 3 (2014): 253–260.

7. Jill K. Clark et al., "Fail to Include, Plan to Exclude: Reflections on Local Governments' Readiness for Building Equitable Community Food Systems," *Built Environment* 43, no. 3 (2017): 315–327; Adrian Morley and Kevin Morgan, "Municipal Foodscapes: Urban Food Policy and the New Municipalism," *Food Policy* 103 (2021); Samina Raja et al., *Local Government Planning for Community Food Systems: Opportunity, Innovation and Equity in Low-and Middle-Income Countries* (Rome: Food & Agriculture Organization of the United Nations, 2021); Roberta Sonnino, "Feeding the City: Towards a New Research and Planning Agenda," *International Planning Studies* 14, no. 4 (2009): 425–435.

8. Hanh Nguyen, "Sustainable Food Systems Concept and Framework" (Rome, Italy: Food and Agriculture Organization of the United Nations, 2018), 1.

9. Joachim Von Braun, "Food Systems—Definition, Concept and Application for the UN Food Systems Summit," a paper from the *Scientific Group of the UN Food Systems Summit*, 2021.

10. Fritjof Capra, "Criteria of Systems Thinking," *Futures* 17, no. 5 (1985): 475–478; Fritjof Capra, "From the Parts to the Whole: Systems Thinking in Ecology and Education," *Elmwood Quarterly* 3 (1994): 31–37.

11. Mia Kang, "Free for all, Organic School Lunch Programs in South Korea," in *School Food Politics*, ed. Sarah A. Robert and Marcus B. Weaver-Hightower (New York: Peter Lang, 2011), 120–140; Jennifer E. Gaddis and June Jeon, "Sustainability Transitions in Agri-Food Systems: Insights from South Korea's Universal Free, Eco-Friendly School Lunch Program," *Agriculture and Human Values* 37, no. 4 (2020): 1055–1071.

12. Mia Kang, "Free for all, Organic School Lunch Programs in South Korea," 125.

13. Since 2006, seventeen regional education superintendents (including provincial and metropolitan levels) have been appointed by direct election.

14. Elementary and middle school (grades 1 to 9, average age eight to sixteen) education is compulsory. High school (grades 10 to 12, average age seventeen to nineteen) is not compulsory, but in 2021, the government made high school a free option with the goal of eventually making it compulsory.

15. Seoul Metropolitan Government, "Seoul Has Accomplished the Three Main Agendas of Universal Education Welfare by Providing Free, Eco-Friendly School Food to all Students from Elementary to High School," February 15, 2021b, https://www.seoul.go.kr/news/news_report.do#view/333899?tr_code=snews.

16. Seoul Metropolitan Government, "Seoul Has Accomplished the Three Main Agendas."

17. Seoul Metropolitan Government, "Seoul Has Accomplished the Three Main Agendas."

18. Gaddis and Jeon, "Sustainability Transitions in Agri-Food Systems."

19. Milan Urban Food Policy Pact, *Milan Urban Food Policy Pact Text* (2015).

20. Seoul Metropolitan Government, *Seoul Food Master Plan* (2017).

21. Seoul Metropolitan Government, *Seoul Food Master Plan*.

22. Lori Stahlbrand, "A Typology of 'Infrastructure of the Middle' in University Food Procurement in England and Canada," *Raizes: Revista de Ciencias Sociais E Economicas* 36, no. 2 (2016): 32–46.

23. Stahlbrand, "'Going the Distance So Our Food Doesn't Have To': Case Studies of Creative Public Procurement at Canadian and UK Universities" (PhD diss., Wilfrid Laurier University, 2017).

24. Stahlbrand, "A Typology of 'Infrastructure of the Middle' in University Food Procurement in England and Canada," 32.

25. Eco-friendly Public Meal Service Team, *A Proposal for the Urban-rural Coexistence Public Meal Service* (unpublished report, Seoul, South Korea, 2019).

26. Seoul Metropolitan Government, *Evaluation Report of Seoul Food Master Plan 2020* (government report, Seoul, South Korea, 2021a).

27. Selugi Son, "Government Response to Support Local Farmers in the Face of COVID-19: A Case of South Korea," *Gastronomica* 20, no. 3 (2020): 74–75.

IV

TOOLS AND CAMPAIGNS FOR SYSTEMS CHANGE

Jennifer E. Gaddis and Sarah A. Robert

This last section presents readers with strategies for school food transformation. The first two chapters provide techniques for others to adapt toward engaging a broad and diverse collection of stakeholders. Chapter 12, "Using Storytelling in the United States to Build Empathy for Change," encourages us to take stock of how school mealtimes are currently experienced by students, food service managers, and school administrators using a composite narrative approach that interweaves individual experiences to craft a specific stakeholder "story" or viewpoint. The authors argue that personal stories from multiple viewpoints are critical for understanding the challenges of school food programs and fostering empathy in others to act.

Chapter 13, "Facilitating Think Tanks to Guide Action and Advocacy in Canadian Teachers' Unions," illustrates an interactive technique used by the British Columbia Teachers' Federation to elicit the expertise of teachers in re-envisioning school food policy. The authors propose pathways to amplify, extend, and advocate based on the rich diversity of work that teachers are already doing within their schools and communities. Importantly, this chapter underscores the need to develop worker power through social justice unionism, which looks beyond the core issues of workers' wages and benefits to broader issues of community well-being.

The final chapters give an inside look at school food transformation. The authors are leaders of two successful state-level campaigns that have become national models. Chapter 14, "The Center for Ecoliteracy's Approach to School Food Systems Change in the United States," charts the evolution of California's School Meals for All Campaign. It details the center's efforts to foster deep collaborative partnerships that led to the California Food for California Kids Network, activate a statewide network of school districts, and identify the most effective levers of change and key voices to amplify the partnerships' goals.

Chapter 15, "Developing Solidarity Coalitions for Universal School Meals and Local Food in the United States," then discusses the more than twenty years of coalition building that united Vermont's anti-hunger organizations, school nutrition professionals, farmers, local food advocates, and others to work together as policy protagonists. The authors explain how they developed messaging, data, and stories to shift public opinion in support of their happy ending: universal free meals and locally sourced food in every Vermont school. They overcame the challenges of partisan politics that have hampered similar efforts in other states and successfully championed their bill through the legislative process.

Taken together, the chapters in this final section show how policy protagonists use the powerful tools of storytelling, participatory research, and organizing to build school food programs that are more caring, connected, and community centered.

12

USING STORYTELLING IN THE UNITED STATES TO BUILD EMPATHY FOR CHANGE

Christine C. Caruso, Lucy Flores, and Amy Rosenthal

We know a good story when we hear (or read) one. This fundamental form of sharing information shows us a path for effectively translating research into action. In common channels for sharing research findings, such as academic articles and policy briefs, the expectation is to aggregate and abstract individuals' experiences, presenting statistics about the number of schoolchildren who do X or describing the systems that mean that American schools do Y. While such abstractions are a necessary part of figuring out and explaining a particular situation, we suggest that stories can provide an important context for these types of findings. And when the goal is political change, stories create empathy in the reader that will spark new or different behaviors that can contribute to social transformation.

Further, stories can especially call attention to the lived experiences of those whom others often do not listen to. A story can help the reader better understand, and empathize with, the difficulties caused by a particular policy or practice, making clearer the case for change and the imperative of action. Stories are also a useful mechanism to highlight and share information that a wide audience might not be aware of. Including the perspectives of diverse people actively participating in all parts of the school food system is crucial to both conceptualizing and achieving more participatory school meals programs that ensure the well-being of students, value workers, and other stakeholders, and contribute to socially just schools and communities.

In this chapter, we describe the purpose and practice of using stories to inspire changes in school food policy and practice. We highlight the power of storytelling in building empathy as well as communicating diverse stakeholders' perspectives and the ways in which advocates have centered stories to effect change in school food and other political arenas. We also present composite narrative as a method of sharing stories collected through qualitative research. Drawing on two research projects that collected and shared stories of those engaged in school food systems, we explain the rationale and process of using this technique and offer three composite narrative vignettes as examples.

STORIES AND EMPATHY

Well-crafted stories introduce the listener or reader to believable characters inhabiting relatable worlds. Stories attract and convince us by developing the texture of lived life through seemingly minute details and by evoking sensory experiences that stimulate the imagination. It is through this believable and relatable portrayal of life that we connect with characters and respond to their circumstances.

Feminist psychologist Carol Gilligan suggests that hearing another person's particular and specific story engenders a "responsiveness" in the listener or reader that is built on care. Her work was motivated, in part, as a response to the "objectivity" that dominated traditional social science of the time. This paradigm did not recognize particulars of experience and strove to be "value neutral," which she came to find to be ethically untenable in the face of great injustices. These culturally dominant notions of neutrality, objectivity, and ultimately abstraction and reductionism obscure the social forces (especially processes of power related to race and gender) that structure social interactions and, in turn, social problems. In Gilligan's work responding to these invisible processes of power, she reflects on the erasure of women's experience and recenters care, relationships, and empathy as positive psychological characteristics.

Gilligan uses interviews to examine the nature of relationships and the role of care in motivating values and choices that are responsive to others' needs. The analysis she presents in her seminal text: *In a Different Voice*, integrates the "voices" from these interviews in the form of short narratives to illustrate the forms of care present in the individuals' experiences, often ones of conflict or challenge. For another person, hearing or reading such real stories of personal struggles is "tied to feelings of empathy and compassion."[1] Gilligan emphasizes that this kind of contextual (as opposed to abstract or objective) understanding is critical—an understanding that centers care and empathy.

Sociologist Marshall Ganz, in his work on public narrative, also emphasizes the connections between narrative, empathy, and personal understanding. He argues that we experience our values emotionally, and so our moral choices can only be made based on our emotions. As a result, it is not enough to *know* that we *ought* to act; we must also *feel* like we *must* act. Ganz suggests that when engaging with narrative, "because we identify empathetically with the character, we experience the emotional content of the moment."[2] In this way, narrative mobilizes the "heart," equipping individuals with the motivation to make the changes that the "head" recognizes as important.

Traditional mechanisms for sharing research findings might clearly contribute to the "head" argument for why a situation should be changed and what to do about it, but they are less convincing at motivating a person's "heart." The abstraction of data in a way that removes the detail and texture of lived experience does not engage our human capacity for empathy. While statistics indicating the breadth of an issue may impress us, and a critique of a policy offers important information on how to change it, they may not be as effective at activating a caring or empathetic response. Narratives that share real experiences, especially when presented with context and in the voice of the individual, may support empathy in the listener or reader and prime them for action in ways that other methods of presenting the rationale for changing policy or practice do not.

While use of narratives may not be common in most academic writing, several advocacy organizations offer evidence of the value of stories to contribute to policy change. Narrative 4 (N4) is a global organization that focuses on young people and elevates the power of their narrative to build empathy and elicit change. They work with educators and youth to facilitate "story exchanges," which "help students understand that their voices, stories, actions and lives matter, and that they have the power to change, rebuild and revolutionize systems."[3] The founders assert that the sharing of personal narratives can help participants "see the world . . . more empathetically through the exchange of personal narratives."[4]

N4 uses this process to build understanding across a broad number of social challenges faced by youth around the world. For example, their ongoing "Empathy Into Action" campaign launched with "Guns and Empathy," a documentary video that captured story exchanges between people on both sides of gun policy debates. Viewers bear witness to the impactful experiences of the participants as they offer their stories of gun-related violence. In an accompanying *New York Magazine* article, the writers document the policy viewpoints and shifts in position, remarkable even if subtle in their difference, inspired by the understanding gained through the story exchange process.[5]

In the school food system, we have also seen the power of stories to influence public opinion and spur political change as demonstrated by recent public discourse around "lunch shaming" practices. Reports of students stamped with a message indicating they need lunch money and cafeteria staff forced to throw meals away instead of giving them to students with negative account balances have fueled public discontent over these practices.[6] In New Mexico, a state senator introduced legislation to ban practices that single out children whose parents owe money for school lunches. He promoted the bill, which ultimately became law, by sharing his own story of growing up in foster homes and having to mop the floor of the cafeteria to help pay for his lunches.[7]

People have responded to individuals' stories of being shamed or forced to shame others with concern for those who have had this experience. These stories engender empathy toward the students and cafeteria staff given how obviously these practices go against commonly held ideals about caring for children. This empathy for children and workers has been channeled into tangible changes in school food policy and practice, such as the New Mexico law and other efforts to end similar practices and, in some cases, the structural conditions that cause them.[8]

It is also important to recognize that policymakers, parents, and the public would not have known about the need to disrupt lunch shaming practices without workers and students sharing their personal stories. Although lunch shaming practices may be widespread, those not working or eating in a school cafeteria would not necessarily be aware of them. Even within the school food system, those who are involved in one element may not know or understand the experience of others. In this case, simply by sharing what had happened to them, workers and students initiated what seems to be a widely desirable and seemingly durable transformation to school food practices. Such surfacing and centering the perspectives of all stakeholders is necessary for understanding the changes the school food system requires.

COMPOSITE NARRATIVE

Once we see individuals' stories as crucial to justifying and encouraging policy change, we must consider how to share them. Narratives can take different forms: they can range from the simple to the complex and draw on all forms of experience, both real and imagined. Thompson and Kreuter lay out three categories of narrative: authentic, fictional, and composite. Authentic narratives relay the information that a researcher has collected about a participant.[9] These are like case studies in that they are the "real" story of someone's experience. Fictional narratives seek to express a targeted message and may be constructed from a variety of sources, primarily the author's "observation and experience," including their imagination.[10]

The composite narrative presents individuals' experiences and perspectives in a blended picture that conveys key themes found across the body of data collected for a given project.[11] It is not a simple and straightforward retelling as in authentic narratives, yet it remains thoroughly humanized and grounded in the details conveyed to the researcher by those sharing their experiences. Composite narratives draw on multiple stories shared by participants, filtered through the reflexive process of the researchers, and grounded in their knowledge of the literature related to the issue. A practical benefit of this approach is the capacity to represent several key themes in a relatively concise form without losing the quality and form of story and natural voice that may add to the reader's understanding of these experiences. At the same time, a major ethical benefit of composite narrative is the representation of contextualized lived experience in an evocative manner without compromising the confidentiality of participants.

The composite narrative vignettes we include in this chapter present the lived experiences of those participating in our projects, with the aim of providing "true" though not "real" stories. The intent is to highlight prevalent ideas and issues expressed by our participants, using details from their reports.[12] The composites are constructed systematically, synthesizing the participants' voices, their context, and the key themes to convey both the content and the texture of their experiences.

Composite narratives can be used as a technique to share findings from projects using diverse methods for qualitative research. Our vignettes are drawn from two large, multi-method projects examining various aspects of school food in the United States. The FoodCorps project "Reimagining School Cafeterias" (RSC) used human-centered design as a methodology to understand and amplify the voices of school food stakeholders from a diverse profile of nine schools and districts across the United States, with an emphasis on students' experiences of their cafeterias and meal programs.[13]

Human-centered design (HCD), the framework used for RSC, is a solutions-oriented approach to design, used in a variety of applications and contexts, including K–12 education. Traditional HCD methods foreground empathy as the initial step in the design process, with the rationale that to effectively design for and with people, one must understand and collaborate with those most impacted by the topic at hand. Equity-centered design frameworks, such as Liberatory Design and Equity-Centered Community Design, more deeply center community members directly impacted by design outcomes, explicitly seeking to advance equity through both the design process and the designed outcome. These flexible, nonlinear approaches integrate history and healing, acknowledgement and dismantling of power constructs, complexity theory, and other equity-driven mindsets and methods into practice. This ensures that individuals and communities with lived experience of the topic lead and control the outcomes of the process.[14]

The second project, "PreK-12 School Food: Making It Healthier, Making It Regional" (MHMR), initiated by School Food Focus, examined meal program operations in six US school districts.[15] MHMR incorporated the qualitative approaches of participant observation, informal and formal in-depth interviews, graphic elicitation, and focus groups. The researchers combined these qualitative findings with quantitative analysis using surveys and secondary institutional data.

While RSC and MHMR used different frameworks for approaching and conducting research, both projects prioritized listening to and learning from community stakeholders whose perspectives are not often heard and demonstrated the power of individual and collective storytelling. Techniques used to gather information and learn from clients in HCD mirror many of those used in critical qualitative research, reflected in meaningful overlaps in the two projects presented here. Specifically, both projects utilized open-ended interviews and conversations, semi-structured interactive group activities, and observations to gain an understanding of student, staff, and other stakeholder experiences of their school meal programs. These techniques aim to collect data drawn from lived experiences and document them in the participants' own words. The researcher also may observe and interact with project participants in their own environments as well as conduct secondary research on topic history and context.

To create composite narratives, the researcher draws on the stories shared by study participants as well as any secondary research, observations, and/or interactions with participants. The first step of developing a composite narrative involves identifying who will be represented and ensuring that the research process elicited enough understanding to allow the reconstruction of truthful stories. The researcher reviews the synthesis of what stakeholders shared, the full set of direct quotations or transcriptions, secondary research on the history and broader context of the topic, and key themes that have emerged. For each stakeholder group represented, the researcher weaves together pieces that build the profile and story of a composite individual, remaining aware of and attentive to misrepresentation. The researcher uses themes as anchoring elements, incorporating anonymized direct quotations and other realistic details that add texture and specificity to the story. The goal is not to create a profile that is all-encompassing of every person's experience in that stakeholder group, but stakeholders should validate the final composite narrative for accuracy. Ideally, composite narratives should be considered alongside the full set of data and contextual learning to provide an informative and nuanced view of people's experiences.

As part of the process of creating a composite narrative, we stress the responsibility of the researcher or story-sharer to consider their own positionality, personal biases, and other historical and cultural contexts. These all affect how the researcher will interpret and present others' stories. We recognize that typically in American, white-dominant culture, individuals with power and privilege facilitate story sharing. The authors of this chapter are no exception—through this very process we, from our social position as academics and experts and having benefited from white privilege, are demonstrating our power to share and frame others' stories. In addition to self-reflexivity and attentiveness to issues of bias, we suggest that when creating composite narratives the researchers offer transparency about their own position (for example, by including a positionality statement explaining how their identities, lived experiences, and other social lenses could influence their research) and look to research paradigms focused on equity for guidance. To the extent possible, the researcher should include those whose stories are being shared as cocreators of the composite narratives. Depending on their interest, story-sharers could collaborate on writing the narratives, provide feedback on drafts, or be credited in a way that is desirable to them.

CAFETERIA VIGNETTES

The composite narrative vignettes that follow share insights from students, food service managers, and school administrators from their respective positions: the nuanced likes and dislikes of students, the Sisyphean-like responsibilities of a cafeteria manager, and the balancing act of school lunch for a principal. We selected these three stakeholder groups as they are some of the most impacted by school cafeterias, while recognizing that many other school food community members, including other kitchen staff, custodial staff, teachers, and caregivers, are integral members of the cafeteria and school meal ecosystem. Constructed from data integrated from our two projects, they present key themes and concepts shared by participants, transformed into stories that reflect their voices and the context of their lived experience.

In the United States, the food served, how it is offered, and the environment in which students eat differs by school district and by school. However, through our research we have noticed broad similarities across schools of varying size, free and reduced-price meal eligibility, racial demographics, and location. The vignettes presented are set in a US middle school (often grades 5-8) with an above-average percentage of students receiving free or reduced-price meals, which is often associated with a higher percentage of students who eat regularly at school as well as a greater recognition of the importance of the meals program as understood by school administrators. We have not defined other specific characteristics of this fictional school as we believe the perspectives presented reflect common themes that are not necessarily attributable to demographic characteristics.

STUDENT VIGNETTE

Mia: Lunch is pretty OK here. I like talking with my friends.

Jayden: Except when it's so loud you have to scream to hear anything. And then the teachers start screaming at us to be quiet, and man, it just gives you a headache.

Mia: Yeah, that really sucks—it's like, this is our only time to relax.

Jayden: It's also really crowded, especially in the part where you get the food, like people always pushing and stuff.

Riley: Yeah, everyone's always pushing and cutting and trying to get through faster so they have more time. That's the worst part—lunch is too short so by the time you actually get through the line you have to decide if you want to talk or eat.

Jayden: I just don't eat—the food is nasty. It's either like "What is that? How long has that been there?" Or it's just straight up gross—one time the middle of my chicken sandwich was just not cooked and that is not ok.

Riley: Oh yeah! Didn't Caitlin find a hair in one of the chicken sandwiches? So nasty.

Jayden: Yeah! She definitely did! I was there and—

Mia: I don't think the food is that gross; it's just boring. It's like always the same thing—like, pizza again? Really?

Jayden: The baked potatoes they had today are the bomb though—you know it's fresh because they open them right in front of you, and you get to pick your butter or cheese or whatever to go on it.

Mia: Ok, yeah, those potatoes are definitely the real deal.

Riley: Yeah, it's like when they used to have that salad bar, that was so good, and you got to choose what you take. Sometimes it's like um, no, thank you, I don't want slimy carrots again today. I like carrots but come on, how can the lunch ladies mess up carrots? It's like, 'Did you even try them?'

Jayden: They definitely don't try the food. Adults would not eat this food.

Mia: But most of the lunch ladies are really nice though. The one who's usually in the middle, the one who's always like "hey, baby doll, how you doing?" She knows I can't eat ham so if it's a sandwiches day she'll always get me a turkey one.

Riley: Yeah, I guess they are trying, but they really need to just, like, ask us what we think. Why do they keep serving stuff we don't like?

Jayden: At my elementary school the food actually got better because they went around with little samples and had people try things at lunch and then we voted. That was cool, and it was like they actually cared what we think.

CAFETERIA MANAGER VIGNETTE

It's 300 percent go go go here in the kitchen. First, you're getting everything ready, then the bell rings, and we have ten minutes to get all the students through. A few years ago, they cut back our staff, so I just don't have as many ladies as I need. We're doing fresh-topped baked potatoes today and whew, it's a challenge—it takes a long time, and a lot of hands, but the kids would just cry if we got rid of 'em.

And that's our job, making sure each child has something that they want to eat, that they get the nutrition they need. And also, just to be that person who notices if they're having a bad day or compliments their new hairdo or just gives them a friendly smile. We just love our students. That's why we're all here—sure isn't for the pay, I can tell you that!

I do wish we heard more from them about what they like or not. Some days I'll have a minute to walk around and ask the kids what they think about things. We'd much rather give them what they want and not have so much waste, if we can do it, you know, within the regs and the budget and all.

I think the teachers see all the waste and judge us. They don't get all the regulations and why we serve what we do. It's like, we're all on the same team, you know? But some are great, they eat the food, and they'll ask us to come in when they're learning about nutrition or they'll bring their class down and we'll do, like, a little lesson on cooking and math.

I wish we could bring the parents in too, show them what we're all about. School food gets such a bad rap; I just want all those busy parents to know, hey, we got this, you don't have to worry about packing a lunch, your child can get something really tasty and healthy from us here. And for free!

The new principal, Ms. Douglas, she really gets it. The last one, I don't think he even knew any of the other ladies' names. I know Ms. Douglas would like to give us a little more time for the lunch period, but there's just so much they're trying to cram into the school day nowadays. But these kids, they just need a break, need some time to socialize and relax.

SCHOOL PRINCIPAL VIGNETTE

In general, I think lunchtime is an important point in the day for our students. Breakfast, too, as far as nutrition goes. It's pretty obvious that if students are hungry they aren't able to focus in class. They can't learn. And when they're hungry, that's when you see more behavioral issues. Our free and reduced lunch rate here is hovering at around 70 percent, so making sure students who need it are able to get their breakfast in the classroom is a priority for us. Custodial doesn't love it—the mess and everything—but I think everyone recognizes why we're doing it. As for lunch, it's also a time for the kids to just be kids and socialize.

The lunch period is also important for the teachers. It's really their only scheduled break during the day. We have other monitors in the cafeteria during lunch. Occasionally teachers will drop in to grab some food, but most of them don't stick around to eat. Thirty minutes isn't much, so they need that time duty-free. I wish we were able to add a few extra minutes to lunch for students and teachers, but it's just not feasible right now given necessary instructional time. But I will continue to evaluate what's possible in future years.

I personally try to be in the cafeteria a few days a week. This is only my second year here, so it's a good way to get to know the students and kitchen staff. In my role, there's a lot going on at any one time, so it would be pretty easy to limit engagement with kitchen staff. When I started last year, it didn't seem like school administration had much of a relationship with the kitchen. Mrs. Hill and her team run their own shop and have a lot to manage with feeding the kids, meeting the regulations. But we're all here to create the best environment for our students, so I try to keep good communication with them, though there's always room for improvement.

And with the students, you can learn a lot about their preferences just by observing and asking questions. In my opinion, the food here is fine. Nothing gourmet, but the choices are good. But kids learn over time that it's not cool to eat school food. There's such a stigma attached to school food that some older kids don't eat anything. Peer influence is huge at this age. Baked potatoes—I think those were today—are semi-popular, though. I also know the food served here looks different from what a lot of kids get at home. I'm not sure how much parents are engaged in the program. I think all of us here would like to increase family engagement.

CONCLUSION

As researchers, we see the information relayed through these vignettes as an important part of understanding the conditions of school meal programs, and as school food advocates we see these stories as both a means to honor the experiences shared with us as well as a call for action. We hope readers find in these narratives a sense of the texture of life in the cafeteria from these various perspectives, giving a glimpse of what it's like to be a student, cafeteria manager, or principal in the US school food system.

It is imperative that practitioners and policymakers prioritize listening to and learning from the stakeholders who are most impacted by the school food system. We also suggest that those researching or otherwise working in school food systems consider stories, potentially through the tool of composite narrative, as a way of sharing what they and other stakeholders know about school food. Sharing stories offers valuable information about the challenges of contemporary school meal programs, and hearing directly from those experiencing them can inspire in others the empathy required to act on these challenges. Understanding and empathizing with each other's experiences is foundational to cocreating a more equitable and just school food future.

NOTES

1. Carol Gilligan, *In a Different Voice: Psychological Theory and Women's Development* (Cambridge: Harvard University Press, 1982), 69.

2. Marshall Ganz, "Public Narrative, Collective Action, and Power," in *Accountability through Public Opinion: From Inertia to Public Action*, ed. Sina Odugbemi and Taeku Lee (Washington, DC: The World Bank, 2011), 274.

3. Narrative 4, "About Narrative 4," Accessed December 30, 2021, https://narrative4.com/about/.

4. Narrative 4, "About Narrative 4."

5. Lisa Miller, "Can a Gun Victim and a Gun Advocate Change Each Other's Minds? An Experiment in Empathy," *Intelligencer*, December 26, 2016. https://nymag.com/intelligencer/2016/12/gun-violence-radical-empathy.html.

6. See, for example, Elisabeth Sherman, "New Mexico Becomes the First State to Ban Lunch Shaming," *Food & Wine*, May 24, 2017, Access from https://www.yahoo.com/lifestyle/mexico-becomes-first-state-ban-134539126.html.

7. Sherman, "New Mexico Becomes the First State to Ban Lunch Shaming."

8. Legislation introduced into Congress would keep schools from singling out students on the basis of their ability to pay for meals or collecting any outstanding debt and makes all meals free for all students, thus preventing any future debt. See Senator Bernie Sanders, "NEWS: Sanders, Omar, Gillibrand, and Moore Seek to Expand and Make Permanent Universal School Meals," May 7, 2021, https://www.sanders.senate.gov/press-releases/news-sanders-omar-gillibrand-and-moore-seek-to-expand-and-make-permanent-universal-school-meals/.

9. Tess Thompson and Matthew W. Kreuter, "Using Written Narratives in Public Health Practice: A Creative Writing Perspective," *Preventing Chronic Disease* 11 (June 2014), https://doi.org/10.5888/pcd11.130402.

10. Thompson and Kreuter, "Using Written Narratives in Public Health Practice: A Creative Writing Perspective," 2.

11. Marcia Stanley Wertz et al., "The Composite First Person Narrative: Texture, Structure, and Meaning in Writing Phenomenological Descriptions," *International Journal of Qualitative Studies on Health and Well-Being* 6, no. 2 (April 2011), https://doi.org/10.3402/qhw.v6i2.5882.

12. Gavin Fairbairn, "Ethics, Empathy and Storytelling in Professional Development," *Learning in Health and Social Care* 1 (March 2002): 22–32, https://doi.org/10.1046/j.1473-6861.2002.00004.x.

13. See the RSC report for a full description of the project: FoodCorps, "Reimagining School Cafeterias: A Human-Centered Design Study," accessed December 30, 2021, https://foodcorps.org/wp-content/uploads/2019/09/Reimagining-School-Cafeterias-Report.pdf.

14. Creative Reaction Lab, *Equity-Centered Community Design Field Guide* (Creative Reaction Lab, 2018).

15. School Food Focus was a national nonprofit organization that worked with school districts to leverage their purchasing power for healthier school meals. It merged with FoodCorps over the course of the Making It Healthier, Making It Regional (MHMR) project. The full MHMR report is available at: FoodCorps, "Case Studies," accessed December 30, 2021, https://foodcorps.org/wp-content/uploads/2022/08/Pre-K-12-School-Food-Making-It-Healthier-Making-It-Regional.pdf.

13

FACILITATING THINK TANKS TO GUIDE ACTION AND ADVOCACY IN CANADIAN TEACHERS' UNIONS

Andrée Gaçoin, Michelle Gautreaux, and Anne Hales

Among the inequities that have been exposed and amplified by the COVID-19 pandemic, access to affordable and healthy food is a growing crisis for many students and their families. In Canada, a survey conducted in May 2020 found that almost one in seven (14.6 percent) Canadians were living in a household with food insecurity, an increase from 10.5 percent in 2018, and with higher rates for households with children than those without.[1] This has contributed to increased attention to the impact of COVID-19 and food security on children's learning and well-being as well as renewed calls for a national school food program.[2] Canada is the only G7 country that does not have a national school food program, and about one in four children attend school hungry on any given day. Advocacy for a national school food program has persisted over several decades and united a variety of groups, including antipoverty organizations, food banks, public health and food policy experts, teachers, parents, and others. The COVID-19 pandemic has amplified this advocacy. While the federal government announced plans to work toward creating a national school food program in Canada in its 2019 budget, progress remains slow.[3]

The current landscape of Canada's school food programs can best be described as a patchwork system, varying greatly between provinces and territories and from school to school. Most school food programs are funded by nonprofit organizations, charities, community groups, and parents [e.g., through Parent Advisory Council (PAC) fundraising] and often rely on volunteer support.[4] In some contexts, provincial government funding is provided, such as the Community LINK (Learning Includes Nutrition and Knowledge) funding in British Columbia (BC), geared toward supporting vulnerable students. As community coalitions such as the BC Chapter of the Coalition for Healthy School Food have recently pointed out, provincial funding is insufficient, and most programs supported by government (81 percent) must seek additional funds from community groups and charitable organizations to meet student needs.[5] Currently in BC, about 75 percent of school districts do have some type of meal program (breakfast, lunch, and/or a "backpack" program) in at least one school.[6] Many students and families rely on these programs for their daily food nutrition needs. As schools shut down in Spring 2020, many schools in BC (and across the world) scrambled to put in place emergency programs to continue providing food to students. Likewise, food banks across Canada have made adjustments and seen a spike in demand.[7,8]

These responses to food insecurity have been necessary emergency measures. At the same time, the pandemic has served to magnify a long-standing issue that many teachers have witnessed and addressed daily in their classrooms: growing food insecurity among students and a lack of any real systemic approach to addressing this need. For example, a 2015 study by the British Columbia Teachers' Federation (BCTF) pointed to a "considerable gap between the needs of hungry children attending public schools and the food programs available to meet their needs."[9] In many cases, it is teachers who step in to fill these gaps. For instance, teachers reported spending on average $29CA/month to bring food to school for hungry students, a figure that resonates with research from the US.[10]

Within the existing food security literature, there is a gap in relation to the role of teachers and teachers' unions on this important issue. To explore food security from the perspective of teachers, the BCTF held a virtual think tank in Fall 2020.[11] As a social justice union, the BCTF has prioritized healthy food for all as a key equity issue that necessitates concrete action to benefit all students and families. This mandate is reflected in research the BCTF conducted in 2012, which foregrounded the widespread issue of students coming to school hungry and teachers' awareness of the gap in services to support them.[12] The impetus for the 2020 think tank came from a BCTF Executive Committee motion that recommended "investigating holding a Summit on Healthy Food for All Students or other teacher research process[13] that investigates issues and solutions related to food insecurity, access to healthy food for students, and culturally relevant and place-based food."[14]

This chapter seeks to address this gap in the literature by providing a detailed overview and analysis of the virtual think tank, which foregrounded teachers' voices in the conversations around food security. In sharing our approach, we invite academic researchers to engage teachers' unions as partners in activist research and provide an example of what such a partnership might look like.[15]

THE BCTF THINK TANK ON FOOD SECURITY: UNION RESEARCH AS ACTIVIST RESEARCH

To deepen understanding of key issues within public education, and propose transformative actions to address those issues, the BCTF engages in what can broadly be termed 'activist research.' Following Jones, activist research is a "framework for conducting collaborative research that makes explicit challenges to power through transformative action."[16] The BCTF, founded in 1917, has a long history as a social justice union. For the union, this is defined as accepting and acting on "our broad responsibility to be involved in the social development of the communities and the province we live in, and we do this in the interests of the children we teach."[17] Guided by a framework of activist research, projects are carried out by a dedicated research department (BCTF Research) within the union, made up of a director, three researchers and two research assistants. Projects are reviewed on an annual basis and reflect the leadership priorities and key objectives of the BCTF in bargaining, education policy, professional practice, and social justice. For instance, the motion that originally led to the food security think tank came from a group of teachers who put forward a need they encountered in their classrooms to the Executive Committee (the BCTF's democratically elected officers representing fifty thousand members). Drawing on a broad range of education research expertise, and quantitative and qualitative methodologies, the BCTF Research team advocates for the development of educational policy, school programs and classroom practice based on teacher knowledges and experiences.

One methodology used to develop the BCTF's approach to activist research can broadly be defined as "issue sessions" in which a group of teachers are selected from across the province to provide their perspectives, experiences, and recommendations on a particular issue. While issue sessions are usually in-person events, the COVID-19 pandemic necessitated rethinking what a participatory research space might look like. The virtual food security think tank was conceptualized as a series of interactive research spaces that enabled dialogue and connection between teachers, community stakeholders and the union. Specifically, there were three events that enabled these connections.

The first event was a province-wide webinar where the BCTF president, Teri Mooring, discussed key issues with experts in food security research, teaching, and advocacy.[18] Mooring was joined by a panel of four community members: Dr. Sinikka Elliott (associate professor of sociology at the University of British Columbia), Samantha Gambling (project coordinator for the BC Chapter of the Coalition for Healthy School Food), Sarah Kim (coordinator of Vancouver Neighbourhood Food Networks), and Denise Nembhard (a home economics teacher and director of Grow Local Society Tri-cities). The conversation created an opportunity for teachers' stories to be told alongside academic and community-based narratives of food security advocacy and action in a public forum where audience members also shared their own perspectives and experiences with panelists. Following the webinar, BCTF Research compiled the rich list of resources and suggestions curated through the Zoom platform's "chat" feature. The list, along with an archived video of the webinar, was shared with participants as well as teachers taking part in a second think tank event.

The second part of the think tank series was a day-long workshop with teachers drawn from across the province currently engaging in food security work through teaching and advocacy.[19] Participants were recruited through an open call to all BCTF members. Interested teachers filled out an application, and eight members were selected to take part based on their experience as well as personal interest in the topic. Three additional teachers were selected to represent the BCTF Executive Committee, the Teachers of Home Economics Specialist Association (whose members engage in food studies in BC public schools), and an Aboriginal perspective on food security and Indigenous food sovereignty.

Workshop discussions were framed by two "power talks," or short focused presentations intended to prompt participant reflection on their own work and experiences. Dr. Jennifer Black (associate professor, Faculty of Land and Food Systems, University of British Columbia) spoke to food security in the context of the COVID-19 pandemic, followed by teacher Maureen LaGroix, who described lived experiences of colonization of Indigenous food systems and efforts to cultivate Indigenous food sovereignty in Haida Gwaii, the unceded and traditional territory of the Haida Nation. The day's discussions fostered collective discovery and learning about the diverse ways that teachers approach food security issues in their schools and local communities. The day's conversations were interpreted in a visual mural, created by Tiaré Jung of *Drawing Change.* Drawing Change[20] is a network of graphic recorders who listen, synthesize, and draw dialogue in real time, enabling participants to see patterns and collective wisdom emerging from group dialogue (see figure 13.1).

The third and final part of the think tank took a "town hall" webinar format to share stories and recommendations from the think tank and bring the event series to a close. The conversation was facilitated by a member of the BCTF Executive Committee, Violette Baillargeon, and featured a panel of two teachers who had participated in the previous workshop. They shared their personal journeys of connecting food security advocacy work to their roles as teachers and guided the discussion by sharing their hopes and aspirations for where teachers and teachers' unions "go from here" with their teaching and advocacy.

Conducted over the course of a month, the multipart event enabled an iterative process of data analysis that, while facilitated by union researchers, was cocreated as the think tank unfolded. The virtual format, necessitated by the COVID-19 pandemic, created new threads of exploration through shared chat messages and interactive whiteboards,[21] and facilitated conversations in group and breakout spaces. The "findings," as presented in this chapter, are intended as the beginning of the conversation, sparks of

13.1 Teachers' perspectives on the impacts of COVID-19 on food security in BC. Live graphic recording by Tiaré Jung, Drawing Change, for the BCTF food security virtual think tank, November 23, 2020.

ideas that aim to facilitate "reflections *within* [food security] movements in order to understand, analyze and improve goals, tactics, structure and processes."[22]

"TRANSFORMING CHALLENGES INTO OPPORTUNITIES": PRINCIPLES FOR ACTION

As teachers discussed their experiences with, and perspectives on, food security in BC public schools, a broad set of principles on which a more just food system should be grounded collectively emerged: rights-based, universal, place-based, and culturally relevant.

"PUBLIC SUPPORT AND INVESTMENT IN THE WELL-BEING OF ALL CHILDREN, NOT JUST CHARITY"

A rights-based approach entails addressing the structural issues that drive food insecurity. For example, while food banks met an immediate need during the COVID-19 crisis, they have been found to be an ineffective "solution" to food insecurity.[23] Food banks are also critiqued for their reliance on a charity model and for masking the need for deeper structural change such as a basic-income approach to poverty reduction.[24]

In the context of school communities, one of the key challenges discussed at the think tank was that school food programs rely on a charity-model, such as partnerships with external community providers or grants to run, as described in this chapter's introduction. Others pointed out how school food programs also too often rely on the passion of a single teacher or the support of one school administrator who can find the time to liaise with a community partner or nonprofit organization to ensure a school food program is successfully run, as most school food programs are created and run at the school level. Not only is this at odds with a rights-based approach, but it also undermines the long-term sustainability of these programs since grant funding must be continuously sought after and is not guaranteed from year to year. The lack of sustained government support and adequate investment makes it challenging to build long-term infrastructure and planning to support school food programs.

Teachers spoke clearly about the need for a rights-based approach to food security in BC to address the shortcomings in current food security policy and school food programming. A rights-based approach frames food security as a central part of the mandate of public education. This involves ensuring access to healthy food for *all* students and supporting food literacy learning for *all* students. Further, a rights-based approach is responsive to the multifaceted impacts that food insecurity has on children, as documented in the research literature.[25]

"UNIVERSAL, NOT TARGETED"

Building on a rights-based approach, the second principle articulated by teachers to guide action is universality. As with the previous statement related to accessing healthy food for all students, this is about "universal access to food (breakfast and lunch) as a community everyday" (teacher participant). Teachers shared how in some schools the school food program is intended for families that struggle to provide their children lunch from home. Students who then access food provided by the school are considered "in need," which can create stigma. Others observed that while many schools have school food programs, participating in the program usually incurs a cost for parents. Recognizing that not all families are able to afford school food programs, many schools offer subsidies, but not all families access them because of potential stigmatization or not knowing how to apply. Programs that are intended for students and families as well as programs that provide subsidy options are both examples of targeted programs, programs that are not universally accessible to all and include targeted measures to certain groups to achieve fuller access.[26] Teachers discussed the need to move toward a universal approach, where all students are covered by the school food program, regardless of financial need. Teachers recognized shifting from targeted to universal school food programs for all as key to addressing the potential stigma that children and families who access school meal programs may face.[27]

Universality also speaks to how learning about food could be a key part of teaching and learning. As one teacher shared, engaging through food creates a "vibrant learning space" and forms "a central part of creating school community." Another teacher described how each class in a school prepared a dish for a shared Thanksgiving meal and how this created a powerful moment of connection grounded within the school community.

Adding on, another teacher observed that all students have "food stories," and an inclusive approach to food security is based on "ensuring everyone's food stories are being told." Throughout the think tank, teachers described ways in which food security extends beyond the provision of school meals and can become a key part of the curriculum. This includes the "preparation and sharing of school meals," "food literacy learning for all students," and connections to outdoor education.

Finally, teachers discussed how working toward a universal approach may also require rethinking the spaces of public education. This could entail "a garden in every school" or more intentionally connecting to agriculture and land-based learning through farm-to-school programs,[28] "partnerships with farmers" in the local community, or "working farming programs."[29] These proposed spaces point to recognizing that "deep system change is needed to build resilience and equity into the future."[30] As one teacher explained, addressing the global climate crisis "starts in the school system" with "educated and informed youth."

"PLACE-BASED AND CULTURALLY RELEVANT": FROM FOOD SECURITY TO FOOD SOVEREIGNTY

A third principle drawn from teachers' perspectives is the importance of place-based, culturally relevant approaches to understanding food security. This principle was discussed within the broader context of settler colonialism and colonization, both in terms of the historical and ongoing impacts on Indigenous food systems and ways of life. A key part of the settler colonial project has been the forcible removal of Indigenous peoples from their lands and onto reserves. This has cut Indigenous communities off from being food sovereign and independent. Indigenous peoples have been prevented from practicing their traditional ways of cultivating food and hunting and forced into a dependency-based food structure, where access to nutritious food is very expensive and often entails driving long distances, particularly in rural and remote communities.[31]

The education system in Canada played a devastating role in the systemic destruction of Indigenous ways of being and living, especially in relation to food sovereignty. In residential schools, food was used as a weapon, a tool of colonial domination to destroy the connection Indigenous children had with their culture and way of life.[32] Indigenous children were malnourished, denied their traditional foods, and forced to consume a highly processed, poor-quality diet. The generational impact and legacy have been the loss of cultural knowledge and connection with land for many, as well as increased food-related health complications and disease.[33] In discussing this painful legacy, teachers at the think tank made the connection to current school food programs, where the lack of culturally relevant food continues to act as a barrier to participation in school food programs for many Indigenous and racialized students.[34]

As a part of decolonization, public schools and education can be reclaimed as sites for resistance and learning to be and do *differently*, as many critical education scholars have pointed out.[35] BCTF teachers attending the think tank echoed this idea as they discussed how, through their teaching, they could challenge the historical and ongoing legacy of colonization and its impacts on their food system. For example, teachers spoke about how taking students onto the land can make space for truth and reconciliation. One teacher spoke about the importance of helping students build a relationship with plants and seeds and shared how she is supporting her students to write stories "from seed to squash," connecting students to teachings about the environment and food sources. Others shared how they have had the opportunity to engage with First Nations elders as part of their teaching about the land, emphasizing the importance of intergenerational relationships with elders and reconciliation through partnerships and sharing opportunities with First Nations. All emphasized the importance of supporting teachers to develop the practice of teaching outside, on the land, independent of the school building. These conversations reflected a commitment to integrate Indigenous ways of knowing and being into teaching and learning, a key part of BC's curriculum since 2015.[36]

In discussing reconnection with land, sustainable agricultural practices, and honoring the knowledge of elders, teachers were articulating how they have the opportunity to engage *food sovereignty* as part of the work of reconciliation through their teaching. Food security and food sovereignty are closely related but distinct in important ways. The notion of food security refers to the goal of eradicating hunger and ensuring all people have access to affordable, nutritious food to meet their dietary needs.[37] Food sovereignty, in turn, is rooted in the idea that "people should thus be given the right to define and decide their own policies and practices around sustainable, *culturally appropriate*, and healthy food production, distribution, and consumption that guarantees equal access to an entire population ... food sovereignty is not just about nutrition, affordability, and access, but also about a connection to history, culture, and the Earth."[38]

Food security and food sovereignty are not necessarily opposed. Indeed, the conversations from the think tank point to how food security can be understood as one part of a broader project of food sovereignty.[39] The focus is then not interrogating the differences between the two concepts but rather bringing a lens of decolonization to food security. This is a critical lesson that emerged from the think tank for the BCTF as a union that will be taken forward to inform our future positions and advocacy on the issue.

PATHWAYS FOR ACTION

While the rich conversations from the think tank, and indeed the diversity of teacher experiences and perspectives from around the province, cannot be reduced to a singular vision for achieving food security, one teacher captured many of the points discussed when describing their vision: "all children in BC have access to healthy, sufficient, place and culturally based foods in a universal program delivered in cooperation with BC food growers, providers and caretakers. Food is the connecting place for community, economic and social health." The think tank offered three potential pathways for working toward this vision: amplifying, extending, and advocating.

AMPLIFYING: FOOD SECURITY AS PEDAGOGY

Teachers are uniquely positioned to bring a pedagogical intentionality and sensibility to food security issues in ways that other stakeholders cannot. From designing the curriculum of food preparation and school garden projects to witnessing how inequitable food provisioning affects young people's well-being and learning, teachers engage in food security issues in innovative ways. Teachers participating in the think tank shared how the day-long workshop was itself a unique space to learn about the diversity

13.2 Teacher visions for food security in BC. Live graphic recording by Tiaré Jung, Drawing Change, for the BCTF food security virtual think tank, November 23, 2020.

of teaching approaches and programs across the province. Many of these approaches are grounded in community- and land-based learning.[40] At the same time, teachers spoke to the need for an ongoing mechanism to share lessons learned and connect with one another. Potential ways to amplify teachers' pedagogical contributions included: sharing food security knowledge and lessons learned from teachers' perspectives (e.g., articles in union publications or in social media); supporting a community of practice for teachers exploring and addressing food security issues; and embedding food security issues in existing union training events.

EXTENDING: PRIORITIZING FOOD SECURITY IN SCHOOL DISTRICT PROGRAMS AND STAFFING

While some teachers are already engaged in food security issues, the COVID-19 pandemic has exposed how food security impacts school communities more broadly. Teachers shared potential paths to extend the work that is already occurring, such as: creating a "making the case" toolkit for teachers to advocate for rights-based, universal, place-based, and culturally relevant school food programs in their local communities; developing a "food justice lens" to guide teaching and learning; designing professional development workshops and other union-created resources on food security issues; and including food security in existing structures within school districts (e.g., advocating for dedicated staffing to address school food security and connecting with community experts to bring food literacy into classrooms).

ADVOCATING: FOOD SECURITY AND POLICY CHANGE

As discussed in the previous section, understanding food security as a part of food sovereignty requires deeper interrogation of our educational systems and structures, and how these can contribute to food security within the broader project of decolonization. In Canada, this work is guided by the recommendations and calls to action from the Truth and Reconciliation Commission of Canada.[41] The BCTF has committed to using these recommendations and calls to action to guide the spirit of all educational initiatives.[42]

The think tank pointed to several potential paths for union-led advocacy that position food security within education for reconciliation. These include: integrating a locally relevant food literacy program into BC's provincial curriculum; engaging with other education stakeholders, such as educational support workers[43] or administrative staff, and communities; advocating for free, culturally relevant, universal school lunch programs;[44] and including a food security lens in new building construction, such as ensuring that school sites include designated school garden spaces and kitchens, as well as less "structured" play spaces and more open spaces for children and teachers to explore and connect with the land.

CONCLUSION

The BCTF's food security think tank conversations confirmed how the COVID-19 crisis has exposed the vulnerabilities of our food systems in meeting the basic needs of all and highlighted the importance of schools as key sites for fulfilling that important social mandate. Schools are key public spaces of community and care, and support students' basic needs in many ways, including the provision of food. While teachers have firsthand knowledge of food insecurity and are among those at the forefront responding to this need in their schools and communities, the perspectives of teachers and teachers' unions are often overlooked in the broader academic literature. This chapter makes an important intervention by showing multiple ways that teachers connect food sovereignty to their role as educators. We hope it provides inspiration to others to engage teachers' unions in conversation, research, and advocacy.

NOTES

1. Statistics Canada, "Food Insecurity During the COVID-19 Pandemic, May 2020," Government of Canada, June 24, 2020, https://www150.statcan.gc.ca/n1/pub/45-28-0001/2020001/article/00039-eng.htm.

2. Children First Canada, "Top 10 Threats to Childhood in Canada and the Impact of COVID-19," September 1, 2020, https://childcarecanada.org/documents/research-policy-practice/20/09/top-10-threats-childhood-canada-and-impact-covid-19; Naomi Dove et al., "Impact of School Closures on Learning, Child and Family Well-Being during the COVID-19 Pandemic," BC Centre for Disease Control and BC Children's Hospital, September 22, 2020, http://www.bccdc.ca/Health-Info-Site/Documents/Public_health_COVID-19_reports/Impact_School_Closures_COVID-19.pdf; UNICEF Canada, "Canada's Kids in Lockdown: Impact of the COVID-19 Pandemic on the Well-Being of

Children in Canada," May 2020, https://oneyouth.unicef.ca/sites/default/files/2020-05/COVID19_RapidImpactAssessment_UNICEF%20Canada_May2020.pdf; Food Secure Canada, "Growing Resilience and Equity: A Food Policy Action Plan in the Context of Covid-19," May 2020, https://foodsecurecanada.org/sites/foodsecurecanada.org/files/fsc_-_growing_resilience_equity_10_june_2020.pdf; Coalition for Healthy School Food Canada (CHSF), "Coalition for Healthy School Food Canada," 2020, https://www.healthyschoolfood.ca.

3. Jess Haines and Amberley Ruetz, "Comprehensive, Integrated Food and Nutrition Programs in Canadian Schools: A Healthy and Sustainable Approach," Arrell Food Institute at the University of Guelph, 2020, https://arrellfoodinstitute.ca/wp-content/uploads/2020/03/SchoolFoodNutrition_Final_RS.pdf.; CHSF, "Coalition for Healthy School Food Canada"; Lynn Roblin, "Why Canada Needs a Universal School Food Program," *Nutrition Connections* (blog), July 27, 2020, https://nutritionconnections.ca/w5h-on-a-universal-healthy-school-food-program-in-canada/.

4. BC Chapter of the Coalition for Healthy School Food, "Attention: Select Standing Committee on Finance and Government Services Regarding 2021 BC Government Budget Priorities" (unpublished letter, June 15, 2020), https://2edb03c8-6d8c-411f-88a8-2708d30ad344.filesusr.com/ugd/e7a651_32c7e5c8f3714eb8bc4c7a767cd6f59c.pdf; Haines and Ruetz, "Comprehensive, Integrated Food and Nutrition."

5. BC Chapter of the Coalition for Healthy School Food, "Attention: Select Standing Committee."

6. BC Chapter of the Coalition for Healthy School Food, "Attention: Select Standing Committee."

7. BC Chapter of the Coalition for Healthy School Food, "Attention: Select Standing Committee"; Breakfast Club of Canada, "Breakfast Club of Canada Sets up an Emergency Fund to Reach out to Children across the Country," Canada Newswire, March 20, 2020, https://www.newswire.ca/news-releases/breakfast-club-of-canada-sets-up-an-emergency-fund-to-reach-out-to-children-across-the-country-849383297.html; World Food Programme, "A Country-by-Country Compilation of Measures Taken to Address the Loss of School Meals Caused by COVID-19 School Closures," *World Food Programme Insight*, March 30, 2020, https://medium.com/world-food-programme-insight/a-country-by-country-compilation-of-measures-taken-to-address-the-loss-of-school-meals-caused-by-6d4ef7849e19.

8. See, for example, Denio Lourenco, "'Most Challenging, Difficult Year': Canadian Food Banks Get Creative to Meet Demand Amid Pandemic," CTV News, October 11, 2020, https://www.ctvnews.ca/canada/most-challenging-difficult-year-canadian-food-banks-get-creative-to-meet-demand-amid-pandemic-1.5141549.

9. British Columbia Teachers' Federation Research (BCTF), "Hungry Students in BC Public Schools and the Adequacy of School Meal Programs to Support Them" (unpublished report, Vancouver, BC, 2015).

10. BCTF Research, "Hungry Students in BC Public Schools," 14.

11. We sincerely thank the teachers who shared their perspectives and experiences as a part of this think tank. Their passion and commitment to food security, and

public education more broadly, is truly inspiring. We also thank the community experts who joined in the discussions, helping to frame key issues and raise further lines of inquiry for our discussions.

12. BCTF Research, "Hungry Students in BC Public Schools."

13. The BCTF has a dedicated research department (BCTF Research) that uses a variety of methodologies to engage in research *with* teachers. The reference to "other teacher research process" allows for flexibility in how members are engaged in research projects with the union.

14. BCTF Executive Committee, "Meeting Minutes" (February 21–22, 2020).

15. For example, one outcome of the relationship forged during the think tank was the BCTF joining the BC Chapter of the Coalition for Healthy School Food as an endorser organization.

16. Denisha Jones, "Research as Resistance: Activist Research as a Framework and Methodology for Social Change," *IGI Global Handbook on Innovative Techniques, Trends, and Analysis for Optimized Research Methods* (2018): 27, https://doi.org/10.4018/978-1-5225-5164-5.ch002.

17. For a description of the various social justice projects the BCTF is engaged in, see British Columbia Teachers' Federation (BCTF), "Social Justice," accessed April 22, 2023, https://www.bctf.ca/topics/services-guidance/social-justice.

18. See British Columbia Teachers' Federation (BCTF), "COVID-19 and Food Security in BC Schools," November 20, 2020, video, 1:21:55, https://www.youtube.com/watch?v=whtud8IWFEs&t=37s.

19. Unless otherwise noted, all direct quotes are from participants at this teacher workshop.

20. See Drawing Change, accessed April 22, 2023, https://drawingchange.com/.

21. Mural, accessed April 22, 2023, https://www.mural.co/.

22. Neil Sutherland, "Social Movements and Activist Ethnography," review of *The Will of the Many*, by Marianne Maekelbergh, *Direct Action*, by David Graeber, and *Networking Futures*, by Jeffrey Juris. *Organization* 20, no. 4 (2013): 627–635, https://doi-org.gate.lib.buffalo.edu/10.1177/1350508412450219.

23. PROOF "Household Food Insecurity in Canada," accessed December 30, 2021, https://proof.utoronto.ca/food-insecurity/.

24. Graham Riches, "Canada Must Eliminate Food Banks and Provide a Basic Income after COVID-19," *The Conversation*, September 10, 2020, http://theconversation.com/canada-must-eliminate-food-banks-and-provide-a-basic-income-after-covid-19-144994.

25. Carinne Deeds, "Food for Thought: How Food Insecurity Affects a Child's Education," *American Youth Policy Forum* (blog), August 24, 2015, https://www.aypf.org/blog/food-for-thought-how-food-insecurity-affects-a-childs-education/; Erin L. Faught et al., "The Association between Food Insecurity and Academic Achievement in Canadian School-Aged Children," *Public Health Nutrition* 20, no. 15 (October 2017):

2778–2785, https://doi.org/10.1017/S1368980017001562; Food Research & Action Center (FRAC), "The Impact of Poverty, Food Insecurity, and Poor Nutrition on Health and Well-Being," December 2017, https://frac.org/wp-content/uploads/hunger-health-impact-poverty-food-insecurity-health-well-being.pdf; Anna D. Johnson and Anna J. Markowitz, "Associations Between Household Food Insecurity in Early Childhood and Children's Kindergarten Skills," *Child Development* 89, no. 2 (March 2018): e1–e17, https://doi.org/10.1111/cdev.12764.

26. Jennifer Black et al., "SD40 School Nourishment Program 2018–2019 Report," Fraser Health Authority, New Westminster School District, University of Saskatchewan, and University of British Columbia, June 2020, http://lfs-jblack.sites.olt.ubc.ca/files/2020/06/BC-School-Lunch-Program-Working-Report-June-2020.pdf.

27. See BCTF Research, "Hungry Students in BC Public Schools and the Adequacy of School Meal Programs to Support Them"; Black et al., "SD40 School Nourishment Program 2018–2019 Report."

28. Farm-to-school programs connect students and teachers to local agriculture with the goals of increasing access to fresh, locally sourced foods in schools, developing food literacy amongst students, and strengthening the local food system. For examples, see Farm to School BC, "Who is Farm to School BC?" accessed April 22, 2023, https://farmtoschoolbc.ca/about-us/what-is-farm-to-school/.

29. Working farming programs connect grade 10–12 students with hands-on experience in all aspects of farm management. For example, see Delta School District, "Farm Roots Mini School on Global TV," February 11, 2016, https://www.deltasd.bc.ca/programs/farm-roots/.

30. Food Secure Canada, "Growing Resilience and Equity," 10.

31. Food Secure Canada, "Growing Resilience and Equity"; Gabrielle Goldhar with Niisaachewan Anishinaabe Nation, "The Interconnected Nature of Food Security and Food Sovereignty," *NiCHE* (blog), May 22, 2020, https://niche-canada.org/2020/05/22/the-interconnected-nature-of-food-security-and-food-sovereignty/.

32. Truth and Reconciliation Commission of Canada, *Honouring the Truth, Reconciling for the Future: Summary of the Final Report of the Truth and Reconciliation Commission of Canada* (Ottawa: Truth and Reconciliation Commission of Canada, 2015), http://www.trc.ca/assets/pdf/Honouring_the_Truth_Reconciling_for_the_Future_July_23_2015.pdf/https://publications.gc.ca/site/eng/9.800288/publication.html; Food Secure Canada, "Growing Resilience and Equity."

33. Food Secure Canada, "Growing Resilience and Equity."

34. See BCTF Research, "Hungry Students in BC Public Schools."

35. Examples include, but are not limited to, Henry A. Giroux, *Theory and Resistance in Education: A Pedagogy for the Opposition* (South Hadley, MA: Bergin & Garvey, 1983); bell hooks, *Teaching to Transgress: Education as the Practice of Freedom* (New York: Routledge, 1994); E. Wayne Ross and Kevin D. Vinson, "Resisting Neoliberal Education Reform: Insurrectionist Pedagogies and the Pursuit of Dangerous Citizenship," *Cultural Logic: A Journal of Marxist Theory & Practice* 20 (2014): 17–45, https://doi.org/10.14288/clogic.v20i0.190890.

36. For more information on British Columbia's redesigned curriculum, see British Columbia Curriculum, "Curriculum Overview," accessed April 22, 2023, https://curriculum.gov.bc.ca/curriculum/overview#key-features. BCTF teachers were involved in this process, and their perspectives and experiences have been documented in another BCTF Research Report. See Andrée Gacoin, *The Politics of Curriculum Making: Understanding the Possibilities for and Limitations to a 'Teacher-Led' Curriculum in British Columbia* (Vancouver, BC: British Columbia Teachers' Federation, July 2018), 48.

37. Georgia Morelli, "The Food Sovereignty Movement Aiming to Put Food Security in Our Own Hands," UNSW Australian Human Rights Institute, 2020, https://www.humanrights.unsw.edu.au/news/food-sovereignty-movement-aiming-put-food-security-our-own-hands.

38. Gabrielle Goldhar and Niisaachewan Anishinaabe Nation, "The Interconnected Nature of Food Security and Food Sovereignty."

39. Georgia Morelli, "The Food Sovereignty Movement."

40. See the book's ancillary materials for examples of teacher-led work and resources that participants shared at the think tank.

41. See Truth and Reconciliation Commission of Canada, accessed April 22, 2023, www.trc.ca.

42. See the British Columbia Teachers' Federation, "Statement of Principles," accessed April 22, 2023, https://bctf.ca/uploadedFiles/Public/AboriginalEducation/StatementOfPrinciples.pdf.

43. In our context, these workers can be broadly defined as members of the Canadian Union of Public Employees (CUPE) and include custodians, maintenance/facilities workers, cafeteria managers, education assistants, among others. See British Columbia Schools CUPE K-12, accessed April 22, 2023, https://bcschools.cupe.ca/.

44. The BCTF is an endorsing organization of the BC Coalition for Healthy School Food, which outlines an approach whereby federal and provincial governments both contribute to expanding existing programs and create new ones. Coalition for Healthy School Food, "Our Guiding Principles," 2018, https://www.healthyschoolfood.ca/guiding-principles.

14

THE CENTER FOR ECOLITERACY'S APPROACH TO SCHOOL FOOD SYSTEMS CHANGE IN THE UNITED STATES

Anne Moertel

The Center for Ecoliteracy, a California-based nonprofit organization, has been engaged in school food systems change for over twenty-five years. Informed by observing living systems in nature, a systems-change approach acknowledges that lasting change occurs when multiple parts of a system are considered: cause and effect, people, and policy, and how these elements interact.[1]

With a focus on building and supporting equitable school meal programs that feature fresh California ingredients, the center recognizes that to create real progress and lasting change, the whole school food system must be considered. By creating deep collaborative partnerships, activating a statewide network of school districts, and identifying the most effective levers of change and key voices to amplify, the center serves as a catalyst for change within the school food system.

In *The Systems View of Life: A Unifying Vision*, Pier Luigi Luisi and Center for Ecoliteracy cofounder Fritjof Capra wrote that "truly sustainable development is based on the recognition that we are an inseparable part of the web of life, of human and nonhuman communities, and that enhancing the dignity and sustainability of any one of them will enhance all the others."[2] The center manifests this idea by engaging students, families, educators, school nutrition directors, partner organizations, food distributors, farmers, and policymakers in school food systems change. Engagement of stakeholders from schools, nonprofit organizations, government agencies, and existing leaders in the field fosters community to build toward common goals. From this approach, shared priorities and opportunities across the system are identified to highlight opportunities that benefit multiple stakeholders.

The center began this work in 1995 with a pilot project to connect school food and garden efforts in Northern California. Three years later, the Center embarked on its first engagement with Berkeley Public Schools in Berkeley, California. Called the Food Systems Project, it was designated as one of four pilot projects of the US Department of Agriculture (USDA) "Linking Farms to Schools" initiative. The project launched a district-wide effort to transform school nutrition service and related curriculum. Using the systems approach, the center led a network of seventeen Berkeley organizations to establish gardens on every public school campus in the city, develop a city food policy, and lead a successful bond campaign for kitchen and cafeteria infrastructure improvements.[3] This led the city of Berkeley to adopt the nation's first district-wide school food policy. This policy, in turn, informed the 2004 federal mandate for every school district participating in the National School Lunch or School Breakfast Programs—that is, nearly every public school district in the US—to implement a wellness policy. Today, school districts nationwide develop and use wellness policies to model healthy habits for the school community and foster a healthy learning environment.[4]

To help catalyze success into the future, and to learn from other successful meal programs, the center convened leading school nutrition experts and practitioners to develop a portable framework that it published in 2004: *Rethinking School Lunch*. This guide provided action-oriented steps for school districts to work toward the goal of serving freshly prepared meals featuring local ingredients. Since there is no single blueprint for reforming school food—every school district is unique—*Rethinking School Lunch* outlines ten interconnected pathways that can help school districts identify which levers of change will help them begin their own transformations: food and health; policy; teaching and learning; the dining experience; procurement; facilities; finances; waste management; professional development; and marketing and communications.[5]

In 2009, the center began a partnership with the TomKat Ranch Educational Foundation, founded by philanthropist and environmental advocate Kat Taylor, to foster a more sustainable food system by transforming school meals in California and prioritizing freshly prepared and locally grown food. The partnership helped to form the California Food for California Kids initiative, the creation of resources to promote fresh, California-grown food in schools, and opportunities for local and state policy change.

SCHOOL NUTRITION PROGRAMS IN CALIFORNIA

The center's work remains focused on California, which is home to the largest number of public school students in the US. California serves 6.2 million children in its public schools, 59 percent of whom were eligible for the free or reduced-price lunch program in the 2020–2021 school year, a common measure of poverty in the US public education system. Almost one in five California children live in households with limited or uncertain access to adequate food, and California consistently reports a higher percentage of children living in food-insecure households than the country overall.[6]

California has a history of progressive school food policy change. In 1988, California voters committed to allocating at least 40 percent of the state budget on public schools and community colleges through the passage of Proposition 98, which also includes specific tests to ensure that the funding remains relatively stable year after year.[7]

At the national level, beginning in 2014–2015, the federal Community Eligibility Provision (CEP) allows schools serving a high number of children living in poverty to provide all students with free meals. California advocates have worked to encourage schools to utilize this provision by formalizing the use of Medi-Cal data (Medi-Cal is California's Medicaid program, a federal program that covers the cost of medical services for children and adults with limited income and resources) to directly certify eligible students (making it easier for schools to qualify as "high poverty") and requiring the highest-poverty schools to implement CEP with Senate Bill 138.[8] By 2021, 38 percent of California's public schools were participating in CEP.

At the same time, anti-hunger advocates recognized that the cost of school meals was not the only barrier to participation. Based on feedback from students and school nutrition professionals, advocates recognized the importance of addressing the stigma surrounding school meals and ensuring that schools were equipped to serve meals that appeal to students. In 2017, the state responded to these critiques by passing Senate Bill 250, the "Child Hunger Prevention and Fair Treatment Act," later superseded by Senate Bill 265, which strengthened the provisions in the original bill.[9] SB 250 went into effect January 1, 2018, guaranteeing all students a school meal of their choice, regardless of whether they could pay. It also prohibited schools from "lunch shaming," the practice of refusing a child a lunch or providing them with an alternate packaged lunch, different from what other children could choose from, if they cannot pay. While this provided a more equitable school meal experience for students, it had the unintended consequence of requiring school districts, as two nutrition directors told researchers, "to pay the debt from their general fund, strapping already struggling schools."[10] According to Senate floor analysis on SB 265, both small and large school districts saw an increase in unpaid meal debt.[11] Barstow Unified School District, which serves approximately 6,300 students, 72 percent of whom are eligible for free or reduced-price meals, reported unpaid meal debt of $16,000 for the 2016–2017 school year and projected $55,714 for the 2018–2019 school year. Los Angeles Unified School District, which serves approximately 608,000 students, 77 percent of whom are eligible for free or reduced-price meals, reported unpaid meal debt of $393,200 for the 2016–2017 school year and projected $2,249,242 for the 2018–2019 school year.[12]

School meal programs, and school kitchen facilities are historically underfunded in the US, and different districts—and schools within those districts—approach this challenge in different ways. Schools with full cooking kitchens can prepare meals on-site but often lack the funding to hire and train labor to prepare and serve freshly made meals. Others, though they were built with full cooking kitchens, don't have the money to repair broken or outdated equipment, and many schools were built without kitchens altogether. This lack of adequate facilities to prepare food, coupled with a lack of professional development and culinary skills training offered to school nutrition professionals, means many schools simply heat or chill packaged products and set them out for students,[13] who often find the food unappetizing.[14] Some school districts utilize a central kitchen to prepare fresh meals in-house and distribute them to school sites. This model allows for the preparation of school meals with more local and seasonal ingredients, and provides freshly made food to students, though it, too, is often packaged, delivered to schools, and reheated on-site.

A variety of these models are used to feed students in California. A 2020 survey report "Are California Public Schools Scratch-Cooking Ready? A survey of food service directors on the state of school kitchens" showed that 31 percent of districts reported high levels of scratch cooking, 53 percent reported some scratch or speed scratch cooking (using a combination of processed and fresh foods), and 16 percent reported little to no scratch cooking.[15] The report states, "While scratch cooking appears to be occurring in districts across the state, rural school districts are more likely to report high levels of scratch cooking than their urban, suburban, or town peers," and "Majority non-white school districts report less scratch cooking. Forty percent of school districts that are majority white enrollment report high levels of scratch cooking, compared to only 27 percent of majority non-white school districts."

Though California grows nearly half of the country's fruits and vegetables, public school students are rarely fed local products. According to the USDA's 2019 Farm to School Census, only 21 percent of the purchasing dollars for school meals in California are spent locally (as defined by each school district), and this percentage drops to 11 percent when excluding fluid milk.[16]

Nationwide, the USDA has found that school meals often cost more to produce than the reimbursements—a phenomenon exacerbated in California because of the higher costs of food and labor.[17] Yet approximately $4.50 was allocated for each school lunch for the 2021–2022 school year,[18] which is supposed to cover equipment, labor, ingredients, and all other costs associated with preparing and serving a school meal. With such minimal funding, school nutrition directors are pressured to get creative with procurement and labor practices while crafting meals that are both appetizing to students and meet USDA nutrition guidelines.

Even with all of these barriers to providing fresh, local meals in schools, improving the school food system presents an incredible opportunity. In California, more than one billion school meals are served each year. This scale creates an opportunity to source food from California farmers and producers, support the school nutrition workforce, and provide students with freshly prepared meals that can support their health and education. The center's history of school food systems change provides effective strategies and lessons learned in the journey to transform school food.

The story of the center, the campaign, and the platform it was built on are described in the following sections. The center, its cosponsors, and over two hundred supporting organizations launched a "School Meals for All" campaign that led, in the summer of 2021, to legislation making California the first state in the nation to adopt universal school meals. Beginning in the 2022–2023 school year, the state will permanently provide free breakfast and lunch to all K–12 public school students. The strategies used in this successful campaign present a model for advocates and policymakers to lobby for and enact universal school meals.

CALIFORNIA FOOD FOR CALIFORNIA KIDS

Today, the center has expanded its reach from one school in Berkeley to a network of over one hundred school districts in California through California Food for California Kids, an initiative that recognizes the leadership and innovation of school nutrition professionals, builds the capacity of school districts to provide students with fresh, locally grown food, and reinforces connections between the classroom, cafeteria, and garden. Membership is free of charge, and the center builds strategic relationships with food service directors and school district leadership to advance food systems change in their school districts. The California Food for California Kids Network serves more than 330 million school meals annually, which together serve one-third of the school meals in the state.

When the center first sought to recruit school districts to build this network, it identified the largest school districts in California with the highest percentage of students qualifying for free or reduced-price meals. The focus was on scale, serving students with the highest need and recruiting districts with a high level of readiness for change. The center also looked to recruit districts that were served by a school nutrition director with the leadership potential to champion the school nutrition program and that had local procurement or scratch cooking programs in place already.

To join, members commit to increasing local procurement and freshly prepared meals; providing garden, culinary, and food system education;

and contributing to the network's data and storytelling development. Each district in the network completes an annual assessment survey to identify its challenges, accomplishments, and goals. In 2020, members rated universal school meals as their top policy priority.

Members of the California Food for California Kids Network gain access to professional development and engagement opportunities, marketing and advocacy materials, and the opportunity to shape a shared political platform. They receive recognition for their leadership and can receive awards for their commitment and innovation. Stakeholders report that the resource they value most, however, is the ability to build relationships with, and learn from, their peers.

In 2022, participating school districts came from thirty-three different counties and represent the diversity of California, including rural districts surrounded by farms in the Central Valley and urban and suburban districts up and down the coast. Some of them are very small, such as one with a single 177-student school site, and some are quite large, including the state's largest, Los Angeles Unified School District, which enrolls more than six hundred thousand students across 1,011 sites. The network represents over two million students, a majority of whom are students of color and qualify for free or reduced-price meals.

This network was born out of the center's "California Thursdays" program, which encouraged school districts to serve freshly prepared meals featuring California-grown ingredients starting one day per week. Through this strategy, districts gradually revamped their practices so that fresh, healthy school meals became the norm. The center provided the *Rethinking School Lunch* framework, technical support, professional development, and marketing resources to support districts in serving and promoting California Thursdays meals.

School districts also participated in "Collective Action Days" to serve California Thursdays meals together on the same day, creating a statewide media campaign to celebrate the program's collective impact. The center continues to foster the community that grew out of this effort through the California Food for California Kids initiative, a growing movement of school food leaders nourishing students with fresh, California-grown meals and ecological education.

STATE ADVOCACY FOR SCHOOL FOOD SYSTEMS CHANGE

The Center for Ecoliteracy's first joint policy endeavor began with a project to apply its *Rethinking School Lunch* framework within the Oakland Unified School District in Oakland, California. The center worked to provide a blueprint, budget, and timeline for transforming the district's school food program to improve student health, well-being, and academic outcomes through a feasibility study that was then adopted in the district's Facilities Master Plan.[19] This master plan provided a basis for bond Measure J, which passed in 2012 with 84 percent public approval, securing $475 million to improve district infrastructure.[20] Measure J provided the funding for Oakland Unified School District to build a central kitchen, instructional farm, and education center.

The center began to work on state-level policy in 2016, collaborating with then–assembly member Susan Eggman and Center for Ecoliteracy board member and California state senator Nancy Skinner on a legislative bill to incentivize California-grown school food procurement. In 2017–2018, this work manifested with a new "California-Grown Fresh School Meals Grant Program" in the state budget with $1.5 million of one-time funding. This was extended in 2018–2019 with an additional $1 million in the state budget.

The center came back to the idea of using public dollars to incentivize California-grown school food procurement in 2019 when three bills focusing on changes to school food were introduced in the legislature focusing on (1) organic procurement, (2) plant-based proteins, and (3) universal breakfast. The center successfully worked with sponsors of the universal breakfast bill to include an incentive for California-grown food and collaborated with the TomKat Ranch Educational Foundation to further encourage the bill authors and sponsors to come together around a single bill. While common ground was fostered, the effort to combine these three competing bills was unsuccessful, and policymakers seemed to lack an understanding of their differences. None were funded during the 2019 legislative cycle.

Through this experience, the center learned how unfamiliar many policymakers were with school meal programs. A broader, multi-stakeholder coalition would be needed to more effectively advocate for state policies to improve school food. So, the center collaborated with the TomKat Ranch Educational Foundation and NextGen California to design a new policy framework that advanced freshly prepared California-grown school meals, including incentives for California-grown procurement, grass-fed beef, organic and plant-based foods, funding for school nutrition staff training and kitchen equipment, and an advisory council. The policy framework was loosely modeled after the 10 cents a meal incentive for local procurement in Michigan and similar programs in Oregon and New York.[21]

The center worked closely with the California School Employees Association (CSEA), the largest union representing school food service workers in the state, to ensure that their priority of providing workers with training and equipment to freshly prepare meals was reflected in this framework. The three organizations then convened a group of forty-three stakeholders representing nonprofits, farmers, food banks, labor unions, and government agencies in October 2019 following the close of the legislative session. The purpose of the meeting was to garner feedback and build support for a policy framework representative of a broad coalition's priorities. Ultimately, efforts to build a unified coalition were unsuccessful, and organizations decided to pursue single-issue bills rather than build a coalition around joint priorities.

Nevertheless, the three organizations committed to advocating for this policy framework focused on educating legislators, the governor's office staff, and budget staff on issues critical to catalyzing school food systems change. The advocacy and lobbying efforts paid off in the governor's proposed state budget in January 2020, which featured $60 million to improve the quality and access to healthy school meals, $10 million for staff professional development, $8.5 million for a Farm to School Incubator Grant Program, and permanent ongoing funding for the California Office of Farm to Fork, the state agency that administers the Farm to School Incubator Grant Program.

Weeks after the budget proposal was released, the coronavirus pandemic hit California, shuttering schools and quickly reprioritizing the state budget. Advocacy efforts pivoted in kind to focus on supporting school districts in serving emergency school meals and providing debt relief for school nutrition department budgets, whose participation had dropped overnight yet whose operating costs were fixed.[22] The center's advocacy was successful in securing $192 million to support emergency school meals and maintaining funding for the state's farm-to-school program.

The onset of the coronavirus pandemic highlighted the importance of school food access for low-income families. As school buildings closed and school nutrition departments pivoted to grab-and-go school meals, media coverage of long lines outside schools and the incredible efforts of school nutrition professionals put a national spotlight on school meals as an essential need for families, many of whom were facing job loss as a result of the pandemic. Building on the accomplishments of the 2020 budget, the attention on school meals, and the top policy priority of the California Food for California Kids Network, the center's focus turned to the audacious goal of achieving universal meals in California.

THE FREE SCHOOL MEALS FOR ALL ACT

In February 2021, California state senator Nancy Skinner introduced Senate Bill 364: The Free School Meals for All Act. Senator Skinner, chair of the Senate's Budget and Fiscal Review Committee, has a long history of social justice and environmental advocacy. As a member of the center's board of directors since 2014, Senator Skinner was aware of the work to be done to improve school meals in California. In 2020, Senator Skinner hired Jessica Bartholow, a longtime anti-hunger advocate, as her chief of staff.

Senator Skinner's 2021 proposal aimed to transform school food permanently so that providing locally sourced, nutritious meals would no longer be a line item subject to politically charged budget negotiations. The proposal was to provide free breakfast and lunch to every K–12 student in California public schools, increase locally sourced meals through a California-grown incentive program, and increase freshly prepared meals through a grant program to provide equipment and training for school nutrition staff.

The bill also aimed to leverage the federal Pandemic EBT program (see chapter 7, "Local and National Responses to the COVID-19 Pandemic in the United States") by creating a permanent food benefit for California students known as "BOOST," the Better Out-Of-School Time program. The BOOST program was developed to ensure that children from low-income families have access to food when schools are closed during breaks and prolonged emergencies.

The Free School Meals for All Act represented the most significant statewide opportunity in the movement for universal school meals in the US: if passed, California could showcase the impact of universal school meals for its 6.2 million public school students and provide a model for future state and federal policy. The center became a cosponsor of the legislation alongside the California Association of Food Banks, NextGen California, the TomKat Ranch Educational Foundation, and state superintendent of public instruction Tony Thurmond.

In collaboration with these partners, the center led an advocacy campaign in support of the Free School Meals for All Act. The team referenced the Messaging Guidance for an Effective School Food Campaign, which surveyed 1,200 US voters in September 2020.[23] The report states: Use "Healthy School Meals for All" in place of "Universal Meals." While the majority of respondents overall supported a policy that ensured that all public school students received school meals, the name "Universal Meals" ranked thirteenth when respondents were asked to choose a name for the policy that they liked. The top-ranked choices were "Healthy Schools, Healthy Kids" (34 percent), followed by "Healthy School Meals for All" (28 percent) and "Nutrition for All" (27 percent). The partners selected "School Meals for All" as the official campaign name.[24]

The "School Meals for All" campaign kicked off in February 2021 with fifteen organizations supporting the policy, including national organizations Food Research & Action Center (FRAC) and Center for Science in the Public Interest (CSPI). As cosponsors of the legislation leveraged existing relationships and connections, they eventually grew the list to a coalition of more than two hundred supporting organizations. The Center for Ecoliteracy gained support from California school districts, nonprofits, and health organizations. The TomKat Ranch Educational Foundation brought on national organizations as well as farmers, ranchers, labor unions, and other members of California's agricultural sector. NextGen California garnered support from climate policy advocates, and the California Association of Food Banks rallied food banks across California as well as faith-based institutions and anti-hunger advocacy groups. These complementary relationships led the School Meals for All Coalition to grow and diversify to include organizations spanning health, education, labor, agriculture, and food banks.

Meanwhile, the nationwide movement for universal meals at the federal level was gaining momentum. Through USDA waivers beginning in March 2020, school meals were made available for free nationwide during the pandemic. This change showcased the unique potential of schools to curb hunger and serve millions of meals each day. Representative Ilhan Omar (Democrat, Michigan) and Senator Bernie Sanders (Independent, Vermont) introduced the Universal School Meals Program Act in October 2019 and put forward the proposal again in May 2021, along with Senator Kirsten Gillibrand (Democrat, New York) and Representative Gwen Moore (Democrat, Wisconsin). However, in conversations with congressional staffers, California School Meals for All cosponsors learned that federal action on a full universal school meals policy was unlikely to happen before the waivers expired at the end of the 2021–2022 school year. That created a new sense of urgency to avoid the sudden loss of this benefit for California families, many of whom do not qualify for free or reduced-price meals under federal guidelines but still struggle to make ends meet due to the state's high cost of living. Federal guidelines state that a family of four with an annual income over $48,470 is ineligible for free or reduced-price school meals, but researchers estimate that a family of four with two working parents in California must make over $112,000 to afford basic necessities.[25]

As the 2020 poll had shown, advancing universal school meals was the top policy priority for members of the California Food for California Kids Network. The center interviewed school nutrition directors about what this policy would mean for their district, school food program, students, and families. For example, Gary Petill, director of nutrition services at San Diego Unified School District, said that "Single parents and spouses of enlisted service members are facing an onslaught of challenges right now. By providing free school meals, we will alleviate some of the burdens on families; many will now be able to afford to pay their rent and utilities, put gas in their car, or even avoid becoming homeless."[26]

The center shared what it learned from network members through fact sheets, articles, social media, and press outreach: (1) a universal meal program could better support students' health and academic success than the current system, in which families who had to apply for free or reduced-price meals ended up falling through the cracks, (2) eligible families were concerned about the stigma of needing support for meals, and (3) some families worried that submitting the application could affect their immigration status.

Members of the advocacy coalition were strategic in explaining how the benefits of the proposed Free School Meals for All Act would extend beyond the students and their families. Stephanie Bruce, nutrition services director at Palm Springs Unified School District, testified to the California Senate Education Committee in April 2021. She argued that the proposed bill would reduce administrative costs and free up staff time for non-administrative tasks. "When our district switched to feeding every student at no cost, we were able to shift the labor of three full-time employees from processing meal applications, sending out letters, and answering phone calls from concerned parents," she explained. "Instead, that staff time is now redirected to creating better tasting, fresher meals that have increased participation." She further explained how the incentives for freshly prepared and California-grown school meals in SB 364 would help schools form meaningful relationships with California farmers that benefit local economies, highlighting that her district, alone, had served one million pounds of fresh California-grown produce to their students since the start of the pandemic."[27]

Labor unions, including the California School Employees Association (CSEA) and Service Employees International Union (SEIU), provided critical support and further underscored the impact this would have on the state's school nutrition workforce. In a letter of support for SB 364, CSEA representatives argued that the bill "could provide more hours, jobs, and pay for food service workers, who are literally putting their lives on the line during the pandemic, to serve meals to our students."

The bill passed with unanimous bipartisan support in the California Senate Education Committee in April 2021. California state senators Brian Dahle and Rosilicie Ochoa Bogh, both Republicans, spoke in support of the Free School Meals for All Act, describing the childhood hunger they had witnessed in their districts and the value of school meal programs. While bipartisan support was not strictly necessary for the bill's passage—Democrats had a supermajority in both the state assembly and state senate—the coalition made an intentional effort to secure Republican support by arranging meetings ahead of the hearing with Republican representatives and their staff. At the California Senate Human Services Committee in April 2021, the bill passed yet again with unanimous bipartisan support, building the momentum for universal meals in California and showcasing the broad support school meals programs have across party lines. The coalition had seized the moment, culminating in the passage of transformational school food policy, but still faced the critical task of securing funding to enact the policy and ensure it would be resilient over time.

ADVOCATING FOR THE ADOPTION OF UNIVERSAL MEALS IN THE STATE BUDGET

In June 2021, policies from the Free School Meals for All Act were proposed in the state budget, but the other components of the proposal were put on hold. The California legislature proposed the following, which became known as the "School Meals for All" package: (1) establishing a universal meals program to serve free breakfast and lunch to every student in California public schools, permanently; (2) funding to train and equip school nutrition professionals to serve freshly prepared meals; and (3) funding farm-to-school initiatives.

Notably, the BOOST program and incentive to purchase California-grown food were not included in the budget proposal. In April 2021, the Biden administration extended Pandemic-EBT through August 2021, which provided additional support for families to access food outside of school and reduced the urgency to pass BOOST in the 2021 state budget.[28] The central focus became passing universal meals and providing schools with funding to support serving healthy, freshly prepared meals.

The California legislature is responsible for passing the state budget that the governor signs or vetoes. While the state had a budget surplus, there were competing proposals around how much to invest in school nutrition. Lobbying legislators to include full funding for School Meals for All in the final budget package was critical. The more than two hundred organizations making up the School Meals for All Coalition advocated by signing letters, raising awareness on social media, highlighting stories via op-eds, and participating in direct lobbying to California governor Gavin Newsom. One school nutrition director organized a letter to Governor Newsom from the superintendents of Long Beach, Sacramento, and Oakland Unified School Districts supporting the School Meals for All package in the budget. Cosponsors held meetings with the administration, legislators, and other policymakers. The center created personalized legislative reports detailing how many students in specific legislative districts would benefit from the School Meals for All proposal—and compared this impact to the governor's initial funding proposal, which would have left out half of the schools in the state.

On July 9, 2021, California officially adopted School Meals for All. Governor Newsom signed AB 130, the education package of the 2020–2021 state budget, which provided $650 million annually to establish a universal meals program to serve free breakfast and lunch to every student in California public schools, permanently. History was made—as the first state in the nation to provide free school meals to all public school students regardless of eligibility, California provided a model for the country to make healthy school meals a part of every child's educational day.

The budget also provided funding for serving more fresh and local school meals. It allocated $150 million to equip schools and train staff to serve freshly prepared school meals. This funding recognized that school nutrition professionals need support in the form of proper equipment and training to serve more freshly prepared and locally grown food in schools. California's Farm to School Incubator Grant Program also received an unprecedented investment through the state budget in the form of $30 million in 2021, with an additional $30 million in 2022. This represents a significant increase from the $8.5 million allocated to the grant program in 2020 and makes California's farm-to-school program the largest in the country, even surpassing the USDA's $12 million farm-to-school program.[29] This funding will support sustainable food procurement as well as projects that provide students with nutrition education, experiential lessons on the food system, and exposure to California agriculture and seasonal foods.

Leading up to the 2022 legislative session, the center reconvened with the TomKat Ranch Educational Foundation, NextGen California, and the California Association of Food Banks to outline a policy platform to strengthen California's school food system and build on the previous year's investments. The Center for Ecoliteracy interviewed school nutrition directors in the California Food for California Kids Network, who shared that their priorities were to ensure funding for School Meals for All, continue to expand the farm-to-school program and support the school nutrition workforce to serve more freshly prepared meals. These priorities were advanced through a 2022 School Meals for All coalition, which consisted of seventy-two supporting organizations. The coalition advocated by lobbying policymakers, supporting testimonies from school district leaders, authoring an op-ed, and sharing the voices of students and school nutrition professionals on social media.

Bolstered by momentum from the 2021 campaign and another state budget surplus, the coalition's advocacy culminated in a record $2 billion to support school meal programs through the 2022–2023 state budget, including:

- $596 million for School Meals for All
- $600 million for kitchen equipment and staff training to support freshly prepared meals
- $611.8 million for enhanced school meal reimbursements from the state
- $100 million to support "school food best practices" (California-grown, freshly prepared, and plant-based meals)
- $60 million for the California Farm to School Incubator Grant Program
- $2.4 million to support the evaluation of the School Meals for All program

Additionally, $45 million was provided to establish the Healthy School Meals Pathway Program, a training program for school nutrition staff to learn scratch-cooking techniques for use in school kitchens.

California school nutrition directors celebrated the historic funding package and the impact of systems-wide investments. Erin Primer, director of Food and Nutrition Services for San Luis Coastal Unified School District, said, "This is an absolute dream to have adequate funding to procure, plan, create, train, and serve amazing food at school. Our students deserve to eat healthy and tasty foods, our staff deserve to use real foods and adequate equipment, and our districts deserve school meal programs that benefit the entire system and the whole child."

With the start of the 2022–2023 school year, California's School Meals for All program went into effect. Kristie To, a high school student in Orange County, California, published an opinion editorial in the *Voice of OC*. She testified to the impact of free school meals:

> My peers and I rely on school breakfast and lunch every day. Many of my closest friends do not have the time and are not in the financial situation to provide themselves with meals to fuel their school day and concentrate in class . . . This new program has alleviated the stress of buying and preparing meals that previously strained students and families . . . Without the burden of being responsible for buying and creating nutritional meals for myself, I can better focus on my education and positions as a student leader. Therefore, I believe all states should follow in the footsteps of California.[30]

LEVERAGING SUCCESSFUL STRATEGIES FROM CALIFORNIA'S SCHOOL MEALS FOR ALL CAMPAIGN

California's 2021 and 2022 state budgets have positioned the state as a model for the nation. The six strategies used in California's School Meals for All campaign can be leveraged by advocates and policymakers to lobby for and enact universal school meals in other local and national governments. First, **seize the moment** to launch your campaign by understanding the political and social landscape you're working within. The pandemic created widespread food and economic insecurity in the US. A national spotlight was cast on the country's safety net programs, including school meals. In addition, the political landscape in California played a role. The state had a budget surplus, and the governor was facing a recall election.

Second, **build strategic partnerships** to form a broad coalition of stakeholders that support the policy change. Cosponsors of the Free School Meals for All Act and the broad multi-stakeholder coalition were critical to the reach and ultimate success of the campaign. Federal advocacy organizations and universal meal advocates in other states collaborated to raise awareness of the California campaign. Funders, in particular those that fund lobbying efforts, were essential to fuel the work.

Third, **use a systems-change approach** to craft policy that benefits multiple groups impacted by the issue. The center's systems change approach helped to craft resilient policy language, build a broad multi-stakeholder coalition, and garner bipartisan support.

Fourth, **leverage a powerful network** of school food champions, and raise their voices to policymakers and in the media. The California Food for California Kids Network provided a platform to gauge key priorities and the feasibility of the policy. The center was able to leverage existing relationships with school nutrition directors in certain legislative districts to connect them directly with policymakers and elevate their voices in the media.

Fifth, present **research and data** customized for your audience to showcase what's possible with their support. With a deep understanding of the school food system, including federal requirements and the status of California schools leveraging federal policies, the center was able to efficiently present data at key moments to policymakers and in the media.

Sixth, design your campaign **brand** and messaging to speak positively to a broad audience. Transformations in school meal programs can make a positive impact on children's health and ensure they have the tools they need to thrive at school. The School Meals for All campaign leveraged best practices to use "for all" rather than "universal" in campaign language, and, consistent with the Center's values of "smart, vital, and hopeful," communications remained steadfast and optimistic throughout the campaign.

NOTES

1. Acknowledgements: Thank you to Abby Halperin for her research contributions to this chapter.

2. Fritjof Capra and Pier Luigi Luisi, *The Systems View of Life: A Unifying Vision* (Cambridge: Cambridge University Press, 2014), https://www.ecoliteracy.org/article/systems-view-life-unifying-vision.

3. The California Legislature's Nonpartisan Fiscal and Policy Advisor, "Bonds," Legislative Analyst's Office, accessed January 10, 2022, https://lao.ca.gov/ballotanalysis/bonds.

4. Food Research & Action Center (FRAC), "FACTS National School Lunch Program," November 2016, https://frac.org/wp-content/uploads/cnnslp.pdf; May Wang, Natalie Studer, and Pat Crawford, "An Evaluation of the School Lunch Initiative: A Report"

(The Chez Panisse Foundation, September 2010), https://www.ecoliteracy.org/sites/default/files/sli_eval_full_report_2010_0.pdf.

5. Center for Ecoliteracy, "Rethinking School Lunch Guide," October 10, 2010, https://www.ecoliteracy.org/download/rethinking-school-lunch-guide.

6. California Department of Education, "Free and Reduced Price Meals (CA Department of Education)," accessed January 10, 2022, https://dq.cde.ca.gov/dataquest/cbeds1.asp?cYear=2020-21&Blah=&Blah=&Blah=&Blah=&Blah=&Blah=&FreeLunch=on&cChoice=StatProf1&cLevel=State&cTopic=FRPM&myTimeFrame=S&submit1=Submit; KidsData, "Children Living in Food Insecure Households," 2022, https://www.kidsdata.org/topic/764/food-insecurity/table#fmt=1168&loc=2,127,347,1763,331,348,336,171,321,345,357,332,324,369,358,362,360,337,327,364,356,217,353,328,354,323,352,320,339,334,365,343,330,367,344,355,366,368,265,349,361,4,273,59,370,326,333,322,341,338,350,342,329,325,359,351,363,340,335&tf=95&sortType=asc.

7. Legislative Analyst's Office, The California Legislature's Nonpartisan Fiscal and Policy Advisor, "*Proposition 98*," 1988, https://lao.ca.gov/Publications/Report/4291.

8. Elyse Homel Vitale, "A Decade of Advocacy Leads to Thousands of Hunger Free California Schools," *Nourish California* (blog), 2018, https://nourishca.org/impact-stories/a-decade-of-advocacy-leads-to-thousands-of-hunger-free-california-schools/; Department of Health Care Services, "What Is Medi-Cal?," March 23, 2021, https://www.dhcs.ca.gov/services/medi-cal/pages/whatismedi-cal.aspx; California Legislature, "SB-138 School Meal Programs: Free and Reduced-Price Meals: Universal Meal Service," 138 Education Code § 49562, 49564, 49564.5 (2017), https://leginfo.legislature.ca.gov/faces/billNavClient.xhtml?bill_id=201720180SB138.

9. California Legislature, "SB-250 Pupil Meals: Child Hunger Prevention and Fair Treatment Act of 2017," 250 Education Code § 49557.5 (2017), https://leginfo.legislature.ca.gov/faces/billTextClient.xhtml?bill_id=201720180SB250; California Legislature, "SB-265 Pupil Meals: Child Hunger Prevention and Fair Treatment Act of 2017," 265 Education Code § 49557.5 (2019), https://leginfo.legislature.ca.gov/faces/billNavClient.xhtml?bill_id=201920200SB265; California Department of Education, "Senate Bill 250 and Senate Bill 265—School Nutrition," October 2019, https://www.cde.ca.gov/ls/nu/sn/senatebill265.asp

10. Trieste Huey and Stephanie Bruce, "Let's Make Free School Meals for All Permanent in California," *EdSource*, May 10, 2021, https://edsource.org/2021/lets-make-free-school-meals-for-all-permanent-in-california/654354.

11. California Legislature, "Bill Analysis," California Legislative Information, September 2019, https://leginfo.legislature.ca.gov/faces/billAnalysisClient.xhtml?bill_id=201920200SB265.

12. California Department of Education, "District Profile: Barstow Unified," accessed January 10, 2022, https://www.cde.ca.gov/sdprofile/details.aspx?cds=36676110000000; California Department of Education, "District Profile: Los Angeles Unified," accessed January 10, 2022, https://www.cde.ca.gov/sdprofile/details.aspx?cds=19647330000000.

13. Jeffrey M. Vincent et al., "Are California Public Schools Scratch-Cooking Ready?: A Survey of Food Service Directors on the State of School Kitchens" (unpublished

report, University of California, Berkeley, Center for Cities and Schools, 2020), https://files.eric.ed.gov/fulltext/ED610527.pdf.

14. Moira O'Neill et al., "Investing in Public School Kitchens and Equipment as a Pathway to Healthy Eating and Equitable Access to Healthy Food," *Journal of School Health* 90, no. 6 (2020): 492–503, https://doi.org/10.1111/josh.12894.

15. Jeffrey M. Vincent et al., "Are California Public Schools Scratch-Cooking Ready?"; Chef Brenda Thompson, RDN, "Chef Leverages USDA Team Nutrition Grant to Develop Healthy Menus for Students," U.S. Department of Agriculture, February 21, 2017, https://www.usda.gov/media/blog/2015/04/30/chef-leverages-usda-team-nutrition-grant-develop-healthy-menus-students.

16. Farm to School Census, "California: USDA-FNS Farm to School Census," U.S. Department of Agriculture, accessed January 10, 2022, https://farmtoschoolcensus.fns.usda.gov/census-results/states/ca.

17. Department of Agriculture, Food and Nutrition Service, "Nutrition Standards in the National School Lunch and School Breakfast Programs; Final Rule. Part II," *Federal Register* 77, no. 17 (January 26, 2012), https://www.govinfo.gov/content/pkg/FR-2012-01-26/pdf/2012-1010.pdf; USDA Food and Nutrition Service, "School Nutrition and Meal Cost Study | Food and Nutrition Service," U.S. Department of Agriculture, October 19, 2021, https://www.fns.usda.gov/school-nutrition-and-meal-cost-study.

18. California Department of Education, "2021–22 CNP Reimbursement Rates—Rates, Eligibility Scales, & Funding," November 9, 2021, https://www.cde.ca.gov/ls/nu/rs/rates2122.asp.

19. Rethinking School Lunch, "Oakland Unified School District Feasibility Study: Executive Summary" (Center for Ecoliteracy, December 12, 2011), https://www.ecoliteracy.org/sites/default/files/uploads/shared_files/RSL_Oakland_Feasibility_Summary.pdf.

20. California Food for California Kids, "Rethinking School Lunch," accessed January 10, 2022, https://www.californiafoodforcaliforniakids.org/rethinking-school-lunch.

21. Ten Cents a Meal for Michigan's Kids & Farms, "Ten Cents a Meal for Michigan's Kids & Farms," accessed January 10, 2022, https://www.tencentsmichigan.org/; George Plaven, "Oregon Lawmakers Expand Farm-to-School Program," *Capital Press*, July 1, 2019, https://www.capitalpress.com/state/oregon/oregon-lawmakers-expand-farm-to-school-program/article_b76103a4-9c3a-11e9-8fb6-2bb6b1519c48.html; Samantha Levy and Kali McPeters, "Growing Opportunity for Farm to School: How to Revolutionize School Food, Support Local Farms, and Improve the Health of Students in New York," Reports and Guides, *Farmland Information Center* (blog), January 27, 2020, https://farmlandinfo.org/publications/growing-opportunity-for-farm-to-school-in-new-york/.

22. See chapter 7, this volume.

23. Center for Science in the Public Interest, "Messaging Guidance for an Effective School Food Campaign" (Center for Science in the Public Interest, December 2020), https://cspinet.org/sites/default/files/attachment/School%20Food%20Messaging%20CSPI.pdf.

24. Center for Science in the Public Interest, "Messaging Guidance for an Effective School Food Campaign."

25. Dr. Amy Glasmeier. "Living Wage Calculation for California." Living Wage Calculator, 2021. https://livingwage.mit.edu/states/06.

26. Gary Petill, "Opinion: Student Meals in California Are Now Free—And Fresh, with Locally Grown Ingredients," *San Diego Union-Tribune*, sec. Commentary, August 6, 2021, https://www.sandiegouniontribune.com/opinion/commentary/story/2021-08-06/free-student-lunch-san-diego-california.

27. Trieste Huey and Stephanie Bruce, "Let's Make Free School Meals for All Permanent in California." *EdSource*, May 10, 2021. https://edsource.org/2021/lets-make-free-school-meals-for-all-permanent-in-california/654354.

28. Phil McCausland, "Biden Administration to Launch Largest Summer Food Program in U.S. History," *NBC News*, April 26, 2021, https://www.nbcnews.com/politics/white-house/biden-administration-launch-largest-summer-food-program-u-s-history-n1265283; California Department of Social Services, "Pandemic EBT," 2020, https://www.cdss.ca.gov/home/pandemic-ebt.

29. USDA Food and Nutrition Service, "USDA Awards $12 Million in Record-Breaking Farm to School Grants, Releases New Data Showing Expansion of Farm to School Efforts | Food and Nutrition Service," U.S. Department of Agriculture, July 15, 2021, https://www.fns.usda.gov/news-item/usda-0158.21.

30. Kristie To, "Student Leader Applauds California's Free School Meals for All," *Voice of OC*, November 30, 2022, last modified December 4, 2022, https://voiceofoc.org/2022/11/to-student-leader-applauds-californias-free-school-meals-for-all/.

15

DEVELOPING SOLIDARITY COALITIONS FOR UNIVERSAL SCHOOL MEALS AND LOCAL FOOD IN THE UNITED STATES

Anore Horton, Faye Mack, Betsy Rosenbluth, and Amy Shollenberger

On a brisk winter morning, students and school staff from across Vermont donned their snow boots and coats, making their way to the state capitol. Inside, school nutrition professionals served locally grown apples and scratch-made parsnip muffins to legislators. Alongside a farmer who supplies much of the food on their lunch trays, students shared their stories about growing and tasting new foods. As a local high school teen ended his testimony, a legislator asked, "Really, what difference does this make to you?" The student paused, then said, "It makes me think what it took to get the food on my plate, and I don't waste it. And when my mom was sick, I did the cooking in the house. And I started a garden at the mobile home park where I live." The legislators went silent. This is our advocacy in action.

INTRODUCTION

In 2021, Vermont state legislators representing all three of the state's major parties developed and championed the Farm Fresh School Meals for All bill—broad-reaching legislation that would establish and fund a holistic and equitable approach to feeding children in school. This bill would bring universal school meals to every public school in the state, fully fund the Farm to School and Early Childhood Network[1] and grants program, and establish a new local food purchasing incentive program. A strong coalition of anti-hunger, school nutrition, farm-to-school, early childhood, and local food advocates and practitioners, who had been working toward this bill for over twenty years, celebrated and supported legislators as they used the coalition's carefully developed messaging, data, and stories to convince their colleagues to support the bill. We are some of the current leaders in this coalition: Anore Horton and Faye Mack lead advocacy work for Hunger Free Vermont; Betsy Rosenbluth works for Shelburne Farms and directs the farm-to-school program, Vermont Food Education Every Day (FEED); and Amy Shollenberger is the founder of Action Circles, a political strategy firm with a campaigning and organizing model of the same name.

Our school food transformation didn't happen by luck but through multiple strategies encompassed in a structured approach called the "Action Circles Model of Campaigning and Organizing." Our coalition is a network of partners from the advocacy, nonprofit, agriculture, and education sectors—united by our shared values and vision for robust, equitable school nutrition programs that welcome every student to eat at school and engage every school community in a local food and farm culture that nurtures children's health, cultivates viable farms, and builds vibrant communities.

We work in the state of Vermont, located in the northeastern region of the US, part of the unceded homelands of the Western Abenaki and Mohican peoples. Vermont is a small rural state with a population of just 643,000. About 25 percent of the state's population lives in Chittenden County where the state's largest city is located. The state is primarily white (94 percent), but the current generation of schoolchildren is 12 percent Black, Indigenous, and people of color—many of them the children of refugees and immigrants from around the world.[2] The state has a deep commitment to its culture of a "working landscape," which includes both agriculture and silviculture as well as a long history of dairy farming. Today, while the dairy industry's family farms struggle under economic pressures, there is a strong local food movement, and communities deeply value the working landscape and connections to the farming community.

At our coalition's core are three entities that don't traditionally work in lockstep across the country (and have sometimes viewed each other as adversaries): school nutrition professionals, anti-hunger advocates, and

15.1 Heartwood Farm of South Albany, VT, proudly displays a "This Farm Feeds Vermont Kids" lawn sign. Credit: Maire Folan for Green Mountain Farm to School.

farm-to-school practitioners. In Vermont, these groups each have separate statewide networks, supported by the School Nutrition Association of Vermont, Hunger Free Vermont, and Vermont FEED. The School Nutrition Association of Vermont is the Vermont chapter of the national trade association and advocacy membership organization that represents the school nutrition profession. Hunger Free Vermont is a statewide nonprofit organization working to end hunger through advocacy and legislation, technical assistance and outreach support of federal nutrition programs, and community engagement in anti-hunger efforts. Vermont FEED is a program partnership of two nonprofits, Shelburne Farms and the Northeast Organic Farming Association of Vermont (NOFA-VT), that engages students with local food systems by connecting classrooms, cafeterias, communities, and local farms. However, in 2003 the School Nutrition Association of Vermont's Board created permanent positions for Vermont FEED and Hunger Free Vermont, creating a space for collaboration led by school nutrition professionals, while adding the capacity of paid farm-to-school and anti-hunger advocates.

Today, members of these Vermont organizations serve as strategic partners creating systemic change, sit on each other's Advisory Boards, and stand together in the movement toward universal school meals with a strong local food connection. This deep partnership did not happen overnight; partnership, trust, a shared vision, and—most importantly—solidarity were built over many years of intentional relationship building, transparent communication, and alignment.

Two grant opportunities from private funders from 2013 to 2018 helped to solidify the partnerships and shared policy goals. In 2012, the Vermont Community Foundation launched a five-year, $5 million campaign to invest in both food access and the local food system, including farm-to-school. In 2013, The Vermont Farm to School and Early Childhood Network and the Vermont Agency of Agriculture, Food, and Markets received grants from this fund for a strategic mapping process to diagram the people, policies, and programs that impact the Vermont farm-to-school system, and to identify the top strategic levers for system change to reach our goal. Through the process, the School Nutrition Association of Vermont, Hunger Free Vermont, and Vermont FEED, along with representatives of forty additional organizations and the Vermont

Agency of Agriculture, Food, and Markets, hashed out a shared goal for all partners that included universal school meals, increased local purchasing, and integrated food systems education. This shared goal reflected how each organization could achieve the change they sought individually, through collaboration and collective action.

The Community Foundation (followed by the Ben & Jerry's Foundation) catalyzed state and local partners coming together under this new integrated goal and made a critical investment in a systems change approach that resulted in shared goals and shared strategies for the partners under the Vermont Farm to School and Early Childhood Network. No longer driven by turf and competition for dollars, partners organized around key levers of change in the farm-to-school system, with a goal that included both ending child hunger in schools (universal school meals) and growing local food systems (farm-to-school programming). Instead of grants to each organization, funders gave the network money to allocate with a peer granting model toward strategies that would forward this shared goal. This approach cemented relationships and trust among partners. It contributed to an attitude of abundance instead of scarcity, even as funds dwindled. As policy had been identified as a key strategic lever for systems change, network funds supported a collaborative legislative agenda for universal school meals and expansion of farm-to-school funding.

Through incremental steps (table 15.1) and various campaigns (table 15.2), we built momentum toward the universal school meals legislation, introduced in 2020, and the comprehensive Farm Fresh School Meals for All bill in 2021.

When our coalition first started to work with Action Circles in 2016, we found that the model gave structure and language to many of the practices and tools we were already using and added to our toolbox. Since Action Circles came on board, our work has seen a tangible increase in both momentum and success. The Action Circles model is designed to build broad and deep leadership within a campaign, which translates to broader movement building. This is represented by the continued expansion of our solidarity coalition, which in 2019 grew to include Vermont-National Educational Association (VT-NEA), the state's largest educators' union. It also has tools to develop strong accountability structures, which help to build trust and solidarity among strategic partners, and it has tools to develop effective

Table 15.1 Incremental steps in providing universal free meals and local food to schools

Year	Universal free meals and farm-to-school milestones
2001	• Burlington School District (the largest in Vermont) becomes the first district in the state to serve universal free breakfast.
2005	• Several school districts unilaterally eliminate reduced-price meal fees, covering the cost through their own budgets.
2009	• Launch of Vermont Farm to School Network.
2012	• Vermont Farm to School Network adopts an integrated goal of advancing both farm-to-school and universal free school meals in a "Virtuous Cycle." • Strategic messaging shifts from "free school meals" to "*universal* school meals" to emphasize the right to food and its fundamental role in education.
2014	• Hunger Free Vermont assists thirty schools with providing universal free meals to seven thousand (8%) students using a federal provision (CEP) that allows higher-poverty schools to serve universal free school meals.
2016	• Sixty-six schools serve universal free meals to 13,900 students (16% of students).
2018	• Seventy-seven schools serve universal free meals (over 20% of students). • In a Vermont Department of Health survey, 87% of schools report that they purchase at least some food from a local producer. Over 50% saw an increase in school meal participation after launching a farm-to-school program.[3]
2019	• More than thirty out of 150 legislators eat lunch or breakfast at a local school on a designated day, celebrating school nutrition.
2022	• 60% of Vermont school food authorities participated in the Local Purchasing Incentive Grants in the first two years. • Over one hundred Vermont farms sell to K–12 schools and early childhood programs.

Note: Tables 15.1 and 15.2 were constructed using Hunger Free Vermont's archives and interviews conducted in 2020 by Anore Horton with Kathy Alexander (past president of SNA-VT and currently the director of Mount Abraham Unified School District and Addison Northwest School District Food Service Cooperative), Doug Davis (past president of SNA-VT, past chair of National SNA's Public Policy and Legislation Committee, and past director of the Burlington School Food Project, 1997–2022), Abbie Nelson (past director of Vermont FEED), and Marissa Parisi (past executive director of Hunger Free Vermont).

message campaigns that are not reactive but rather focus on the "happy ending" to the story we want to write.

LEAD WITH A HAPPY ENDING

One foundation of the Action Circles model is to articulate the vision of the "happy ending" an organization or coalition is working toward. Articulating a happy ending means that everyone involved knows what the end goal is and what it will look like to meet that goal; we will know when we are done. This articulation also allows the organizations and coalitions to invite varied groups into the work if they are committed to the "happy ending" and shared principles, which we will detail shortly.

Farm Fresh School Meals for All embodies the happy ending our coalition has been working toward for over twenty years. We have a clear vision: school nutrition programs as an integral part of our education system, universally available for all students, made from locally produced food that students are aware of and value and are prepared with skill by professionals who are well-compensated and respected for their crucial roles in children's health and learning. The 2018 results of a Vermont Department of Health survey of all schools to evaluate progress toward the Farm to School and Early Childhood Network goal show that four out of five schools have at least some farm-to-school activity, and 87 percent of schools reported that they purchased at least some food from a local producer. Over 50 percent of schools saw an increase in school meal participation when a farm-to-school program was launched.[4] School meals are wholesome, delicious, culturally responsive, and support children in building a positive connection to food, agriculture, and to their community. All children, regardless of their family income, are able—and *want* to—eat school food.

Another way we have long articulated and explained our vision is as a continuous "virtuous cycle." If all we wanted to do was make sure children did not go hungry at school, we could push for universal school meals while ignoring the content of those meals. However, in our virtuous cycle, universal school meals, packed with locally grown produce, meat, and dairy that students have had hands-on experience with, sustains the farming economy of every Vermont town—where the school cafeteria is almost always the largest communal gathering place and the largest "restaurant." And the connection to those delicious, fresh, nourishing, local school meals make school cafeterias the cool place to eat, increasing student participation and bolstering school meal program finances. Kids get healthier and learn better, and schools draw down more funding to purchase even more local food—the virtuous cycle continues and expands, and the whole community benefits. Our research partnership in 2016 with the University of Vermont Department of Education showed that school food and learning are interconnected to further support coalition messaging.[5]

Our coalition understands how this happy ending helps fulfill key organizational commitments for each partner. The School Nutrition Association of Vermont, Hunger Free Vermont, and Vermont FEED have differing core missions: representing the interests of school nutrition professionals, permanently ending hunger, and engaging youth in building and promoting a resilient food system. Our happy ending links these missions together, is key to our success as partners, and drives our commitment to stay in solidarity with each other year after year. The organizations each know that one partner alone cannot change the school food system, and that the different policy, program, and funding pieces all work together to elevate school meals and make the cafeteria experience the best it can be for our students, school nutrition professionals, farmers, and communities. We have committed to working together toward our happy ending, sharing leadership on different incremental steps and priorities along the way.

The happy ending is also a key component of the accountability structure and of building effective strategy. When one of the coalition members suggests a strategy or when a legislator proposes an amendment or policy, we can ask—does it lead to the happy ending? If we cannot articulate how that strategy or policy proposal will lead to the ending we want, we know it is not one we can support.

The development and launch of the Universal School Meals Campaign was a monumental point in our work. It meant we could end the practice of "lunch shaming," in which students with negative account balances (unpaid meal debt) are singled out in potentially embarrassing ways, and eliminate the stigma associated with free school meals for hundreds of thousands of Vermont children and their families. When our campaign began in 2019 the concept of universal school meals was largely unknown to the general public. In January 2020, the Vermont Legislature became the first in the nation to introduce a universal school meals bill. Passing this legislation became more politically feasible after the COVID-19 pandemic, since most schools in Vermont and around the country served meals at no cost to all students during the 2020–2021 and 2021–2022 school years, which dramatically increased public awareness of and support for universal free school meals.[6]

OVERVIEW OF THE LEGISLATIVE PROCESS

The Vermont legislature is a part-time citizen legislature made up of a 150-member House of Representatives and a thirty-member Senate. Legislators only receive a stipend and often hold full-time paid jobs. There are three major parties represented in the State House: Democrats, Republicans, and Progressives. Legislators have no staff and no private offices; the body prides itself on being open and available to the public. The legislature meets from January to May each year, with rare special sessions during other parts of the year. Bills are sponsored by legislators and are introduced in either the House or the Senate (called a chamber). Once introduced, a bill is then sent to a committee based on the bill's subject matter. The committee may then choose to pursue the bill, take testimony, discuss the bill's details, and recommend amendments to it. The committee will then vote on the bill and, if it passes, it may be sent to other committees based on its subject matter before ultimately being voted on by the full chamber. If the chambers come to an agreement, the bill passes the legislature and is sent to the governor, who can choose to sign it into law, allow it to become law without their signature, or veto it.

Vermont's legislature uses a legislative biennium–a two-year term of legislative activity. This means that if a bill is introduced in the first year of the biennium, the legislature has two legislative sessions in which to consider the bill before it must start over from the beginning. However, if a bill fails to pass during the two years of the biennium, it must be newly reintroduced and start from scratch.

To prepare for what we expected to be a four- or five-year legislative campaign, Hunger Free Vermont established a group of key stakeholders to serve as the Universal School Meals Campaign Strategy Team. Many of the organizations and individuals at the table had worked together in various ways over many years, and some were brand new to the group. Our first step was to develop a set of shared principles for the campaign. The Action Circles model uses Shared Principles as a set of agreements that serve as a foundation for any decision-making throughout a campaign. It is the list of requirements that must be met, and cannot be compromised, in achieving the happy ending.

Shared Principles serve four important purposes. The process of developing the Shared Principles creates alignment and trust among the various individuals and organizations at the table. Tensions are surfaced and worked through at the start, rather than in the heat of a legislative session or intense negotiations with a short timeline. They also serve as a helpful reference tool when a new organization joins the effort; they must agree to the principles to join the coalition. Finally, they allow advocates and lobbyists to make decisions throughout the campaign quickly. We know that our coalition will not support any changes to legislation that violate our Shared Principles. So, advocates who are testifying or working closely with legislators can respond in the moment to proposed changes on behalf of the group. It also protects against the group splintering or having its members pitted against each other when legislators or other interest groups inevitably propose compromises. Shared Principles also act as a key component of our accountability structure. The group agreement is that no member will agree to anything that does not adhere to the principles. It is possible to change the principles if the situation changes, but if the exercise is done well at the beginning, the principles should withstand shifting situations.

We formalized a set of Shared Principles for Vermont's Universal School Meals Campaign in 2019. We have repeatedly experienced their power in action as when Vermont's Hunger Councils, representing over one thousand community leaders from every corner of the state, unanimously approve the universal school meals campaign. The boost in support for universal school meals did not translate to legislative action after the bill was introduced in 2020. The COVID-19 pandemic slowed the bill's progress, and by the summer of 2020, it had completely transformed the way that meals were being served, along with how educators, state government, and individuals across the state were talking about the importance of school meals.[7]

No one seemed quite sure how the pandemic and related economic recession would impact state budgets and property taxes—the primary source of education funding in Vermont. Many new residents moved to Vermont in 2020, including many families with school-aged children, potentially increasing the property tax pool. However, a record number of people in Vermont were struggling with hunger, and many people had lost jobs. Would there be a public appetite for increasing property taxes to pay for school meals? Were the school folks in our coalition still willing to push for greater public spending on school nutrition programs when the whole education system was in chaos?

Hunger Free Vermont pulled together the Universal School Meals Campaign Strategy Group to check in. We wanted to make sure that everyone still thought that moving forward with the Universal School Meals Campaign in 2021 was a good idea and to see if the pandemic had shifted anyone's perspective on key aspects of the bill, like how to pay for it. We were prepared for a challenging meeting with many perspectives. We didn't expect to fully come to an agreement in just one meeting. However, at the start of the meeting we revisited our Shared Principles:

1. We will work together to make two meals available to every Vermont public school student on every school day, with no direct charge to any student to get the meals.
2. Our campaign and the solution to get to universal school meals must be respectful, equitable, and systemic, so we will work together to ensure that:
    a. School meals are accessible to every student—the goal is that all students participate in their school nutrition program.
    b. No student or family will be shamed or singled out for any reason related to school meals.
    c. The collection of income information from families will not be tied to school meals and will be collected from every family.
    d. Meals will be established as part of a child's educational day.

3. To maintain high-quality school meals, we believe all schools should be in the National School Lunch Program and School Breakfast Program.
4. We believe the state revenue source for universal school meals should not be regressive and will not require a cut to other important programs.
5. We will work to ensure that the statewide solution to achieve universal school meals will not rely on corporate sponsorship or other forms of charitable contributions.
6. We believe and will work to ensure that universal school meals will enhance the local economy through increased local purchasing for school meals.
7. We believe that school nutrition professionals should be recognized and engaged as major contributors to the integration of universal school meals into the educational day.
8. We believe that the Vermont Agency of Education must be supported financially to ensure adequate capacity to achieve universal school meals in Vermont.

Going down the list, one by one, we collectively reaffirmed that these principles still fit and felt true. Guided by the principles, we unanimously agreed to keep moving forward with the campaign, and that it was more important than ever. No one suggested a single change to the bill.

The universal school meals bill was subsequently reintroduced in 2021, and by February, interest in the bill was picking up steam in the State House. We found that most legislators were with us in theory; they loved the idea of universal school meals and understood why it was important. They shared our happy ending. However, some were worried about the cost. One of the suggestions that we received from multiple legislators was to take an incremental approach. Vermont had already made school meals free for students whose household income falls below 185 percent of the federal poverty line, so why not go to 300 percent next? Our Shared Principles include equity and universality—creating a new economic indicator for who gets free meals and who doesn't is not equitable, does not further destigmatize eating school meals, and does not create a universal program. It was clear that the proposal violated our Shared Principles, and we were able to respond with confidence that it was not a path that our coalition could support. While it can be tempting in the moment to say "yes" to a legislative compromise that may guarantee a "win" sooner, it was easy for us to say "no" because we had our Shared Principles to use as the foundation of our advocacy and decision-making.

Taking all the time we needed to bring a wide range of coalition members together to create and commit to a set of Shared Principles, and circling back to reconfirm them as the advocacy landscape shifts, has proven to be our most important practice for maintaining the trust of our important partners over the long haul of a major legislative campaign.

CURRENT STORY ANALYSIS AND DEVELOPMENT OF SHARED MESSAGING

The Action Circles Model uses story-based strategy as a theory of action. The coalition learned from this model that the way to develop an effective strategy is to change the public narrative about school food. We believe that all students can enjoy nourishing meals at school prepared by respected professionals and feel connected to that food while providing a consistent market for local farmers. Instead of focusing on the shortfalls and challenges of our current school food system, we ask, "What would it look like if school meal debt was eliminated? If cafeterias had the staffing and infrastructure needed to process locally grown ingredients into school breakfasts and lunches? If sharing communal meals in classrooms and cafeterias was a daily experience embraced by students, teachers, administrators, and staff? If students experienced how local food is grown and cooked? And if the people who run school meal programs were fully included in school districts' decision-making because everyone understands that eating is elementary to education?"

We used Current Story Analysis to uncover the places where the current message frames and talking points about school food were not serving us. Then, we worked together to create new messages, effectively "rewriting the story" so that it would lead to the happy ending we wanted. After a few rounds of editing together, we agreed on four simple message frames: (1) universal school meals mean that every student can eat at school every day; (2) eating is elementary to education; (3) cafeterias can be inviting, simple, and satisfying spaces; and (4) no student should learn what hunger feels like at school. We further developed three to four talking points for each message frame, which we tested and trained people to use.[8] We practiced saying the talking points out loud and noted when they felt forced or unnatural. We also tried using them word for word when talking with family and friends in natural conversation (without telling them we were testing talking points) and captured their feedback.

We then used the messages in presentations to the community, in our public communications, in the media, when working with schools, and when talking with legislators. Our messages began to resonate and build across the state and in the State House. Legislators told our story to each other and to us, as though it was their own story that they had been telling for years. While the legislature was considering the Farm Fresh School Meals for All bill during the 2021 legislative session, our messaging about school meals and local food kept reappearing in news stories from journalists and in op-eds that we did not draft. School nutrition professionals, state agency staff, and others also used our solidarity coalition's language when testifying to the legislature.

As our school food stories were repeated, shared, and treated as more and more self-evident, the old and disempowering stories that challenged our "happy ending" and the assumptions that supported it started to disappear. By the 2021 legislative session, we were no longer being told that the quality of school meals was poor or that people didn't want their children eating them. Even more importantly, our emphasis on equity and collective responsibility—that "every student should have access to the same things while at school, whether it is educational opportunities or food"—was silencing what had been one of the most common objections to our vision: that individual parents ought to be responsible for feeding their own children and it was somehow immoral not to make them do it. The question became *when* Vermont would make the policy leap and begin providing universal free school meals instead of *if* it should do so.

ENGAGING PEOPLE CONTINUOUSLY AND THROUGHOUT THE COALITION

The Action Circles Model includes a variety of engagement levels. Individuals and organizations can move through circles based on whether they wish to contribute to, for example, higher-risk actions or leadership, and depending on the stage of the campaign, their comfort with different kinds of activities, and what is going on in their own lives. This can include a wide variety of actions, such as serving school nutrition recipes in the State House cafeteria; bringing taste tests to committee hearings (farm-to-school snacks, of course!); children singing garden songs for the House devotional, and students sharing their personal stories.

Importantly, we encouraged leadership from school nutrition professionals and used coalition resources to amplify stories that prefigured the "happy ending" we were all working to achieve. Take, for example, Chris Parker, a professional chef turned school nutrition director who serves free school meals made with Vermont ingredients to all students in his district. He became a vocal Farm Fresh School Meals for All champion over the course of two years. As he deepened his engagement with the coalition, he regularly shared his story with the media and his school board. He also testified in the State House in support of increased investment in school nutrition programs statewide. We celebrated his success by helping him connect with local and regional media eager to tell a local good news story about the school district.

The Action Circles model works when the individuals and organizations leading the campaign are willing to share power with others and share ownership of the campaign and the issue. When we shared power and ownership, we made our campaign and our movement stronger. We saw this process play out over the years in the core coalition of Vermont FEED, Hunger Free Vermont, and the School Nutrition Association of Vermont. Natural turnover of staff and key school champions like students, teachers, and school nutrition professionals meant that high risk-takers and leaders of this effort changed many times over the years. This was especially true with the School Nutrition Association of Vermont, which does not have any paid staff. The board president is the public face of the organization, especially in the State House and in the media. This role transitions to a different person every year, with their own skills, style, and experiences. With intention, we successfully welcomed successive new board presidents into a leadership role in the advocacy effort while also maintaining space for the former board presidents to stay engaged at a high risk or leadership level. This proved to be very helpful because there were school nutrition professionals across the state who engaged in advocacy and were comfortable speaking to the media, testifying, and calling up their legislators.

Vermont's part-time citizen legislature only meets five months of the year, so it's easy to lose momentum with the public and with supporters. Also, change can take time. We have been advocating for the state to fully invest in the Farm to School and Early Childhood Grant Program for many years. Through transparent and consistent communication and opportunities for engagement at all levels, the Farm to School and Early Childhood Network maintained strong support and a growing cadre of champions ready to act when needed. Engagement opportunities included signing a supporter card to be shared with their representatives, inviting supporters to low-stakes meetings with their representatives, sharing a post on social media or submitting a letter to the editor, or signing their organization or business on to a letter. It kept our core base of coalition members engaged when the legislature was not in session and ensured that supporters were not contacting their representatives for the first time when we had a big request to make.

BUILD A PLATFORM AND LET THEM STAND ON IT

The Action Circles model uses a strategy called "Build a Platform and Let them Stand on It." We created a situation for policymakers and decision-makers to become the heroes of the story when they do what we are asking them to do. For example, we invited legislators to speak at our annual Farm to School and Early Childhood Awareness Day at the State House and during National Farm to School Month. Rather than ask our strongest champions to speak, we asked those who were supportive but not yet champions. By giving them a speaking platform with other leaders (and sometimes talking points), they developed into champions of the bill to be celebrated.

Because we are sharing power, the organizations within the coalition don't need "credit" for getting more funding or getting a bill passed. Thus, we could celebrate any policymaker who decided to champion our cause. As a result, we were able to develop champions of all parties and backgrounds, similar to how the coalition is made up of people who come to these issues from a variety of perspectives.

In 2015, the Vermont Farm to School and Early Childhood Network celebrated Farm to School month by inviting legislators to eat lunch at an elementary school in Burlington, Vermont's largest city.[9] Two state senators saw firsthand the impact of farm-fresh free school meals for all. That day, students made kale pesto from their school garden and offered taste tests in the cafeteria. Nearly all the students chose to eat school lunches made with produce from Vermont's abundant fall harvest. As the senators were leaving the school, they talked about how surprised they were that students were eating the healthy foods and how excited they were by the positive culture in the lunchroom. The experience inspired them to ask where to direct state funds so that all Vermont cafeterias could become such inviting and positive places. That moment led to the legislature funding a pilot program to help schools launch universal meal programs through the state's Farm to School Grant Program, the first state-level investment in universal school meals in the US.

Universal school meals remain integrated into the Vermont's Farm to School Grant Program and the work of the Vermont Agency of Agriculture Food and Markets. The pilot program proved that schools with universal meal programs were able to purchase significantly more local food. Still to this day, these state senators tell the story of the 2015 school lunch visit and the pilot program it inspired.

This speaks to the power of personal connection with legislators and other government officials. In our advocacy work, we approached these powerful stakeholders as individual human beings with a variety of pressures on them at any given time. For example, the Vermont state director of child nutrition programs had valid concerns about how to support hundreds of schools navigating the complex transition to universal school meals without more staff. We recognized her as the leader of an overworked team without capacity to fully respond to school districts' requests for technical assistance. As the director of a department housed within the Vermont Agency of Education, she was also responsible for communicating the agency's main concern to the legislature: that without the incentive of free school meals, parents and guardians would refuse to provide the income data currently collected in school meal applications, which is widely used in the US as a proxy for poverty to determine federal funding for school food.

Yet we also recognized her steadfast commitment to making sure students have access to food in school. Through listening, asking questions, and honoring her position within the structure of state government, we found ways to not only address her concerns but to champion her department's need for an additional full-time position in the bill. We worked hard to get this new position passed, even though the universal school meals legislation didn't pass in 2021. Midway through the 2021 legislative session, her comments on the bill became less oppositional with more reference to "what the advocates would say." By the 2023 legislative session, the Agency of Education was providing data and testimony that aided passage of the bill.

We also found it important to take the time to authentically celebrate successes large and small and to thank everyone involved. For example, in 2013, the Vermont legislature passed a bill that eliminated the reduced-price category for school lunch, making Vermont the first state in the nation to eliminate the reduced-price meal category. The bill signing marked a major milestone five years in the making. Rather than jump right into another campaign, we spent a year thanking legislators, celebrating, and sharing the impact that their work was having across the state. We made sure that legislators had the experience of knowing that their work was making a difference in the lives of their constituents and that they were appreciated for it.

BUILDING ON SUCCESS

Over the course of our coalition's twenty years of working together, we have continued to act from hope rather than from fear. We lead with a happy ending that is solutions focused. This has enabled us to make significant strides at the state level (see table 15.2) and helped strengthen a national movement that leverages the work of our solidarity coalition.

After our 2013 victory eliminating all reduced-price meal fees, we shared our strategies, campaign documents, and research at national conferences and with partners across the country. By 2021, seven additional states[10] had followed Vermont's lead by eliminating all reduced-price school meal fees. In the last two years, more states have taken this action, or jumped past it to fund universal free school meals. As of April 1, 2023, legislatures

Table 15.2 Summary of legislative campaign and state budget allocations

Year	Legislative activity and state budget allocations
2005	• Launch of legislative campaign to eliminate the reduced-price breakfast fee.
2006	• Vermont becomes the first state to create a Farm to School Grants Program.
2008	• Statewide elimination of the 30-cent reduced-price breakfast fee.
2010	• Launch of statewide campaign to eliminate the reduced-price lunch fee.
2013	• Vermont becomes the first state to eliminate all reduced-price meal fees.
2016	• Launch of campaign to increase Farm to School Grants Program funding. • Legislature increases funding for Farm to School Grants Program and includes a pilot project to help barely CEP-eligible schools provide universal school meals (the first state-level appropriation for universal school meals in the US) while increasing their local food purchasing.
2018	• State funding increases for the Farm to School Grants Program for the third year in a row and expands to support early childhood programs.
2019	• Partners develop the Universal School Meals Campaign principles, message frames, and strategy. • Senator Debbie Ingram agrees to sponsor the universal school meals bill.
2020	• Universal School Meals legislative campaign officially launches in January. • Introduction of Local Purchasing Incentive bill in both the Senate and House. • COVID-19 pandemic upends Vermont's legislative session.
2021	• New legislative champions introduce universal school meals and local food purchasing incentive bills. Led by longtime school meals champion, Senator Robert Starr, the Senate Agriculture Committee combines both efforts into S.100, the Farm Fresh School Meals for All bill. • Legislature passes Local Purchasing Incentive Grant Program. • Universal school meals passes the Senate but the session ends before the House passes the bill.
2022	• Universal school meals bill passes for 2022–2023 school year with a mandate to report back on financing options during the following legislative session. • Farm to School and Early Childhood Grants funded at $500,000.
2023	• H.165, a bill to make Universal School Meals permanent in Vermont and provide dedicated permanent funding, was passed with overwhelming tri-partisan support and signed by the governor.

in thirty (out of fifty) states and the District of Columbia were considering—or have already enacted—permanent universal free school meals.[11]

The COVID-19 pandemic contributed significantly to creating this policy window for universal free school meals (see chapter 7, this volume). However, by pursuing an integrated goal of advancing both farm-to-school and universal free school meals in a "Virtuous Cycle," our solidarity coalition has helped foster a national movement for "values-aligned universal school meals."[12] According to the National Farm to School Network, as of December 2022, 79 percent of states that had introduced universal school meals legislation had also enacted at least one local food purchasing policy.[13]

At the national level, our ongoing work and the strong relationship we have built with Vermont's congressional delegation led to the introduction by US Senator Bernie Sanders (Independent, Vermont) of the national universal school meals bill in 2019—a bill our coalition partners helped draft—and to its regular reintroduction since then. From our perspective, state anti-hunger, school nutrition, and farm-to-school advocates have forged a powerful national movement that eventually will make a federal universal school meals program inevitable.

NOTES

1. This network was created in 2008 to coordinate efforts to engage PK–12 students and school communities in a local food and farm culture that nurtures children's health, cultivates viable farms, and builds vibrant communities.

2. U.S. Census Bureau, Decennial Census 2020, PL 94–171, Table P1, Vermont, https://data.census.gov/table?g=040XX00US50&tid=DECENNIALPL2020.P1; The Annie E. Casey Foundation, Kids Count Data Center, "Vermont," accessed April 23, 2023, https://datacenter.aecf.org/data?location=VT#VT/2/0/char/0.

3. Vermont Farm to School & Early Childhood Network, "2018 Vermont Integrated Food, Farm, and Nutrition Programming Data Harvest" (Vermont Department of Health, October 2018), https://vermontfarmtoschool.org/resources/2018-vermont-integrated-food-farm-and-nutrition-programming-data-harvest.

4. Vermont Farm to School & Early Childhood Network, "2018 Vermont Integrated Food, Farm, and Nutrition."

5. Josiah Taylor, Bernice Garnett, M. Anore Horton, and Ginger Farineau, "Universal Free School Meal Programs in Vermont Show Multi-domain Benefits," *Journal of Hunger & Environmental Nutrition* 15, no. 6 (2020): 753–766, https://doi.org/10.1080/19320248.2020.1727807.

6. See chapter 7, this volume.

7. See chapter 7, this volume.

8. To see this campaign artifact, see Hunger Free Vermont, "Key Messages," Universal School Meals Vermont, last updated January 2020, https://www.universalschoolmealsvt.org/messaging-frames.

9. For more information on Burlington's School Food Project, see Doug Davis, Dana Hudson, and members of the Burlington School Food Project, "Going Local: Burlington, Vermont's Farm-to-School Program," in *School Food Politics*, ed. Sarah A. Robert and Marcus Weaver-Hightower (New York: Peter Lang, 2011), 162–182.

10. Colorado, Maine, Maryland, Minnesota, New Mexico, New York, and Oregon. New Hampshire, North Carolina, and North Dakota cover the reduced-price co-pays for breakfast only. Washington, DC, covers the cost of reduced-price lunch, along with universal breakfast. Washington covers reduced-price breakfast co-pays for all students and reduced-price lunch co-pays for students in grades K–3. Data provided by the Food Research & Action Center. (Data for 2021).

11. Permanent universal school meals have been enacted by the state legislatures in California, Maine, Minnesota, and New Mexico, and by ballot initiative in Colorado. Temporary universal school meal programs are currently in place in Connecticut, Massachusetts, Nevada, and Vermont.

12. The National Farm to School Network is the largest nonprofit organization in the US working to advance farm-to-school programs in K–12 and early child education settings. It advocates for values-aligned school meals built on six shared community values: economic justice, environmental justice, health impact, prioritizing racial equity, respecting workers and educators, and animal welfare. See National Farm to School Network, "Our Values," June 2021, https://assets.website-files.com/5b88339c86d6045260c7ad87/613797bd05726e5c091c5280_OurValues.pdf.

13. National Farm to School Network, "State Universal Meals Policies Can Strengthen A Just and Resilient Local Food System," December 2022, updated April 2023, https://assets.website-files.com/5c469df2395cd53c3d913b2d/642b2bc519f5a1184e10255f_Universal%20Meals%20Policies%20can%20Strengthen%20a%20Just%20and%20Resilient%20Local%20Food%20System%20(3).pdf.

CONCLUSION

Jennifer E. Gaddis and Sarah A. Robert

School food politics is everywhere. Beyond the legislative chamber where policy is crafted or the corporate food lobbyist's portfolio, a whole ecosystem of policy protagonism (or policy protagonists) is flourishing. Smallholder farmers are forming cooperatives and securing government contracts that allow them to nourish young people with food that is healthy, safe, and sustainably produced. Young people—from Argentina to Sweden and beyond—are protesting and organizing together for school food justice.[1] School food workers in South Korea and Ghana are striking to demand higher pay and greater respect for their essential labor.[2] And parents are fighting their local school boards to ensure students are given enough time to eat their meals and culturally relevant food.[3] This is just a small sampling of what we see happening, and we know from talking with and learning from others that possibilities abound.

Feeding students during the school day involves the work of many different stakeholder groups. Yet only a select few (mostly policy elites) see themselves as doing "political" work and subsequently claim power in the policymaking process. In the preceding chapters, however, we learn from and about a multitude of stakeholders (mostly *not* policy elites) who are intervening with the state in the way Silvia Federici encourages in the foreword to this collection. These policy protagonists are making sense of and doing political work within and across local, national, and global levels to transform school food systems.

PUSHING THE FIELD OF SCHOOL FOOD POLITICS FORWARD

Our desire to raise awareness of the political economic systems influencing who feeds whom, what, how, when, and for what purpose builds on the foundation laid over a decade ago by *School Food Politics*, which included essays from scholars and practitioners from all six continents.[4] In preparing this volume, we took the same inclusive approach to authorship while charting a pathway toward a feminist politics of food and education. We found ourselves asking big questions: How can school food programs and policies play a transformative role in the food movement? What makes school food a positive experience for students, parents, and education and food chain workers? How might we reimagine school meals and the spaces where they are prepared and served in ways that support community well-being? What policy mechanisms and organizing strategies are necessary to achieve these goals? How might students, teachers, food service workers, and other members of the school community be supported as leaders in this movement? How might different theoretical frameworks and/or theories of change enhance, enliven, and advance our understanding of school food politics? How might we reframe school food as an anti-capitalist, feminist, ecological concern and, in doing so, open new pathways for organizing?

So, in June 2020, we issued a call for a new book: *Transforming School Food Politics around the World*. We received forty-five abstracts and selected those that best connected to the themes of the volume: systems change, policy protagonism, and the feminist politics of food and education. We rejected those that had a narrow focus on nutrition, public health, or development. We also rejected those with an extremely top-down approach that lacked the voices of grassroots policy protagonists. We prioritized chapters that uplifted real-life examples of transformative school food politics and submissions from the Global South. Unfortunately, as the COVID-19 pandemic progressed and posed tremendous and unequal challenges, several authors were no longer able to complete their chapters. This included authors from Aotearoa New Zealand (Māori authors), Australia, Botswana,

Ghana, Philippines, and Sweden. The final composition of this collection reflects not only these changes to authorship but also our own positionality as academics based at institutions in the US with strong connections to practitioners and organizations in the US and Canada.

STRATEGIES AND PRIORITIES FOR EXPANDING THE FIELD

What we and our collaborators have offered through this book is a set of tools for analyzing school food systems and a collection of empirical examples that showcase the creativity and dedication of people and communities who affirm the transformative potential for broadscale policy protagonism and engagement with the state. Many authors began their chapters with a brief explanation of the social organization of their national school meal program—the early history, evolving goals, funding, and local implementation—with a particular emphasis on the stakeholders involved in shaping who feeds whom, what, how, and for what purpose. In doing so, they demonstrate how historical and place-specific context shapes both the problems with school food systems and the possibilities for transformation. We see this as fundamental to both the academic discussion of school food politics and enriching for policy protagonists whose efforts may benefit from a stronger historical understanding of the school food system they seek to transform.

We have learned from chapter contributors and through our own research on school food politics that we must be creative and collaborative to build this knowledge base. For example, in chapter 1, Alexis Agliano Sanborn, the US-based award-winning filmmaker of the documentary short *Nourishing Japan*, leveraged her background in Japanese Studies and familiarity with the Japanese school lunch system to coauthor a chapter with Professor Katsura Omori, a leading Japanese academic whose research and teaching focuses on food education, local food, and traditional cuisines in school meals. Their combined backgrounds made for a powerful writing team that was able to highlight the rich contextual specificities of Japan's school meals that would be of most widespread interest to an international audience. In chapter 5, Raven Lewis, a high school student from the US, partnered with her mentor, Jarrett Stein. His experience with academic writing and long-standing relationship with Rebel Ventures enhanced Raven's first-hand account and resulted in a more robust story of the organization and its impact.

It is our strong belief that community perspectives are an important form of knowledge, and we encourage practitioners to share their policy protagonism more widely. In chapters 14 and 15, leaders of two state-level campaigns for universal free school meals in the US tell their own organizational histories. They do the valuable work of identifying the multiple stakeholders and levels of governance that impact their school food systems, articulating their organizations' goals and strategies for change, and reflecting on lessons learned. Combined authorship from academic and community partners offers another approach to building collective knowledge of school food politics and systems change, as we see in chapters 2, 6, 7, and 12.

We also want to uplift the potential for community research to advance a feminist politics of food and education. In chapter 8, Prerna Rana, uses her training as a PhD student in civil society and community research to direct our attention to grassroots struggles and community-level experiences that center students' right to food and the role of women in feeding them a midday meal. Likewise, the British Columbia Teachers' Federation (chapter 13) provides an example of how organizations can engage in creative, community-based participatory research to elevate the experiences and knowledge of teachers and other overlooked stakeholder groups.

People in the Global North have much to learn from the Global South (see chapters 3, 8, 9, and 10 in this collection) about school food politics. We urge scholars and activists to seek out opportunities to learn from those who are doing this work. The United Nations' report *The State of School Feeding Worldwide* offers a useful starting point.[5] It is published every two years and includes inspirational examples of school food organization and innovation from a wide range of global contexts. Moreover, we see tremendous value in transnational dialogue and cross-country comparisons, and the ability to learn from a rich diversity of places and scholars is growing through these coordinated efforts. Yet many academic studies and primary source materials (e.g., newspapers and government documents) that shed light on school food politics may go overlooked due to language barriers. Chapters 1, 3, 4, 8, 9, 10, and 11 in this book do the important work of translating data from Japanese, Spanish, Finnish, Hindi, Portuguese, and Korean for an English-language audience. Additional collaborative scholarship and translation of primary source materials into multiple languages (not just English) would further the field of school food politics and bolster transformative efforts worldwide.

Knowledge of school food politics comes in many forms. We wish to underscore the importance of embodied knowledge and lived experience, which many of our authors access through different techniques such as autoethnography (chapter 5), oral histories (chapter 10), and composite narratives (chapter 12). Organizational records and other texts, too, are vital sources of information that require communal efforts to create and maintain. To this end, we encourage individual policy protagonists, organizations, and coalitions to document, archive, and make available the artifacts that represent their work.

TRANSFORMING SCHOOL FOOD POLITICS THROUGH CARE AND COMMUNITY

Our goal in this book was to highlight instances of transformative school food politics, which we believe is not possible without policy protagonism, itself an act of care that can be used to produce more caring food and education systems. When we care about school meals, we must care for and about not only the children who eat them but also the cooks and cafeteria workers, teachers, agricultural workers, and others whose labor they depend on. And through our school food systems, we must care for the natural environment on which all life depends. This core belief is threaded through the many chapters of this book and their multifaceted engagements with the concept of sustainability, which is foundational for enacting a feminist politics of food and education that centers care.

Care is a powerful form of acting in community—even at the national level—with implications for how we feed children in school. The feminist transformation we seek is one that comes from a diversity of stakeholders contributing their situated knowledge, questioning who holds power and who claims power, and forming collaborations to increase policy protagonism. We hope readers will have gained a deeper appreciation of school meals as central to the infrastructure of daily life that sustains and nourishes communities currently and into the future. We further hope that readers will recognize care as a form of power with the potential to bring about transformative change when people act in community with one another to renegotiate who feeds whom, what, how, and for what purpose.

NOTES

1. See the introduction to this volume for more on the Argentine student protest. Students at the Globala School in Stockholm, who have eaten meat-free school lunches since 2008, organized together to democratically design a program that reflected their values and concerns. Magnus Naess, personal communication with the authors, February 9, 2021. The Milwaukee school lunch justice campaign is another example. See Marriam Mackar, "Fresh over Frozen: MPS Students Fight for Better School Lunches at School Board Meeting," *TMJ4 Milwaukee*, January 12, 2023, https://www.tmj4.com/news/local-news/fresh-over-frozen-mps-students-fight-for-better-school-lunches-at-school-board-meeting; Isaiah Holmes, "Student Activists Demand Lunch Justice in Milwaukee Schools," *Wisconsin Examiner*, April 2, 2022, https://wisconsinexaminer.com/2022/04/02/student-activists-demand-lunch-justice-in-milwaukee-schools/.

2. For more on the South Korean strike, see Kim Na-yeon, "Non-Regular School Cafeteria and Care Workers Go on Strike Today," *The Kyunghyang Shinmun*, March 31, 2023, http://english.khan.co.kr/khan_art_view.html?artid=202303311712097&code=710100. For more on the national school caterer strike in Ghana, see *JoyNews*, "School Feeding: Some Basic School Pupils Bemoan Poor Quality of Food amid Strike by Caterers," April 28, 2023, video, 8:29, https://www.youtube.com/watch?app=desktop&v=-jSNwN8Ld98.

3. For an example of parents fighting for longer lunch periods, see Amy Bounds, "BVSD Parents Advocate for Longer Elementary Lunches," *Boulder Daily Camera*, December 31, 2022, https://www.dailycamera.com/2022/12/31/bvsd-parents-advocate-for-longer-elementary-lunches. For an example of parent advocates advocating for culturally relevant meals, see Kaylee Domzalski, "Inside Latino Parents' Push for Healthy, Culturally Appropriate School Lunches," *Education Week*, April 29, 2022, https://www.edweek.org/leadership/inside-latino-parents-push-for-healthy-culturally-appropriate-school-lunches/2022/04.

4. See Sarah A. Robert and Marcus B. Weaver-Hightower, *School Food Politics: The Complex Ecology of Hunger and Feeding in Schools around the World* (New York: Peter Lang, 2011).

5. See World Food Programme, *State of School Feeding Worldwide 2022* (Rome: World Food Programme, 2022), https://www.wfp.org/publications/state-school-feeding-worldwide-2022.

ANCILLARY MATERIALS

To facilitate an ongoing platform for co-learning and to support educators who are teaching with this book, we have built an extensive collection of online supplemental resources and curriculum. These materials include primary documents, images, short videos, and printable handouts. To access these materials, please visit the ancillary materials tab on the MIT Press website for *Transforming School Food Politics around the World*.

ANCILLARY MATERIALS

CONTRIBUTORS

Alexis Agliano Sanborn is an independent researcher with a background in Japanese studies. She directed the award-winning documentary short *Nourishing Japan* (2020), which explores the impact of food education and the school lunch system on Japanese communities. She received her AM from Harvard University in Regional Studies of East Asia and an MPA from New York University.

Lisa Altmann is the director of school nutrition for Rowan-Salisbury Schools (RSS) in North Carolina. RSS is a K–12 public school system, and she has been with the system for more than twenty years.

José Arimatea Barros Bezerra is professor at the Faculty of Education of the Federal University of Ceará, Brazil. He is a pedagogue, specialist in popular health education, doctor in education, postdoctoral fellow in history, and school feeding policy researcher.

Islandia Bezerra is an associate professor at the Faculty of Nutrition/FANUT—Federal University of Alagoas/UFAL. She is also a lecturer at the Latin American School of Agroecology/ELAA. Nutritionist, with a Masters and PhD in social sciences. Post-Doctorate at the Universidad Autónoma de Chapingo/UACh, Mexico.

Jennifer Black is an associate professor of food, nutrition and health in the Faculty of Land and Food Systems at the University of British Columbia where she leads the Public Health and Urban Nutrition Research Group. Her research aims to understand how food is connected to the complex social and contextual factors that shape the health of individuals, communities, and the environment.

Brooks Bowden is an assistant professor at the University of Pennsylvania, where she serves as director of the Center for Benefit-Cost Studies of Education. She is an editor at *Educational Evaluation and Policy Analysis*. Her work focuses on mitigating barriers related to poverty and vulnerability as well as improving the relevance of evidence for policy and practice through the consideration of resources required to successfully serve students.

Christine C. Caruso is an affiliate faculty of Public Health Sciences at the University of Connecticut School of Medicine, where she is a member of the UConn Collaboratory on School and Child Health. Her work aims to uplift community members' voices and expertise through community-based participatory research and advocacy addressing health equity, food systems, labor and working conditions, and environmental justice.

Cristiane Coradin is a lecturer at the Paulista State University Júlio de Mesquita Filho—UNESP, Faculty of Agricultural Sciences of Vale do Ribeira—São Paulo. PhD in Environment and Development, Master in Rural Extension. She is a researcher and social activist, addressing topics such as family farming, agroecology, health, socio-environmental conflicts and injustices, gender relations and intersectionalities.

Rebecca Davis is a former teacher; a research associate in the families and children policy area at MDRC, a nonprofit research organization; and an affiliate of the Center for Benefit-Cost Studies in Education. She studies ways in which social, governmental, communal, and educational systems can help to mitigate hardships of poverty and improve the health and well-being of children and families.

Sinikka Elliott was an associate professor in the Department of Sociology at the University of British Columbia (UBC) and a cherished colleague, mentor, and teacher before she passed away in May 2021. She came to UBC in 2017 from North Carolina State University, which she joined in 2008 after completing her doctorate in sociology at the University of Texas, Austin. Sinikka had an international reputation as a scholar of family, inequality, and health and cared deeply about the well-being of children and their food experiences at school.

Rachel Engler-Stringer is a professor in the Department of Community Health and Epidemiology in the College of Medicine at the University of Saskatchewan and a researcher with the Saskatchewan Population Health and Evaluation Research Unit. She convenes the School Food Working Group of the Canadian Association for Food Studies. She currently leads a curriculum-integrated universal school lunch program intervention study, a study examining promising school food programs in every province and territory, and an Indigenous school food program development project.

Debbie Field is the coordinator of the Coalition for Healthy School Food, a network of more than 260 nonprofit organizations that advocate for the development of a universal, cost-shared healthy School Food Program for Canada. Debbie is also an associate member of the Centre for Studies in Food Security, Toronto Metropolitan University, and visiting teaching faculty in the MPP program McGill University Max Bell School of Public Policy.

CONTRIBUTORS

Lucy Flores is a design strategist dedicated to cocreating a more equitable and joyful food system. She is the founder of Studio Magic Hour, a collaborative design studio working to advance equity in the food system, and a former equitable design fellow at Hopelab. Previously, she led innovation initiatives at FoodCorps, a national nonprofit that partners with schools and communities to nourish kids' health, education, and sense of belonging. She is a member of the Design Justice Network, Equity Army, and AIGA.

Andrée Gaçoin is director of information, research and international solidarity at the British Columbia Teachers' Federation. Her research focuses on developing a unique, in-depth, and contextualized exploration of education in BC from the perspective of teachers. Andrée is particularly interested in using research as advocacy to uphold and strengthen an inclusive public education system.

Jennifer E. Gaddis is an associate professor of civil society and community studies at the University of Wisconsin-Madison and the author of the award-winning book *The Labor of Lunch: Why We Need Real Food and Real Jobs in American Public Schools* (University of California Press, 2019). Gaddis is an advisory board member of the National Farm to School Network and has written op-eds on school food politics for popular media outlets such as the *New York Times, Washington Post, USA Today, The Guardian*, and *Teen Vogue*.

Michelle Gautreaux is a senior researcher at the British Columbia Teachers' Federation (BCTF). Most recently, her work has included a critical examination of policing programs in schools and their impact on teachers who identify as Indigenous, Black, and People of Color. Prior to joining the BCTF, Michelle spent eight years as a classroom teacher, teaching both primary grades and adult education.

Anne Hales is a senior researcher at the British Columbia Teachers' Federation. Her research supports the BCTF's ongoing advocacy for free, inclusive, and quality public education, and is currently focused on union engagement, teacher mentorship, and teachers' mental health.

Karin Hjälmeskog is a docent in Didaktik (curriculum studies) at Uppsala University.

Anore Horton is the executive director of Hunger Free Vermont, whose mission is to end the injustice of hunger and malnutrition for everyone in Vermont. Anore leads the coalition bringing statewide permanent Universal School Meals to Vermont and serves on the boards of Community of Vermont Elders and Vermont Businesses for Social Responsibility.

Kristiina Janhonen is a docent in home economics science, with extensive experience in education, food studies, and school meals. She currently works as a senior researcher at the Finnish Institute for Health and Welfare.

Jennifer LeBarre has been a leading advocate for improving school nutrition programs in California and nationally for nearly twenty years. She served as executive director of Student Nutrition Services for Oakland Unified School District prior to joining the San Francisco Unified School District, where she currently serves as interim head of policy and operations.

Raven Lewis is currently an undergraduate student, studying marketing at Georgia State University. Raven wrote her chapter for this volume while attending high school at the Creative and Performing Arts High School of Philadelphia, where she majored in film and graphic design, while also working at the nonprofit Rebel Ventures as a Cinematographer.

Faye Mack is a committed advocate for a more equitable food system. Currently, she is the executive director of Food Co-op Initiative, a nonprofit organization that provides information, training, and technical assistance to communities working to open their own retail food co-op. Prior to this role, and during the writing of this book, Faye was the advocacy and education director at Hunger Free Vermont and helped lead the coalition bringing statewide permanent Universal School Meals to Vermont.

Marjaana Manninen, senior adviser, education, works as an expert and senior advisor at the Finnish National Agency for Education (EDUFI). Marjaana has a long background in education having worked as a teacher at comprehensive and upper secondary schools and as the head of education of a municipality prior to the position at the Finnish National Agency for Education.

Brent Mansfield currently teaches Edible Education at a public school in Vancouver's West End. He is a cofounder of LunchLAB, a curriculum-aligned lunch program in which middle school student leaders work with chefs to create a delicious, healthy meal for fellow students to enjoy. He is a BC Chapter Steering Committee member of the Coalition for Healthy School Food.

Anne Moertel is a writer, designer, and advocate working at the intersection of health policy and public education. She leads communications at the Center for Ecoliteracy, a cosponsor of California's "Free School Meals for All Act." The organization successfully advocated for California to become the first state to adopt universal school meals in 2021. Previously, Anne led communications at the San Francisco Unified School District on safe and equitable food access during COVID-19 school closures and served as Creative Director for Healthy Schools Campaign from 2011 to 2019.

Katsura Omori is a professor at Yamagata University, and she received a doctoral degree of education from Tokyo Gakugei University. She teaches methodology referring to food education at school using local resources, such as school lunches, traditional cuisine, seasonal food, local farmers, and producers. She also works with home economics teachers and school dieticians to provide effective programs for food education at local public schools.

Prerna Rana is a PhD student in civil society and community studies at the University of Wisconsin Madison. She has experience as a development practitioner working with community organizations in rural India on issues like gender empowerment, financial inclusion, and sustainable agriculture. Her current research utilizes a critical lens to understand community power and organizational partnerships in the third sector.

Margaret Read is senior director of impact and evaluation at Partnership for a Healthier America, a national nonprofit organization devoted to transforming the food landscape in pursuit of health equity. At the time of writing this book chapter, she was at Share Our Strength evaluating the pandemic's impact on food and nutrition security and federal nutrition assistance programs. Previously she was a researcher at the Rudd Center for Food Policy and Health where her work focused on the school meals, school wellness policies, and the emergency food system.

Emmanuelle Ricaud Oneto is a temporary lecturer in anthropology of food at the Agronomy and Food Institute (Institut Agro), Dijon, France, and a research fellow at the Laboratory of Political Anthropology (LAP), Paris. She obtained her PhD in Social Anthropology at the School of Advanced Studies in Social Sciences (EHESS), Paris, in 2022. She is a member of the research group "Cantinégalité" (CMH-INRAE) working on school food programs and the research group Justice and Indigenous Peoples (JUSTIP) at EHESS, National Center for Scientific Research (CNRS). Her work focuses on the interconnection between public policies and Indigenous food systems, identity, and political and cultural concerns.

Sarah A. Robert is an associate professor in the Graduate School of Education and affiliated faculty member in the Department of Global Gender & Sexuality Studies at the University at Buffalo (SUNY). Dr. Robert examines the relationship of policy/politics and gender in global, South American, and US contexts focused on three areas: teachers' work, school food, and curriculum/textbooks. She is the author of the award-winning books *School Food Politics: The Complex Ecology of Hunger and Feeding in Schools Around the World* (Peter Lang, 2011) and *Neoliberal Education Reform: Gendered Notions in Global and Local Contexts* (Routledge, 2015).

Betsy Rosenbluth is the director of farm to school at the Shelburne Farms Institute for Sustainable Schools and coordinates the Northeast Farm to School Collaborative. Her work focuses on policy, capacity building, and resource development to grow robust farm-to-school programs, which rebuild healthy food systems and cultivate links between classrooms, cafeterias, and communities.

Amy Rosenthal has been researching school meals and working with school food practitioners for over a decade. Amy is currently a social science research analyst with the US Department of Agriculture Food and Nutrition Service. (She contributed to this publication in her personal capacity. The views and opinions expressed are her own and do not necessarily represent the views of the Food and Nutrition Service, USDA, or the US Government.)

Ludmir dos Santos Gomes is a teacher in the high school professional education network in the state of Ceará, Brazil, as well as a business administrator, specialist in logistics, and master and doctor in education.

Sônia Fátima Schwendler is a professor in education at the Federal University of Paraná, Brazil, acting at the Postgraduate Program in Education. Currently, she is Queen Mary University of London's Visiting research fellow and the Institute of Education—University College of London's affiliate researcher. She has experience in participatory action research, based on studies and actions carried out with social movements and rural women in the field of education, gender studies, agroecology, and climate justice.

Amy Shollenberger is the founder and CEO of Action Circles, a political strategy firm based in Vermont. She developed the Action Circles model of campaigning and organizing to bring a feminist perspective to political work.

Courtney Smith is the senior vice president of program research, innovation and impact at Share Our Strength, a national nonprofit organization dedicated to ending hunger and poverty. Her work focuses on identifying and promoting adoption of effective strategies, policies, and programs that center the needs of families and communities facing food and economic insecurity.

Seulgi Son is a doctoral candidate in urban and regional planning at the University of Michigan, specializing in sustainability transition in food systems with a particular focus on governance and societal mechanisms. Her research centers on planning strategies to bolster transformative aspects of grassroots food initiatives and increase accessibility and equity of healthy food options.

Jarrett Stein is the university assisted community school director of health partnerships and social ventures at the Netter Center for Community Partnerships at the University of Pennsylvania. Prior to this, Jarrett worked as a middle school nutrition teacher in West Philadelphia with the Netter Center's Agatston Urban Nutrition Initiative.

INDEX

Note: Page numbers in italics followed by *f* and *t* refer to figures and tables, respectively.

Aboriginal people, 45, 237
Action Circles Model of Campaigning and Organizing (US), 274, 277, 279, 282, 285–288
action pathways for BCTF
  advocating food security and policy change, 245–246
  amplifying food security as pedagogy, 243–245
  extending prioritizing food security, 245
action principles for BCTF
  place-based and culturally relevant as, 241–243
  public support for all children as, 239–240
  universality, rights-based approach to, 240–241
activist research, 235–239
afasi mikuna (lazy food), 66
Agatston Urban Nutrition Initiative (US), 105

agrarian reform, 186–191, 196n6, 197n9, 197n13
agriculture, xii, 9, 11, 187–189, 192–194, 206
agroecology, xxxvi, 146, 185–186, 192
Agroecology Journeys (Brazil), 186, 197n13
airplane food, 50
Akshaya Patra Foundation (APF) (India), 159, 161
Alameda County Community Food Bank (US), 138
Altmann, Lisa, xxxiv, 108, 115, 303
American Recovery Act (2021), 140
American Rescue Plan (ARP) Act, 130
APF. *See* Akshaya Patra Foundation
Are California Public Schools Scratch-Cooking Ready? survey, 255
Association of Realtors (US), COVID-19 response and, 119

Baillargeon, Violette, 237
Barbara & Edward Netter Center for Community Partnerships (Netter Center) (US), 97–100
Bartholow, Jessica, 260
Basic Education Development Index (IDEB) (Brazil), 172, 182n16
Basic Law on Food Education (2005) (Japan), 5, 9–11, 22
BCTF. *See* British Columbia Teachers' Federation
Ben & Jerry's Foundation (US), 277
Berkeley Public Schools, 252
Better Out-Of-School Time program (US). *See* BOOST
Bharat Gyan Vigyan Samiti (India), 149
Bhopal, 153
Biden-Harris Administration, 140–141, 264
Bihar, 153–156
bijao leaf *(Calathea sp.)*, 63
Black, Jennifer, xxxiii, 237, 303
Bogh, Rosilicie Ochoa, 263
BOOST (Better Out-Of-School Time Program) (US), 260–261, 264
Brazilian Miracle (1964–1973), 170
Brazilian school food politics
  agroecology in, 6, 185–187, 196n5
  feminist agroecology and the PNAE in, 187–191
  feminist pedagogy of care for life and, 193–195
  final considerations of, 195–196
  food sovereignty and culturally relevant food in, 191–193
Bread Riot, 117
BRICS (Brazil, Russia, India, China, South Africa), xxv
British Columbia Teachers' Federation (BCTF), 234–237, 242–246, 248n13, 250n44
Bruce, Stephanie, 263

Buenos Aires, youth and school food politics of, xviiii-xxi
Build a Platform and Let Them Stand on It, 288–290
Burke County Public Schools, 135–136
bus routes, 135–136

CACFP (Child and Adult Care Feeding Program) (US), At-Risk Afterschool Meals of, 131
California, school nutrition programs in, 253–256
California Food for California Kids Network, 218, 253, 256–257, 262
California School Employees Association (CSEA), 259, 263
California School Meals for All Campaign, 218, 262, 267–268
California Senate Education Committee, 263
California Thursdays® program, 257
California-Grown Fresh School Meals Grant Program, 258
Canada's Food Guide (CFG), 39
Canadian school food program (SFP)
  background and methods of, 41–44
  core goals of, 45–55
  improving justice as core goal of, 41–46
  inclusive vision of wellbeing as core goal of, 38–40
  national school meal program in, 2, 29–32
  vision of childhood as core goal of, 33–37
Capra, Fritjof, 251
care
  in community, 299–300
  feminist pedagogy and, 193–195
  in meal preparation and, 34–36
  use in transforming school food politics, xxviii-xxvix

INDEX

Career and Technical Education (CTE) (US), 105
CARES (Coronavirus Aid, Relief, and Economic Security) Act (US), 128, 130
care work, invisible, xxix, 36–37, 44
Ceará, Brazil, 169, 173, 180–181, 182n17
CECANE (Collaboration Center for School Food and Nutrition) (Brazil), 181
Center for Ecoliteracy (US)
  advocating for universal meals and, 264–267
  approach to school food systems by, xxxviii, 218, 251–253
  California Food for California Kids and, 256–257
  Free School Meals for All Act and, 260–264
  school nutrition programs in California and, 253–256
  state advocacy for school food system change and, 258–260
  successful strategies for school meals for all campaign and, 267–268
Center for Science in the Public Interest (CSPI) (US), 261
Central Food Technological Research Institute (CFTRI) (India), 162
centralized kitchen, 145, 157–161
centros de estudiantes (student councils), 19
chemical food *(comida química)*, 65
Child and Adult Care Feeding Program (CACFP) (US), At-Risk Afterschool Meals of, 131
Child Hunger Prevention and Fair Treatment Act (US), 254
children, as social actors, 32–34
chisan chisho (local production, local consumption), 9
CHSF. *See* Coalition for Healthy School Food (Canada)

civil society organization (CSO). *See* CSO coalition, solidarity for universal school meals (US)
  building a platform for, 288–290
  building on success for, 290–282, *291t*
  engaging people continuously for, 286–288
  introduction to, 273–279
  lead with a happy ending for, 279–281
  overview of legislative process for, 281–285
  shared messaging for, 285–286
Coalition for Healthy School Food (CHSF) (Canada), xxiii, 29, 40, 46
Collaboration Center for School Food and Nutrition (CECANE) (Brazil), 181
Community Eligibility Provision (CEP) (US), 253
community fabric, vi–viii
Community Foundation (US), 276–277
community kitchen (comedores populares), 57–58
composite narrative, xxxvii, 217, 220, 223–226
consumer, of school meal, xxxii, 13, 102
Contestado Settlement (Brazil), 185–186, 197n10
coriander *(sacha culantro)*, 54, 63, 173, 175
Coronavirus Aid, Relief, and Economic Security (CARES) Act (US), 128, 130
corporate food industry, school meals and, xxiv, 146, 202
COVID-19 pandemic in the United States
  bus routes as meal delivery sites during, 135–136
  congressional response to, 127–130, *129t*
  home delivery during, 136–137
  pairing food with essential goods during, 137–138

COVID-19 pandemic in the United States (cont.)
  policy response during, 139–141
  providing school meals during hybrid learning during, 138–139
  San Francisco school food distribution during, 125–126
  school food system response to, 130–133
  US national school meal programs during, 126–127
  walk-up, drive-thru, curbside delivery of meals during, 133–135
COVID-19 pandemic worldwide
  gender inequality in Canada during, 44
  Japanese food production and, 19–21
  rapid response by school nutrition departments to, 118–120
  school food programs and, xxi
CSO (civil society organization)
  current role of, 158–159
  history of, 151–156
  as stakeholder in school meal programs, xxiv
Current Story Analysis, 285–286

Dahle, Brian, 263
Dalit, of India, 153, 157–158
da Silva, Luiz Inácio Lula, 171
DC Central Kitchen, 137
de Castro, Viveiros, 62–63
Dewey, John, xxxiv, 85
Dhanbad appeal, 149
Dixon, Kevin, 95–96, 101
Document of Aptitude (DAP) (Brazil), 189
DoorDash (US), 136
Drawing Change (Canada), 237, 244f

Education Ministry's School Lunch Campaign (CME) (Brazil), 170
Eggman. Susan, 258

Elliott, Sinikka, xxxiii, 31–35, 236, 304
Emiliano Zapata Encampment (Brazil), 186, 197n9
Empathy Into Action campaign (US), 222
empathy, building through stories, 220–223, 222n8
empowerment
  of farmers, xxxi, xxxvi, 169, 172–178, 190, 206, 295
  of parents, xxiv, 7, 30, 40, 59, 157, 177, 295
  of school nutrition workers, xxxiv, 75–76, 108
  of women, xxvi–xxviii, xxxvi, 186–187, 190–195
  of youth, xix, xxxi–xxxii, 75–76, 85, 87, 95–97, 101–105, 280
environmental health, 40
equity, as core goal, 41–46
Equity-Centered Community Design, 224
Escherichia coli O-157, 22
ethnographic fieldwork, during school lunches, 48–50
Everitt, Tracy, 38
Executing Entities (EEx) (Brazil), 188

Facebook, 140
fairness, improvement of, 41–46
Families First Coronavirus Response Act (FFCRA) (US), 132
family farms
  Brazil
    buying school food from, 172
    cooperative experience of, 173–174
    history of school feeding in, 170–171
    Mandala enterprise of, 174–180
    national procurement standards of, 169–170
    policy shift and PNAE transformation in, 171–172
    working with PNAE and, 175–180, 188–191

INDEX

South Korea
    innovative school food procurement in, 208–210
Vermont
    Farm Fresh School Meals for All in, 273–279, 288
Family Medical Leave Act (FMLA) (US), 132
FAO (Food and Agriculture Organization of the United Nations), xxxvii, 170
Far Bars, 97–98
Farm to Fork, California Office of, 259
Farm to School and Early Childhood Network (US), xxxviii, 273, 276–279, 288–289, 292n1
Farm to School Census 2019 (USDA), 255
Farm to School Incubator Grant Program (US), 259, 265–266
fast food, vi
Federal University of Ceará (UFC), 180–181
Federation of Prefectural School Lunch Associations of Japan, 8, 19
FEEST (Food Empowerment Education Sustainability Team) (US), 105
FEMA (Federal Emergency Management Agency) (US), 137
feminist agroecology
    Brazilian school food politics and, 185–187
    the PNAE and, 187–191
feminist politics, xxvi, xxix, 75, 296, 299
Field, Debbie, 44, 304
Finland's sustainable food education
    a course for sustainability transformation for, 86–87
    food education in, 84–86, 89n4
    school mealtimes and
        current framework of, 79–80
        pragmatism and food sense in, 84–86, *86f*

        road to sustainability of, 80–84, *83t*, 90n6
    sustainable food education in, 77–79, 90n11
Finnish Law on Compulsory Education, 79
Finnish National Agency for Education (EDUFI), 79Finnish National Nutrition Council, 79
First Nations, 27, 45, 242
First Nations' Development Institute (US), Native Farm to School Project of the, xxvii
FNS (USDA Food and Nutrition Service, US), 125–127
food
    as culturally relevant, 191–193
    feminist politics of, xxix
    understanding production of (Japan), 19–21, *20f*
food allergy
    in Japan, 6, 21
    in Peru, 60–61, 65
Food and Agriculture Organization (FAO), of the United Nations, xxvii, 170
Food and Finance High School (US), 105
Food Banks, California Association of, 261
Food Connect (US), 137
food education
    in Finland, 84–86
    in Japan's school lunch program, 9–11, *11t*
    in Vermont Farm to School and FEED programs, 276–278
food industry
    in Brazil, 170–171
    profiting from nutrition-fortified items by, 39
    respect for (Japan), 17–18
Food Policy for Canada and Federal Budget (2019), 46

Food Research & Action Center (FRAC) (US), 261
food security think tank. *See* think tank
food sense, xxxiv, 78, 84–87, *86f, 88t*
food sovereignty, xxviii, 185, 191–193, 237, 241–243
Food Systems Project (US), 252
food systems, analytical framework for, 202–206
food waste, 16–17, 78, 80–82, 117, 212
FoodCorps (US), xxxvii, 224, 231n15, 305
free meal site, 138–139
Free School Meals for All Act (US), 260–264
Free Trade Agreement, 206
frontier, Indigenous schools as, 56

Gaddis, Jennifer E., 45
Gambling, Samantha, 236
Ganz, Marshall, 221
garden
  agroecological, 194
  home, 54, 57, 61, 63–66, 173–175, 273
  kitchen, 161, 163, 186, 187, 190, 195
  school, xxii, xxvii, 5, 15, 40, 105, 241, 243, 246, 252, 256, 289
Gardner, Jason, 107
General Agreement on Tariffs and Trade (GATT), 204
Gibson, Tre'Cia, 96–97, 100–103
Gillibrand, Kirsten, 262
Gilligan, Carol, 220–221
Glass of Milk Program *(Programa Vaso de Leche)* (Peru), 58
Global School Feeding Policy, xxii
godowns (government storage units), 152
Good Food Purchasing Program (US), 134, 202
Government Appropriation for Relief in Occupied Area (GARIOA) (Japan), 7
grab-and-go sites, 125, *132f,* 138

Gram Sabha (village assembly), 149, 153, 164n3
Great East Japan Earthquake (2011), 23
Grow Local Society Tri-cities (Canada), 236

Hachijojima Fisheries Cooperative (Japan), 18
Haida Gwaii (Haida Nation), 237
Halperin, Abby, 268n1
happy ending, 279–281
Healthy, Hunger-Free Kids Act (HHFKA) (US), 126
healthy deliciousness, xxx, xxxii, 101, 103
Healthy School Meals Pathway Program (US), 266
Hernández, Carolina, 114
home delivery, COVID-19 and, 126, 136–137
Home Grown School Feeding Program (UN), 202
Humala, Ollanta, 58
Human-centered design (HCD), 224–225
Human Development Index (HDI), 17
hunger, in relation to poverty, xxi, 7, 32, 141, 171–173, 274. *See also* Free School Meals for All Act
Hunger Free Vermont, 276, 278, 281, 283
hybrid learning, meals during, 138–139

In a Different Voice (Gilligan), 221
India, activism and partnerships in
  civil society and government activism in, 149–151
  current role of civil society organizations in, 158–164, 167n39
  history of civil organizing in, 151–156, 165n13
  nutrition gardens in, 163–164
  politics of midday meal scheme in, 156–158

INDEX

Indigenous food system, 237, 241–243
Indigenous people, xxvii, 2, 38–39, 45–47, 50, 56, 59–61, 63, 67, 69, 72, 172, 176, 180, 241–242, 274
Indigenous Women of the Amazon Agenda, 60–61
infrapolitics of subaltern group, 55
Integrated Child Development Services scheme (India), 156
Integrated Program for Sustainable School Canteens, in Côte d'Ivoire, xxvii
intellectual appetite (Japan), 13–14
Interethnic Association for the Development of the Peruvian Jungle (AIDESEP), 60
International Society of Krishna Consciousness (India), 161–162
Ishizuka, Sagen, 9
issue session, 236–239

Jan Swasthya Abhiyan (India), 162
Japan school lunch program
  food education in, 9–11, *11t*
  future of, 21–23
  historical development of, 6–9, 24n14
  proper nutrition in, 12
  school lunch system in, 1–2
  seven objectives of, 11–21, *20f*
  whole systems approach to, 5–6, 23n4
jobs, in school food, 45–46
Jung, Tiaré, 237, *238f*, *244f*
justice, improving core goals of, 41, 44
just school food economy, 145–146

Kaba, Tiguida, 95
Karnataka Food Commission (India), 162
Kauer, Jane, 97, 103
Keep Kids Fed Act of 2022 (US), 141
Kichwa, 56–57, 64
Kim, Daejoong, 204
Kim, Sarah, 236

kitchen-cum-store, 151, 165n11
Kreuter, Matthew W., 223

labor of lunch, 32, 36
Labor of Lunch, The (Gaddis), xxviii
LaGroix, Maureen, 237
Landless Women, 36, 187–191, 197n11
Landless Workers' Movement (MST) (Brazil), 35–36, 169, 173–179, 181n1, 182n19, 186, 198n29
Latinx/Latin American community, 114
lazy food *(afasi mikuna)*, 66–69
Learning Includes Nutrition and Knowledge (LINK) (Canada), 234
Lewis, Raven, xxxiv, 95–96, 297–298, 306
Liberatory Design, 224
Licensed Agencies for Relief in Asia (LARA), 7
life cycle, 15–16
Liné, Thibaud, 43–45
Linking Farms to Schools initiative (USDA), 252
low-income household, food for, xxiii, 114. *See also* hunger, in relation to poverty
Luisi, Pier Luigi, 251
Lula da Silva, Luiz Inácio, 171
lunch shaming, 222–223, 254, 280

Máíjìkì, 56
Maijuna (Amazonian Native community), 53–69, 69n2, 70n7, 74n53
Making It Healthier, Making It Regional (MHMR) (US), 224–225, 231n15
mandala enterprise, 174–181
Martha's Table (US), 137
McAteer Culinary Center (US), 136–137
MDMS. *See* Mid-day Meal Scheme
Measure J (US), 258
Medi-Cal (US), 253
Messaging Guidance for an Effective School Food Campaign (US), 261

mestizo people *(wiracocha)* (Peru)
  sudado de pescado as meal for, 56, 63
  definition of, 55–56
  logistics of schooling and, 61–62
  school food and becoming, 62–64
MHMR. *See* Making It Healthier, Making It Regional
Michel's Bakery, 99, 105
Mid-day Meal Scheme (MDMS) (India), 150–164
MIDIS (Ministry of Development and Social Inclusion) (Peru), 59, 61
Milan Urban Food Policy Pact, 146, 207–208
Ministry of Agriculture, Forestry, and Fisheries (MAFF) (Japan), 10
Ministry of Development and Social Inclusion (MIDIS) (Peru), 59, 61
Ministry of Human Resource Development (India), 156, 158, 162
monosodium glutamate *(ajino)*, 65
Moody, Lynn, 109, 114–115
Moore, Gwen, 262
Mooring, Teri, 236
Mother Allowances Program (Peru), 58
MST. *See* Landless Workers' Movement (Brazil)

N4 (Narrative 4), 221–222
Napuruna (Amazonian Native community), xxxiii, 2, 54–69, 70n7, 74n53
National Curriculum Standard, food education in Japan, 10
National Food Assistance Program (PRONAA), of Peru, 58
National Food Security Act (2013) (India), 155
National Fund of Education Development (FNDE) (Brazil), 181, 183n27, 185
National Institute of Nutrition (NIN) (India), 162
National Nutrition and Food Safety System (SISAM) (Brazil), 172

National Programme of Nutritional Support to Primary Education (NP-NSPE) (India), 151
National School Feeding Campaign (CNAE) (Brazil), 170–171
National School Feeding Program (Peru). *See* Qali Warma
National School Feeding Program (PNAE) (Brazil). *See* PNAE
National School Lunch or School Breakfast Program (US), 252
National School Lunch Program (NSLP) (US), 32, 42, *129t*
National School Lunch Tournament (Japan), 18
National School Meals Act (South Korea), 204–205
Nationwide School Lunch Network (South Korea), 204–205
Native Farm to School Project (US), xxvii
natural food, 64–65
nature, appreciation of (Japan), 15–16
Nembhard, Denise, 236
neoliberalism, xxv, xxix
  in Brazil, 190
  corporate food industry and, xxiv-xxv, xxix
  in India, 164
  in Japan, 8
  in Peru, 59
Netter Center (University of Pennsylvania). *See* Barbara & Edward Netter Center for Community Partnerships
Newsom, Gavin, 133, 265
NextGen California, 259, 261
New York Magazine, 222
non-GMO (non-genetically modified organism), 209
Northeast Organic Farming Association of Vermont (NOFA-VT), 276
Nourishing Japan, 297

INDEX 317

nutrition garden (India), 163–164
nutritionism, 38–39

Omar, Ilhan, 262
Orbon (South Korea), 206
organic product, 82, 163, 186, 205–209, 258

P-EBT (Pandemic Electronic Benefit Transfer program) (US), 130, 140
Panchayats (grassroots body of governance) (India), 149, 157, 164n2
Pandemic Electronic Benefit Transfer program (P-EBT) (US). *See* P-EBT
Paraná (Brazil), xxxvi, 186, 197n13
Parker, Chris, 287
Partaking of Life: The Day Little Mii Became Meat (Japan), 15
partnership, community, 117–118
pedagogy
  amplifying: food security as, 243–245, *244f*
  feminist care for life as, 193–195
  food sovereignty, culturally relevant food and, 191–193
People's Union for Civil Liberties (India), 152
Peruvian Amazon, school food politics of
  community autonomy in school food policy in, 2–3
  Indigenous logics related to schooling in, 61–64
  infrapolitical discourse among Maijuna in, 67–69
  negotiating school food for, 64–67
  overview of school meals program, 57–61
  regional context of, 56–57
  school food politics of, 53–56, 69n1, 69n3, 70n4
Petill, Gary, 262
pishtaco (outsider) (Peru), 67

PNAE (National School Feeding Program) (Brazil), xxxvi, 169–181, 185–196, 202
policy protagonism, in school food politics, xxx–xxxix
poverty, in relation to hunger, xxi, 7, 32, 141, 171–173, 274. *See also* Free School Meals for All Act (US)
pragmatist learning theory, xxxiv, 78–79
Primer, Erin, 266
private commercialized service, school meals as, xxiii
Project Pledge Philly (US), 104
Proposition 98 (US), 253
Public Distribution Scheme (India), 156
public good, school meals as, xxiii
public meal centers (South Korea), 201–202, 209–210
Pugh, Allison, 34, 49

Qali Warma (National School Feeding Program) (Peru), xxxiii, 53–55, 57–69
Quechua (Peru), 53, 69n2

Rebel Crumbles, 99–106, *99f*
Rebel Market, 104–105
Rebel Ventures (US), 34, 95–105
Reimagining School Cafeterias (RSC), 224
Rethinking School Lunch, 252, 257–158
Revolution Foods, 134–135, 137
Right to Education Act (RTE) (India), 150, 164n4
Right to Food (RTF) campaign (India), 152–156, *155f*
Right to Food Act (India), 158
Rowan-Salisbury School District (RSS), summer meal program in, 110–111
RTF. *See* Right to Food (RTF) campaign (India)

San Francisco Peace Treaty (1951) (Japan), 7
San Francisco Unified School District (SFUSD). *See* SFUSD
Sanders, Bernie, 230, 262, 292
Sandler, Jen, xx
Scheduled Castes, 153, 157
Scheduled Tribes, 153, 157
School Breakfast Program (SBP) (US), 126, *129t,* 252
School Feeding Council (CAE) (Brazil), 172, 182n11
School Food Committee (CAE) (Peru), 59
School Food Focus (US), 231n15
school food politics
  policy protagonism in, xxx–xxxii, 295
  pushing forward, 296–297
  transformation of, xvix–xxx, 217–218, 299–300
  youth engagement in, xviiii–xxi, 300n1
school food program
  global overview of, xxi–xxv
  mobile methods of delivery of, 107–110, 133, 135–137, 139
  women's empowerment and, xxvi–xxvii, 187, 190
  youth empowerment and, 85, 87, 101, 105
school food worker
  Finnish sustainable food education and, 78–80, 84–85
  in India, 157–162
  student appreciation vignette for, 36, 228
  working conditions of, xii–xiii, 117
School Lunch Act of 1954 (Japan), 5, 7, 9–11
School Lunch Association Act (Japan), 8
school lunch center, 21–23
School Lunch Enforcement Ordinance (Japan), 7
school meals
  financing of, xxiv
  national level
    activism and government partnerships in India, 149–151, 156–158
    introduction to, 1–3
    school food policy in Japan and, 5–23
    school food politics in Brazil and, 185–187
    school food politics in Peruvian Amazon and, 53–69
    school food programs in Canada and, 29–47
    school food system change in the United States and, 251–253
    sustainable food education in Finland and, 77–79
  political goals and impacts of, xxv–xxvii
  as public good or private commercialized service, xxiii
School Meals for All Coalition (US), 262, 264, 266
  successful strategies of, 267–268
School Meals for All package (US), 265
School Nutrition (Kitchen) Garden Guidelines (India), 163
School Nutrition Association of Vermont, 276, 280, 287
Scott, Tim, 97, 104
scratch cooking, 1, 34, 113, 255
Seamless Summer Option (SSO) (US), 126–127, *129t,* 130–131
Self Help Group (SHG) (India), 160–161
Senate Bill 138 (US), 253
Senate Bill 250 (US) (Child Hunger Prevention and Fair Treatment Act), 254
Senate Bill 265 (US) (School Nutrition), 254
Senate Bill 364 (US). *See* Free School Meals for All Act

Seoul (South Korea), public meal centers in, 201–202, 209–210, *209f*
Seoul Food Civic Council, 212
Seoul Food Master Plan, 203, 206–208, 212
Seoul Metropolitan Government, 146, 203–212
Service Employees International Union (SEIU), 263
SFP. *See* Canadian school food program (SFP)
SFUSD (San Francisco Unified School District), food management during COVID-19 by, 125–126, 134–137
Shared Principles, Action Circles model of, 282–285
Ship Shape Community Center (Canada), 135
Shollenberger, Amy, 274
Skinner, Nancy, 258, 260
Smart Snacks, 126
SNAP (Supplemental Nutrition Assistance Program) (US), 130
social wealth, state controlled, vi–vii
South Korea, urban-rural supply chains in
  eco-friendly school lunch program of, 204–206, 215n14
  public food procurement in, 211–213, *211t*
  Seoul food masterplan of 2020, 206–208
  urban-rural coexistence public meal service in, 208–210
  urban-rural supply chains for, 202–203
Spanish-speaking community, 114
SSO. *See* Seamless Summer Option
stakeholder
  definition of, xx–xxx
  as policy protagonists, 295
  understanding and inclusion of, 224–225
State of School Feeding Worldwide, The (UN), 298

Stein, Jarrett, xxxiv, 95, 97, 297, 308
stigma, 41–42
story-based strategy, as theory of action, 285–286
storytelling
  for building empathy for change, 219–220, 230n8
  cafeteria manager vignette and, 228
  cafeteria vignettes and, 226–227
  for coalition building, 257
  composite narrative for, 223–226
  empathy and stories for, 220–223
  school principal vignette and, 229
  student vignette and, 227–228
Summer Food Service Program (SFSP) (US), 126, 130
Summit on Healthy Food for All Students (Canada), 235
Supplemental Nutrition Assistance Program (US). *See* SNAP
Supreme Court (SC) (India), 149, 152–154, 156–157
Sustainability transformations, xxxiv, 86, *88t*
Systems View of Life, The (Capra and Luisi), 251

Tamba-Sasayama School Lunch Center (Japan), 18
Tassinari, Antonella, 56
Taylor, Kat, 253
teachers' union, 138, 234–235, 237, 246
tehsildar (land revenue officer), 154
Ten Cents a Meal Program (US), 202
think tank
  on food security, 235–239, 245–246
  food security to food sovereignty in, 241–243
  guiding action and advocacy in Canadian teachers' union, xxxvii, 217, 233–235, 247n11, 248n15
  pathways for action from, 243–246
  principles for action and, 239–240

think tank (cont.)
  universal, not targeted rights-based approach to, 240–241
Think&EatGreen@School project (Canada), 40
Thompson, Tess, 223
Thurmond, Tony, 261
Time magazine, 139
To, Kristie, 257
TomKat Ranch Educational Foundation (US), 253, 258–261
trade union, xxxv, 161
traditional cuisine
  in Japan, 18–19
  in Peruvian Amazon, 53–54, 57–58, 60–67
transformative school food politics, xxix, xxxii, 85, 296, 299–300
Transforming School Food Politics Around the World, 296
Truth and Reconciliation Commission of Canada, 245

UCPM. *See* Urban-rural Coexistence Public Meal Service Program (South Korea)
UFEF (Universal, Free, and Eco-Friendly School Lunch Program) of South Korea, 202–213
UNICEF (United Nations International Children's Emergency Fund), 8, 29, 170, 204
United Nations (UN), World Food Programme of, xx–xxi
United Nations Children's Fund. *See* UNICEF
United Nations Sustainable Development Goals, xxvii
Universal, Free, and Eco-Friendly School Lunch Program (South Korea). *See* UFEF
universal school meals, xxiii, xxxii–xxxv
  in Brazil, 171–172, 180
  in Canada, 44, 46–47, 245–246
  COVID-19 and, 76, 140–141, 292
  developing coalitions for (US), 273–278, 281–285
  in India, 153–154
  in Japan, 2, 5, 23
  principles of action for, 239–241
  School Meals for All (US) and, 256–267
  in South Korea, 201–202, 204–206
Universal School Meals Campaign (US), 280–283
Universal School Meals Program Act (US), 262
universality, 31, 43, 44, 240–241
University of British Columbia, 236, 237
Urban-rural Coexistence Public Meal Service Program (UCPM) (South Korea), 201, 208–210, 209f
US (United States)
US Agency for International Development. *See* USAID
US Department of Agriculture. *See* USDA
USAID (United States Agency for International Development), 57–58, 170, 204
USDA (US Department of Agriculture), 110–111, 117–119, 125–130, 140–141, 252, 255
USDA Food and Nutrition Service (FNS). *See* FNS

Vancouver Neighbourhood Food Networks, 236
Vermont, developing solidarity coalitions in
  overview of legislative process in, 281–285, 290
  universal school meals and local food in, 273–279, 278t
Vermont Community Foundation, 276

INDEX

Vermont Department of Health survey, *278t*, 279
Vermont Farm Fresh School Meals for All Bill (2022), xxxviii, 273, 277, 286
Vermont Farm to School & Early Childhood Network, 273, 276–279, 288–289
Vermont FEED (Food Education Every Day), 274–276
vertical lunch, 14–15
Via Campesina, xxiv, 196n29
village assembly (Gram Sabha), 149, 153, 164n3
village council (Gram Panchayats), 157
Village Education Committee (VEC) (India), 157
virtuous cycle, 279–280
Virus, Amy, 98, 102

WFP. *See* World Food Programme
White House Conference on Hunger, Nutrition, and Health 2022, 141
WIC (Special Supplemental Nutrition Program for Women, Infants, and Children) (US), 117
Williams, Hope, 135
World Food Programme (WFP), of United Nations (UN), xx-xxii
World War II, 6, 81

youth
 as beings not becomings, 32
 as consumers, xxxii
 as entrepreneurs, xxxii, xxxiv, 100–105
 as leaders, 101
 as policy protagonists, xix
 school food politics and, xviiii
 as stakeholders in Canadian SFP's, 32–37
youth power, 101–102
Yum-Yum Bus (YYB)
 background for, 107–110, 123n4
 community partnerships with, 117–118
 COVID-19 and, 118–120
 cultivating trust in, 114–115
 design of, 110–114, *112f*, 123n6, 123n7
 in-district support for, 115–117
 resources for building of, 120–122, *121t*
YYB. *See* Yum-Yum Bus

Food, Health, and the Environment

Series Editors: Robert Gottlieb, Henry R. Luce Professor of Urban and Environmental Policy, Occidental College

Nevin Cohen, Associate Professor, City University of New York (CUNY) Graduate School of Public Health

Keith Douglass Warner, *Agroecology in Action: Extending Alternative Agriculture through Social Networks*

Christopher M. Bacon, V. Ernesto Méndez, Stephen R. Gliessman, David Goodman, and Jonathan A. Fox, eds., *Confronting the Coffee Crisis: Fair Trade, Sustainable Livelihoods and Ecosystems in Mexico and Central America*

Thomas A. Lyson, G. W. Stevenson, and Rick Welsh, eds., *Food and the Mid-Level Farm: Renewing an Agriculture of the Middle*

Jennifer Clapp and Doris Fuchs, eds., *Corporate Power in Global Agrifood Governance*

Robert Gottlieb and Anupama Joshi, *Food Justice*

Jill Lindsey Harrison, *Pesticide Drift and the Pursuit of Environmental Justice*

Alison Alkon and Julian Agyeman, eds., *Cultivating Food Justice: Race, Class, and Sustainability*

Abby Kinchy, *Seeds, Science, and Struggle: The Global Politics of Transgenic Crops*

Vaclav Smil and Kazuhiko Kobayashi, *Japan's Dietary Transition and Its Impacts*

Sally K. Fairfax, Louise Nelson Dyble, Greig Tor Guthey, Lauren Gwin, Monica Moore, and Jennifer Sokolove, *California Cuisine and Just Food*

Brian K. Obach, *Organic Struggle: The Movement for Sustainable Agriculture in the U.S.*

Andrew Fisher, *Big Hunger: The Unholy Alliance between Corporate America and Anti-Hunger Groups*

Julian Agyeman, Caitlin Matthews, and Hannah Sobel, eds., *Food Trucks, Cultural Identity, and Social Justice: From Loncheras to Lobsta Love*

Sheldon Krimsky, *GMOs Decoded: A Skeptic's View of Genetically Modified Foods*

Rebecca de Souza, *Feeding the Other: Whiteness, Privilege, and Neoliberal Stigma in Food Pantries*

Bill Winders and Elizabeth Ransom, eds., *Global Meat: The Social and Environmental Consequences of the Expanding Meat Industry*

Laura-Anne Minkoff Zern, *The New American Farmer: Immigration, Race, and the Struggle for Sustainability*

Julian Agyeman and Sydney Giacalone, eds., *The Immigrant-Food Nexus: Food Systems, Immigration Policy, and Immigrant Foodways in North America*

Benjamin R. Cohen, Michael S. Kideckel, and Anna Zeide, eds., *Acquired Tastes: Stories about the Origins of Modern Food*

Karine E. Peschard, *Seed Activism: Patent Politics and Litigation in the Global South*

Jennifer E. Gaddis and Sarah A. Robert, eds., *Transforming School Food Politics around the World*